NR*

D0941317

NR*

THE ROCK ART OF TEXAS INDIANS

Panther Cave. Copied July 10, 1937. Scale: 1/4″ to 1′

This large panther, or cougar, can easily be seen from the top of the cliff on the opposite side of the canyon. Further comments concerning this pictograph are included in the caption for Plate 23.

THE
ROCK ART
OF
TEXAS
INDIANS

Paintings by FORREST KIRKLAND

Text by W. W. NEWCOMB, JR.

UNIVERSITY OF TEXAS PRESS : AUSTIN & LONDON

LIBRARY

MAR 1 3 1978

UNIVERSITY OF THE PACIFIC

341827

Western
Americana

tall
E
78
T4
K59

Library of Congress Catalog Card No. 66-15697
Copyright © 1967 by the University of Texas Press
All Rights Reserved
Manufactured in the United States of America

For Gleny

PREFACE

Curiosity may not have as dire consequences for the anthropologist as for the cat of the ancient maxim, but it can involve him in unexpected matters, diverting him into strange paths leading to lands he never intended to visit. Such has been my experience with the rock art of Texas Indians. For many years I had been aware that prehistoric Americans had painted and carved rock surfaces, and I was beguiled by the few rock paintings I had seen. But I had no intention of pursuing the subject. After all, prehistoric rock art was the concern of archeologists, art historians, or some other sort of specialists, hardly a matter for an ethnologist interested in the development and nature of recent Indian cultures. But as soon as Frank Wardlaw, director of the University of Texas Press, showed me the Forrest Kirkland collection of paintings, I knew that this was a subject I would pursue if ever given the opportunity, and when the University purchased the collection and I was invited to prepare a text to accompany publication of the Kirkland paintings, there was only one possible answer. I had to pursue this byway.

If my curiosity had been less and my modesty or my knowledge more, I might not have plunged so willingly into the subject of Indian rock art. The task appeared to be a simple one that would soon be followed to its end, but I found that this assumption was a mistake; the subject is recalcitrant and the work to be done almost limitless. The rock art of Texas is not fully known in a descriptive sense, and comparative and analytical studies which depend upon such knowledge are only barely begun. The fascinating and challenging Pecos River style paintings, for example, warrant exhaustive study, but the total number of sites with paintings in this style is unknown, even on the Texas side of the Rio Grande. What may lie on the Mexican side is almost a complete mystery. In short, this book is not and cannot be a definitive treatment of the rock art of Texas. Nor can it lay claim to being a pioneering effort, since A. T. Jackson's *Picture-Writing of Texas Indians* (1938) deserves that distinction.

This book is, rather, an attempt both to reproduce the rich and diversified rock art of a large region in a visually comprehensible and relatively compact manner, and to fix this art in its proper cultural context. Kirkland's superb paintings lend themselves admirably to the first aim and provide a mighty stimulus to accomplish the second. Consequently, I have attempted to provide the reader with what information is available about the artists responsible for Texas' rock art—their archeological affiliation or tribal identity, their age, and the essentials of their cultures. Though such information is often fragmentary and sometimes almost nonexistent, it helps establish a threshold from which this art may be more meaningfully viewed. I have not been timid about suggesting the motives behind this rock art. I know I have thus set out on a dangerous course studded with pitfalls, but if the serious investigator fails to suggest an explanation, the way is left open to those who traffic in the sensational and fantastic rather than in the reasoned surmise and the thoughtful deduction.

Many people have generously assisted and encouraged me in the writing of this book. Curtis D. Tunnell and Dee Ann Suhm Story, both former curators of anthropology of the Texas Memorial Museum, have been particularly helpful, critically reading the manuscript and giving me many useful suggestions. Chapter 4 has benefited materially from the suggestions and criticisms made by Professor T. N. Campbell, of the Anthropology Department, The University of Texas. This chapter has also profited from conversations both in the field and in Austin with Dr. Terence Grieder, of the Art Department of the University, and with Dr. David Gebhard, director of the Art Gallery of the University of California, Santa Barbara, both of whom have made intensive and extensive studies of the rock paintings in the lower Pecos River country. Mr. and Mrs. Fred R. Campbell, owners and guardians of the Paint Rock site, have very kindly gone over Chapter 7 and helped to make it more fully accurate. King Harris, co-founder with Forrest

Kirkland of the Dallas Archeological Society, has generously assisted with Chapter 1. Mrs. Willena C. Adams, technical reports editor, and Mrs. Idella P. Browning, secretary, both of the Museum staff, deserve special words of thanks for the many hours they labored over the manuscript and for their constant encouragement. Through illness and many difficulties Mrs. Forrest Kirkland has maintained her very lively interest in the work she and her husband accomplished. She has given help and advice freely and it is gratefully acknowledged. Finally, many thanks and much gratitude are due my wife, Gleny, whose patience, tolerance, and understanding sustained me throughout this work.

W. W. Newcomb, Jr.

Texas Memorial Museum
Austin, Texas

CONTENTS

PLATES

(Color Plates in Italics)

PHOTOGRAPHS

MAPS

TABLE

FIGURE

THE ROCK ART OF TEXAS INDIANS

CHAPTER 1

FORREST KIRKLAND AND HIS PAINTINGS

One of those chance occurrences which afterward seem fated started Forrest Kirkland and his wife Lula on the absorbing adventure of copying the rock art—the paintings and petroglyphs—of Texas Indians. In August of 1933 the Kirklands attended a family reunion and fish fry on the Llano River a few miles below Junction, Texas. While Forrest and his father were examining arrowheads the children had picked up in a nearby field, the elder Kirkland told his son of some Indian rock paintings he had seen along a bluff above the Concho River near Paint Rock, some thirty miles east of San Angelo, when he had stopped there while on a fishing trip. Knowing that Forrest, who was both an artist and collector of fossils and Indian relics, would surely enjoy these mysterious paintings, the father urged him to stop to see them on his way back to Dallas. Forrest had, in fact, heard of the Paint Rock paintings but that was long before the archeological bug had bitten him, and he had never taken the time to see them. Now he decided to take his father's advice. He said of this visit (1934):

Arriving in Paint Rock about sundown we lost no time locating the place. No one being in sight we entered the gate, drove to the camp ground, and pitched camp for the night. A hurried look over the cliff and at the paintings convinced me that no one with whom I had talked had seemed to fully appreciate the significance of these pictographs. We decided that night to make some copies with my water colors, which I always take with me on trips. Copies, we thought, would add interest to our little Indian collection which was growing so rapidly. Accordingly, we set to work early the next morning and by 10:00 A.M. I had carefully filled two 8 x 10 spaces with interesting groups and Lula had done almost as many in pencil. The colors and designs were copied accurately but no attempt was made to draw to a scale or include every figure in a design. Our sole object was to get a few Indian pictographs for our collection.

The designs Lula had copied in pencil, I later worked up in water color to match the two I had made on the spot. These were framed and hang today on our museum walls. They are the seed from which, I believe, one of our most worthwhile aspirations has grown.

We didn't make a careful survey of the complete group of paintings while we were there, but only a casual inspection showed they were badly weathered. Some had

been injured by sightseers and many of them had been totally destroyed by ruthless vandals. Here was a veritable gallery of primitive art at the mercy of the elements and the hand of a destructive people. In a few more years only the hundreds of deeply carved names and smears of modern paint will remain to mark the site of the paintings left by the Indians.

Every time I looked at these copies which we hung in our little museum, this question came to mind. Why shouldn't I return to Paint Rock and carefully copy every picture still remaining on the cliff and so save them for future generations? Lula and I talked it over. She thought it was a good thing to do. I went to the library for information but found almost nothing on the subject — just two short articles in the Texas Folklore Society publications. Evidently no one had given the subject much thought. What was at first merely a suggestion in my mind soon became a solemn command. I am a trained artist able to make accurate copies of these Indian paintings. I should save them from total ruin.

So it was definitely decided that we would drop everything at the first slack season of the summer and go to Paint Rock to copy the paintings. It was a serious undertaking for me. I felt my almost total lack of knowledge on the subject. I could do the drawing well enough but were my eyes trained to see what I should see? I read all the books I could find that told about primitive paintings, especially those on the walls of caverns in Europe, and in that way tried to prepare myself for the task.

Not only did Forrest Kirkland return to copy the pictographs at Paint Rock, but he and his wife were to spend every moment he could steal from an active business for the remainder of his life in copying the rock art of Texas. Kirkland must have realized, perhaps dimly at first but with sure conviction, that everything he had done and been before was training for this immense task. He had found his mission and it was an all-consuming one. Never again did he paint landscapes, save once as payment for the privilege of copying rock art. Never again did he search for fossils, and even the quest for arrowpoints had lost its appeal. Talented, energetic, dedicated, and singleminded, he became a zealot in his determination to record and preserve the rock art of Texas.

Born November 24, 1892, on a farm near Mist, in southeastern Arkansas, Olea Forrest Kirkland

FORREST KIRKLAND

was educated in the local grammar and high schools, and attended Hendrix College in Conway, Arkansas, for a year. He studied commercial art for a short time in Battle Creek, Michigan, before being drafted for World War I. Although a childhood bout of what appears to have been rheumatic fever left him with a damaged heart, and hiking with a heavy pack made him dizzy and white with fatigue, he was sent to France as an infantryman. On board ship he contracted mumps and as soon as the troopship docked at Le Havre he was placed in a British hospital and later in a British convalescent camp. In the hospital the British managed to lose his papers, and it was not until the war was over that he was able to officially establish his identity; as a result of this loss Kirkland was not paid even the pittance a private was due. He enjoyed the convalescent camp, however, for he liked to meet and talk to strangers, and there were men of many nationalities there. They in turn must have been charmed by this young Arkansan who spoke an interesting dialect and had a rare talent for getting on with people.

Nearly penniless but with time to spare in the convalescent camp, Kirkland spent all but his last cent to buy watercolors and paper. With these he painted scenes of the surrounding countryside and sold them to fellow soldiers, a practice he kept up throughout the two years he spent in France. When he had recovered from the mumps he was assigned to the 120th Infantry, but after a company commander had seen one of his sketches he was attached to the intelligence section of the 2nd Battalion and served as a map maker there for the remainder of his stay in Europe.

Discharged from the service in 1919, and feeling himself too old to complete his disrupted education, Forrest Kirkland moved to Dallas, where he went to work for an engraving firm. By 1925 this largely self-taught artist had established his own business, an advertising-art studio which specialized in making intricate drawings of industrial machinery for catalogue illustrations. Such illustrations had to be accurate in the smallest detail, yet the artist had to draw them quickly if he was to turn a profit. At this Kirkland became a master. Working freehand with an airbrush he could rapidly translate complex blueprints of cotton ginning, oilfield, and other equipment into attractive and realistic pictures. He was blessed with a mechanic's understanding of machinery as well, and occasionally pointed out to engineers weaknesses in their designs. Throughout his adult life Kirkland committed himself fully to whatever he was doing, and for years labored twelve and fourteen hours a day, seven days a week in his studio. After the business was established and he could take vacations, he labored as long if not longer at his pleasures.

Soon after he started his own business a young woman came to work for him. Lula Mardis was born in Fisher County, Texas, on a ranch almost under the shadow of the Double Mountain. She too was an artist, had studied at the Art Institute in Chicago, and had had practical experience doing art work for a department store in Birmingham, Alabama. Besides helping with the art work in the studio she kept the firm's accounts and did many of the other chores for the bustling, growing business. After five years she and Forrest were married, and thereafter they shared their work, hobbies, and ultimately their interest in Indian rock art. On their camping trips in later years she did much of the driving and all the photography. The photographs in this volume are only a sample of her artistry with the camera. She was also camp cook and explorer, and occasionally did some of the preliminary work on the pictograph copies. Though most of what is said here refers to Forrest Kirkland, and though the paintings reproduced in this volume are his, they would scarcely have been possible without the help of his devoted wife.

During the busy, hard-working, early years of his business career Kirkland continued to paint watercolor landscapes. He soon became well known in the Dallas area for them and received several awards in competitions. He was a lifelong member of the Dallas Art Association, and in 1933 was listed in the *American Art Annual* — the "Who's Who" of American art — published by the American Federation of Arts. He painted his landscapes solely for his own pleasure, not because he hoped to sell them, for he felt that if he did his pleasure in them would be spoiled and painting would become just work. After he had achieved recognition in the field of watercolors and had mastered the medium to his own satisfaction, his interest in it began to wane. Significantly, Kirkland never worked in oils. He was impatient to complete whatever he was doing and he could do a watercolor of a Dallas slum, a favorite subject, between home and office whereas an oil painting would have pre-empted days of his precious time. The speed with which he could paint an exquisite watercolor or produce a meticulous drawing of complex industrial machinery was to stand him in good stead when he turned his talents to copying rock art.

His interest in fossils began one day in 1932 when a friend brought to the studio a section of a beautiful specimen of an ammonite, an extinct form of mollusk related to the pearly nautilus. Kirkland, always possessed of a curious, inquisitive turn of mind, was keenly interested in it. He knew his friend would not part with the specimen, but he said, "Give it to me," and receiving the expected answer, retorted, "I'll just go out and find one for myself then." And he did. First, Kirkland bought and borrowed all the books he could find on geology and paleontology, and when he had assimilated their information, he obtained a geological map of Texas so that he could locate and visit promising fossil localities. Lula was enthusiastic, and their weekend excursions to fossil sites were soon broadened into full-scale camping trips. In the next two years they collected and identified hundreds of fossils. Among them were some fossils Kirkland could not identify but believed might be impressions of jellyfish. Though friends scoffed at this notion, with characteristic perseverance he sent a specimen to R. S. Bassler of the United States National Museum, who reported that Kirkland had discovered an impression of a jellyfish not known previously in this country. As a result Kirkland sent a brief article and photographs to *Natural History* magazine, which published them in the April, 1941, issue as a "letter to the editor" (Vol. XLVII, No. 4, p. 243). Kenneth E. Caster, a paleontologist at the University of Cincinnati, saw the letter and ultimately made a study of this new fossil material, though the war postponed publication until 1945. In his paper Caster (1945) set up a new family, Kirklandae, to accommodate the new genus and species (*Kirklandia*

texana Caster) for the jellyfish which Kirkland had found.

Most friends were incredulous that the Kirklands should have such a bizarre hobby as fossil collecting, and some probably wrote the couple off as demented when in later years they took to camping in inhospitable places to copy ancient markings on rocks. But a few shared their interest in fossils, and as a result the Dallas Fossil and Mineral Club came into being, and Kirkland was for a time its president. But while collecting fossils the Kirklands had often discovered Indian arrowheads and other artifacts, and gradually their interest in archeology surpassed their interest in fossils. As a result, Kirkland helped organize the Dallas Archeological Society and was its president until his death. The club met twice a month, and as often he had a lecture prepared for it. He was an excellent public speaker, holding audiences spellbound even when talking on subjects which would normally hold slight interest for them. Under Kirkland's guidance the Society also started a bimonthly publication called *The Record*, and although it was intended primarily for the entertainment of its members, its quality was such that libraries and museums were soon requesting copies. Kirkland was a frequent contributor (see Bibliography), as he was to other archeological journals.

Predictably, the Kirklands read everything they could find in this new field of interest, and from the beginning they recognized that archeological specimens had a story to tell and were not merely baubles which collectors could boast about to one another. Mrs. Kirkland recalls (letter to writer, dated August 24, 1964):

We collected all the publications and books on the subject, from universities, second-hand book stores, new book stores, anywhere we could get them, from all over the country, from Washington to Austin and the west. And we *studied* them. Forrest suggested, shortly after the Dallas Archeological Society was formally organized, that when they went exploring, no matter what, to always keep records and write about what they found.

Kirkland practiced what he preached, even insisting that his wife also keep field notes since, as he said (1934): "It will be interesting to compare the two sets of Notes and see how differently a man and a woman view the happenings on an archeological trip." Mrs. Kirkland kept diaries of their summer camping trips from 1934 through 1939. She kept no diary during the brief trip of 1940, and wrote only a few words about their last trip in 1941. These fascinating accounts are quoted at length here.

The winter of 1933–1934, after the Kirklands had visited Paint Rock, must have dragged on interminably for them, and not until the twentieth of June could they get away from business for the trip to Paint Rock. Kirkland (1934) described their work there and the procedure they were to follow at the scores of sites they later visited:

When we arrived in Paint Rock, late in the afternoon of June 20th, the whole place about the paintings seemed changed. A new fence had been built around the ranch and a keeper's house stood beside the gate. At once, I saw we might have trouble getting into the place. We didn't stop at the gate, but instead drove on to town and then learned from an ice man that the place was a part of a ten section ranch owned by a Mr. Sims. The old gentleman still lived in the ranch house some distance from the highway, but his son, O. L. Sims, now County Judge, lived in town. I also learned that Judge Sims was an authority on Indians, that study being his hobby. I knew at once he was the man to see.

I found him just as he was leaving his office, evidently rushing out to meet his wife, but he took enough time to listen to my plan and to explain the gate-keeper and the new rules they had been forced to make about entering the ranch. It seems that cattle rustlers of a new kind have sprung up in recent years, far more efficient than the famous rustlers of pioneer days. They will drive a fast truck into a ranch at night, corner a drove of sheep or a herd of cattle, load up, make a quick get-away, and dispose of their loot to a string of associated markets and restaurants along a regular route. To combat these outlaws a keeper had been placed at the gate and no one was allowed on the ranch without a written permit. Judge Sims was much interested in my plan to copy the paintings and gave me a letter that would get us past the gate-keeper.

Not long after sun-up the next morning we were on the grounds mapping out our work. It was decided that in order to keep all the drawings uniform I should do the actual painting. Lula would go ahead and make a careful survey of the cliff and assist in any other way possible. It was decided to start at the west end of the cliff and proceed towards the east, copying the paintings as much as practical in the order they appeared on the rocks. The copies were to be made one-eighth actual size, a careful record was to be kept of the designs too badly mutilated to be made out; and each drawing should include the complete design exactly as it was made by the original artist.

My procedure was first to measure the rock on which a group of paintings appeared, then to draw the outline of the rock to scale on my board; then to measure the principal figures in the design and draw them in pencil to the same scale. The remaining parts of the design were carefully copied freehand. This procedure was continued until two boards were filled with pencil sketches of the paintings. Then returning to the first group and preparing my water colors, I painted in all the backgrounds which represented the rocks on which the paintings were made. These backgrounds were given only a general color, no attempt being made to represent the variations of color on each rock. Then sitting before each group of paintings I carefully checked my pencil sketch to see that it was accurate, and colored the drawing as nearly like the original Indian painting as my skill and colors would allow. This procedure was followed until the last group of paintings had been copied. . . . I copied in all one hundred and twenty groups. Forty-one groups, fifty-two single drawings, and ten handprints were so badly mutilated that they could not be copied.

It took three days to copy the Paint Rock pictographs, and after the Kirklands spent Sunday with Judge Sims, three vacation days still remained.

They headed first for Sanco, a small town about forty miles north of San Angelo, near which they knew of an archeological site. After collecting some artifacts there, they turned their Model-A Ford toward Fort Chadbourne, a few miles to the east. Not only had they seen some interesting artifacts gathered from this region, but Judge Sims had shown them a tracing of some Indian petroglyphs taken from a boulder in the vicinity. Their experience there was typical of the difficulties which often beset their path. As Kirkland recorded it (1934):

What is left of the once thriving little city of Fort Chadbourne is scarcely worthy of a name. The depot, large enough to serve a town of 2,500 people stood apparently deserted; a dilapidated two-story school building raised its vacant bell tower about the mesquites that covered the valley; and one large store building still remained to mark the west side of what was once the square. This building, once divided to accommodate a drug store, hardware store, and general merchandise establishment, is now one huge desolate room about 90 x 100 feet. It is arranged for a dance hall, with an orchestra stage on one side and a cold drink stand and a few groceries on the other. The proprietor and his family lived in a small space, curtained off in one corner.

We asked for cold Cokes but the stand was out of ice so we contented ourselves with spending a few minutes in the shade, exchanging remarks about the dry weather and the dilapidated building. I had hoped to get some information from some of the natives about the location of the Indian petroglyphs but we were the only people in town except for the lady in the store, who had never heard of Indian carvings. Presently two cars drove up and four men came in and ordered drinks. No mention was made to them about the lack of ice and the drinks were apparently enjoyed by all.

The eldest of the men, thin, wrinkled, and one-eyed, looked suspiciously at Lula and I. He was a typical "hayseed" and seemed a little dubious of Lula's trousers. I could easily see that we were "forners" to him. Thinking that he might know about the petroglyphs I asked if he knew anything about a cave in those parts with Indian pictures on the wall. He refused to talk and the other men knew nothing of such a cave. He only muttered something and eyed me with his one good eye.

Finally, he said "Look here stranger; I aint tellin' nothin'. What you lookin' for, gold or silver?"

"I'm not hunting gold or silver," I explained. "I'm just an artist and want to copy the Indian paintings on the walls of the cave."

"Wall, that might be" he replied "but I shore aint sendin' nobody up any of them canyons where one of my friends is bottlin' up a batch."

I went to the car, got my Paint Rock sketches, lined them up against the wall, and put on a real show for the folks. The old man was dumfounded. He even crawled along the floor before them so as to get a better view. This sold him completely and he became so friendly before we left that he invited us to spend the weekend at his house. But he knew nothing of the petroglyphs.

Years later the Kirklands were to "get" the Fort Chadbourne petroglyphs; in 1934 they had to satisfy themselves with prospecting for new archeological sites before returning to Dallas. On their homeward way, however, they lunched by the road in a shady place a few miles west of Breckenridge. Judge Sims had assured Kirkland that the paints used for the paintings at Paint Rock did not originate in Concho County, and Kirkland remembered that he had once near Breckenridge picked up some limonite, an oxide of iron that could have served as a pigment. Now, while eating, his eyes fastened on a series of gullies washed into the gray clay of a hillside, so after lunch and a short rest the two explored the hill.

. . . there in this one gully we found every color used by the Indians at Paint Rock, with the exception of black, which, as I have said, must have been charcoal. At the top near the surface of the ground was a thin layer of light gray chalky substance which appeared almost white when marked on a rock. A few inches below this was a similar layer, except it was of a lemon-yellow tint. At other levels in the clay were other deposits of oxide of iron, ranging in color from orange, through bright red, deep violet and brown. Some lumps were hard but much of it was as soft as chalk and perfectly free from grit. The supply seemed almost unlimited.

I searched the ground around the deposit but found no indication of Indian habitation. From the sack of color which I collected from the deposit, I selected a grade of twelve colors. When ground and mixed with glue and glycerine, this material made an excellent water color; although the shade of each color became several shades darker than it appeared when used as a pastel. To further test the use of the colors, I copied some of the Indian paintings with them and found they matched almost exactly the original colors used by the Indians. The discovery of this deposit so perfectly completed our week's work that we arrived home, still thrilled at the grand climax to our first serious archeological expedition. (Kirkland, 1934)

When Kirkland copied the Paint Rock pictographs he did not know of any other places where similar paintings might be found. But that winter he sent J. E. Pearce, chairman of the Department of Anthropology at The University of Texas, black and white photographs of the paintings he had made. Pearce was enthusiastic about Kirkland's work and invited the Kirklands to visit him in Austin before A. T. Jackson left for a summer in the field. Jackson was then collecting data for his work on *The Picture-Writing of Texas Indians* (1938), and Pearce thought a meeting of the two men should be profitable for both. Lula Kirkland wrote (1935):

We went down and showed him the original paintings and enjoyed a very pleasant visit with them. Mr. Jackson considered getting Forrest to go with him on field trips as an artist, to paint the pictographs. But we preferred to go out on our own during our vacations. Mr. Jackson suggested that if we could take a month off it would be well to go to the Hueco Tanks Indian paintings near El Paso, or if we had a shorter time to go to Meyers Springs, near Dryden, Texas, west of the Pecos.

With these leads the Kirklands could hardly wait to be off for the field, but it was July 20 before they

could get away, and at that only two weeks could be spared from the business.

They drove first that summer to Paint Rock to check the accuracy of the previous year's work and to add a few miscellaneous paintings they had omitted. Then taking Jackson's advice they headed for Meyers Springs. By the time they had obtained permission to visit the site it was dark and they could not reach it that night, so as soon as they could find a flat place they set up their cots and ate supper by flashlight. They were so excited and eager to see the pictographs they could scarcely sleep. Up at daybreak, after a hurried breakfast they were on their way to the Springs.

The paintings (Plates 70–79), different from those at Paint Rock, were of much interest, and Kirkland immediately set to work. While he was making preliminary measurements, the ranchman and his family arrived for a visit, and only after a lengthy conversation could Kirkland get back to his work. Fortunately, the visitors warned the Kirklands that their car, parked on a Bermuda grass plot on the canyon floor, would be in danger of being washed away if it should rain up the canyon. That afternoon it did rain, and within an hour the water was several feet deep over the flat rock on which they had been standing to copy the paintings.

We were feeling rather discouraged and disgusted for it continued to rain at intervals, and since the canyon was dammed below the cliff the water would only run off to a small extent since the dam kept it backed up. That night we had to sit in the car and try to sleep. A most uncomfortable way to try to sleep. I said try—for that is all you can do, you become so cramped after a few minutes in one position you awake and there are a limited amount of positions you can get in.

July 24, Thursday. Were we glad when day came! The canyon had run down so we could see the rocks we had to stand on. They were covered with slimy mud as slippery as if they were greased, but we had to get those pictures! Donned bathing suits, and with bare feet Forrest made a careful attempt to get to the paintings to finish drawing them. By taking a step, then carefully placing our bare feet so as to rub off the slimy mud and get a toe hold, we managed to make our way along the wall and finish the drawing that day.

Unfortunately we had a sunny day, I say unfortunately because the water in which we worked outside the shadow of the cliff reflected the sun on our tender skins uncovered by the bathing suits, and before we realized it we were badly sun burned. We had worked in the shadow of the cliff so did not dream of this happening. (Lula Kirkland, 1935)

Kirkland was not able to finish his copies until the twenty-fourth, but on the next day they hurried to Alpine and Sul Ross College, where Victor Smith of its faculty was said to know the location of some pictograph sites. He told them of some paintings in the Davis Mountains, and by Sunday noon, July 27, they had arrived at Fort Davis. While copy-

The Kirklands at a campsite.

ing rock paintings in this region the Kirklands made a discovery which was often to prove highly useful in making out dim paintings. In an exceptionally low shelter under a huge rock they found some small black animal pictures (Plate 89):

The spaces under the rock were no more than a few inches to a foot in height, and the Indians had evidently used them like a fireplace as they were smoked almost black. The animal paintings were painted on this smoked rock surface *in black*. You can imagine the difficulty we had in seeing them. Someone had been there previously, however, and chalked an outline around some of the clearer pictures in order to make photos of them. The chalking obscured some of the detail and we wanted to see what was underneath, so Forrest decided to try washing the chalk off. As soon as the rock was wet the little animals popped up clearer than ever, and we began finding other animals as we wet the rock. Many that we later found had not been seen before. Unfortunately the chalk would not wash off but the attempt to get it off gave us a very valuable idea for future use. From then on when detail was hard to make out we found by wetting the rock with water the picture and all bits of paint, with a few exceptions, would be bright and clear for as long as it was wet. (Lula Kirkland, 1935)

Hearing of another pictograph site northwest of Fort Davis and having copied all the pictographs they could find in the Fort Davis vicinity (Plates 89, 90), on July 30 the Kirklands headed for the Rock Pile Ranch.

All afternoon we followed the rocky road up and down mountains, through canyons and narrow valleys until it became a mere trail. Going down one steep mountain we struck a rock hard and found later that we had broken the cap over the end of the radius rods and just missed breaking a rod. We saw only one ranch house, but a few dim trails led off the main road at intervals. These people seldom go out to the "big" cities. Just before sundown we arrived at the Rock Pile Ranch house, in a high mountain

valley, almost under the shadow of old Sawtooth. Almost in the yard and back of the house was a huge pile of granite rocks as high as one hundred feet, and several hundred yards in front of the house was another huge pile even higher. From these the ranch got its name. . . . What an Indian's paradise that rock pile must have been! Among the huge rocks many as large as good sized houses I found shelters and caves of a variety of shapes and sizes, some connected by corridors of varying widths and heights. High up in the rock pile I found a large pine tree growing in dirt lodged in a crevice. Crevices among the rocks also held water, like cisterns. (Lula Kirkland, 1935)

Kirkland rapidly copied the paintings in the shelters of the rock piles (Plates 91, 92), and with only a few days of vacation left, they headed for the lower Pecos River country many miles to the east, where they had heard other pictographs were to be found. He copied the pictographs of Mile Canyon, near Langtry, on August 2 (Plates 9, 10) but his reaction to these distinctive paintings is not recorded, and on the following day they had to leave for Dallas.

The following summer, 1936, the Kirklands were able to spend almost a month copying pictographs, the greater part of it in the lower Pecos River country. This year too, they had a new automobile, a 1936 Dodge sedan. In previous years they had driven a 1929 Model-A Ford coupé, an ideal car in most respects because its high clearance allowed them to go places most automobiles could not go. But the coupé was cramped, particularly when they wanted to sleep in it. The Dodge was roomier, if somewhat lower, and it was used for all of their subsequent field work. An ice chest and a chuck box which made a table when opened were fastened to the running board. A two-burner Coleman stove, two folding cots, campstools, and a five-gallon water jug rounded out their camping equipment. Having only a mosquito bar to cover their cots, they slept in the car when it rained.

Leaving Dallas on the Fourth of July, they copied the pictographs in the Lehmann Rock Shelter, near Doss in Central Texas, on the fifth (Plates 111, 112), and continued southwest. After exploring some of the canyons in the lower Pecos River country, Kirkland was copying its paintings by the eighth. They remained in Val Verde County through the sixteenth of the month, Kirkland painting thirteen places (Plates 1–3, 11–14, 16, 19, 43–46) in this interval—a prodigious quantity considering the complex nature of the pictographs and the heat, dust, and other difficulties with which they had to contend. A glance at Mrs. Kirkland's Diary (1936) illustrates well the conditions under which they worked. On July 12, for example:

. . . after a hurried lunch we started for a location on the banks of the Rio Grande. Mr. McBee (the landowner) was to show us the way but while we were getting water from a tank, he went on and left his wife to show the way. On the way we had to burn out a wasp's nest to get through a gate. We arrived at the place where we had to stop the car. We had been told we would have to go through a bat tunnel to get to the shelter we wanted. The old Southern Pacific railroad dump along the canyon wall was the road we had to go to get there. The tunnel had been made in the cliff by the railroad. Since its abandonment it had become the roosting and breeding place of millions of bats. It was fairly light, but the stench of the bats in the tunnel was very disagreeable and sickening. I was scared the first trip through. It wasn't so the return trip, but the last trip the next day made me sick. Our clothing even smelled of that nasty tunnel. We found the shelter but the pictures were rather crude and scarce. Forrest drew all of them before we left for the car.

That night while we were fixing the cots some wild animal came up in the bushes and growled. It wasn't a wolf and from all evidence since, it must have been a panther. We went on to bed since we couldn't see anything, but was I scared! I knew it was unlike a coyote to do this growling and not quite like a panther not to scream. He (or she) sounded like a mad tomcat but many times louder. He evidently smelled us and the food, and growled because we prevented him from getting to it. We went on to bed, however, and I tried hard not to go to sleep, but did doze occasionally, to be awakened by this animal growling again. All night long he circled our car and occasionally growled nervously as if he was very angry. I could smell him too, when he came to a certain spot in his rounds. I never in my life was so glad for daylight to come.

Most of the pictograph sites were difficult to get to, and some required considerable ingenuity.

. . . the descent into [Rattlesnake] Canyon was so steep and difficult he [Forrest] had to let his paint box down with a rope and climb down after it. I followed him soon and having no rope I took along a pair of trousers, tied up the end of one leg, placed my camera outfit and our lunch in it, and while holding to one end I slid down the rocks. It is far too difficult to climb in and out of canyons to get a bite of lunch so we usually carried it with us. The pictures in this canyon, by the way, were on the back wall of a small grotto-like shelter. A beautiful mural of Indian designs interwoven with their representation of the human figure in costumes. It was dimmed by the many years of sun and wind action but had not been mutilated by white man and with study, Forrest was able to get all the designs. He worked all of this day (July 14) on the drawings.

. . . Late in the afternoon . . . a rainstorm came up and I tried to let Forrest know about it. I had returned to the car ahead of him when I saw the rainstorm coming. It seemed to have been raining some time on the draws at the head of the canyon so I feared it might get up and Forrest would be marooned in the shelter. Did you ever see an ocatillo? If you have, you can imagine what a predicament I found myself in when I tried to run through a thicket of them in a high wind. The ocatillo is usually found on rocky ledges along the banks and top edges of canyons and rocky hillsides. It has the appearance of a bunch of almost straight canes an inch or so in thickness and closely studded the entire length with half-inch or longer thorns, loosely stuck in the ground. In a high wind they were whipping around in all directions and since they grew only a few feet apart, in places it was difficult to walk through them. I tried running through. (Lula Kirkland, 1936)

Finishing the Rattlesnake Canyon paintings on the fifteenth (Plates 1–3) the Kirklands spent one more day in the lower Pecos River country, copying pictographs on the Brown Ranch (Plate 19).

We found the way easily enough but it was not easy to get over the road. The last half of it was practically impassable and often we had to stop and pull rocks out of the way or one of us would have to stay out and tell the other just how far to go this way or the other, so we could get by. We met a Mr. Skiles, the man who lives on the ranch, who rushed up to us with a gun across his saddle. When he learned that we had stopped at his house and got directions from his wife, and that we had been told about the pictures on this ranch by his wife, he was very friendly. After finding the shelter in which we thought the pictographs were we ate a bite and prepared for our afternoon's work. It was raining in several directions so we were in a big hurry. Forrest got his water colors and board and I my camera and away we went. Almost to the canyon one of my shoe soles came off back to the heel. I was afraid I would step on a thorn or that it would trip me, and wondered what in the world I could do. Forrest gave me a string off a rag he had in the paint box. I tied the sole on winding it over and around my foot— but still it would slip off. I eventually arrived at the shelter after one of the most difficult descents and ascents of a canyon we had yet encountered. High up on the canyon wall was the shelter. A small one badly weathered but some very very interesting pictographs.

. . . We were thirsty after our hasty scramble and discovered that in our rush to get to the shelter we had forgotten to bring our waterbag. All the water we had was a small bottle in the paint box that he had brought along to paint with. The heat was intolerable and the mosquitos made you miserable with their buzzing and stinging. We decided to take a tiny swallow of the water at a time and wait as long as we could before taking another and maybe we could manage to finish the pictures before we had to return to the car. The water was hot and not overly clean but how good it tasted. We found a hole in a rock with some water in it left by a recent shower and though it

Plate 1. Rattlesnake Canyon. Copied July 13, 1936. Scale: 9/32″ to 1′

was full of animal life Forrest managed to get enough water from it together with some from the bottle to finish the pictographs.

. . . we decided to get out of there before night. We were badly crowded for time but by hurrying we managed to get over the most difficult part of the road before all daylight left us. We stopped by the side of the road and prepared a few bites to eat by flashlight. We had passed a ranch house on the way out, but left it about 1½ miles behind. While we were getting settled for the night here came the rancher from the house all out of breath. He had seen our car lights going on and off and said he thought we might have been a son he was expecting, in trouble of some kind. Really I think he wanted to see who we were and he had walked all that distance to see. (Lula Kirkland, 1936).

On the seventeenth the Kirklands drove to Alpine, sought advice from Victor Smith about the paintings that remained to be copied, and spent the night at Fort Davis before making a swing through the Big Bend. Kirkland copied the pictographs at Bee Cave and Chalk Draw on the nineteenth (Plate 81), Agua Fria (Plate 82) on the twentieth, Comanche Springs (Plate 83) and Study Butte (Plate 84) on the twenty-first, and Glenn Spring (Plate 85) and Hot Springs (Plate 85) on the twenty-second and twenty-third, all in Brewster County. Heading north, he copied the rock art near Balmorhea (Plates 93–96) on the twenty-fourth, and after a side ex-

PLATES 1, 2, 3

This intricate group of pictographs is in a small shelter in the east wall of Rattlesnake Canyon near its mouth. High above the flood level of the canyon, the shelter is about forty yards long and twenty feet deep. The back wall rises abruptly from the floor for about two feet, then rounds back and up and over into the ceiling without a seam. Limestone is weathering off in thick flakes from the overhanging edge and has destroyed some of the designs about two-thirds of the way down.

The paintings begin about four feet from the floor and extend well up on the ceiling to a height of eight feet. Instead of copying the pictographs in their present dim colors an attempt was made to use the original colors. This made it possible to follow each design even where there is much superimposition. The designs were treated with water where it was necessary to determine their exact shape. Only the parts of designs that could positively be made out were included in the copy.

PLATE 3

Shelter 2. About two hundred yards up the canyon from the main shelter and on the same side are two other shallow shelters. About level with the bottom of the canyon, they are flooded with every rain. The first had a few very dim Pecos River style paintings on the ceiling, but they were much too dim to copy. The second contained these few, very clear, historic pictures and handprints in bright red.

SHELTER 1

Plate 2. Rattlesnake Canyon. Copied July 13, 1936. Scale: 9/32″ to 1′

SHELTER 1

SHELTER 2

Plate 3. Rattlesnake Canyon. Copied July 14, 1936. Scale: Shelter 1, 9/32″ to 1′; Shelter 2, 5/16″ to 1′

cursion through the Guadalupe Mountains and on to Carlsbad, New Mexico, copied the pictographs at Blue Mountain (Plates 96, 97) in Ector County on the twenty-ninth before turning homeward.

In 1937 the Kirklands were able to get away from Dallas by July 3, the lower Pecos River country once again being their destination. On the way Kirkland copied the paintings at Paint Rock Springs (Plates 113, 114) on the Llano River, and those in the Frio Canyon (Plate 15). Disappointed that rock art was so scarce in the Hill Country, they hurried on to the lower Pecos, remaining there eight days (July 7–14). In this interval Kirkland filled fourteen boards (Frontispiece, Plates 20–28, 47–49, 64). Returning to Dallas by a different route, he copied the petroglyphs near Roscoe in Nolan County (Plate 115) and the rock art near Breckenridge (Plate 121).

Again in 1938 the Kirklands spent the month of July in Val Verde County copying its rock art, and between the fourth and the twentieth of the month Forrest filled twenty-eight boards (Plates 4–8, 17, 18, 29–34, 50-53, 55–63, 65, 69). By now they had copied the paintings at most of the better-known and more accessible sites, so that these copies not only represented much meticulous painting but a tremendous amount of arduous climbing and hiking under very trying conditions. For example, after copying the pictographs they found in several shelters (Plate 29) they decided to walk down Pressa Canyon in hopes of finding more paintings.

The canyon was almost filled with trees and underbrush and we found the walking better in the center of the stream bed regardless of the huge boulders and rocks we had to clamber over for a greater part of the way. The sun was almost directly overhead, the trees gave hardly any shade, the limestone rocks and boulders had been scoured to whiteness by the many waters that had been over them, and they reflected back the white hot heat of the sun in a blinding glare. They were almost as hot as the top of an old iron stove with a fire in it.

But on we went, finding here and there an open stretch of canyon in which the walking was good. Finally when the sun was beginning to throw a shade on one side of the canyon, we found high up on the sunny side a narrow shelf above which were some tiny animals, human and deer pictures in red, unlike anything we had discovered before [Plate 53]. Forrest decided he would try to get them before the bit of shade along the ledge disappeared and so that we would not have to make the tiresome walk back again. He had to work with his back in the sun, but managed somehow to get them done in all that intolerable heat. If we could have had a breeze it would have relieved us much. . . . After a bit of rest we started our long hot walk back to the car up the canyon. When we did get there we were so completely exhausted and so thirsty we just flopped down in the dirt and sat there until we gained enough strength to get in the car and find a place to camp for the night.

On the way out we found an old stunted live oak that afforded enough shade for ourselves and car, and there we stopped. Putting out the cots, we removed all unnecessary clothing and lay there and just rested for more than an hour. Away in the night some animal awoke us barking real hoarse. We shined his eyes with the flashlight, Forrest saw the bulk of his body, and we decided it was a fox who had discovered us. He ran away, but returned later and barked again. We went back to sleep and let him bark. (Lula Kirkland, 1938)

Copying the petroglyphs in Lewis Canyon (Plates 56–63) a few days later was also trying work. Lula Kirkland recorded (1938):

Never have I worked under more trying circumstances. First the sun caused a steaming heat to come from the rocks and later the rocks were as hot as if they had a fire under them, the glare even with smoked glasses was bad and the reflected heat from the hot rocks became almost intolerable. Still we worked on. There was no shade near to give a minute's relief and hardly a breath of air could be felt. We crawled under a bush for a bit of very thin shade and ate our lunch. Back to work we went, but about 4:00 o'clock we had to quit. The sun seemed as if it was baking our brains, the water we had would not quench our thirst, and it became so unbearable we had to walk down to the river to the waterhole and crawl in the shelter and stay for an hour or more. When we came out we felt better, some thunderheads had collected, and it was thundering rather heavily. We started to work again but had hardly finished a board full when it started raining. We made a shelter for our boards, Kodak, etc., with rocks piled together which kept them dry until the rain continued with more force when we decided we were going to get wet anyway so might as well go to the car. It was about a half a mile up a difficult steep trail—a trail filled with small rocks and rubble that rolled and turned with every step you made on them. I put my Kodak in the top of my old straw hat—I tied the strings tight under my chin—my handbag and an extra pair of shoes I had under my arm. It was pouring down rain by that time and rushing up that cliff was a breath-taking task without it raining in your face. I held my hand over a hole in my hat to keep the rain out, and when I got to the car I didn't have a dry thread on me. My hat string had drawn up till it was choking me, but only a small amount of water got on my head. When the rain slacked a bit we changed to dry clothes, crawled in the car, rested, and went to sleep from sheer exhaustion while the rain continued.

Days were sometimes wasted in searching for paintings which did not exist or were disappointing after they were found. Though clothes were torn from their backs, the Pecos waded and rewaded, innumerable canyons climbed into and out of, and blazing heat and choking dust remained their constant companions, this remarkable couple doggedly clung to their mission. With reluctance even, they left the sweltering canyons of the lower Pecos River to return to Dallas at the end of the month.

By this time word of Kirkland's paintings was spreading, and in 1938 the Addison Gallery of American Art in Andover, Massachusetts, exhibited them. In subsequent years his paintings were exhibited at the Buffalo Museum of Science (1940) and the Dallas Museum of Fine Arts (1943). Kirkland also prepared oversized copies of some of the more intriguing pictographs and used these over and over again in the lectures he was requested to give on the subject.

The month of July, 1939, found the Kirklands again on the trail of rock paintings. Before returning to the lower Pecos River region they copied the rock art of several Central Texas sites (Plates 117, 122, 123). By the twelfth of the month six more boards of paintings (Plates 35-37, 41, 54, 80) had been made in the lower Pecos River region, and on the following day the Kirklands headed for Balmorhea, where they had heard of more pictographs. Failing to find these, they visited again with Victor Smith in Alpine, copied the pictographs at Indian Water Hole (Plate 80), then visited Presidio on the Rio Grande before turning westward for the Hueco Tanks and its famous pictographs.

All who drive westward from Alpine to El Paso are impressed with the distance and the land. So too was Mrs. Kirkland (1939), who remarked that

The thing that impressed me most about the miles we traveled from Marfa to El Paso was the many, many miles of semi-desert, I might say desert that has little or no water; it hardly affords life to the lizards and rattlesnakes. Texas is a large state but so much of this country is apparently so worthless. At all times we were in sight of near and far mountains, beautiful with the haze in the distance and varicolored when near. The Rio Grande is a green line of vegetation, after we drew near to it, with large blue mountains, forming a formidable looking barrier across in Mexico. Sand dunes with stunted mesquites filled the valley where irrigation had not reached. From McNary on to El Paso we saw river water running in irrigation ditches with green fields of cotton and feed stuffs. I remember how sweet the clover smelled. The highway stretches out in a straight line for miles and miles up the valley, for the greater part between rows of cottonwood trees. The longest avenue of trees I've ever seen before.

After a brief stop in El Paso they continued on to Hueco Tanks, Mrs. Kirkland describing them (1939) as:

Small mountainous piles of granitoid rock, sticking up out of a desert valley, surrounded by other small mountains. These huge piles of rocks catch rain water in holes or crevices in rock called tanks, and keep it there clean and sweet many months after a rain. It is a veritable oasis in the desert.

They pulled up at the largest water hole and, eager to see the paintings they had heard so much about, immediately began to search for them. Some of the first they found were in

what is called the Comanche Cave. . . . The air that greeted us was icy cool and so refreshing. On a huge rock up near the top of the cave was one large rock on which someone had printed, no one knows how many years ago, the sign "WATTER HEAR." Underneath through a gap about four feet wide was a huge cistern of water, ice cold. The slanting rock leading up to the cistern was polished to a glassy surface by the many feet, Indian and white, that had gone up for water. Reclining on the cool rock with the cool air coming from the cave was a delightful experience after our climbing over the hot rocks looking for pictures, and over our heads on the top or the ceiling of the shelter the Indians had painted pictographs. Over them hundreds of names are written and printed, the earliest date I saw was 1849. . . . Walking and climbing up and down and around the huge rocks we found most of the pictures near the ground level and near mortar holes. With night coming on we chose a place to camp and called the day ended. (Lula Kirkland, 1939)

Recording the many pictographs of Hueco Tanks was a tremendous task, but with Kirkland diligently painting and Mrs. Kirkland scrambling up and down the rocks locating new sites, photographing various shelters, and taking care of the camp chores, they had completed the copies on twenty-six boards (Plates 124–149) by the end of the month.

It was the most productive summer of painting they had had or were to have. Although they spent two more summer vacations copying rock art, they had visited the major sites in the state and Forrest Kirkland's health appears to have been failing. July of 1940 found them once again in the lower Pecos River country, where they found a few more paintings to reproduce (Plates 38–40), but their vacation was brief. Mrs. Kirkland fell and injured her back and had to return to Dallas for treatment. Kirkland copied only a few other petroglyphs (Plate 116) in Nolan County during the remainder of the summer.

The next year, 1941, two weeks in July were devoted to recording the paintings and petroglyphs of the Panhandle. They had planned to go back to the Pecos and Devils rivers but heard the region was having so much rain that they did not do so. The rock art of Rocky Dell in Oldham County was copied first (Plates 150–152), then the scattered petroglyphs of the region (Plates 153–160) before they drove south to Fort Chadbourne, where Kirkland copied one last design (Plate 120). That winter he finished an article about the rock art of the Panhandle for the *Bulletin of the Texas Archeological and Paleontological Society* (Forrest Kirkland, 1942b). Soon after, he was felled by a heart attack.

He was forty-nine years old when he died, April 2, 1942. He had attempted what no one else had dared, and he had succeeded beyond the dreams of any. He had copied most of the rock art then known in Texas. His heroic, self-imposed task was completed.

CHAPTER 2

AN INTRODUCTION TO ROCK ART

Sketchy figures painted on rock walls and crude forms scratched on boulders may hardly qualify as art to some people. At the outset, then, it is necessary to describe what is meant here by art as well as rock art and to discuss something about the nature of each and their roles in human society. For our purposes, art is that segment of culture which consists of socially transmitted skills and their products — written and oral literature, plastic and graphic representation, music, drama, and dance — by which experience is interpreted and made intelligible. By rock art is meant graphic representation on natural rock surfaces, in caves and rock shelters and on boulders. Apart from painting, and perhaps tattooing, of the human body, it is probably the most ancient of the graphic arts and has been widely practiced by men on all continents. The terminology employed for various kinds of rock art has been rather loosely used in the past, but it is now customary, and followed here, that "petroglyph" refers to figures which are carved, incised, pecked, or otherwise engraved into the surface of a rock, and "pictograph" to figures painted on a rock surface. "Petrograph" is occasionally used as a synonym for petroglyph.

For our purposes, a culture may be regarded as an organized body of knowledge, beliefs, habits, customs, institutions, rituals, games, tools, and other artifacts which distinguish a particular group of people. All mankind participates in one or another culture, but only man possesses culture, since it depends upon unique intellectual abilities peculiar to our species (White, 1959: Chapter 1). Although man is a distinctive kind of animal, he is still an animal driven by the forces common to all organisms, and culture may be practically viewed as man's way of satisfying these needs. "It is a means of obtaining need-serving materials from nature, a means of defending one's self and one's group against enemies, a means of combatting disease, of finding protection from the elements, etc" (White, 1947:182). Every culture is a system, a coherent, self-consistent organization of related parts. No segment or aspect of it floats free, so to

speak; each is responsive to and affected by other segments, as in turn it affects them. Art is not independent of other aspects of a culture but is closely and intimately related to them. It cannot be otherwise of course; how could the art of any people be anything but a reflection of the physical and cultural world in which they are immersed? The way peoples exploit their environments, the ways they are organized to make their technological systems work, and the means by which they explain and interpret their experiencing of the world and the cosmos, find expression in their art. An art form, such as rock painting, may then be viewed as one of the means by which a people interprets experience, as well as a reflection of that experience.

As an aspect of culture, art is uniquely human; no other animal produces art. This is not to deny that men may view the works of various creatures as aesthetically pleasing. A spider's web may be a work of art to a naturalist. But the spider is not an artist nor his silken trap art according to our usage. It becomes art when a man, in a dance, mimics a spider spinning a web or draws a picture of the web. This conception of art also recognizes that the artist and his art are part of an ongoing tradition or traditions. Obviously this is so and it might be unnecessary to raise the point were it not that the creativity and originality of artists have been much emphasized in the Western world in recent years. So much have they been emphasized that the erroneous impression is sometimes given that a new style of painting, for example, has sprung full blown from the palette of a genius without precedent or antecedent. But as Carpenter (1942:30–31) has put it:

If the artist were wholly free to create, why should not each of his creations be completely unique, instead of showing a manner appropriate to a school or group, which in turn takes its ordered place within a phase or style pointing back to its predecessors and forward to its successors? Even El Greco and Van Gogh, however erratically different from their contemporaries, fit intimately their particular time and place within the evolution of painting. It is of course the old dilemma of the freedom of the human will: we may act freely according to our judgment, choice, and desires; but our judgment, choice, and desires are motivated and conditioned by our own past and by the present world surrounding us.

Haag (1960:219) has said much the same sort of thing for music:

The important point is the continuum in music; each musical style is drawn from the idiom of the preceding period. The artist's greatness lies in the manner in which he renders his interpretation of the style. In every creation the fathering musician is also the son of the grandfather and his work will show some inheritance from that generation. The modern composers, Klebe and Berg, are as much the offspring of Schonberg as jazz-pianists Bruebeck and Wilson are the descendants of Morton, but all these creative artists carry the "genes" of Mozart and Beethoven.

There is no room here to examine further the artist's role in his artistic milieu. Suffice it to say that the art of any people is viewed here like any other aspect of culture, as a body of habits, beliefs, practices, and products passed on from one generation to another. New elements enter the artistic stream from time to time by developments from within and by borrowings—diffusion—from without. Old elements are superseded, to be forgotten, lost, or regarded as passé.

The traditional nature of art implies its evolution, meaning that any art form changes through time, one form or style growing out of another. Rock art is particularly pertinent to this discussion since the Ice Age cave art of Europe has long been recognized as a classic example of the evolution of an art form. In its simplest terms (in time, increasing knowledge may complicate this sequence) there was a progression from crude, outlined, monochromatic paintings to skillfully executed, naturalistic, polychrome paintings, to abstraction and simplification in later stages of the evolution. It is interesting and perhaps of considerable theoretical importance that the rock art of one region of Texas underwent a somewhat similar evolution (see Chapter 4). Whether all graphic art forms, if developing without external stimuli, would pass through roughly the same stages remains a matter for debate. In general terms, there seems to be a natural progression from early groping and experimentation, through complication and maturity, to ultimate mastery within consciously or unconsciously imposed limits. A redefinition of purpose or goal follows, usually marked by the eradication of nonessentials and a return to fundamentals, which is to say a turn toward abstraction or stylization.

While art forms evolve and progress in this sense, it is inaccurate to view art in general as having evolved from something simple and crude, naive and unskilled among prehistoric peoples to something sophisticated and superior in modern civilizations. Culture in the larger sense has evolved and progressed in that it has developed progressively better ways of exploiting the environment. Modern European civilization, for example, has evolved far beyond its Upper Paleolithic forerunner in the ways in which the forces of nature have been harnessed. But there has been no corresponding progress in art; modern European artists would be hard put, in fact, to "improve" upon the naturalistic portrayal of game animals as drawn by some of the Upper Paleolithic hunters. Art serves the culture or civilization of which it is a part and in many ways reflects that of which it is a part. But there is no such thing as a paleolithic stage in art any more than there is a neolithic or Iron Age stage. (For varying viewpoints see White, 1947; Munro, 1963.) Though primitive peoples produced much of the rock art discussed in this volume, they were primitive in a technological sense, not necessarily in an artistic one.

There are, nevertheless, vast differences between the arts of primitive cultures and those of modern industrial civilizations. Industrial civilizations obviously have a much wider range of materials and tools with which to express themselves. The musical instruments of a modern orchestra, for example, are complex and diversified and their manufacture is far beyond the technical capabilities of hunters or fishermen. In cultures with wildfood subsistence patterns and rude technological systems in general, occupational and professional groups are also lacking. Such societies cannot afford the luxury of full-time artists as can industrialized societies; those who paint and dance and sing in primitive cultures can do so only in a part-time capacity. The surprising thing is that such part-time artists often became so skilled. Perhaps of more importance, modern Western artists can, and do, benefit from the artistic traditions of many exotic cultures in addition to their own. Their art is increasingly cosmopolitan, derived from many disparate sources. But artists in primitive cultures are for the most part too isolated and provincial to have a wealth of artistic diversity and choice to draw upon. They can rely only upon their own relatively homogeneous artistic traditions; a multiplicity of schools or styles can hardly exist. It is for this reason that the art of primitive peoples is such a fertile field for studying the mainsprings of art; it is less encumbered, less complex, and its basic nature is more easily perceived.

Different cultures emphasize and pursue different artistic activities with varying degrees of intensity. Some may neglect the plastic arts, others music, or one art may be practiced avidly, another tepidly, and so on. In the case of rock art some peoples have engraved and painted rock surfaces through many centuries, even millennia; others have seldom or never done so. Those cultures which have a long tradition of painting or engraving rocks and which pursue this form of artistic expression ardently are naturally apt to become skillful at it. On the other hand, those peoples who only occasionally practice rock art, or engage in it for the slightest of reasons, are apt to produce less skilled works. The magnificent European cave paintings are the result of many generations of artistic experience, of trial and error; the lively Bushman paintings may be too, though they cannot be traced as well through time; other long-followed rock art traditions could be mentioned. But much of the world's rock art, and certainly some of that found in Texas, has every appearance of having been produced by novice artists who had little experience in ornamenting rock surfaces and who could not have profited from any very deep accumulation of artistic knowledge and experience.

Tempting though it may be to label what appears to be a crude and unskilled drawing inferior to an accomplished one of another culture and region, this sort of judgment has to be avoided. Our appreciation and comprehension of rock art, or any form of primitive art for that matter, may suffer when the work is evaluated by the canons of European or American taste. One people may have been inspired to paint their pictures for magical and religious reasons, another to commemorate successful hunts, still others as an idle pastime. As the motivation differs, so too will its artistic expression. Looked at this way, evaluation of one artistic tradition by the canons of another becomes absurd and meaningless. Greyhounds bred for running ability are hardly to be faulted because they are poor retrievers. Every artistic style or school, however crude or skilled, has behind it an idea, often vague, seldom explicit, of what that art should be. In the rock art of one culture the aspiration may be to portray game animals exactly as they appear in nature, in another the portrayal of an animal's actions may be of paramount importance, elsewhere the important thing may be to depict symbolically the animal's essence or soul—and so forth. To allege, for example, that Upper Paleolithic Franco-Cantabrian paintings are superior to Bushman paintings of South Africa because animals are portrayed more realistically, is to confuse and distort our comprehension of both art forms. There is no reason to suppose that the Upper Paleolithic Europeans and the Bushmen were moved to paint rock surfaces for the very same reasons, and there is even less reason to suppose that the Bushmen wanted to attain the realism of the Franco-Cantabrian artists. Or to shift the argument, Franco-Cantabrian art should not be labeled "backward," "underdeveloped," or "inferior" to Bushman art because it lacks the lively scenic groupings of the latter. Comparisons are important, and analytical investigations of rock art are sorely needed, but it is impossible to objectively evaluate art apart from the culture of which it is a part. As White (1947:182) has put it:

There is and can be no absolute standard in terms of which all forms of government, ethical systems, religions, forms of family, etc., [including art] can be measured or evaluated. They are not relative to each other; each is relative to its own situation. It is meaningless to ask, which is better, a hammer, shovel, needle, canoe or bicycle. It all depends upon what you need and want. An ethical code that works well among preliterate hunters might—and almost certainly would—be out of place in highly developed agricultural, or industrialized, communities. A religious system suited to a pastoral life would not fit a seafaring and horticultural people such as the Polynesians. We see, then, that it is unjustifiable to attempt to compare the same non-technological aspect of a number of different cultures with each other and to evaluate them against each other apart from their respective contexts, the cultural *wholes*.

Inevitably, one of the first questions a person asks when confronted with a spectacular example of rock art is why was it produced. Although answers are frequently a matter of probability rather than solid fact, a great deal is known about the motivations of prehistoric artists and the role of art in their cultures. Art is, by definition, a way of interpreting experience. Specifically, it should be pointed out that men of every culture or civilization have needs which cannot be satisfied by things or products appropriated from the physical world. Nor are these needs trivial; the cliché that man does not live by bread alone is an understatement. Had he not found ways of serving these other, "intraorganismal" needs he might not have survived at all. In a general way these needs fall into two categories, one of which may be called "spiritual." Man must feel, or, rather, each culture must equip its members with the feeling, that the struggle for survival is worthwhile and that his efforts will be rewarded. Man realizes that the business of making a living is difficult, that getting along with his obstreperous fellows is no mean feat, and that frustration, misfortune, and defeat are his constant companions. As White (1959:9) puts it: "He requires companionship, courage, inspiration, hope, comfort, reassurance, and consolation to enable him to continue the struggle of life." Although these needs must be satisfied from within, they are very much a part of man's adjustment to the external world. The hunter equipped only with a spear is a poor match for a lion, but the spear-bearing hunter garbed also in the mantle of courage and confidence is a dangerous foe for half-a-dozen lions.

Besides these spiritual requirements, there is another class of needs which might be called, for want of a better term, entertainment. Reconciliation to a struggle which is onerous and brief can still leave life dull, featureless, and boring. Man needs to have the tedium broken; he flourishes best when he can look forward to special events and when he can ornament his world with exciting and beautiful objects. To put it succinctly, men need to excite and be excited, to create and to admire that which they have wrought.

Men have an array of devices with which to satisfy these intellectual and moral needs: mythology, religion, philosophy, lore, and art. Art, then, is part of man's attempt to reassure and console himself; it is a way of illustrating and visualizing man's conception of himself, his world, and his cosmos; it is part of his effort to come to grips with and adjust to the external world; it turns a drab and cheerless existence into one charged with drama and excitement; it renders satisfactory or satisfying, and comprehensible, what may otherwise be regarded as forbidding or intolerable. As the term is used here, art may be distinguished as a separate aspect of culture, but it is obvious that virtually every other aspect or component of culture is apt to be permeated with one or another form of art. The farmer's hoe may be fashioned in what is considered to be a pleasing shape, the recitation of a myth may be accompanied by music or dancing, a magical ritual may require that a picture be painted on a rock, and so forth.

It is apparent that many rock paintings and petroglyphs are analogous to the fossilized bones of bygone animals in that they are all that survives of ancient ceremonies, rituals, and other activities. They are the bare bones of something once fuller and fleshed out. This comparison is not intended to imply that all rock art is but a part of some larger ceremonial complex. Some was quite surely produced for itself as entertainment, and not as a by-product or part of other activities. Unfortunately, many investigators, when lacking clues to the motives behind a particular form of rock art, are all too apt to fall back on the "art for art's sake" explanation. Many of the hasty and crude pictographs in Texas, for example, seem to be the products of idle play, but such judgments obviously should be made with caution, not as a handy refuge for the puzzled.

Rock drawings and engravings hold a fascination for many people, particularly archeologists, because they are a unique type of archeological specimen. They are unique because they reveal otherwise hidden aspects of past cultures. Normally the archeologist must reconstruct a bygone culture from the relatively few more-or-less-indestructible material remains he has been able to recover from his excavations. Through these he is able to gain a knowledge of the material, mechanical ways in which a people lived, and by inference may come to understand a great deal about their economic, social, and political institutions.

As V. Gordon Childe (1951:13) has cogently remarked:

The archaeologist collects, classifies, and compares the tools and weapons of our ancestors and forerunners, examines the houses they built, the fields they tilled, the food they ate (or rather discarded). These are the tools and instruments of production, characteristic of economic systems that no written document describes. Like any modern machine or construction, these ancient relics and monuments are applications of contemporary knowledge or science existing when they were fashioned. In a liner results of geology (oil, metal-ores), botany (timbers), chemistry (alloys, oil-refining), and physics (electrical equipment, engines, etc.) are combined, applied, and crystallized. That is equally true of the dugout canoe fashioned by Stone Age man from a single treetrunk.

Again, the ship and the tools employed in its production symbolize a whole economic and social system.

But material remains, whether of a ship or a spear point, do not directly or indirectly reveal much, if anything, about the beliefs and feelings, the hopes and fears of a people. The spear point is mute when one asks if its maker danced to call down the rain or to increase the stock of game. The dugout canoe, or the inferred social system with which it is connected, fails to divulge how the supernatural powers were swayed to come to the aid of man. Such things may be disclosed, however, in a people's rock art. The artist paints a picture of himself or his fellows engaged in a rain dance or symbolically slaying game; he can, of course, depict any objects, events, mythological creatures, abstractions, or ideas which are familiar to him.

Rock art does not, of course, reveal all that the anthropologist would like to know about prehistoric cultures. In fact, it discloses all too seldom its purpose and role, and frequently reflects equivocally the culture of which it is a part. As Anati (1961:22) has noted: "the study of rock art is infinitely more complex [than archeology] for here we deal not with objects themselves, but with pictures of objects and sometimes with the representation of totally intangible realities." Besides such inherent difficulties and perplexities, all too frequently it is difficult or impossible to associate a particular form of rock art with a known prehistoric culture. Though pictographs or petroglyphs may be present at a site where more conventional archeological remains are found, this does not necessarily mean they are associated. Even when cultural debris has accumulated in a cave or rock shelter to the extent that it covers some or all of the wall art, lacking other evidence we can be sure only that the art predates the other cultural material. Fortunately, the subject matter of the rock art may help to fix its associations, and occasionally carvings, sketches on small slabs, or the like are also found among other cultural material so that the affiliations of the pictographs or petroglyphs can be determined.

Although the association of rock art with known prehistoric cultures is often poor and our understanding of it fragile, rock art often opens the doors to comprehension, and we can fleetingly glimpse the shadow of what we seek. For no matter whether the artist's subject is a recognizable object or an abstract figure, it inevitably mirrors the social and cultural world of which it was a part. Thus, the Archaic hunter in the lower Pecos River region of Texas might paint a picture of a deer with a conventionalized body composed of stripes or cross-hatches, but he usually makes evident his interest in deer tracks by carefully and naturalistically depicting the hoofs. And, so long as the art is fairly skilled and realistic, it provides much information about the physical and culturally visible portions of the artist's world. He may depict the game animals which are crucial to his group's survival, the weapons used in hunting, the manner of using them, and the methods of hunting. He may portray his kinsmen, their dress, dwellings, and multifarious activities. Oddly, there is very little rock art anywhere in the world which takes for its subject the physical features of the land or its vegetation. Rock art is primarily concerned with animals, men, their tools and equipment, and nonnaturalistic figures and designs. Even when it is composed of undecipherable geometric figures, careful study may reveal some significance in them and something about the people who produced them. In Nevada and eastern California, as an illustration, there are hundreds of petroglyph sites whose petroglyphs are largely composed of geometric forms. A thorough investigation has revealed that these sites were situated near game trails, and that "the glyphs themselves, or the act of making them, were of magico-religious significance, most probably a ritual device to insure the success of the hunt" (Heizer and Baumhoff, 1962:11). We would like to know more about such petroglyphs of course, but at least their general significance has been fathomed. Occasionally, rock paintings even reveal the customary outlook, or other attitudes and beliefs of a people. The lively, scenic panoramas of Bushman art, for example, disclose a joy in living and an atunement with the natural world which was a basic ingredient of that culture.

Despite the possibility that studies of rock art might yield a unique kind of information about America's prehistoric inhabitants, few thoroughgoing investigations were made until relatively recent years. Scientific archeology got under way in the United States only in the last decades of the nineteenth century, even later in many other parts of the hemisphere. Understandably, archeologists were more concerned with potsherds and projectile points, burial mounds and house structures than they were with strange, scattered scratchings and daubings on rocks. Pictographs and petroglyphs could hardly be collected for study in the laboratory, they were difficult to copy accurately, and there was often no way of connecting them to the more usual archeological manifestations of prehistoric Indians. Fascinating though they might be, they seemed to promise little help in the task of reconstructing the story of prehistoric America. In 1886, however, Garrick Mallery published *Pictographs of the North American Indian* and followed it in 1893 with *Picture-Writing of the American Indians,* both volumes dealing in part with the nature and distribution of rock art. But the investigation of American pictographs and petroglyphs languished after Mallery's pioneering beginning, and even today there are some regions of the Americas in which the rock art is poorly if at all described, and not analyzed at all. Interest has been quickening in recent decades, however, sparked perhaps by Steward's survey of the *Petroglyphs of the United States* in 1937. A number of careful and intensive studies of local rock art areas are now appearing, such as the one by Heizer and Baumhoff (1962) for Nevada and eastern California, and by Schaafsma (1963) for the Navaho Reservoir District in northwestern New Mexico and southern Colorado. In the near future a relatively complete descriptive knowledge of North America's rock art should be available, thus making possible a better overall idea of the extent of certain styles, their relationships to each other and to archeological complexes, and their interpretation in general.

The difficulties involved in recording rock art and in making such data available have hampered somewhat the development of these studies. There is no standard method of copying rock art; each technique has its own advantages and shortcomings and its critics and defenders. In general, three methods of recording rock art are used: tracing of the painting or petroglyph, photographing, and copying with scale drawings. Tracings have the advantage of reproducing the forms of rock art exactly, though they duplicate the colors of paintings no more or less accurately than artists' copies. Kirkland (1937b:97) believed that "the chief advantage of tracing is that this method can be used by anyone not skilled in making drawings. The difficulties encountered, however, in obtaining tracings of very large designs, and designs high above the floor, and the very bulky copies that result, make the method unsatisfactory for use on a large scale." Tracings are also often unmanageable in the laboratory or office, and must be copied on a reduced scale before they can be used for comparative purposes or published. Tracings also fail to record the nature of the surface on which the paintings were placed.

Photography, particularly color photography, is

favored by many investigators because it is rapid and can be a fairly accurate means of reproduction. Willcox (1963:2), for example, believes that

In recording and reproducing rock art for publication the most important thing, in the present writer's view, is that the reader should get a true impression of how the work looks on the rock. This is why photography, especially in colour, is preferable to tracing or artist's copies where it is practicable. If complemented by careful tracing so much the better.

Unfortunately, color photographs of dim rock paintings often reveal nothing more than pretty patches of color and so are unsatisfactory for comparative and analytical purposes. Photography can also distort color values as well as proportions, and fail to record significant parts of paintings. Photographers, incidentally, seem to have been the chief culprits in treating some Texas pictographs with kerosene and similar substances in order to bring out their colors, ruining the paintings for subsequent investigators (Forrest Kirkland, 1937b:94).

Artists' scale reproductions of rock paintings are apt to be less accurate than tracings or photographs even though they are meticulously copied. It is not that copyists intentionally falsify what they see, but the aesthetic-cultural framework through which they see can warp perception so that they may omit what is present and add what is not there. Artists may also consciously distort reality in that, as Kirkland did, they reproduce colors as they seem to have been originally rather than as they appear after hundreds or thousands of years. There is no doubt that this practice is justified for paintings which are on the verge of being obliterated. Artists' copies may also intentionally minimize what may be distracting backgrounds, forcing the paintings to stand out as they never did in reality. The justification of this practice is that it serves to focus attention on the art itself. Artists' copies also have the advantage of being relatively permanent, easy to use for comparative purposes, and, as Gebhard (1960:14) notes:

The free-hand copying of pictographs and petroglyphs has an additional advantage in that it forces the recorder to minutely study the panels. By doing so he will often be able to discern parts of the drawings which otherwise might fail to attract his attention. Within certain limitations it is also possible to suggest reconstructions of obliterated areas of the drawings and the brilliance of the original coloring.

Kirkland (1937b:98) preferred scale copies of rock art

because we were fortunate enough to have the professional skill, and because this method, when properly used, overcomes almost every objection raised to tracing and to photography. Every design that can be clearly seen and reached for measurement can be accurately copied to scale, and designs too high to be measured can be drawn freehand almost as accurately as a photograph. Every design can be shown in the same scale without distortion and without a distracting background. The copies are small and of uniform size.

There is probably general agreement that for some sites and types of rock art, one copying technique may be superior. But in another region with a different art some other technique may be best, and, ordinarily, for a fully recorded site there will be copies in several techniques.

As a professional artist working before adequate color film had become available, Forrest Kirkland, not surprisingly, found scale copies to be the best technique for recording rock art. He attempted to make his copies as faithful as was humanly possible, and he succeeded admirably. Persons who have been able to compare Kirkland paintings with the actual pictographs or petroglyphs have found his reproductions remarkably accurate. His only shortcoming seems to have been an occasional tendency to simplify or leave out some minor portions of paintings (Grieder, 1965:9,14). This "failing" has been noted only in his recordings of the lower Pecos River region, where some pictograph panels are very intricate and omissions are common and probably inevitable. No two people see exactly the same forms or colors in these dim rock paintings, and no matter how scrupulous the artist, his version is bound to differ in some respects from the work of another artist. In Texas, sites presenting this problem occur only in the lower Pecos River region, where the paintings are complex and apt to be superimposed over one another.

Kirkland worked out his own techniques for copying pictographs, and explained it fully (1937b:98–102):

Water color was chosen as a medium because water color board is most suitable for careful pencil drawings, the color can be quickly and accurately matched and applied over the pencil sketch, and will dry immediately. Since the copies are intended to be filed away as a permanent record, only the best standard materials are used. Our colors are chosen from an absolutely permanent palette of a reliable make, and our paper is hand made English linen mounted on six-ply board. All copies are made on uniform size cards, eleven by fifteen inches, which is one-fourth of a standard water color board. This size is ideal for handling and storage, and has proved a very convenient shape for copies at most locations. When the copies are finished, these boards can be sealed in cellophane envelopes, and with reasonable care, should remain unchanged almost indefinitely.

The size and type of the pictures at a location determine the scale. For the sake of easy comparison, however, we try as often as possible to use the same scale on all pictures at one place. Very large pictures can, of course, be reduced successfully to a much smaller scale than very small or complicated designs. One-half inch to one foot is the usual scale for large designs, although one and one-half inches to one foot is best for groups or small pictures. When the pictures are continuous, or almost so,

PECOS RIVER
SITE 1   No. 1

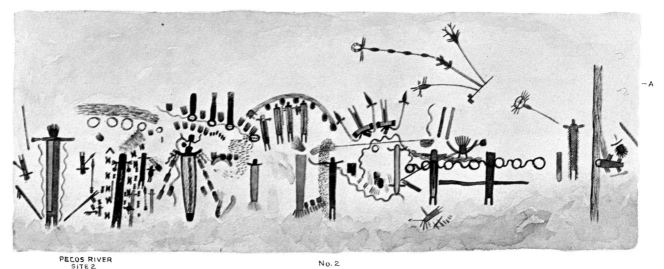

PECOS RIVER
SITE 2   No. 2

Plate 4.   Pecos River. Copied July 10, 1938. Scale: Site 1, 1/4″ to 1′; Site 2, 3/16″ to 1′

PLATE 4

No. 1. Pecos River, Site 1. These red paintings are under an overhanging bluff on the west side of the Pecos River. The pictures are about halfway up the cliff just above a small sloping ledge on which the artist could stand while painting. They get the full force of the morning sun and are wet by blowing rains from the east. Yet they are still quite clear except for the handprints on the left, which probably were never very clear. The rock is flaking badly and has affected the pictures in several places.

No. 2. Pecos River, Site 2. This shelter on the west bank of the Pecos River is about two hundred feet long, fifty feet deep, with a back wall about twenty feet high. Cultural debris appears to be six or more feet deep on its floor. Pictures have been painted continuously over the back wall from the floor to more than eighteen feet high in places. But those near the floor are so badly over-painted and damaged from being rubbed against that only a few can now be made out. The designs at the top are dim but sufficiently clear for copying. The exact color, however, was difficult to determine in some places because of dust collected on them. The heavy collection of dust was caused by an oil which had been painted over the best designs, evidently by someone who wanted to intensify their color for photographing.

PLATES 5 and 6

Pecos River, Site 2. Plate 5 joins Plate 4 at A, and Plate 6 at B, to form a continuous panel. Plate 4, No. 2, follows the bottom part of No. 1 after a gap of about ten feet. The interesting but very dim feather design in Plate 6, No. 2 is followed on the right by human figures and other elements, but they have been exposed to the weather and are so far gone that they could not be copied.

Plate 5.   Pecos River, Site 2. Copied July 10, 1938. Scale: 3/16″ to 1′

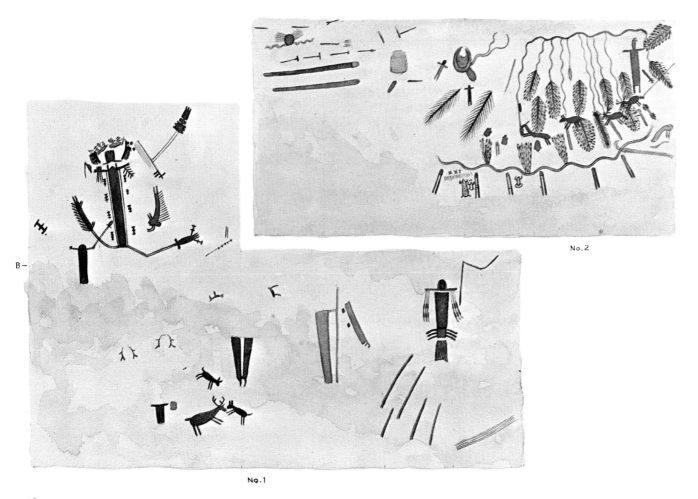

No. 2

No. 1

Plate 6.   Pecos River, Site 2. Copied July 10, 1938. Scale: Nos. 1–2, 3/16″ to 1′

on a long wall, a scale is chosen that will fit the group to a series of boards or plates, as we call them, so that no important design will be divided, and so the group can be reconstructed in its true relations by placing the plates end to end. To do this requires considerable measuring and planning before the copies are begun, but the plan has worked out remarkably well at every site where the pictures were continuous. If a blank space is on such a wall, a break is shown in the copy and the distance omitted is noted on the plate. If for any reason, a picture has to be moved from its correct position, a note is always attached explaining the alteration. Where the designs are scattered about over the wall or cliff so that the above procedure is impractical, they are copied or numbered as nearly as possible in their order from left to right.

Our actual procedure at a location is as follows:

1. A careful survey of the location is made to determine the number and type of designs to be copied.
2. The walls are measured, the scale chosen, and the designs to go on each plate determined.
3. The section allotted to the first plate is divided in convenient spaces, usually three or four feet, depending on the scale, and marked with upright sticks. (We avoid chalking the wall if possible). This greatly simplifies the work of copying.
4. Each design in this section is carefully measured and copied to scale on the plate in pencil. The accuracy of the final copy depends entirely on the skill of the artist and the care with which he performs this operation.
5. When every design on the first section has been copied in pencil, the general tone of the background is painted in. No attempt is made to show small imperfections in the rock or slight variations of color, which would only confuse the Indian designs.
6. Seated in front of each design, we recheck its copy for accuracy, match its color, and paint it in on the plate. For the sake of legibility, it is necessary, in most cases, to use stronger color than is now found on the paintings. As a rule, we try to make our copies about the strength of the original paint. Slight breaks in lines and figures from flaking or other injuries are disregarded in the copy, but no part of a picture is ever added that we cannot be positively certain about.
7. The above procedure is continued with each section until the entire group is copied. Then, a careful survey is made of the location for artifacts, mortars, burnt rock hearths, and other cultural indications.
8. Photographs are made of the shelter or cliff and of any other objects of interest at the location.
9. Notes are made of the location and of every interesting thing observed during our survey of the grounds. The kind of rock on which the designs are painted, the condition of the designs, the colors used, the over-lapping of designs, and any other unusual feature of the paintings, are carefully recorded in these notes. A condensed draft of these notes and the photographs made at the location are later attached to the back of the copies. The original notes are filed away as a permanent record of the survey.

The Notes to which he referred are an invaluable supplement to Kirkland's paintings and not merely captions for them. Many are several hundred words long and contain much more information than the usual caption. This material has been freely quoted in the text, and plate captions in this volume are derived from Kirkland's Notes, though in most cases they have been considerably condensed. Virtually all his Notes have been used either as captions or quotations in this text. It should be noted that Kirkland was quick to criticize his own work, and this trait is revealed in some of his comments in the captions (Plate 100, No. 7, and Plate 109, No. 3, for example).

Petroglyphs and pictographs are here regarded as cultural objects or artifacts, amenable to scientific study and analysis just as are spear points, pottery vessels, marriage customs, and political habits. But there is another way of viewing rock art, a humanistic one in which paintings and engravings are regarded as works of art to be described, evaluated, and criticized in subjective terms. Although the former approach has been adopted here, the latter has much merit; possibly there are art critics and others who could communicate their sensitive and perceptive reactions to rock art in such a way as to arouse an understanding and appreciation of it which could be gained in no other way. The error would be to confuse the two roads to understanding—for the anthropologist to employ the subjective, sometimes visceral jargon of the art critic, the humanist to masquerade his highly personal, ethnocentric bias under the banner of scientific detachment. To divorce the two approaches is not as easy as it might seem; eminent anthropologists have erred in this respect, and probably all investigators have their favorite style or like individual works which it is difficult for them not to overvalue.

Although Kirkland made every attempt to record Texas' rock art fairly and honestly, it is quite obvious that he was strongly drawn to certain pictographic styles and, as an artist, was uninterested in most petroglyphs. The present writer must also admit to a strong personal attraction for certain rock paintings and much less enthusiasm for other rock art. Conceding this bias is an admission of personal taste, not of any particular perceptual incapacity. That viewers hundreds or thousands of years later find one or another form of rock art appealing is indicative of the timelessness and universality of art. Fortunately, much rock art and much that Forrest Kirkland reproduced can be enjoyed in and of itself within our own aesthetic milieu.

CHAPTER 3

A SURVEY OF THE WORLD'S ROCK ART

One or another form of rock art is found on every continent, and in western Europe men were painting cave walls perhaps as long ago as fifty-thousand years. Despite its worldwide distribution and antiquity, much of the world's rock art is poorly known, partly because descriptions of it—when they exist at all—have frequently been buried in obscure publications, partly because its study has often been regarded as belonging to some nether discipline, lying fallow somewhere between art history and archeology. No one, so far as the present writer is aware, has attempted a study of rock art on a worldwide basis; indeed there are very few studies of even hemispheric scope. At the same time an appreciation of the rock paintings and petroglyphs of any area lacks perspective and depth unless it can be related to or placed against the backdrop of the rock art of other regions. It is much like trying to understand the nature and character of poodles while remaining ignorant of other dogs. For this reason it has seemed imperative that before focusing on the rock art of Texas, a brief though admittedly superficial survey of the rock art of the rest of the world should be made.

It is often alleged that rock art, or most of it, has been produced by hunting peoples, and, by inference, that hunters have some sort of mysterious inner compulsion to paint or engrave rock surfaces. The cave murals of France and Spain, painted by Upper Paleolithic hunters, and the well-known Bushman art of South Africa, also the product of a people of a hunting and gathering culture, are often cited to support this contention. But many hunters in various parts of the world have not ornamented rock surfaces to any extent—some Plains tribes of North America for example—and many people whose subsistence was partially or wholly based on something other than wild game have produced rock art. The pastoral people who were authors of the widespread Bovidian rock paintings of North Africa immediately come to mind in this connection. While there is, then, no necessary association between rock art and hunting cultures, it is accurate to say that peoples with a wild-food subsistence

pattern are more apt to have a tradition of rock painting and engraving than are agricultural or other people of more complex subsistence patterns. The reasons are hardly mysterious: hunters or hunters and gatherers are usually nomadic or seminomadic and are apt to frequent or camp in caves and rock shelters, whose surfaces often invite painting or engraving. And, apart from hides and bark, these people are not likely to have other materials or surfaces available for this form of art. Sedentary agriculturalists and other more technologically advanced civilizations, on the other hand, seldom use caves or rock shelters for habitations, and ordinarily have many other kinds of surfaces and materials readily available for painting or inscribing, from house walls to paper and canvas. They may decorate rock surfaces, and peoples of every cultural stripe have done so, but such art seldom becomes an elaborate, avidly practiced, significant tradition with them. It is peoples with wild-food patterns of subsistence who have cultivated rock art most assiduously all over the world, and it is primarily this art with which we are concerned.

Western Europe[1]

By thirty thousand, perhaps as much as fifty thousand, years ago men of the modern type had come to stay in Europe. The last great surge of glaciation had passed its peak, and these men were better equipped to cope with the rigors of a still difficult environment than had been men of the Mousterian and the earlier Lower Paleolithic cultures. Though probably subdivided into a number of tribes or similar groups varying somewhat from one another in their ways of life, these Upper Paleolithic people were all skilled hunters of the rich assortment of big-game animals which then roamed Europe. Three major cultural phases succeeded one another in the Upper Paleolithic era of western

[1] This section is based on the following works: Bandi and Obermaier (1953), Bégoüen (1929), Bégoüen and Breuil (1958), Breuil (1952), Cartailhac and Breuil (1906), Christensen (1955), Frobenius and Fox (1937), Graziosi (1961), Kühn (1956), Maringer (1960), Maringer and Bandi (1953), Windels (1950).

Europe, first a widespread Aurignacian phase, then in parts of Europe a Solutrean, which seems to have been brought by invaders, followed by a Magdalenian, whose termination about 10,000 B.C. brought the Upper Paleolithic to a close. The Aurignacian has been subdivided into an early Périgordian stage, succeeded in most areas of western Europe by a middle or true Aurignacian, and then capped by a Gravettian phase. The most spectacular remains left by these Ice Age hunters are paintings and engravings found on the walls and ceilings of caves, first appearing in the Périgordian at the very beginning of the Upper Paleolithic.

Europe's rock art is concentrated in the Cantabrian Mountains of northern Spain, the Dordogne Valley and adjacent regions of south-central France, and in the Pyrenees of southwestern France. Hence, it is usually designated Franco-Cantabrian art. Although it is not as widespread as were the Upper Paleolithic cultures of which it was a part, there is no question that it was executed by men of these cultures. This statement can be made because a multitude of engraved and painted tools and objects of bone, ivory, horn, as well as decorated small stone slabs have been found in association with Upper Paleolithic materials. Many of these objects of "minor art" are identical to the cave paintings in style and manner of expression. Some of the engraved stone slabs seem even to have been models or preliminary sketches for wall paintings. Cultural debris covering paintings has accumulated at a number of sites, and this fortunate circumstance has also aided in determining the associations of various paintings, as have the superimposition of paintings and the stylistic development of the paintings themselves.

It was a child, five-year-old Maria, daughter of a Spanish nobleman, Don Marcelino de Sautuola, who discovered these cave paintings in 1879. The Sautuolas lived in the small town of Santillana del Mar, which lies in hilly country about twenty miles southwest of Santander on the northern coast of Spain. Don Marcelino had taken along his small daughter on a visit to the cave, and while she was playing there her candle happened to light up a painting of a red bull. Maria excitedly called her father, and incredulously the pair stared at the painting. Then they examined other walls and ceilings, and to their astonishment saw a large number of paintings and engravings. There were bison—bulls, cows, and calves—in all manner of poses, wild boars, and herds of horses. Most of them were in a small chamber about eighty-eight feet from the opening, the rest at the far end of the cave almost a thousand feet from the entrance.

That these animals had been painted by Upper Paleolithic artists is established fact today, and it was apparent to Don Marcelino that such must have been the case. But try as he might he could not convince prehistorians that Ice Age men could possibly have been such skilled artists; they denied the antiquity of the paintings. Ultimately Don Marcelino was held up as a forger, swindler, and worse. Denied access to scientific meetings, the last years of his life were passed in gloomy bitterness. If the cave of Altamira had remained the only site of Upper Paleolithic paintings, scientists might still doubt their authenticity. But in the last decade of the nineteenth century paintings were discovered in a number of French caverns—La Mouthe, Pair-non-Pair, and Marsoulas—loath though prehistorians were to accept them. Finally, in 1903, Abbé Henri Breuil, a young assistant to the French prehistorian Emile Cartailhac, after clearing out the cultural debris in two caves, Font-de-Gaume and Les Combarelles, near Les Eyzies in the Vézère Valley of southern France, was astonished to find that both contained numerous paintings of animals. The authenticity of Ice Age art could no longer be doubted.

Since the discovery of Altamira, paintings have been found in more than one hundred caves in the Franco-Cantabrian region. Altamira remains one of the richest caves, equalled or exceeded only by the spectacular cave of Lascaux, discovered at the beginning of World War II. Situated near Montignac in the Vézère Valley, the entrance shaft was opened when a storm uprooted a tree. Four boys noticed the newly reopened cave, scrambled down the narrow entrance shaft almost twenty feet, and were amazed to find themselves standing in a chamber whose walls were covered with a breathtaking collection of animal paintings. It was subsequently discovered that Lascaux is a complex cave with several levels and a number of chambers, most of which contain entrancing frescoes. In terms of sheer number of animals portrayed, the Lascaux cave is unsurpassed. Both Altamira and Lascaux were hermetically sealed for many years, so that darkness, constant humidity, and the lack of human or other disturbance has preserved the

PLATES 7 and 8

Pecos River, Site 14. This medium-sized shelter very near the top of a cliff is at the mouth of a canyon on the west side of the Pecos River. At one time almost the entire back wall was covered with pictures, but heavy soot has completely covered all except those at the west end. The designs of Plate 101 were badly affected by the soot, but they were still sufficiently clear to be readily copied. The designs above the center of the copy extend well up onto the rounding ceiling. The long designs in the center and the one on the right are almost directly overhead. The center, shaft-like design was painted solid red and then covered with white opaque dots. The copies may be joined at A to show the continuous panel of paintings.

Plate 7.   Pecos River, Site 14. Copied July 19, 1938. Scale: 1/4″ to 1′

Plate 8.   Pecos River, Site 14. Copied July 19, 1938. Scale: 5/16″ to 1′

ancient murals with remarkable freshness. Franco-Cantabrian murals were habitually painted on inaccessible and secluded cave walls, and this circumstance has led to their preservation. Perhaps other men in other regions painted on rock surfaces as early as or earlier than men in western Europe, but if such was the case their work disappeared long ago because it was not situated in places where it would be preserved.

Franco-Cantabrian art followed an interesting developmental course through the thousands of years it was produced. The early Aurignacian artists had few technical artistic traditions to rely on, and their early engravings and paintings were crude outlines or silhouettes. No attempt was made to convey depth or perspective, and the contours of animals' bodies went unnoticed. Only the profile of animals was drawn and at first only the legs on the near side were shown, but antlers and horns were depicted in front view, giving the heads a skewed, odd appearance—a twisted perspective. The paintings at La Grèze in the Dordogne Valley are good examples of this early style. They are, incidentally, known to be early as they were buried by debris from the later Solutrean and Magdalenian and were not discovered until these deposits were excavated. Engraved animals in silhouette with but two visible legs are accompanied by polychrome paintings of the same style, all being rather stiff and static. By the late Aurignacian, progress had been made toward more naturalistic representations of game animals. All four legs were now shown, and heads and antlers were depicted in realistic perspective. The Aurignacian paintings at Lascaux, for example, show considerable development over those at La Grèze and are particularly noteworthy because there are no superimpositions, as there are at other sites in France and Spain in this same style. The Lascaux paintings display much more action, with galloping wild horses, some of which are of monumental size.

By mid-Magdalenian times the progress that had been made in depicting animals naturalistically reached its climax. Artists were now masters of shading, and the fur, muscles, and contours of animals are exceptionally lifelike. Often the artists, as on the ceiling at Altamira, even took advantage of natural protuberances of rock to enhance the realism of their painting. But by late Magdalenian times, the artist had turned his back on the goal of depicting animals as realistically and naturally as possible; he had, in fact, come so close to attaining this goal that further progress was hardly possible. Paintings were now simplified, the essential features of animals being portrayed by a few sure strokes.

It is apparent that Franco-Cantabrian artists were not concerned with pleasing the aesthetic sensibilities of their audience. On the contrary, the location of their paintings was more likely to inspire feelings of awe and mystery, particularly, we may conjecture, if young hunters on the threshold of maturity were allowed to gaze on shadowy paintings lighted only by flickering torches or stone lamps during the course of solemn ceremonies. In a number of paintings wounded animals or animals pierced by spears are depicted. In a few caves where clay was abundant, animals were modeled and spears actually thrown at them, as the riddled models attest. Hence, the desire to slay game is believed to be one of the motives behind this art. Perhaps single hunters or small parties of hunting companions preparatory to the hunt sketched pictures of the animals they hoped to secure, or symbolically acted out the drama they soon hoped to consummate. But this was not the only purpose of the paintings, as there are cases in which the probable motive was that of increasing the supply of game. Gravid bison unmarred by wounds occur, and clay models of a bull bison in the act of mounting a waiting cow have been found. Other examples might be cited. Basically, the belief probably was that by painting or engraving a picture, fashioning a bas-relief, or by making a three-dimensional model, control was or could be gained over that animal. Thus, it was likely believed that if the animal was portrayed as pierced by a spear, or the pictured animal was symbolically slain, so too would the hunter be able to kill the real animal. Such imitative or homeopathic magic is well known among many modern-day hunting peoples and others and, as will become evident, was one of the principal motives for much of the world's rock art.

If power or control over a game animal could be secured by painting its likeness on a wall, it would be logical to believe that power over humans could be gained in the same way. Whether or not this reasoning is correct, human representations are scarce in Franco-Cantabrian paintings, and those depicted are caricatured so that individuality could not be ascertained. Masked human figures garbed in animal disguises are occasionally encountered, however, and these are generally thought to be drawings of shamans or priests. In some caves a number of paintings are superimposed over one another even though there were vacant surfaces nearby. In other instances a painting of one kind of animal has been altered so that it has become another species. The explanation seems to be that certain locations were regarded as particularly sacred and powerful. If animals were painted on a wall, the correct magical formula or ritual followed, and the subsequent hunt was successful, then it seems likely that before some later hunt precisely the same magical routine would be performed at ex-

Pecos River, Site 14, showing the artist copying the principal paintings of Plates 7, 8.

actly the same place. Thus, the superimposition of animals and the alteration of pictures becomes comprehensible.

In general the Franco-Cantabrian art is characterized and set apart from the mural art of other regions by several features. In marked contrast to Bushman art, for example, there are few scenic groupings. Each animal or occasionally several animals were painted as separate entities, as things in and of themselves. Though there may be hundreds of animal paintings in a single cave, each one is isolated, unrelated to others. Absent too is any suggestion of ground, sky, or background. Animals are usually depicted in static poses; they seldom run or gambol as they do in Bushman art. In sum, Franco-Cantabrian was a grandiose and remarkable form of rock art, a monumental legacy of an ancient people.

With the end of the Ice Age and the withdrawal or extermination of many game animals from western Europe, the tradition of engraving and painting pictures in caves waned. One might say that the old magic failed. The reindeer had followed the ice sheets northward and the last mammoth had long since been slaughtered despite all the magical practices men might perform. The people of Europe had to change their ways, adapt their lives to the new conditions, and though rocks were sporadically decorated in the ensuing Mesolithic period, the old tradition was forgotten. Only in Scandinavia and northern Russia are there rock engravings and paintings which may, at least in part, owe their origins to the ancient Ice Age art of western Europe.

This Arctic rock art consists mainly of animal pictures pecked or ground into flat stone surfaces. Remnants of paint on some suggests that a few at least were once painted. At first these engravings were thought to date from the Bronze Age, as do many rock engravings of southern Scandinavia, but it has now been realized that they are distinct from the Scandinavian ones. While their exact age is unknown, at several places Bronze Age petroglyphs are superimposed over them, and their content also plainly reveals that they are a product of a hunting and fishing people, not of farmers or herders.

Arctic art is quite varied, ranging from naturalistic to stylized forms, apparently a result of the large area in which it is found as well as the considerable span of time over which it was produced. What appear to be the oldest examples in northern Norway are distinctly naturalistic; toward the south increasing stylization is apparent. As with Franco-Cantabrian paintings, Arctic art seems to have had a magical purpose, for the pictures are usually located in remote and inaccessible places, as on steep cliff faces reached only with difficulty. Concern with fertility of animals is expressed in some pictures and hunting magic seems to be expressed in others. It may be noted in this connection that the "life-line," a line extending from an animal's nose or mouth to the heart or perhaps lungs, is encountered quite often in these pictures and that this same motif is found in American rock art, with at least one example being known in Texas. The earliest and northernmost Arctic art is strongly reminiscent of the late Aurignacian art of western Europe. There could be no direct connection between these two art forms, separated by so many years and by such a great distance over which there are no connecting links. But it has been suggested (Maringer and Bandi, 1953:159–163) that the sources of Arctic art reach back to the late Aurignacian of central Russia, which persisted with but slight change until the end of the Upper Paleolithic.

Eastern Spain[2]

Along the eastern coast of Spain, never more than seventy-five miles or so inland and extending from the vicinity of Barcelona southward to Cadiz, are a number of rock shelters containing an ancient mural art of a distinctive kind. Called Spanish Levant, Levantine, or East Spanish art, it is a product of the Mesolithic period, dated between 10,000 and 5000 B.C. Though considerably more recent than Franco-Cantabrian paintings, some investigators see a relationship between the two traditions in that some of the animal paintings of the Spanish Levant are similar to those of the Franco-Cantabrian, particularly those of the Périgordian period. The twisted perspective appears in both, as does a tendency toward scenic groupings (Maringer and Bandi, 1953:137–138).

The Levantine paintings are located under rock ledges and in small shelters, suggesting a somewhat different motivation than that of the murals painted in dark, remote caverns. Still, these shelters are located in remote and isolated situations not used as habitation sites by the artists, so this art may also have been born of magic. Unlike the Franco-Cantabrian, Levantine art is addicted to portrayal of human figures—running, hunting, dancing, at war. Frobenius and Fox (1937:24) characterize this style as emphasizing "not only a feeling for composition but a very live conception of movement, haste and speed—in direct contrast to the general immobility of the francocantrabrian paintings and engravings." Actually, several ways of depicting the human figure have been found, each distorting the body in one way or another, but all are alike in their passion for portraying lively action. Whether or not this variation is a matter of the evolution of form or is a function of regional or tribal differences has not yet been completely resolved. Some of the human figures are clothed and adorned, and many are depicted carrying or using bows and arrows, representing, incidentally, the earliest known usage of this weapon (Kroeber, 1948: 663). Most Levantine figures, whether animal or human, are also quite small, up to a foot or so in height, none being life-size or larger. These angular and often sketchy paintings are usually monochromatic, normally a reddish brown or black, occasionally white. None of the polychromes of Franco-Cantabrian art is present.

While the affiliation of Spanish Levant art with the Franco-Cantabrian would seem to be remote or nonexistent, it is, on the other hand, stylistically similar to some found in North Africa, the Sahara, and South Africa. In fact, eastern Spain, Morocco, Algeria, and Tunisia may prove to be a single entity so far as rock art is concerned (Graziosi, 1941: 279).

Africa[3]

Next to the Ice Age art of western Europe, the rock art of South Africa is probably the most widely known of any in the world. Though it well merits its wide acclaim, more recently discovered paintings and petroglyphs in the Sahara and elsewhere in Africa are equally deserving. It is, in fact, becoming clear that Africa is one of the great rock art regions of the world, though much of it is not yet adequately described, or perhaps even discovered, and the age and distribution of certain rock art styles pose questions for which there are not yet answers. The striking similarity between the Spanish Levant paintings and the Bushman art of South Africa, for example, raises intriguing problems and many speculations. Connections between the two regions have not yet been convincingly demonstrated, but rapidly accumulating information may alter this situation. How early rock art was produced in Africa also poses a difficult, perhaps insoluble problem. Africa, unlike western Europe, does not have plentiful limestone caves whose walls could have preserved paintings for many millennia. Instead, petroglyphs and pictographs were often placed in exposed situations, where the elements more rapidly destroyed them. Also, unlike the situation in Europe where favorite subjects of paleolithic artists were Ice Age mammals that later became extinct, Africa's Pleistocene fauna did not undergo mass extinction, so that animals portrayed in rock art are of relatively little help in dating. Finally, as in many other areas of the world, evidence is often lacking to connect particular forms of rock art to known archeological complexes.

In northern Africa scattered rock art sites extend from Mauritania and Spanish Sahara eastward to the Nile Valley, and from the Mediterranean

---

[2] The following discussion draws upon: Christensen (1955), Frobenius and Fox (1937), Graziosi (1941), Maringer and Bandi (1953), and Kroeber (1948).

[3] The following section is based on: Bleek and Stow (1930), Bleek and J. and M. Van der Riet (1940), Breuil (1955a, 1955b), Burkitt (1928), Clark (1954, 1957, 1959), Cole (1965), Cooke (1957), Forde-Johnston (1959), Friendly (1963), Lhote (1959), McBurney (1960), Obermaier (1931), Rhotert (1952), Rosenthal and Goodwin (1953), Walton (1957), Willcox (1956, 1963).

coast deep into the Sahara Desert and the Sudan. The rock art of this tremendous region is quite variable, was undoubtedly painted and engraved over a considerable span of time, and is attributable to a number of different peoples. How ancient the oldest work is has not been conclusively established, but that people lived in parts of the Sahara now completely desiccated is indicative of some antiquity, as is the fact that they portrayed an extinct giant buffalo (*Bubalus antiquus)* and animals which can no longer survive there, such as the elephant, rhinoceros, and hippopotamus. Petroglyphs are more common than paintings, doubtless because they have survived better. Some of the most striking, and earliest, petroglyphs are life-size outline engravings of game animals, generally placed on vertical rock surfaces. Usually seen in profile, animals portrayed include the giant buffalo, the zebra, elephant, giraffe, leopard, donkey (presumably wild), and many others, including men. Animals are skillfully represented in naturalistic poses, although various features such as humps and legs may be exaggerated. A product of a hunting people or peoples, petroglyphs of this kind are found along the southern side of the Atlas Mountains from Tunisia on the northeast to Spanish Morocco on the west. Petroglyphs which are probably related to these, or rather, are likely the product of related hunting people, have been found in the plateau of Tassili n'Ajjer, a sandstone plateau in the Sahara in southeastern Algeria, in the Fezzan province of Libya, and eastward at scattered sites to the Nile. Many other petroglyphs have been found throughout North Africa, some apparently earlier than these naturalistic engravings, many others produced in later times by Neolithic herding peoples, and still others by more recent folk.

Rock paintings are also widespread in North Africa, though their relationships and sequences are not well known. One of the most completely reported and a major center of rock art is in the Tassili n'Ajjer. Thousands of human and animal figures are painted on its rock surfaces. The earliest paintings were made by a hunting people, apparently about eight thousand years ago (Lhote, 1959:204). These paintings are of small human figures with exaggerated large round heads executed in "violaceous" ocher (*ibid., 193).* Figures often carry bows or peculiar trident spears. Oddly for a hunter's art, animals are uncommon in the early paintings and the few represented are mostly elephants and wild sheep. Subsequently, figures increased in size, several colors were employed, more care was taken with the paintings, and animals became more common. According to Lhote, at some point in its history this tradition was influenced from an Egyptian source, and a new and more vigorous style resulted. In a final phase drawings of humans became gigantic with heavy forms less carefully rendered. Many animals were portrayed, giving a good idea of the fauna that then existed in the Sahara. Included are paintings of elephants, giraffes, wild oxen, hippopotamuses, wild sheep, wart hogs, lions, and ostriches.

This art was succeeded by that of a pastoral people at Tassili whose favorite subjects were their cattle. Two species, the African ox (*Bos africanus)* and the thick-horned ox (*Bos brachyceros)* are depicted, usually in large herds escorted by herdsmen. Painted in flat tints or outlines, these cattle are naturalistically portrayed with great attention paid to anatomical detail and action. These pastoral people were also hunters who painted the abundant wildlife as skillfully as they did their cattle. Lhote (1959:201–202) discovered evidence at a number of sites that these Bovidian artists had contacts with Egypt, and he believes that they came from the east.

Paintings similar to those found in the Tassili n'Ajjer are widespread in northern Africa, particularly those of Bovidian artists who may have wandered over a vast region seeking pasturage for their stock. More than a thousand miles east of Tassili n'Ajjer, in the Libyan Desert, for example, a pastoral people also painted and engraved boulders and rock walls. This art is similar to that of the pastoralists of Tassili, and it also had some sort of affiliation to the Egyptian civilization (Rhotert, 1952). An earlier hunting people also left engravings on the rocks of this region. Even farther east, in the Diredawa area of Ethiopia, naturalistic rock paintings of pastoralists have been discovered. The dress and weapons of the human figures portrayed in these paintings are similar to those of the present Hamitic people of the region, but the cattle lack the humps of modern Zebu cattle. But in a later series of paintings both humped cattle and camels are depicted, dating them within the historic era (Breuil, 1934; Clark, 1954: 295–315). Other protohistoric and historic inhabitants of North Africa have also ornamented its rock surfaces. Paintings of chariots pulled by horses drawn in a distinctive "flying gallop" pose characteristic of Mycenaen art of Crete have been found at a number of places in the Sahara and by this evidence are dated after 1200 B.C. There are many other pictographs and petroglyphs of horses and camels, the latter usually shown with riders. Many of these are comparatively crude, done in small scale, and date from quite recent times, since camels (dromedaries) were introduced into Africa after A.D. 500.

Few rock paintings have been found in Kenya, but in 1960 on the slopes of Mount Elgon near the Uganda border a number of paintings were discovered on the walls of a protected shelter (Cole, 1965:242–244). These red and white paintings depict cattle, apparently domesticated and lacking humps of the region's recent cattle. The floor of the shelter lacked any cultural debris, so the affiliations of the artists are unknown. One of the few human figures appears to be armed with a bow and arrow, and it seems reasonable to ascribe these paintings to a pastoral people. The horns of the cattle in these rather crude drawings are emphasized, and one has a fork as though it was intended to be a deer's antler. But deer have not been present as far south as Kenya for several hundred thousand years at least, and it seems likely that artificial deformation is involved, an old and common practice in this part of the world. Petroglyphs are also rather scattered and uncommon in East Africa, and are unlike the naturalistic outline engravings of North Africa. They consist mostly of lines, geometric designs, and cup marks or cup-shaped depressions ground into rocks. Petroglyphs of the same general sort are found in Zambia, in the Katanga region of the Congo, and on into Angola. Their age, cultural affiliations, and purpose are still in doubt.

In Tanganyika and Northern Rhodesia, now Zambia, rock paintings again become more common, apparently representing the northern border or terminus of the area of rock painting generally known as the Bushman area. This region may be likened to a giant fishhook, its tip in South West Africa, curving south around the formidable Kalahari Desert, its shank stretching northward from the Cape of Good Hope some two-thousand miles into central Tanganyika. The bulk of its rock art was undoubtedly the work of the Bushmen and their ancestors, the small-sized, hunting and gathering people who once roamed over much of southern and eastern Africa. But much remains to be learned about the archeological associations of the rock art of this tremendous region, as well as about the art itself. It has undergone stylistic changes through time and has regional variations. The Bushmen seem to be represented archeologically by a Wilton culture, which began about 2000 B.C. and lasted until recent times in some areas of southern and eastern Africa. But it is now known that at least some rock art of eastern Africa was produced earlier —4300 B.C. if a radiocarbon date stands up—by a Nachikufan culture centered in Zambia and Tanganyika (Cole, 1965:237–239). And there is a good possibility that prehistoric and historic people in this vast region other than Bushmen also participated in this rock art tradition. In short, the protohistoric and early historic Bushmen seem to have been the greatest exponents of a lively form of rock art, but they may not have been its creators or its only practitioners.

While the age of the oldest Bushman paintings is not known with any precision, it has been estimated that surviving examples could surely reach back five centuries and "an age of twenty centuries [is] quite possible, but longer than this unlikely for rock paintings or petroglyphs under the conditions in which they are found" (Willcox, 1963:51). Many of the paintings are historic, and in fact Bushmen continued their ancient tradition in northern Bechuanaland until 1917. But, harried and decimated, the remaining groups were ultimately confined to the inhospitable Kalahari Desert, where suitable rock surfaces are virtually absent. Apparently a few groups continued for a time to paint on animals' hides, but the custom has been completely abandoned and the Bushmen remember nothing of their ancient art today.

Practicing no agriculture and maintaining no herds or flocks, the Bushmen were hunters, fishermen, and gatherers. In the days before they were driven into the more desolate parts of southern Africa by Bantus and Europeans, small nomadic groups must have led a relatively bountiful, easy life though they had but a Stone Age technology with which to secure their subsistence. Wherever available, the Bushmen camped in rock shelters, and in this tremendous area there are thousands of them, most of which are only a few yards long and a yard or so deep. Where shelter walls are smooth they are frequently painted with lively scenes of men and animals, and many other rocks and boulders in exposed places are inscribed with petroglyphs. Although a wide array of subjects are portrayed in this rock art, most paintings—as could be expected of a hunting people—are of game animals or humans engaged in various activities. They painted virtually every animal of the rich African fauna known to them, including elephants, giraffes, rhinoceroses, zebras, buffaloes, leopards, lions, birds, reptiles, and fish. Their favorite subjects—elands, rheboks, springboks, and hartebeests—were also apparently the principal game animals in their diet. Animals in both the paintings and petroglyphs are realistically depicted with what can only be described as consummate mastery. The Bushmen obviously were keen observers of the animal world about them and were amazingly adept at recreating the likenesses of this fauna on stone surfaces. While the animals the Bushmen drew are not as active and lively as their human figures, particularly in their earlier paintings, animal drawings, whether of single animals or well planned compositions, are always fresh and different, never stereotyped. Notable and "unparalleled in any other rock art in the world and indeed not equalled in any art until the fifteenth century in Europe was the Bushmen's mastery of foreshortening" (Willcox, 1963:82). Not only does foreshortening occur in paintings but in petroglyphs as well. In contrast to paintings of animals, human figures are portrayed less naturalistically with, as

Willcox says (*ibid.*), "some deliberate exaggeration by way of emphasis." Facial features, for example, are never indicated and the body is conventionalized. Although the human figure is shown in several ways, most are depicted with heavy calves, thighs, and buttocks. Humans, often in groups with women exhibiting the characteristic steatopygia of the Bushmen, are shown engaged in a wide assortment of activities from fishing and hunting scenes to dances and battle scenes. All in all, Bushman art is an exceptionally lively, vital art.

They seem to have painted the walls of the shelters they transiently occupied for a variety of reasons. Unquestionably a great many are commemorative in the sense that they recount events, or tell stories about hunting incidents, encounters with Negro or European invaders, and the like. But there are other paintings of half-men, half-beasts which seem to deal with mythology, and at some sites the Bushmen painted pictures on top of each other, sometimes three and four deep. This is strong presumptive evidence that such walls were particularly important, possibly sacred, and that the art was in part a magical or religious one, or that the act of painting rather than the result itself was important.

When a Western observer first encounters Franco-Cantabrian art the usual impact is incredulity that ancient and technologically primitive men could produce such masterful works of art. A second reaction is a question: Why did they paint such murals? The impact of Bushman art is quite different. The observer is immediately seized with the realization that this is an art which boldly reflects the nature of a Stone Age people. It is an ebullient, effervescent, merry art, recording a life lived joyously as part of and hand in hand with the natural world. Inquiries into its purpose seem almost superfluous; the viewer is tempted to share its delights rather than wonder at its rationale.

Australia [4]

The continent of Australia, isolated for many millennia from the mainstream of cultural developments and sparsely populated by men who had but a meager assortment of weapons and tools with which to exploit a generally harsh environment, might seem an unlikely setting in which rock art would flourish. But rock paintings and petroglyphs have been reported from nearly every part of the continent, as well as from the even more remote island of Tasmania. Some of Australia's rock art may be of venerable age, though how ancient remains a

[4] This section is based on the following works: Berndt (1964), Davidson (1936), Elkin (1949), Elkin and C. and R. Berndt (1950), Mountford (1954, 1961), Simpson (1953), Spencer and Gillen (1899, 1904).

matter of conjecture. Perhaps of more significance, the aborigines continued to produce rock art down to modern times with the result that its purpose and role in native cultures is better understood than it is in most areas of the world. In general it played a surprisingly important part in native life; it "permeates all aspects of the aborigines' life. It is the vital medium through which they keep alive their philosophies, their laws and the stories of their creation" (Mountford, 1954:11).

The most distinctive of the continent's rock paintings are found in caves along the western edge of the Arnhem Land plateau in northern Australia. These are rather static, life-size or larger polychrome paintings of birds, fish, reptiles, kangaroos, and other animals, with only occasional anthropomorphic representations. Some at least are quite recent, as natives remember when they were painted. Aptly termed X-ray art, "the aborigines painted not only what they saw, i.e. the external form of the creature, but also what they could not see, yet knew to be there, the skeleton, lungs, hearts and other internal organs" (Mountford, 1961:6). What amounted to a simple version of this idea was occasionally employed in North America to indicate the heart and a "heartline" to the mouth, and the same basic idea crops up in rock art in other areas. But in western Arnhem Land it was carried to extremes. Some of the larger X-ray paintings are made up of thousands of fine, colored lines, and when friezes of these figures, up to a hundred feet long, cover the walls and ceilings of rock shelters the effect is quite striking.

Also found in western Arnhem Land, often in the same caves in which there are examples of X-ray art, are paintings of stick-like, animated human figures in red. Both men and women are depicted—dancing, hunting, and fighting. The natives attribute them to a mythological fairy people who lived in the rocks, the Mimis, and stoutly maintain that they are not responsible for them. Paintings of more malignant spirits, the Mormos, are also found in this region. Up to eight feet tall, most have enormous genitals. Apparently both the beneficent and malignant representations were painted to illustrate myths and tales while they were being told. Mountford (1961:6) has pointed out that many of the Mimi figures have a startling resemblance to some Spanish Levant, northern Saharan, and Bushman paintings. They antedate the X-ray paintings, but exactly when they were painted and by whom is a mystery.

Some of the most elaborate rock paintings of the continent are found in the Kimberley region of northwestern Australia. Two kinds of rock art are found here, an earlier one possibly associated with the Mormo spirit paintings of western Arnhem Land (McCarthy in Berndt, 1964:41). These graceful, life-size anthropomorphic figures usually wear odd headdresses and are armed with boomerangs and spears. The later paintings are complex polychrome murals of totemic beings, the Wandjina. These are supernatural beings who are held to be responsible for rain, lightning, rainbows, the succession of seasons, and the fecundity of plants, animals, and man. All of the Wandjina are of a single style although there is considerable variability in size and minor details. Curiously, all lack mouths and it is incomprehensible to the natives that they could be painted otherwise.

On the head is a red and white or yellow oval band, which encircles the face, and from its outer edge radiates a fringe of red lines tipped with black. This headband represents a strip of red ochre and fat, such as is commonly applied to the head and face of Aborigines today. The eyes and nose form one unit, usually in red, with long eyelashes encircling both eyes. Body and limbs have a thick red or black outline, covered with red stripes which represent falling rain. The hands and feet are large, and the latter lie on top of each other to expose the soles. Toes and fingers vary in number from three to seven. The genital organ is indicated in the female Wandjina, but not in the male. . . . The general effect of Wandjina is one of great mystical power vested in a kindly spirit possessing no dangerous attributes. (McCarthy in Berndt, 1964:41-42)

In western Arnhem Land there are other cave paintings which the aborigines view as the actual bodies of various totemic food animals. By acting out a traditional ritual which involved whipping the painting with a branch, it was believed that the totemic spirits would be forced out of the painting into the world and thus replenish the supply of that particular creature. In this same region enemies could be slain by painting their likenesses on cave walls and then reciting certain magical incantations over them.

The rock art of the northern parts of Australia has apparently been stimulated by sporadic contacts with Indonesia and Melanesia, and the number of styles, motifs, and the range and combination of colors is greater than in more remote parts of the continent (Mountford, 1961:7; McCarthy in Berndt, 1964:37-40). Over much of central and southern Australia rock paintings seem to be simpler and more abstract, and in some regions limited to spirals, concentric circles, wavy lines, and the like. Petroglyphs are common in Australia and may also be of considerable antiquity. The earliest and most widely distributed form of petroglyphs are simple grooves abraded in rocks, scattered irregularly over the surface or arranged in simple designs. These were succeeded by an outline style, the greatest development of which took place in the Sydney-Hawkesbury River region of eastern New South Wales. Here engraved outlines of men, animals, birds, and fish are often immense, reaching lengths

of sixty feet. These appear to be in sacred locations and are presumed to have been produced for ritualistic and religious purposes. A third phase of engraving rocks seems to have spread from northwestern Australia to other parts of the continent. Linear and geometric designs replaced the naturalistic figures of the earlier period. Most of these figures are small and seem to have been hastily and carelessly made. Great numbers of them have been found. A fourth phase, in which rocks and boulders were pecked, lasted until the time of European occupation. In this widespread style all sorts of animals were depicted, as well as mythical creatures and humans engaged in hunting, fighting, dancing, and making love. They seem to be related to the Mimi style of rock paintings, and their location at sacred totemic centers suggests that they too were associated with religious beliefs and practices.

South and Middle America

Rock art has a widespread distribution in the Americas, from Alaska to Argentina and from the Atlantic to the Pacific coasts. Much of it is the product of recent or historic Indians, but some rock surfaces were carved and painted at least several thousand years ago and a few perhaps much earlier. Considering the immense area and the span of years involved, it should not be surprising that American petroglyphs and pictographs are tremendously varied. Some are as crude and primitive as the sidewalk scribbling of children and probably about as significant. At the other extreme are complex and intricate designs which no doubt represent the results of long-practiced traditions pursued for reasons which were of considerable importance to the artists. Unfortunately, the rock art of some regions, particularly in South America, has not yet been adequately described. This is partly because much of it is not visually very spectacular, but its often remote location and the preoccupation of archeologists with other matters are also factors.

South American rock art is ordinarily classified into four geographical groups: Patagonian, Ando-Peruvian, Colombian-Venezuelan, and Brazilian (Boman, 1908, 2:815–855; Rouse, 1949:495). Rock paintings and painted petroglyphs have been found in many caves and rock shelters in Tierra del Fuego, Patagonia, and extend to south central Chile. Most seem to be rather crude, but depict a considerable variety of geometric designs, human hand- and footprints, simple human figures, and bird and animal tracks. Most rock art in this region is prehistoric, though its cultural affiliations and age have not yet been well worked out. The Ando-Peruvian region includes the southern and central Andes, extending from Chile and Argentina to Bolivia and Peru. Both pictographs and petroglyphs occur and are found in rock shelters and in the open. Much of this region's rock art was apparently associated with the advanced civilizations which developed there, and the art seems to be peripheral in the sense that its subject matter and motifs had first been developed and worked out in other media. The rock art is quite variable and is frequently complicated. It runs the gamut from realistic portrayal to conventionalized figures. Scenic groupings are also present. Depiction of animals, birds, and humans rather than geometric figures seems to be characteristic of the region as a whole. Rouse (*ibid.*) states that

Pictures of the llama are most common in the central part of the area. As one moves north into Peru, feline figures become more important; to the south, the typical design is an entanglement of irregular curved lines. Most of the drawings of scenes are in Northwest Argentina, while North Chile is characterized by enormous petroglyphs, which are often traced in the desert sands rather than on rocks, or by planting stones in the ground.

In the Colombian-Venezuelan region rock art is found almost solely in mountainous areas. Both paintings and petroglyphs occur, in the open and in caves and rock shelters. Animals and humans are common subjects; unlike in the Ando-Peruvian region, details of clothing and ornamentation are not depicted and scenic groupings are lacking (*ibid.*, 498). In Huila, south of Bogotá, Colombia, some of the rock art figures are said to resemble the goldwork of the Chibcha, the great native civilization of that area. Pérez de Barradas (1914) has described this and seven other zones of rock art in Colombia, none of which seems to represent highly significant traditions in the native cultures. Apparently much of this rock art is partially or wholly ancillary to art of other media.

The rock art of the Brazilian region is not well known. Rouse (1949:499) believes that there are

centers of concentration near the headwaters of the various tributaries of the Amazon, in the region around Pernambuco and Natal in Brazil, in the Guianas, and in the West Indies. Engraving is more common in the northern part of the area and painting in the south. Pictures of fish, animals, and human beings seem to be characteristic; they are drawn in a schematic fashion which contrasts with the detail of the Highlands. Such designs are often presented only in part, in the form of faces or of faces and bodies. Simple geometric figures, such as the circle and the spiral, are also common.

A distinctive manner of depicting the human face in petroglyphs is found in Puerto Rico in the West Indies and in Chiriqui in Panama, raising the possibility that there was a widespread Caribbean area of rock art (Holmes, 1888:22; Fewkes, 1903, 1907; Frasetto, 1960).

The focus of archeological interest throughout Middle America, from Panama to the Valley of Mexico and beyond, has been quite understandably on the spectacular remains of the great civilizations that once dominated much of this area. While the artistic traditions of the Maya, for example, were well developed and distinctive, neither they nor other Nuclear American civilizations emphasized the custom of painting or engraving natural rock surfaces. This does not mean that they never practiced this art form, only that it was not of great significance to them. Consequently, very little rock art has been reported from this region, and distinctive styles seem to have been practiced nowhere widely or through a considerable period of time.

North America

Both pictographs and petroglyphs are more common in the arid lands of western North America than they are in the eastern forested sections of the country. Chances for preservation, particularly of pictographs, are of course better in arid regions. Suitable rock surfaces are also more numerous in dry-land regions since they are less apt to be covered with vegetation and soil. Petroglyphs have a wider distribution than pictographs, not because pecking, incising, or grinding figures on rocks was a more congenial or satisfactory form of expression, but because paintings and drawings are much more perishable, hence have not so often survived the vicissitudes of the years. Despite climatic differences and the differential availability of suitable rock surfaces, petroglyphs and pictographs have been recorded from all but a handful of states. As of 1946, only Alabama, Connecticut, Delaware, Florida, Indiana, Louisiana, Mississippi, New Hampshire, and South Carolina lacked rock art of any kind (Tatum, 1946).

In far North America—Alaska and Canada—pictographs appear to be absent and petroglyphs rare, the latter being reported on Kodiak Island (Heizer, 1947) and at one site ninety miles inland from the Arctic Ocean (Solecki, 1952). Their rarity may be a result of a severe climate and a thinly scattered aboriginal population, but it is entirely possible that many rock art sites have not yet been discovered or reported. In the region covered by the Canadian Shield, which stretches from Hudson Bay south in an arc along the northern shores of the Great Lakes then northward into the Labrador peninsula, a considerable number of rock paintings have been found on vertical rock surfaces, always near the waterways which were the chief avenue of travel (Dewdney and Kidd, 1962; Stanton, 1947). The paintings are mostly red, but traces of black and white pictographs have been found. Game animals, such as moose and bear; canoes and wigwams; and what appear to be mythical creatures, such as thunderbirds and a pipe-smoking moose, are common subjects (Dewdney and Kidd, 1962:111). Many of the paintings are apparently associated with places thought to have been inhabited by supernatural beings; others may represent messages to other men or gods. Since these rock paintings are exposed to severe weathering it seems unlikely that any of them are over four or five hundred years old.

Petroglyphs are common along the Pacific coast from southeast Alaska to northern California in the region occupied in historic times by tribes of the distinctive Northwest Coast culture. In southeast Alaska, in the area inhabited by the Tlingit, Keithahn (1940:132; also see Emmons, 1908) found that the rather abundant "petroglyphs were made by the forebears of the present native inhabitants of the region, that they originated here, that they came to have a religious significance relating to the food supply, and that out of them was evolved the present striking Northwest Coast decorative art." Farther south among the Quinault of Washington, boys undergoing puberty rites painted pictographs of mythical water monsters they had seen in visions (Steward, 1937:413; Cain, 1950).

The central valleys of California lack pictographs and petroglyphs, and the pictographs of the coastal region have little in common with the rock art of nearby regions. The Sierra Nevada mountain range seems to have served as an effective barrier against the westward spread of petroglyphs from the Great Basin. In the Santa Barbara and Tulare areas, for example, some simple elements of the pictographs are shared with the petroglyphs of eastern California but most are distinctive.

Foremost is the practice of outlining figures of one color with one or more borders of a different color. We also find many figures made up of a series of dots instead of solid lines. There are a number of geometric elements—herringbones or feathers, alternating straight bands of color, zigzags, and others which are worked into designs so elaborate as to defy analysis. (Steward, 1929:222–223)

Another distinctive region is in the southern section of the state extending into Baja California, where the principal pictographic design "is the zigzag in various arrangements and combinations" (Steward, 1929:222; Hicks, 1959:64). The purpose and meaning of these pictographs is explained by the girls' puberty ceremony and other ceremonies of the Luiseño and Cupeño, historic tribes of the area. Both tribes held elaborate puberty ceremonies which were concluded by the girls' racing to a rock on which they painted these designs. There also seem to have been other ceremonies during which rocks were painted with various designs (True, 1954). Most of the California pictographs seem to be of recent origin, although evidence of superimposition at a few sites indicates that at least some of them may be older.

Petroglyphs are probably more numerous in the arid Great Basin region of western North America than anywhere else in the hemisphere. Pictographs, on the other hand, are relatively rare even though climatic conditions would seem to favor their preservation more than in most areas. Some of the Great Basin petroglyphs appear to be quite ancient, others recent (Steward, 1937:417). Heizer and Baumhoff (1962) were able to establish a series of petroglyph styles in Nevada and eastern California, tentatively dating the earliest Pit-and-Groove petroglyphs between 5000 B.C. and 3000 B.C. These investigators believe that these simple and unobtrusive petroglyphs are "spread over most of western North America and perhaps even farther" (p. 209) but that in some regions they seem to have a much more recent date. A Great Basin Curvilinear style is said to have begun somewhat later—three or four thousand years ago—but if it is associated with the ancient Desert Culture, as seems likely, its age could be considerably greater (Steward, 1929:220; Baumhoff, Heizer, and Elsasser, 1958; Heizer and Baumhoff, 1962:205–207). Heizer and Baumhoff have distinguished other petroglyph styles in the Great Basin, but of more significance for our purposes, they have argued very convincingly (1962:239) that

petroglyphs in Nevada and eastern California are evidence of the purposeful and rational action of prehistoric peoples. They are not aimless "doodling," nor are they deliberate and planned expressions of the artistic impulse. We think that we have proved that petroglyphs in the area we have studied are to be understood as a part of the economic pursuit of hunting large game (deer, antelope, and mountain sheep). . . . Thus, petroglyphs are part of the magical or ritual aspect of taking large game.

In the desert and plateau land of the Southwest, petroglyphs and pictographs are relatively common. The custom of painting and engraving rocks was well established among the historic Pueblo peoples, reaching back to their Basket Maker beginnings sometime around the advent of the Christian era (Steward, 1937:421). Some of their petroglyphs are evidently clan symbols (Colton and Colton, 1931) commemorating dangerous journeys, but commemoration was not the only purpose behind the rock art of this region. Pictographs which are part of this Puebloan tradition occur at two sites Kirkland visited, Hueco Tanks near El Paso and Rocky Dell in the Panhandle, and are discussed in Chapter 8. Other Southwestern peoples, such as the Navahos, carved and painted rock surfaces, often in styles and motifs which are related to those of the Pueblos. Portrayal of the hunchbacked flute player, an ancient deity in the Southwest and of the Pueblos, for example, also occurs in Navaho and Apache art. A representative hunchbacked figure occurs at Hueco Tanks.

On the walls of the caves in which Basket Makers, the first farmers of the Southwest, lived are often found "simple anthropomorphic figures with triangular bodies and squarish heads, usually in red" (Steward, 1937:421 and Plate 4A). Steward believed that "a people living on the Colorado Plateau in eastern Utah borrowed this simple Basket Maker art and developed it with extraordinary success." Whether or not this was actually the case, the pictographs of the Colorado Plateau are impressive and a few of them in size and in the lavish use of color, are vaguely reminiscent of some of the Pecos River style pictographs of Texas (see Chapter 4). Steward (1937:421) says:

These striking figures are sometimes carved, sometimes painted, sometimes both [Plates 100, 101, 102]. Often whole canyon walls are covered with imposing galleries of regal and unearthly beings which may be gods or may be men. When painted, they are often in three and four colors; when carved and incised, they are executed with a care and precision unequaled elsewhere. The square-shouldered bodies are surmounted by squarish heads which may well depict masks (but no masks have ever been found in pre-Columbian Southwestern archeological sites) and which are surmounted by antlers of different kinds, "feathers," and other ornaments which are undoubtedly identifying symbols. The faces usually have eyes, a refinement rare among petroglyphs elsewhere, and below the eyes are two thin lines, which strangely resemble but are certainly not connected with the "tear marks" on faces in Tiahuanacoid drawings in ancient Peru. Earrings and necklaces are shown in great profusion and often the body bears elaborate designs.

The absence of boulders, ledges, cliffs, and other suitable rock surfaces in many parts of the immense interior plains of North America has limited rock art to scattered and spotty localities. Nonetheless the many pictographs and petroglyphs of considerable variability in this region suggest that a number of different peoples, possibly through a long period of time, painted and incised its rocks. Outstanding rock art sites include Writing-on-Stone on the Mild River in southern Alberta, Pictograph Cave in southern Montana (Mulloy, 1952; Renaud, 1936), Dinwoody Canyon in Fremont County, Wyoming (Gebhard and Cahn, 1950), Castle Gardens, south of Moneta in central Wyoming (Renaud, 1939), Whoop-Up Canyon in northeastern Wyoming, the Red Canyon district in the southern Black Hills, Inscription Rock on the Smoky Hill River near Ellsworth, Kansas (Wedel, 1959:483), and others, including several sites in the plains region of Texas, to be discussed in Chapters 7 and 8.

Petroglyphs are more common than pictographs in the plains and were executed by an assortment of techniques—pecking, rubbing, grinding, and incising. They are similarly variable in subject matter, ranging from simple to complex geometric designs and including many representations of various kinds of animals and humans. Some petroglyphic styles appear to be widespread, although no definitive studies of these have yet appeared (Wedel, 1961:276).

The less common pictographs are usually in red, but black, white, and other colors have also been found. As with the plains petroglyphs, no comparative or analytical study of these pictographs has yet been made. At least one style or type of pictograph, the so-called shield-bearing warriors, has an immense distribution, and others may be found which are equally far-flung. Shield-bearing warriors have so far been discovered in southern Alberta, Canada; Montana; Wyoming; and Utah where they are associated with the Fremont culture (Wormington, 1955:186; Secrist, 1960; see also Wedel, 1961:276). Kirkland reproduced a number of these shield-bearing warriors from the Hueco Tanks site near El Paso (discussed in Chapter 8), thus extending the range of these figures considerably. At Hueco Tanks they appear to be historic, but at other sites they are dated much earlier.

Although there are many scattered petroglyphs and some surviving pictographs east of the Mississippi, nowhere does it appear that they played a particularly significant role in aboriginal cultures nor do they seem to have been part of any well-developed tradition. If there are widespread types or styles of petroglyphs and pictographs, they have gone unrecognized. A few designs and motifs have a wide distribution, in fact are not restricted to the eastern United States, but their age and significance are in doubt. Among these are carved hand- and footprints. We learn, for example, that

Petroglyphs occur throughout southern Illinois and along the streams which border this area. The carved human footprints occur abundantly here, through Indiana and Ohio, and along the Tennessee and Cumberland rivers. They are also found up the Mississippi and Missouri rivers. . . . The designs appear to have been pecked and ground into the sandstone to produce a most realistic effect, indicating that the foot or hand was actually used as a model. In a few cases it appears that they were also painted. (Merwin, 1937:79)

Many of the petroglyphs of the eastern United States have been known for many years, with the result that a tremendous amount of fiction and legend has sometimes grown up about them. The famous Dighton Rock on Narragansett Bay, Massachusetts, is perhaps the most extreme and famous case: the petroglyphs on this rock have inspired almost six hundred articles and books. Some have used the petroglyphs to "prove" the European origin of American Indians, others have insisted they pointed the way to buried pirate treasure. "Scholars" have "successfully translated" them as Scandinavian, Scythian, Hebrew, Phoenician, Egyptian, Persian, Libyan, Trojan, Chinese, and Japanese symbols. And finally, some have asserted that these petroglyphs were made by God, not man. These incredible interpretations were examined and summarized by Edmund B. Delabarre (1928), who concluded that Dighton Rock and similar New England petroglyphs were made by Indians after the arrival of Europeans. This dating and Delabarre's conclusion that they were purposeless may be called into question, but his rational approach to the subject has laid to rest the more bizarre and naive speculations.

In worldwide perspective, North America may be characterized as a region in which many different people at various times sporadically engraved and painted rock surfaces. In a few places and probably for varying reasons, some people elaborated and cultivated this art form. Where this took place, distinctive and original styles developed. But no style of rock art was as widespread as that of the Bushman in Africa, and no tradition was or probably could have been practiced for as long as was that of the Franco-Cantabrian art in Europe. The rock art of Texas fits our general characterization well; many paintings and engravings, spasmodically produced by a variety of prehistoric and historic peoples, have been found within the borders of the state. And in a region centering around the juncture of the Pecos River with the Rio Grande, as will become evident in the following chapter, there flourished one of North America's most distinctive and earliest pictographic centers.

In sum, men of many cultures on every continent through many thousands of years have painted and engraved rock surfaces. They have done so for a variety of reasons but usually, it would seem, for practical, down-to-earth purposes. The striking diversity in the world's rock art suggests that men have repeatedly and independently invented this mode of artistic expression. But the example of other or earlier artists has also frequently stimulated them to try their hand at its practice.

CHAPTER 4

THE LOWER PECOS: ANCIENT PAINTINGS

Shrouded with the dust of centuries, embellishing walls of shelters and overhangs which peer vacantly at the desolate, sun-scorched canyons of the lower Pecos River country is a stunning array of rock paintings. The most common, distinctive, and oldest style of paintings has been variously termed Val Verde Dry Shelter Culture (Kirkland, 1939:47), Pecos River Focus style—after a presumed association with this archeological complex (H.C. Taylor, 1948:74; Graham and Davis, 1958:78), and Pecos Style (Gebhard, 1960:9). They will be referred to here as Pecos River style. Geographically these paintings are confined to a limited area centering around the junction of the Pecos with the Rio Grande (Map 1). Most are within the borders of modern Val Verde County in the drainage systems of the Rio Grande, lower Pecos, and Devils rivers. But a few have been found on the Mexican side of the border in Coahuila (H. C. Taylor, 1948:84); one known site is in northeastern Terrell County in the Pecos drainage (Plates 41, 42) and some at Meyers Springs, also in Terrell County, are either Pecos River style or are very closely related to it (see Chapter 6). Because of the amount and variety of rock art in the lower Pecos River region, discussion of it has been divided between two chapters. The earlier Pecos River style paintings are discussed here; the later pictographs, principally of a Red Monochrome style, and the petroglyphs are taken up in Chapter 5.

Kirkland copied pictographs at forty-three sites in Val Verde County, thirty-five of them containing Pecos River style paintings, and he knew of but was unable to visit six other sites (1939:47–48). Jackson (1938:165–239) listed forty pictograph sites in Val Verde County, a large majority of which had Pecos River style paintings. In a survey of the Diablo (now Amistad) Reservoir for the Texas Archeological Salvage Project, National Park Service, Graham and Davis (1958:80) located forty-nine pictograph sites, thirty-eight of which are in the Pecos River style, as well as four other sites at which this and later styles are represented. In short, more than forty Pecos River style pictograph sites

are known, but this is not a complete inventory since new ones continue to be found. At some sites there are only a few scattered Pecos River style paintings, but in some of the larger shelters paintings may almost completely cover the walls, extending along them for more than one hundred feet (Kirkland, 1939:51). Exactly how many walls of shelters and overhangs once bore Pecos River style pictographs cannot, of course, be determined, but in the lower Pecos River region they are still amazingly common and must once have been ubiquitous.

Though there have been fluctuations between more and less arid conditions in the lower Pecos River region, the climate does not seem to be significantly different today than it was when the Pecos River style pictographs were executed. This region is semiarid, rainfall during the past forty-five years averaging a little over fifteen inches annually, most of it falling in the summer, when high temperatures reduce its effectivity enormously. Except for the Rio Grande, Pecos, and Devils rivers, water is extremely scarce. The many rugged, steep-walled canyons are normally dry, although standing water may sometimes be found in bedrock water holes in canyon floors, and there are a number of springs in the area. It is hardly surprising that human occupancy of the region was concentrated near the rivers.

The lower Pecos River region is in a transitional environmental area and perhaps this had a bearing on its attractiveness to prehistoric man. To the southwest, including most of West Texas, southern New Mexico, and great reaches of northwestern Mexico, lies the Chihuahuan Biotic Province (Blair, 1950). A generally arid area of great physiographic diversity, it contains many mountain ranges, desert basins, river valleys, and arid plains. This physical diversity is reflected in an equally varied flora and fauna. In the basins a thin cover of grasses may be found, or sometimes typical desert shrubs such as creosote bush (*Larrea*), and catsclaw (*Acacia roemeriana*). At higher elevations there are more grasslands and at elevations over five thousand feet cedar, oak, piñon, and other trees occur. A greater

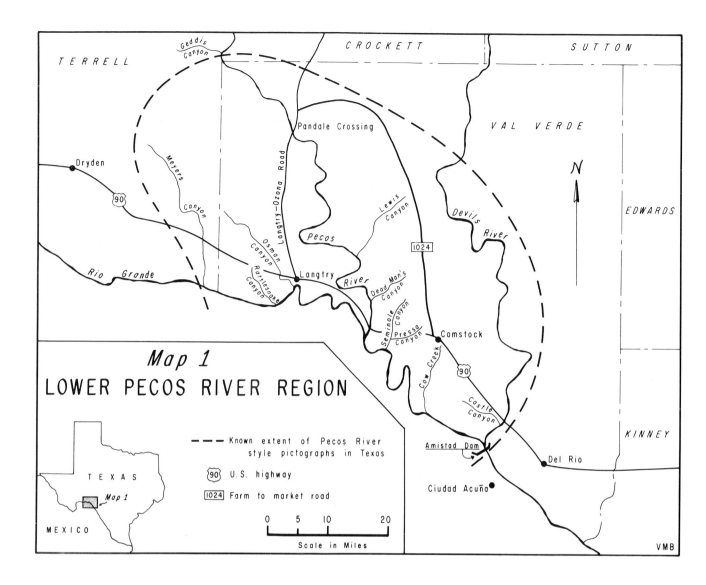

Map 1
LOWER PECOS RIVER REGION

- - - Known extent of Pecos River
      style pictographs in Texas

90   U.S. highway

1024   Farm to market road

0   5   10   20
Scale in Miles

variety of mammals is found in this region than in any other in Texas, though the roster of game animals which could figure prominently in human subsistence is not large. Deer are the most common large game animal. Grizzly bear, mountain sheep, and pronghorn (*Antilocapra americana*) are present, but their remains have not been found in archeological sites so far as this writer has been able to determine. There may have been a few bison in this province in historic times, at least sporadically, and apparently they were more common in earlier centuries (Reed: 1952, 1955).

To the northeast of the lower Pecos lies the Balconian Biotic Province (Blair, 1950), sharply demarcated on its southern side by the Balcones Escarpment. The Escarpment and the Pecos River have formed an effective barrier across which many species of vertebrates have been unable to pass. Although much of this limestone plateau is now badly overgrazed, it originally supported many good grazing grasses and extensive prairies. Today the principal vegetative features are scrub forests of Mexican cedar (*Juniperus ashei*), Spanish Oak

(*Quercus texana*), and stunted liveoak (*Quercus virginiana*). The fauna was diverse, species from east and west occupying this broad ecotone and, important to hunting peoples, the plateau supported fairly dense concentrations of deer and bison.

To the southeast of the lower Pecos River lies the Tamaulipan Province, an area with a semiarid climate, long hot summers and mild winters. The dominant vegetation is thorny brush such as mesquite (*Prosopis juliflora*), and cacti such as prickly pear (*Opuntia lindheimeri*). In terms of animals useful to subsistence, this was probably the poorest of the three regions. Bison seldom ranged this far south and other large game animals were not abundant.

The environment of the lower Pecos River country was, then, relatively harsh but it was also varied and endowed with a substantial assortment of plant and animal resources. Men had to adjust their lives to perpetual aridity, high temperatures, and to be willing to utilize a wide range of animal and plant foods, few of which were ever abundant.

Nearly all of the Pecos River style pictographs

No. 1

No. 2

THIS FIGURE RAISED 4″

No. 3

Plate 9. Langtry. Copied August 2, 1935. Scale: No. 1, 1/48; No. 2, 1/16; No. 3, 1/32

are in shelters in which there are or were midden deposits—accumulations of cultural debris, dirt, and trash—or are immediately adjacent to burned-rock middens, composed of fire-cracked hearthstones and also dirt and cultural debris. There is little doubt but that the peoples responsible for the middens, or parts of them, were also the artists who executed the pictographs. Middens and other archeological sites excavated in the lower Pecos River region reveal two major prehistoric cultural divisions: an early Paleo-Indian occupation, and a long, slowly changing Archaic continuum (Kelley *et al.*, 1940:162; Kelley, 1950a:72; Epstein, 1963:116–121). Peoples of Paleo-Indian cultures, the earliest known in the Americas, were hunters of mammoth, mastodon, bison, and other now extinct animals. They used distinctively pressure-flaked flint projectile points, as well as an assortment of other stone and bone tools. Only two sites, Bonfire Shelter near Langtry and the Devil's Mouth Site on a terrace at the juncture of the Devils River with the Rio Grande, have yielded Paleo-Indian artifacts. Bonfire Shelter was a bison-kill site, so situated that

PLATE 9

No. 1. These paintings are all that remain of what were once a large number of pictographs in Eagle Cave, Mile Canyon, near Langtry. They originally extended some fifty yards along the back wall from the south corner of the shelter. At this corner the pictographs are about ten feet from the floor and have been protected, but about thirty feet from the corner the floor rises to within a few feet of the pictographs and from that point on, only indefinite smears of color remain.

No. 2. These pictographs are on the south wall near the outside corner of a shelter near Eagle Cave on the opposite (east) side of Mile Canyon. The paintings were uncovered when a trench was dug along the wall.

No. 3. These pictographs are on the south wall of a small shelter high on the bluff overlooking the Rio Grande below the mouth of Mile Canyon. The animals at the bottom and the almost horizontal bar above them are quite clear, but parts of the fringed and black figures had to be treated with water before they could be copied. Evidently the animals are much more recent than the figures above them. More designs had been painted at the other end of the shelter but they were too faint and eroded to be copied.

39

Paleo-Indian hunters were able to drive or stampede an extinct species of bison (*Bison antiquus* or *B. occidentalis*) over its overhanging cliff. A radiocarbon date obtained from charcoal in its extensive bone deposits yielded a date of 10,230 ± 160 years before the present. The attractiveness of this site as a bison "jump" is demonstrated by the fact that an Archaic people thousands of years later used it in the same way to secure modern bison (Dibble, 1965). No evidence has ever been found that the widespread Paleo-Indian hunters, either in the lower Pecos region or elsewhere, practiced pictography. There are no pictographs in the immediate vicinity of the Devil's Mouth Site (Johnson, 1964:92–93), and though the walls of Bonfire Shelter seem to offer suitable surfaces for painting, no pictographs are found there. In addition, the subject matter of the Pecos River style pictographs, or of any of the pictographs in the region for that matter, is foreign to what is known about Paleo-Indian peoples. They were bison hunters, perhaps depending upon the herds as exclusively as did historic Plains Indians, yet there is not a single bison depicted in the Pecos River style pictographs. Pecos River style artists, so far as they were concerned with animals, emphasized deer and cougars, neither of which had any known significance to these Paleo-Indian hunters. There is no reason to believe, then, that any of the pictographs in the lower Pecos River region were painted by Paleo-Indians.

In the last decade or so, accumulated archeological evidence has revealed that a common cultural pattern, presumably connected historically, once blanketed a tremendous amount of territory in arid and semiarid North America and perhaps extended into adjoining regions. An early manifestation of this Western Archaic, or Desert Culture, at Danger Cave in Utah has been dated at more than eleven thousand years ago (Jennings and Norbeck, 1964), and other early sites in Nevada, Colorado, and Arizona are known. As century succeeded century a divergency of cultures developed from this common base, adapted to local environmental situations and influenced in various ways by other cultural traditions. But in some remote and isolated regions the Western Archaic persisted relatively unchanged for many millennia. The Archaic culture of the lower Pecos River was situated in such a region, and though minor alterations and changes occurred, from beginning to end it retained its affiliation with the Western Archaic tradition. The Western Archaic was characterized by considerable if not preponderant dependence on wild-plant foods, collected by nomadic people who had a penchant for living, or camping, in caves and rock shelters. So far as material remains are concerned, it was distinguished by "the atlatl, large oval and stemmed (but not fluted) projectile points, the grooved club, the absence of grooved axes and celts, the metate and mano, net carrying frame and/or conical burden basket, fiber sandals, both twined and coiled basketry . . . plaited matting, fur cloth, twisted fiber, and cordage" (W. W. Taylor, 1956: 220).

In recent years it has become clear that the Archaic cultural remains in the lower Pecos River region accumulated over a long span of time. The dim beginnings of this culture seem to date from about 6000 B.C. and it persisted until A.D. 600 or later (Johnson, 1964:92–99). It was an exceedingly conservative tradition. As Johnson (1964:97) has pointed out, there was "a more or less uniform Archaic culture from beginning to end, the major changes through time thus far noted being simply changes in the shapes and styles of projectile points." On the basis of these changes this long Archaic continuum is subdivided into an Early, Middle, and Late Archaic. However described terminologically, it was a self-contained, inward-looking tradition, anciently adapted and committed to a relatively static existence in an unchanging world. Introduction of the bow and arrow, sometime between A.D. 600–1000, presaged a quickening of cultural change, possibly population movements and end of the old tradition as such. But many of the essentials of this way of life persisted into historic times among Coahuiltecan and related peoples, disappearing only with the subjugation and extermination of these tribes in the eighteenth and nineteenth centuries.

Archaic sites in the lower Pecos River region are common; those so far excavated include the Fate Bell Shelter (Pearce and Jackson, 1933), Murrah Cave (Holden, 1937), the Shumla caves (Martin, 1933), Eagle Cave (Davenport, 1938), Centipede and Damp caves (Epstein, 1963), and the Devil's Mouth Site (Johnson, 1964). These are all located in Val Verde County, but other sites in adjacent areas contain related materials. A number of dart point types, for example, are shared with Archaic cultures of the Edwards Plateau to the northeast (Suhm *et al.*, 1954:52), and the lower Pecos Archaic is also closely allied to the cultural complex found in Frightful Cave in the Cuatro Ciénegas basin of Coahuila, Mexico, some two-hundred airline miles to the south. W. W. Taylor (1956:220) states that the differences between the Coahuila materials and those of the lower Pecos "are not large, nor are they very numerous in comparison to the similarities. Certainly the two cultural complexes are phrasings of a single basic culture, and closely related phrasings at that." Rock shelters near Alpine in Brewster County, far to the west, have also been reported to contain artifacts related to those of the lower Pecos (Kelley *et al.*, 1940:86-87), and no doubt similarities

View from Eagle Cave across canyon. Note Shelter No. 2 in opposite wall. See Plates 9, 10.

and relationships to other archeological complexes will be discovered in time. The significant point to note here is that the long Archaic tradition of the lower Pecos River region was the local expression of a widespread cultural pattern, distinguished from it by a number of unique traits. Pictographs are one such trait. Though frequently associated with cultures of the Western Archaic, nowhere was this art form cultivated more assiduously or did it develop further than in the lower Pecos River country.

All but a very few of the prehistoric lower Pecos pictographs belong either to the Pecos River or Red Monochrome styles, the latter to be taken up in the following chapter. In several cases Red Monochrome paintings are superimposed over Pecos River paintings, demonstrating that the Pecos River style is older. Internal evidence also suggests this conclusion since the older atlatl (spear thrower) is often depicted in the Pecos River style paintings, the more modern bow and arrow in Red Monochrome pictographs. The evidence is also quite clear that the Pecos River style pictographs were drawn by artists of Archaic culture. The presence of atlatls, darts, and rabbit sticks (grooved clubs) are a persistent and emphasized characteristic of Pecos River style paintings; they have also been recovered from Archaic archeological deposits in the region. Fragments of bows, arrows, and arrowpoints occur in these sites, it is true, but they are concentrated in the upper levels of cultural refuse and seem to have appeared in later times (Kelley, 1950a: 72). Pecos River style paintings are also invariably found in shelters in which there is Archaic cultural

debris, or such remains are close by. Finally, in a shelter near Langtry in Mile Canyon (Plate 9, No. 2) Pecos River style paintings, which have been tentatively assigned to an early Period 1, have been covered by midden debris. Kirkland (Notes, Plate 9) remarked that

The debris is at least six feet deep in this shelter. It may be eight feet deep in places and extends more than a foot above the top of the pictographs in the back of the shelter. The height of the pictographs is two and one-half feet where they are exposed. Assuming that they were painted to within one foot of the floor level, which is most unlikely, it means that four or more feet of dirt and rock has been added to the floor of the cavern since the pictures were painted.

How long it took to accumulate such a quantity of rubble is unknown, but the presumption is that the pictographs have considerable antiquity. Unfortunately, relic hunters have dug so many holes and trenches in this shelter that there is little possibility of positively establishing the exact nature of the cultural debris. A superficial examination of the much-disturbed remains, however, revealed basketry, matting, sotol quids (chewed fragments of the stalks, some still bearing tooth marks), and the like, some of which are almost surely Archaic.

The Pecos River style paintings utilized a number of colors in highly interesting combinations. Depending upon which subdivision of the style they belong to, one color was often used to outline another, and alternating lines of colors are common. A dark red was the most frequently used color, and next in descending order of frequency were

No.1

No.2

Plate 10. Langtry. Copied August 2, 1935. Scale: Nos. 1–2, 1/32

PLATE 10

This panel of paintings is in a shelter near those illustrated in Plate 9, No. 2. The floor is not piled up with debris, as it is in many shelters, and the pictographs are high on the back wall. Thus protected, every design is still complete except the left end of the black figure in the center of No. 2. Gray dust covered the entire group so that individual designs could not be clearly seen until treated with water. When dampened, however, they appear clear and sharp and are so copied. The entire back of the shelter is covered with one continuous design, and when No. 2 is placed to the right of No. 1 so that the *A's* coincide, the design appears just as it is in the shelter.

black, light red, yellow, orange, and white (Kirkland, 1939:52). The red, orange, and yellow shades were obtained from ocher, the black appears to be carbon, and the white was derived from a clay.

As many as five different colors have been used on one group of pictures; but three colors seems to be the limit used on any one picture. White was the least used of all the colors. In two or three instances, it appears that soot was scraped from the wall to get the effect of white; but white paint was used in at least five shelters. (Kirkland, 1939:54)

Colors were applied in liquid form with a brush, or were used dry after the pigment had been molded into a crayon. In the Fate Bell Shelter in Seminole Canyon two pieces of yellow ocher (limonite) were found; both are triangular crayons, the larger being about fourteen inches long. The ocher had been ground to a powder, mixed with water, molded into the desired shape, and allowed to dry before use. Other bars and lumps of ocher have been found, as well as manos and metates on which the pigments were ground (Pearce and Jack-

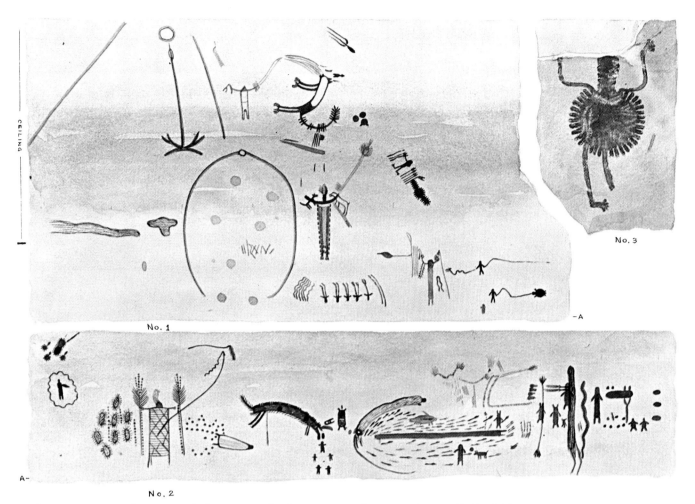

Plate 11. Seminole Canyon, Shelter 3. Copied July 10, 1936. Scale: No. 1, 3/16″ to 1′; No. 2, 5/32″ to 1′; No. 3, 3/8″ to 1′

son, 1933:55–56, Plate XIb). Grease or fat was apparently used as a binder on occasion, but there is doubt about whether it was always used in preparing paints and crayons. Paintbrushes have been recovered, made in several cases from sotol leaves which were folded lengthwise, then wrapped, and the ends shredded. In one instance red pigment still clings to the shredded end. In other cases the ends of "woody stalks" were shredded for brushes (Schuetz, 1961:183).

The most conspicuous figures in the Pecos River style paintings are intricately costumed and painted anthropomorphic beings. They have been variously interpreted as depicting dancers, shamans, and mythical beings. Strikingly varied, they range in height, for example, from less than a foot to overwhelming figures almost fifteen feet tall, and such variation is indicative of their diversity in other respects. This variability suggested that there was some sort of internal development in the paintings. The occasional superimposition of anthropomorphic beings strengthened this possibility. But it was not

PLATE 11

Nos. 1 and 2. These paintings are in a small shelter on the west bank of Seminole Canyon. The present floor is uneven and about ten feet below the bottom of the pictures, but it seems to have been level and much higher at one time. Much of the design is on the ceiling, and even when the floor was level it must have been ten to fifteen feet above the floor, necessitating a scaffold for painting. The paintings are in good condition, but because of their elevation most could not be accurately measured.

No. 3. This figure is only four feet from the floor, and the copy is therefore quite accurate.

TABLE 1
A Tabular Comparison of the Distinguishing Characteristics of Pecos River-Style Shamans[1]

Characteristic	Period 2 (Total No.:46)		Period 3 (Total No.:83)		Period 4 (Total No.:10)	
	No. of cases	Per cent of occurrence	No. of cases	Per cent of occurrence	No. of cases	Per cent of occurrence
Height:						
10' and over	6	13	0	0	0	0
6'-9'11"	13	28	9	11	3	30
3'-5'11"	17	37	48	58	7	70
Under 3"	10	22	26	31	0	0
Headless	19	41	8	10	1	10
Fingers	31	67	48	58	5	50
Feet and/or toes	12	27	34	41	10	100
Legs	29	63	67	81	3	30
Profile	8	17	6	7	0	0
Monochrome	36	78	5	6	1	10
Bichrome	8	17	57	69	3	30
Trichrome	1	2	21	25	6	60
Atlatl and dart	25	54	25	30	4	40
Darts	15	33	21	25	2	20
Rabbit sticks	29	63	20	24	2	20
"Prickly pouches"	33	72	38	46	8	80
Pouches extend from arm	22	48	22	27	2	20
Associated with animals	13	28	17	20	2	20
Associated with humans	32	70	61	73	6	60
"Feather clusters" at hip	8	17	0	0	0	0
Sinuous lines	8	17	40	48	3	30
Stylized projectile points	0	0	20	24	5	50
Winged figure	0	0	7	8	0	0

[1]One hundred sixty-two anthropomorphic figures were considered to be shamans. Of these, forty-six were ascribed to Period 2; fourteen others were tentatively assigned to Period 2 but are not tabulated. Eighty-three shamans were attributed to Period 3; eight others were tentatively classified as Period 3 but are not tabulated. Ten shamans were assigned to Period 4; one other seemed to have Period 4 affiliations but is not tabulated. None of the tentative Period 1 figures have been tabulated.

The process by which the number of periods and the features which characterize them were arrived at is difficult to describe because it was a product of a subjective hunch. To validate this hunch a list of features of the shamans and objects associated with them was compiled. It had been thought that there were two phases or periods of painting, but during this compilation it was realized that there were more. The existence of two middle periods (and less surely an earlier and later one), then, is not an artificial construct even though it is the relative, not absolute, frequency of a number of characteristics which establishes the periods. There may be, of course, distinguishing features which have not been recognized, and subsequent work may reveal that there are more subdivisions than have been recognized here. Oddly, some distinguishing features are blatantly obvious only after they are recognized. How so many people, including the present author, could be familiar with stylized projectile points yet not recognize what they symbolized is a case in point. One can only conclude that there may be other obvious yet hidden characteristics and symbols in these paintings.

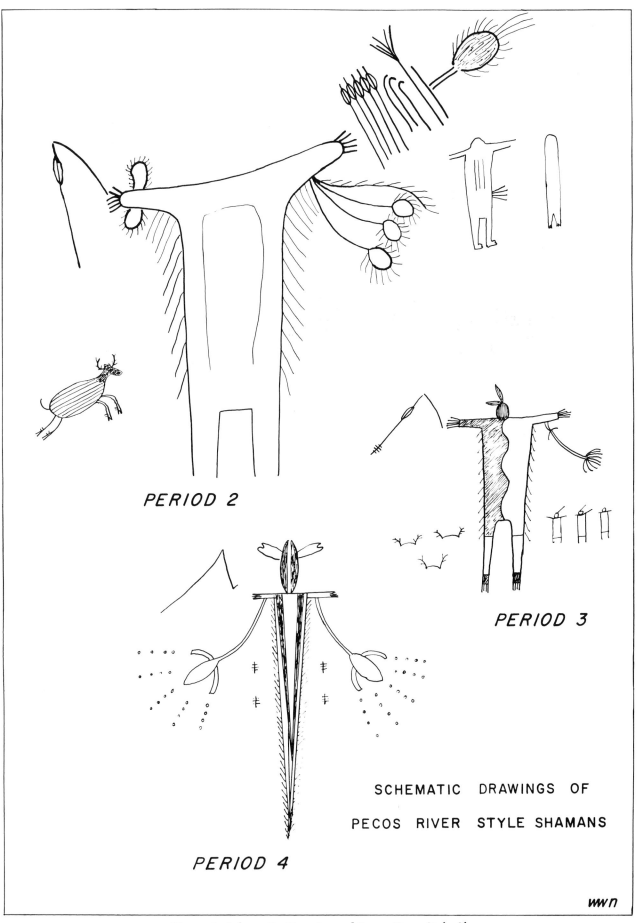

PERIOD 2

PERIOD 3

PERIOD 4

SCHEMATIC DRAWINGS OF
PECOS RIVER STYLE SHAMANS

Figure 1. Schematic Drawings of Pecos River-Style Shamans

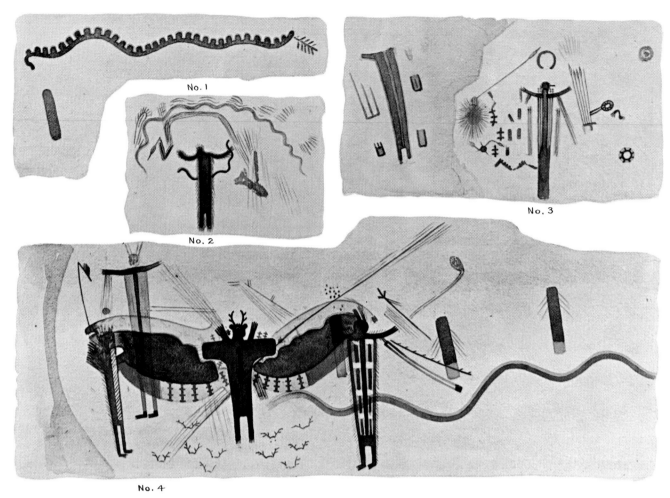

No. 1

No. 2

No. 3

No. 4

Plate 12.　Seminole Canyon, Shelter 4. Copied July 10, 1936. Scale: Nos. 1–4, 3/8″ to 1′

PLATE 12

The Fate Bell Shelter in Seminole Canyon is 150 yards long and its greatest depth is about 40 yards. Paintings were once almost continuous just above floor level for the entire length of the back wall, but they have been almost completely destroyed by overpainting, smoke, spalling of the rock, and general wear and tear by occupants. Parts of designs can be made out all along the wall, but none are complete. All copies were painted stronger than the designs now appear; an attempt has been made to approximate the original colors, judged by the places that are still clear. Nothing has been included that could not be certainly made out. Lines and designs that are broken by flaking of the rock have been completed where enough still remains to be certain of the original position; otherwise they have been left out or blurred.

No. 1. This design is low on the wall just outside the south end of the shelter and is very dim, due no doubt to its exposure to the sun and rain.

Nos. 2 and 3. An offset in the ceiling forms a second wall at the south end of the shelter, just about as high from the floor as one can reach. Because of the height, paintings on this wall have been protected, but about a third of the pictures were too dim from age or smoke to be made out, and these that were copied were very dim.

No. 4. This panel is one of the clearest in the shelter and could be seen to be copied very accurately by wetting it in places. It is on the sloping ceiling above the second wall.

until the characteristics of each of these anthropomorphic beings, as well as the objects and animals in close proximity to them, were tabulated that the existence of two major substyles of painting and possibly two others was revealed (see Table 1). These substyles form a developmental and chronological sequence which have been given "Period" designations. In addition to the elaborately costumed anthropomorphic beings, Pecos River style paintings contain many other human figures. But most of these seem to be ordinary men, in the sense that they are not elaborately costumed and are almost always subordinated to the dominant, central figures either by being inferior in size or by being grouped around them. In order to name and distinguish between the two kinds of anthropomorphic beings, the intricately costumed and ornamented central figures have been designated "shamans." The probabilities are good, as will be shown, that these beings were in fact intended to represent shamans, that is, individuals who possessed special knowledge of the supernatural world and more than ordinary ability to deal with it. It is possible, however, that they were intended as something else,

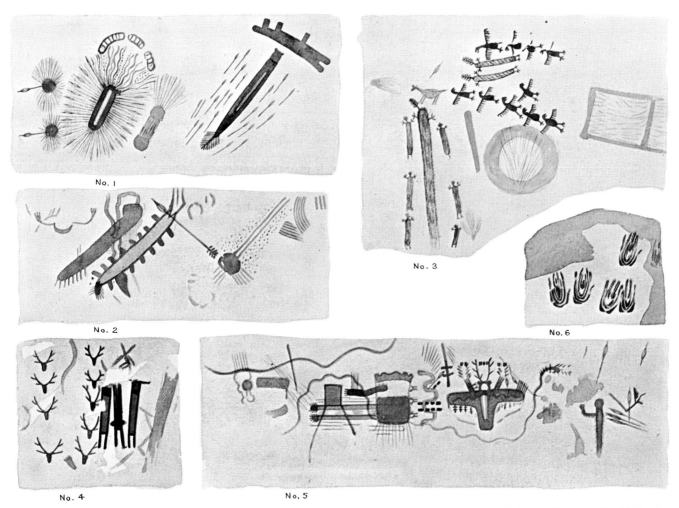

Plate 13.   Seminole Canyon, Shelter 4. Copied July 10, 1936. Scale: Nos. 1–2, 3/8″ to 1′; No. 3, 3/4″ to 1′; No. 4, 1/2″ to 1′; No. 5, 1/4″ to 1′; No. 6, 3/4″ to 1′

so this designation is in part a matter of convenience.

What appear to be the oldest Pecos River style paintings, tentatively assigned to Period 1, are illustrated in Plate 9, No. 2. The figures in this painting are crude and done in a light red or red-orange monochrome, but a yellow crescent-shaped object is present above the head of the central figure. This is the painting that had been buried by at least four feet of cultural debris, and Kirkland regarded it as very old. In another example (Plate 53, No. 2), the half-circle, or crescent-shaped, band of color is attached to or held over the head by the figure's arms. Other possible occurrences of Period 1 paintings are found in Plate 16, Nos. 1 and 3. Kirkland (1939:72) characterized these as "simple, solid, light red figures lacking the detail and individuality of the later work." In one instance (Plate 16, No. 3) eight figures holding each other's hands as if in a dance have been overpainted by what is probably a Period 2 painting. Badly weathered and very dim are a number of paintings which extend for about fifty yards along a cliff at the head of Pressa Canyon (Plate 64). Partly under a vivid historic painting,

PLATE 13

Nos. 1, 2, and 5. These designs are on the second, offset, wall in the Fate Bell Shelter. No. 1 is very dim but was distinct while wet.

No. 3. This small group of Fate Bell pictographs is very dim. The birds had been painted with a small brush, but the deer and plume-headed figures were made with a sharp crayon.

No. 4. This is the only design on the back wall of the Fate Bell shelter sufficiently complete to warrant copying.

No. 6. These handprints are remarkable because they were made by painting a design in the hand and then stamping it on the wall. No other handprints were found in the Fate Bell Shelter, and since the color is still very clear it would seem that they belong to a later culture than the rest of these pictographs.

Forrest Kirkland at pictograph site in Mile Canyon. See Plate 10.

nine faint anthropomorphic beings are visible. Most lack heads, and though cruder than those of Plate 16, No. 3, they resemble them. None of these figures tentatively ascribed to this initial period have objects associated with them which are characteristic of the typical shamans. Crude figures such as these have the earmarks of first attempts at this form of artistic expression. If they were not present, it would have to be assumed that they existed at one time, either in the lower Pecos River region or elsewhere, or in some other medium of expression. But Kirkland found so few of these crude figures to record and they bear such a distant relationship to the more distinctive features of later shamans that little more can be said of them. Kirkland even concludes that (1939:72):

if the very elaborate polychrome pictures evolved from these, we have been unable to trace the development. The highly evolved figures appear to be as often buried or badly weathered as the simpler forms that should have preceded them; and the more realistic figures from which the conventional ones should have evolved, are not found at all. The present evidence, therefore, although by no means conclusive, points to an outside development.

While Kirkland is undoubtedly correct in the sense that the remaining Pecos River style paintings do not reveal every step in a developmental series, the main direction of development can be shown, from the crude beginnings already mentioned, through a well-executed realistic style, to a conventionalization, and finally to a highly stylized, abstract form. The fact that "highly evolved figures"

are sometimes badly weathered while simpler, presumably earlier forms are sometimes fresh and clear may well be a function of local conditions rather than age. Wetness, soot, and later occupancy of shelters, to name a few factors, have much to do with whether or not paintings will be bright, faded, or completely obscured. Since shamans are intricately attired or painted it is difficult to determine when they are relatively naturalistic depictions and when conventionalizations.

Shamans first take on their highly distinctive form in Period 2 (see Figure 1). The style is essentially outline, although the body may be filled in with lines or stripes, or may be a solid color (Plate 24, large figure on left, for example). Kirkland seems to have had the shamans of this period in mind when he described them as possessing

an extremely elongated figure, sometimes with sides parallel, but usually broader at the shoulders, with arms on opposite sides of the body, extended at right angles or slightly raised; the legs, if present, extending downward in line with the outside edge of the body. . . . The fingers and toes are indicated with from three to five parallel lines extending straight out from the ends of the arms and legs. (1939:55)

Shamans are ordinarily painted in a dark purple-red pigment, more rarely in an orange-red.[1] Only eight Period 2 shamans are painted in two colors. In the central figures in Plates 24 and 25, for example,

[1] See Table 1 for the number of occurrences and percentage of occurrence of the major characteristics which distinguish the shamans of each Period.

Fate Bell Shelter, Seminole Canyon, looking down the canyon. See Plates 12, 13, 14.

panels of gray may be found, and there is one aberrant Period 2 figure in yellow, black, and red (Plate 25, far left).

More than 40 per cent of Period 2 shamans are over 6 feet tall and six of them are over 10 feet. This is in sharp contrast to Period 3 shamans, none of which exceed 9 feet in height. Period 2 figures are usually drawn in full-front view, but in eight cases either both feet point in one direction or the arms are shown on one side of the body, suggesting a side view. One of the most intriguing figures to be found in the Lower Pecos River country is the "man in gray," a naturalistic painting of a robed and hooded human depicted in profile (Frontispiece). It undoubtedly belongs to Period 2, but it does not seem to represent the usual type of shaman and has not been tabulated as such. Attempts to depict the human figure in side view decline in Period 3 paintings, with only a very few shamans portrayed with feet pointing in a single direction and none with arms on the same side of the body.

Many Period 2 shamans lack heads, though not necessarily headdresses, and facial features are never portrayed. Fingers may be absent and almost three-fourths of Period 2 shamans lack feet or toes. Thirty-seven per cent have no legs. Occasionally (eight instances) a figure of this Period is depicted with what appears to be a cluster of feathers or a feathered sash worn low on the body, so that he gives the impression of being costumed in a low-waisted flapper dress of the twenties (Plates 14, 23, 32, No. 2). This "sash" is confined to shamans of Period 2. A distinctive "horn" headdress, that is,

two rather blunt projections extending upwards from the outside margins of the head, also seems to be confined to Period 2 paintings (Plates 22, lower right; 23; 24; 25; 33, Nos. 1 and 2; 36, No. 2; 49, No. 10).

Most of the objects associated with the shamans of Period 2 are realistically portrayed and others seem to be, though it is impossible in every case to state just what they are. In the right hand or suspended in mid-air close to the hand in more than half of the Period 2 shamans is an atlatl, or throwing stick, with a feathered dart in position ready for launching. Kirkland referred to it as a "broken flowering plant" but as Kelley (1950b:73) has pointed out: "that the darts shown in place with the instrument are actually darts cannot be doubted, however, since they are repeatedly shown piercing animals. The atlatl is just as obviously that, therefore." Attached to or suspended from one or both arms in nearly three-fourths of the Period 2 shamans are objects which vary considerably but usually resemble prickly pear pads, a series of sticks, or fringed bags or pouches. The resemblance to prickly pear pads would seem fanciful were it not that hollowed-out pads with sewn edges have been recovered from archeological sites in the area. In the left hand or near the hand, a series of feathered darts arranged parallel to one another are recognizable in 33 per cent of Period 2 paintings. In 63 per cent of the examples, several straight or curved objects similar to the rabbit or fending sticks found with Archaic Pecos River archeological materials are next to the darts. Finally, to the right of these ob-

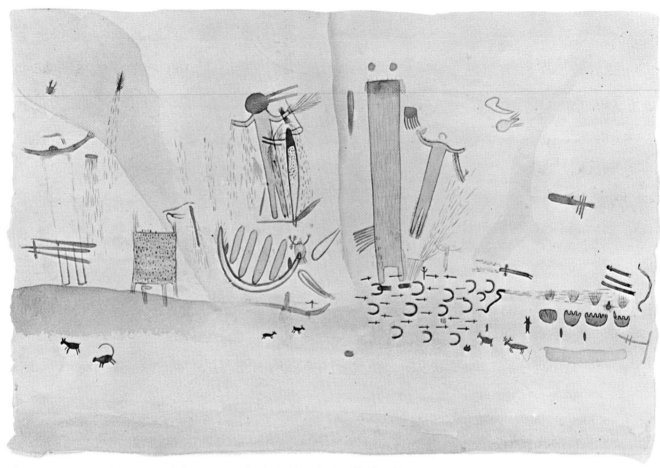

Plate 14. Seminole Canyon, Shelter 4. Copied July 9, 1936. Scale: 5/32" to 1'

PLATE 14

These very large designs are high on the sloping wall at the north end of the Fate Bell Shelter. They are fully exposed to the morning sun and to blowing rains from the east and southeast. In view of this exposure it is surprising that so many of the designs and figures can still be made out. The lower figures were no doubt near the floor level at one time, but the floor has washed out and they are now ten to twenty feet above the ground and most of the figures extend about twenty feet above even the original level of the floor. They were certainly painted from some kind of scaffolding. The length of the designs was carefully measured but their height had to be estimated.

PLATE 15

Nos. 1, 2, 3, and 4 (upper). At the head of Frio Canyon, north of Leakey, above some springs in a high bluff, is a long, shallow shelter. A few black pictographs are still dimly visible on its back wall. Only two marks (No. 2, upper left) and three crosses are in red (No. 3). A few other pictures may once have been on the cliff, but now are only dim black splotches of color. It was necessary to wet the pictures before accurate copies could be made.

Not numbered (lower). These paintings are on the ceiling in the central part of the Fate Bell Shelter in Seminole Canyon about ten feet above the present floor level. They are unique in that they appear to have been done almost entirely with crayon. The orange-red and yellow colors are brilliant, but are laid over the smoke-covered ceiling and do not show up very plainly. The bodies of several figures are lighter than the ceiling and seem to have been coated with an application of light gray clay or mud.

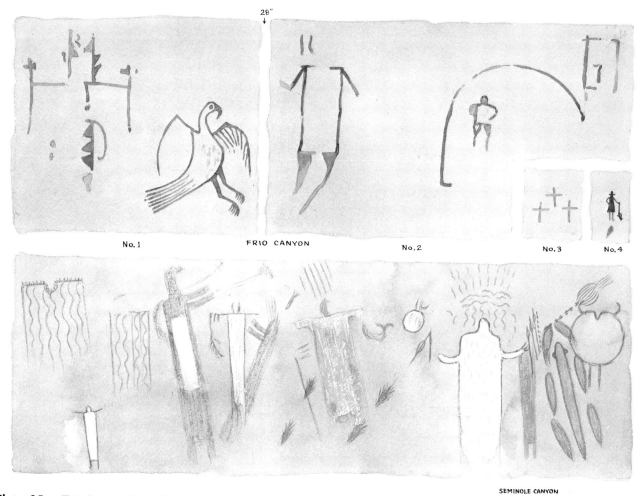

No. 1   FRIO CANYON   No. 2   No. 3   No. 4

SEMINOLE CANYON

Plate 15. Frio Canyon. Copied July 5, 1937. Scale: Nos. 1–4, 1/2″ to 1′. Seminole Canyon, Shelter 4. Copied July 11, 1937. Scale: 1/4″ to 1′

Frio Canyon. See Plate 15.

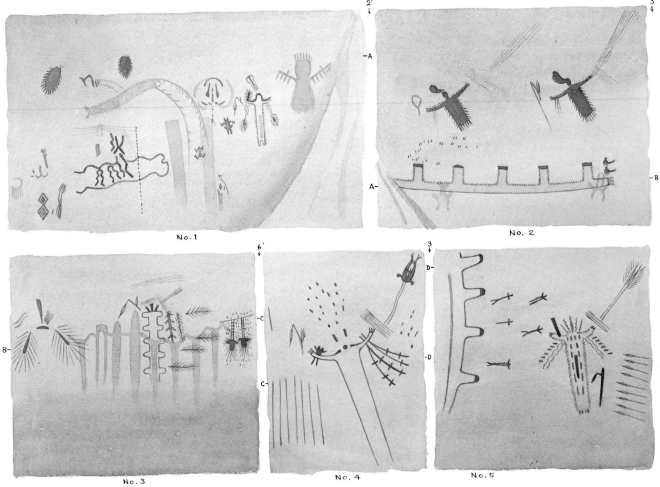

Plate 16. Shelter at Railroad Tunnel. Copied July 12, 1936. Scale: Nos. 1–5, 3/16″ to 1′

jects, often attached to them, and extending outward from the arm is a line or series of lines at the end of which is an object, again resembling the pad of a prickly pear or a fringed pouch. Almost half of the Period 2 shamans exhibit this feature.

Earlier investigators, lacking information from a large number of examples, assumed that shamans were usually depicted in conjunction with animals. Although animals are more often found in association with Period 2 shamans than with those of subsequent periods, this is so in only 28 per cent of Period 2 paintings. In short, the association of animals with shamans is not usual or even frequent in any period. The most common animals found with Pecos River style pictographs are deer, apparently of the white-tailed species. They are invariably diminutive (about the size of a small dog) in relation to the nearby shamans of Period 2. "The body is usually oval; the legs straight lines placed so as to express action; the toes are pictured, as are also horns, ears, and tail. The animals are generally represented in droves extending across the shelter wall" (Kirkland, 1939:62). Their bodies are often depicted as striped or crosshatched and are usually pierced

PLATE 16

This panel of paintings is in a shelter high up on a bluff overlooking the Rio Grande, a few miles below the mouth of the Pecos River. All figures in the shelter were clear enough for copying except a few badly weathered ones to the right of No. 5. The copy was made so that when the corresponding letters on the five sections are placed together, the panel's parts will be in correct relationship to one another.

PLATES 17 and 18

Below the mouth of Seminole Canyon on the Rio Grande, overhanging cliffs twenty to forty feet wide extending for over two hundred yards, provided a surface for these paintings and those of Plate 69. Only the upper half of the overhang has a smooth enough wall for painting. Most of this space shows signs of paint, but the pictures on only about 150 feet remained clear enough to be made out. The paintings in these two plates form a continuous panel when joined at the designated alphabetical points.

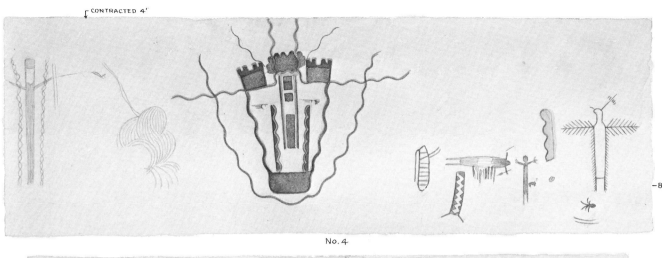

No. 4

No. 6

Plate 17. Rio Grande Cliffs. Copied July 15, 1938. Scale: Nos. 4 and 6, 1/4″ to 1′

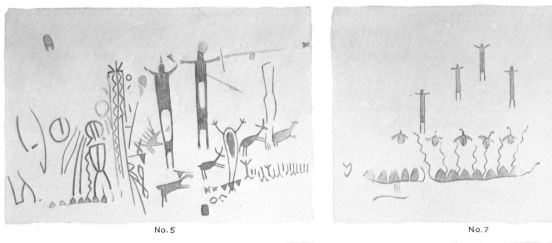

No. 5

No. 7

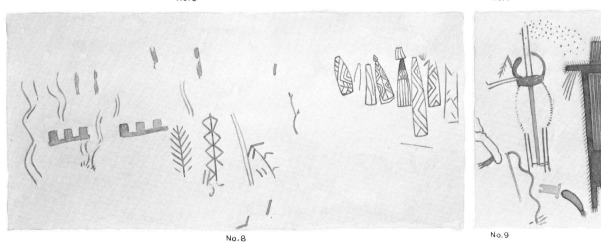

No. 8

No. 9

Plate 18. Rio Grande Cliffs. Copied July 15, 1938. Scale: Nos. 5,7,8,9, 1/4″ to 1′

by an atlatl dart or spear, ordinarily in the heart or forequarters. In one instance (Plate 23) a dart has penetrated a hind foot, lending the picture an unmistakable touch of humor, at least from our point of view.

Cougars or pumas (*Felis concolor*) are more conspicuous in Period 2 pictographs than are deer, though they appear with less frequency. Kirkland (1939:60) noted that:

many of the animal pictures are exceptionally realistic. This is especially true of the puma, or Mexican lion, which seems to have held an important place in the culture. One life-sized picture of this animal is remarkable for its graceful pose and realism. The average picture, however, is fairly crude with long body, graceful, erect or arching tail; but with stiff straight legs. The mouth is usually open, ears erect, and bristles raised. Claws are usually present; but the eye is seldom expressed.

In contrast to the representations of deer, cougars are seldom of small size in relation to the anthropomorphic figures, and in several instances are huge; one measures almost nine feet from nose to base of the tail, which arches an additional ten feet (Plate 26, No. 1). None of the large cougars are associated with shamans of other periods; in fact, cougars are virtually nonexistent in later periods. Two diminutive bushy-tailed quadrupeds occur with two Period 3 shamans (Plate 35, No. 2) and they may be intended as cougars. In another case three small animals which appear to be cougars are painted near an anthropormorphic being which has affiliations with Period 3 shamans, although this figure was not tabulated as one (Plate 42, No. 3).

Subordinate anthropomorphic figures are associated with shamans much more frequently than are animals, both in Period 2 and later periods. But in Period 2 the peripheral human figures are apt to have little obvious connection to shamans (Plate 46, Shelter 2, for example). In Period 2, as well, several shamans are apt to be found close to one another as if engaged in a single activity (Frontispiece, Plates 23, 24, 25, for example). In Period 3 paintings, subordinate anthropomorphic beings are often grouped around shamans in a way which strongly suggests that they represent some sort of supporting cast (Plate 19, figures to right of central figure). Virtually no human figures which can be associated with Period 2 shamans are pierced by darts. In only one case do darts even touch a human figure (Plate 25, under and above black figure), and it is not in a prone or upside-down position as are those of later periods (Plate 28, No. 1, left, for example). A rarely depicted, rotund creature associated with Period 2 shamans may or may not be intended as human. Two examples are from Panther Cave (Plate 24, far right; Plate 25, far right). An oval figure, pierced by a dart and superimposed over a Period 2 shaman vaguely resembles this pair and

also appears in Panther Cave (Frontispiece). Another round and profusely fringed object at another site may represent the same creature (Plate 40, No. 1, upper left).

Period 2 paintings are a highly distinctive form of Pecos River style rock art. While only a few of the features which characterize it are lacking in other Pecos River paintings, the frequencies of most characteristics set it apart, and when all are taken together the Period is an easily distinguishable form of the Pecos River style rock art. That Period 2 paintings are relatively early is demonstrated by the fact that they are never superimposed over Period 3 or Period 4 pictographs; in one instance a Period 2 shaman, unfortunately somewhat atypical, is superimposed over figures which apparently should be referred to Period 1 (Plate 16, No. 3). Period 3 shamans are occasionally painted over those of Period 2, thus establishing their chronological position (for example, Plate 24, lower-right quadrant, black-and-red-masked being superimposed over parts of several Period 2 figures; Plate 25, red-outlined black figure superimposed on Period 2 painting).

More than half of the anthropomorphic figures considered to be shamans belong to what has been designated as Period 3. In a number of respects these shamans are quite different from those of Period 2. Almost 70 per cent are painted in two colors, 25 per cent in three, and the use of black is much more common (see Table 1). Bodies usually contain panels of color and provide a good means

PLATE 19

These paintings are in a small shelter in a deep canyon that empties into the Pecos River northeast of Langtry. The shelter, high up in the canyon wall and very difficult to reach, is about twelve feet wide and one hundred feet long. The paintings are on the back wall above a natural shelf three and one-half feet high and one foot wide. There is a shallow midden deposit on the floor and a number of round mortar holes in the shelf and in rocks on the floor. The ceiling is so badly smoked and flaked that the tops of some of the designs are very dim; the bottoms of the designs also fade into the background.

PLATE 20

High up on the cliff above the Rio Grande not far below the mouth of the Pecos River is a large shelter once known as Painted Cave, now usually referred to as Parida Cave. About one hundred yards long and fifty yards deep, it has a small spring in the back which the Indians no doubt used. Relic hunters have vandalized the cave's extensive cultural deposits to such an extent that they can no longer yield reliable information about its ancient occupants. The cave has comparatively few paintings, perhaps because of the wall's roughness. All of the paintings are dim but there is no overpainting, and with one or two exceptions every design could be clearly made out.

CONTRACTED 3'6"

No.1

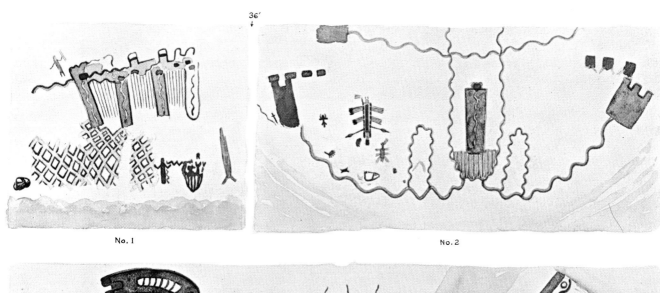

A –

No.2

Plate 19. Brown's Ranch. Copied July 16, 1936. Scale: Nos. 1-2, 1/4″ to 1′

36′

No.1

No.2

– A

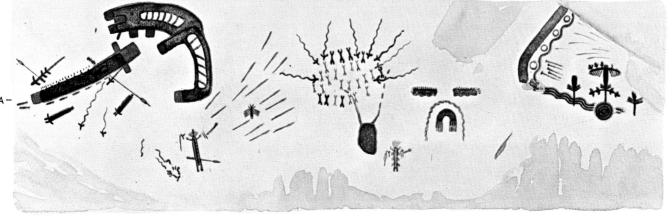

A –

No.3

Plate 20. Painted Cave. Copied July 7, 1937. Scale: Nos. 1–3, 1/4″ to 1′

Forrest Kirkland at work in small, nearly inaccessible shelter. See Plate 19.

for quick identification. But there are many variations on this theme: the body may be half one color and half another (Plate 31, No. 1), sinuous lines of color may ornament the body (Plate 35, No. 1, far right), and figures are frequently fringed. As noted earlier, Period 3 shamans are rarely of heroic size; 89 per cent are under six feet in height. Only 10 per cent of the Period 3 shamans lack heads, in contrast to more than 40 per cent in Period 2 who do, but, as in the earlier period, facial features are never depicted. Fingers are portrayed about as often as they are in Period 2, but legs, feet, and toes are depicted more often. What appear to be feathers have become popular as headdresses and may be regarded as typical of this Period. An antlered headdress is associated exclusively with a peculiar variation of the shaman. In it wide, squared-off "wings" extend horizontally outwards from either side of the body at about shoulder level, and hands and arms project upwards above them (Plates 12, No. 4, central figure; Plate 13, No. 5; Plates 2 and 33.)

An atlatl with dart in place is less frequently shown with Period 3 shamans. The distal end of some of these darts, as well as others not associated with atlatls, now have three or four short parallel lines intersecting the shaft at right angles to it (Plate 31, No. 1, for example). Intended to represent a projectile point, or perhaps a foreshaft, this conventionalization appears without the rest of the dart in many Period 3 and Period 4 paintings. That dart points should be portrayed in this manner seems strange until it is realized that to the artist the manner of hafting the point to the dart shaft may have been of greater significance and interest than the shape of the point itself. Thus, the artists may have been depicting this feature rather than the projectile point (Plate 12, Nos. 3, 4; Plate 6, No. 1 upper left). Stylized projectile points do not occur in any Period 2 paintings and in only 20 per cent of the Period 3 paintings, but they are prominent in paintings of five out of the ten shamans assigned to the final Period 4.

The other paraphernalia associated with shamans is often more difficult to recognize than that of Period 2 because it is more simply or hastily executed. There is also a decline in the number of darts, rabbit sticks, and "prickly pouches" portrayed with shamans, as Table 1 reveals. Indeed, there is not an instance in which a Period 3 shaman is equipped with all the objects traditionally thought of as typical of shamans. The highly variable fringed or prickly pouches of Period 2 continue to be varied when they are depicted in Period 3, and there seems to be a tendency for them to be elongated, apparently with long tassels or fringes, in contrast to Period 2. The fringed pouch projecting outwards from the end of the arm shows much variation. Though present in only 27 per cent of Period 3 shaman pictures, it may be given great emphasis in them (Plate 38, No. 1, figure at right, for example). In a few cases sinuous lines are associated in one way or another with Period 2 shamans. In Period 3, nearly 50 per cent of the shamans are accompanied by such lines. These have often

Panther Cave. View of shelter from opposite side of canyon. Note man standing on lip of shelter. See Frontispiece and Plates 23, 24, 25, 26.

been interpreted as snakes, and some undoubtedly are, but they occur in so many different contexts and are so varied that it is probably best to attempt no interpretation. Suffice it to say that they are additional distinguishing features of Period 3 shamans.

As has been noted, in Period 3 shamans are less frequently associated with animals than in Period 2, and when animals are shown — deer for example — the head and antlers (Plate 13, No. 4) or the antlers alone are apt to be depicted (Plate 12, No. 4, bottom) rather than the entire animal. Other humans are associated with shamans somewhat more frequently than in Period 2, and these peripheral humans are more closely related to the central figures. In some paintings they seem to represent dancers (Plates 19, No. 1; 38, No. 1; 30, No. 1), in others they appear to be enemies who have been pierced by darts (Plates 20, No. 3, left; 4, No. 2, left side), or prone enemies surrounded by stylized projectile points (Plate 19, No. 1, left of central figure). Period 3 shamans are occasionally superimposed on earlier Period 2 figures, and there seems to be a tendency at some sites for Period 3 paintings to be applied over other Period 3 paintings (Plates 1, 2, and 8). This practice can hardly be attributed to a dearth of fresh surfaces on which to paint, but must be the result of special qualities of these locations. No Period 3 paintings are superimposed on Period 4 work, and no Period 4 painting was painted over an older pictograph.

Period 3 shamans are for the most part easily distinguishable from other forms of Pecos River art.

Though numerous and quite variable, present evidence does not indicate that the Period should or could be further divided on stylistic grounds. Period 3 shamans are often more simply drawn than their precursors, though they seem scarcely less naturalistic. It is in associated objects that there has been a shift away from naturalistic portrayal — the antler now may serve for the whole deer and the conventionalized projectile point for the dart.

Tentatively distinguished from Period 3 paintings are a small number of paintings of shamans which are so conventionalized that they probably should be set apart from Period 3, and are thus designated as Period 4. They are a step or stage beyond the bulk of Period 3 figures stylistically. There is no positive evidence from superimposition that they were the latest or last of the Pecos River style pictographs. The most extreme example is found in Plate 34, No. 2 (left figure), in which the shaman has become a balanced geometric design. If this were the only Pecos River painting extant, it would be impossible to know what it represented. But a close examination reveals that the atlatl and dart are suspended in mid-air as usual and that much-magnified prickly pouches are suspended from the arms in the familiar way. It was probably this figure Kirkland was referring to when he remarked that the shaman was "subject to so many modifications and conventionalizations that it sometimes loses its human aspect and becomes merely a design" (1939:58). A shaman in Black Cave (Plate 28, No. 1), while not similar to the Plate

34 figure in detail, parallels it in symmetry and is an extreme example of the use of stylized projectile points. They are employed on the headdress, as design elements on the body, and cascade from one hand to another object decorated with the stylized projectile point motif. Another tentative Period 4 shaman nearby (Plate 28, No. 2) also illustrates the lavish usage of the projectile-point symbol. These two shamans are unique in the use of streams of red dots which apparently are intended to represent the forces which issue from the shaman's weapons. Another tentative Period 4 shaman (Plate 5, far right) is also decorated with stylized projectile points. This figure, as well as several other Period 4 shamans, utilizes dots or circles as bodily ornaments (Plates 28, No. 1; 19, left figure and upper figure on right). These do not occur on any other Pecos River shamans. Other characteristics which seem to typify Period 4 shamans are the utilization of three colors in a single figure and a tendency to omit or minimize legs, feet, arms, and fingers. None of the Period 4 shamans have been overpainted, nor are they superimposed on any other pictographs. Stylistically, then, these few shamans represent the most developed form of Pecos River art, and the probabilities favor their being the most recent of the Pecos River style pictographs.

In addition to shamans and the various objects which accompany them, there are a number of other objects or forms which appear only occasionally and cannot be said to be characteristic or typical of one or another period. Some of these appear to be animals (Plates 38, No. 2, right of center; Plate 11, No. 2, center, for example), others geometric figures or designs (Plate 17, No. 4, center; Plate 20, Nos. 1, 2, for example). Among the most intriguing is a figure that might be likened to a sparsely toothed comb or a boat (Plates 40, No. 1; Plate 39, No. 2). These two figures are associated with Period 3 shamans, but other similar objects are affiliated with Period 2 paintings (Plates 14, 16, Nos. 2, 5). What they represent is unknown. Not as visibly evident as these enigmatic figures are circles, sometimes with lines radiating from them, occasionally pierced by darts (Plate 11, No. 2, upper left; Plate 13, No. 1; Plate 22, lower left, for example). Some may be plants, but the majority appear to represent something else.

The Pecos River style pictographs, as revealed by analysis of the shamans, show an internal development from what appears to be crude beginnings to a realistic, usually monochrome style, to a polychrome, somewhat stylized form, to final conventionalization and abstraction. While the two middle periods can readily be distinguished, there is really no abrupt break between periods. A few paintings cannot be placed surely in any period, and, assuming that no distinguishing features went unnoticed, it seems best to regard these as transitional between periods. If there is a gap in a developmental sense, it is between the ill-defined, poorly represented paintings of Period 1 and those of Period 2, for Period 2 paintings suddenly blossom from undistinguished seed into a highly developed and distinctive substyle. Running through all the Pecos River style paintings is also a single manner of expression, difficult to define, but so clear and persistent that it is impossible to mistake this kind of rock art for any other. Kirkland (1939:71) says that it "is not its individual figures and forms; but the skillful way these elements have been combined into elaborate, beautifully balanced designs and compositions" that is the outstanding artistic achievement of the Pecos River paintings.

PLATE 21

Nos. 1, 2, 3, and 4 (upper). These pictographs are on the left wall near the floor of Parida Cave. Note the crayon drawings in Nos. 1, 2, and 3. The body of the figure in No. 4 is painted around a natural bridge in the rock wall. This is one of the very few cases in which an Indian has taken advantage of a natural rock shape to construct a picture.

Nos. 1 and 2 (lower). Slick Trail Shelter is at the mouth of a small canyon entering the Rio Grande below the mouth of the Pecos River. The paintings are in a small, shallow shelter with a smooth back wall. This wall has been completely covered with pictures and overpainted in some places many times. The floor evidently once extended up to the base of the pictures, where they are now badly worn and smeared. Also, water has run down from above and destroyed many paintings. The pictures copied were chosen from the least weathered sections, but none of them were in good condition.

PLATE 22

(Upper). Lookout Shelter is at the mouth of Seminole Canyon opposite Panther Cave. It is long and shallow with a very high overhang, affording poor protection from blowing rains. The lower corner of the shelter ends abruptly high up the cliff and commands an excellent view for some distance down the Rio Grande and also up Seminole Canyon. The rocks at this point are worn slick as if by the feet of many Indians on lookout duty—thus the name, Lookout Shelter. Only these few pictures had been painted on the wall. In the shelter, however, were several large rocks almost completely covered with grooves and tree-like designs, evidently cut into the rock by Indians sharpening tools.

(Lower). Panther Cave is on the east wall of Seminole Canyon at its mouth. It is a large shelter showing signs of occupation, but there is no deep deposit on the floor. There are many shallow mortars in the rocks under the shelter. These designs are in a shallow extension to the right of the main shelter. A few paintings to the right of this group have been destroyed.

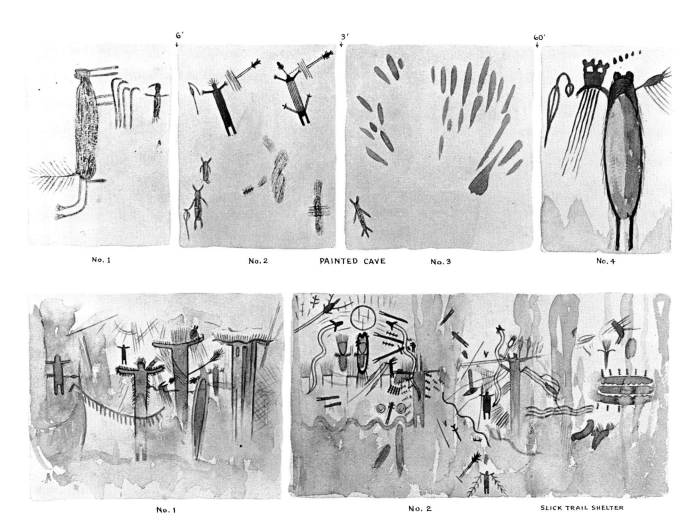

No. 1   No. 2   PAINTED CAVE   No. 3   No. 4

No. 1   No. 2   SLICK TRAIL SHELTER

Plate 21. Painted Cave. Copied July 7, 1937. Scale: Nos. 1–4, 1/2″ to 1′. Slick Trail Shelter. Copied July 8, 1937. Scale: Nos. 1–2, 1/4″ to 1′

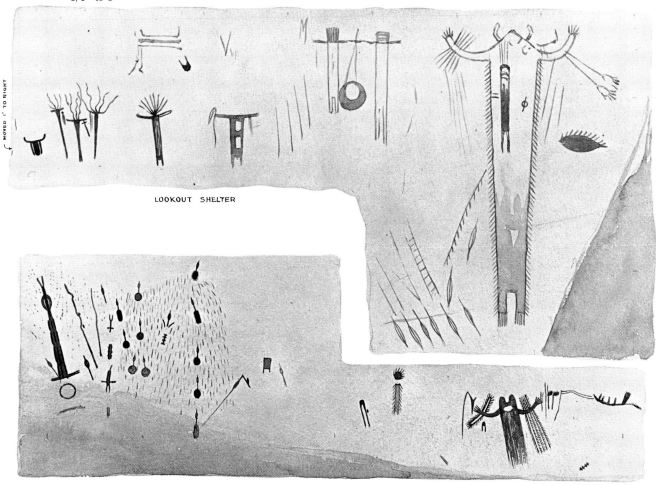

LOOKOUT SHELTER

PANTHER CAVE

Plate 22. Lookout Shelter. Copied July 8, 1937. Scale: 7/8″ to 1′. Panther Cave. Copied July 9, 1937. Scale: 1/4″ to 1′

View from Pecos River, Site 8, showing juncture of Pecos River with the Rio Grande. See Plate 31.

The existence of two definite and two probable periods of painting related to each other in a developmental sequence suggests that the Pecos River style of rock art embraced a considerable span of time. A sophisticated and complex art form could hardly have run its course in a few score years, and from what is known about other aspects of this culture, one would judge that it was a slow development. There seems to be no reason why we cannot assume that the pictographs of Period 1 and Period 2 date from one of the earlier manifestations of the tradition, perhaps several millennia before the birth of Christ. Whenever the development of these rock paintings began, it had apparently run its course by A.D. 1000.

The Life of the Pecos River Artists

The men who painted the Pecos River style pictographs were gatherers, hunters, and fishermen, unacquainted with gardening and probably not unlike the historic Coahuiltecans of northeastern Mexico and southern Texas in subsistence habits (Newcomb, 1961:29–57). At first glance it would seem impossible for a people to do more than eke out a wretched and precarious livelihood by depending upon the bounty of such an inhospitable environment. Actually, for a small population intimately acquainted with this land—its plants and animals, their potentialities and habits—it could provide an adequate and varied subsistence.

No large game animal was plentiful enough in the lower Pecos River region that a dependable subsistence could be based upon it. Deer were the most important game, though their remains are not common in archeological sites. The frequency with which herds of them appear in the pictographs probably reflects their importance though not necessarily their numbers. No Pecos River style pictographs depict bison or antelope although both animals were at least sporadic visitors to the region. Two extensive bison-bone deposits have been excavated in Bonfire Shelter, near Langtry, the lower deposit equated with the Paleo-Indian hunters already mentioned, the upper, which is stratigraphically separated from the lower, referable to an Archaic context. But the intrusion of bison into this country must have been unpredictable and infrequent. Other animals whose remains have been found in midden deposits, and which were presumably utilized for food or other purposes, include raccoon, gray fox, coyote, cottontail rabbit, pocket mouse, and ground squirrel. Turkey and quail bones are occasionally encountered, and horned toad and probably other lizards may have been eaten. Fishbones are common, particularly those of catfish; fish must have played a significant role in the diet. Snail shells of a large terrestrial genus (*Bulimus*), often charred, are found in large quantities in many middens and presumably were consumed (Pearce and Jackson, 1933:129–132). Mussel shells are less commonly found.

The scarcity of deer and other animal bones in midden deposits suggests that though such game may have been avidly sought, a diversity of wild plant foods provided the bulk of the diet. The most important plant food seems to have been sotol (*Dasylirion texanum* Scheele), a spiny-leafed plant of the lily family. The large sotol crowns, from which the leaves grow, were baked in pits or earth ovens, apparently in a fashion similar to that practiced by historic Indians of the region (Newcomb, 1961:115–116). At the Fate Bell Shelter in Seminole Canyon, for example, Pearce and Jackson (1933:Map III, pp. 16-17) found seven such pits in which were fragments of sotol leaves, ashes, and burned limestone rocks. The bulb of lechuguilla (*Agave lechuguilla*) and other agaves were probably prepared for consumption in the same manner. Other important plant foods were mesquite beans; tunas, or fruit, of the prickly pear; and a large assortment of seeds, nuts, and fruit. Included among these were black persimmons, acorns, Mexican walnuts (*Juglans microcarpa*), hackberries, huajillo beans (*Pithecellobium pallens*), which are similar to mesquite beans, beans of the catsclaw, seeds of wild onions, and grass seeds. A characteristic feature of the shelters and other open sites in the region are mortar holes, often deeply worn in rock ledges or large boulders. It was in these that nuts and seeds were reduced to meal. A quart of crushed Mexican walnuts, for example, was recovered from one mortar hole (Pearce and Jackson, 1933:42). A few Mexican buckeye nuts (*Ungnadia speciosa*) and many seeds of the Texas mountain laurel or mescal bean (*Sophora secundiflora*) have been found in Pecos River middens. Both are inedible, but the mescal bean, containing highly toxic narcotic alkaloids, was employed—eaten—in religious rituals by a number of historic tribes. It was probably so used by the peoples of the lower Pecos River.

Because many of the shelters in which the remains of this lower Pecos River culture have been found are exceptionally dry, many wood, fiber, and leather artifacts have been preserved (Schuetz, 1956, 1961). The basic weapon of hunters was the dart or spear propelled by the atlatl, or throwing stick, the remains of which have been recovered from occupation sites. Slightly curved, grooved, flat rabbit sticks also have been found. They may have been thrown at smaller game or used as clubs. The chief tool for grubbing sotol and other vegetable foods was a simple digging stick pointed at one or both ends. Wooden shovels or scoops may have been used for the same purpose, though the charred condition of many of them indicates household usage (Schuetz, 1961:179–180). Wooden fire hearths, fire drills, wedges, stakes, drills, needles, and shuttles have also been found. Stone manos for grinding nuts and seeds in bedrock mortars have been found, and a diversity of flint tools, from choppers and axes to knives, scrapers, and points, were used.

Bone and antler were fashioned into awls, flakers for chipping, scrapers, needles, beads, and pen-

Hanging Cave in Paint Canyon. See Plate 32, Nos. 1 and 2.

dants. Extensive use was made of sotol, lechuguilla, sacahuisti (*Nolina texana*), apocynum, and other vegetable fibers. Several kinds of fiber sandals have been found, and matting, basketry, and nets were also manufactured from these materials. Twigs bent with fiber cords suggest that snares for catching small game were used; cradles made of sticks and fibers have been recovered; pouches or bags were woven from vegetable fibers, and skin bags have also been found; even the hollowed-out pads of prickly pears seem to have been used for the same purpose. Leather fragments, including a leather apron, suggest something about attire, and fur robes or blankets made by interweaving fur in strands of cordage were also used. Fragments of stone pipes and what appear to be cane cigarette holders indicate that smoking was known. All in all, a rather complete inventory of the material culture of the people of the lower Pecos River can be made. It suggests a relatively elaborate material

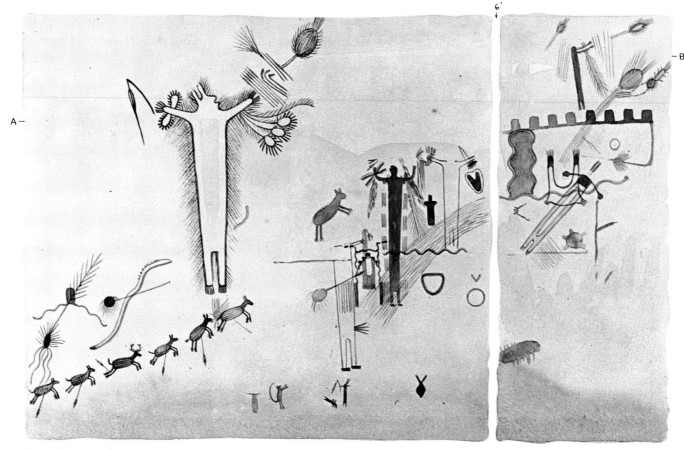

Plate 23. Panther Cave. Copied July 10, 1937. Scale: 1/4″ to 1′

culture for a hunting and gathering people and ingenious use of the materials available in this environment.

Recent cultures with a means of exploiting nature similar to that of the Archaic cultures of the lower Pecos River region allot the hunting chores to men and the gathering duties to women, or to women, children, and elderly men. Such a division of labor is virtually inevitable since bearing and rearing children restricts the physical activities of women, while men are stronger, less encumbered biologically, and generally better fitted for the ardor of the chase. So far as food supply was concerned, however, the women likely could be depended upon to collect considerable foodstuff, though it might be but seeds, tubers, and roots. With dependence on wild foods, and a lack of control over food supply as a consequence, not only was total population limited by the availability of these plants and animals, but population must have been dispersed. Seasonally it may have been possible and advantageous for a relatively large group of people to join forces for communal rabbit or deer drives. Or, perhaps following a particularly abundant harvest of mesquite beans or prickly pear tunas, a considerable number of people could meet

PLATE 23

Paintings cover the entire wall and part of the ceiling of Panther Cave, reaching more than twelve feet above the floor. The designs at each end of the shelter have been exposed to the sun and blowing rain and are very dim, but under protected parts of the shelter the color is still remarkably bright. The paintings at the lower end of the cave have been used as the Frontispiece in this book. They are actually continuous with this plate. A seep spring in the ceiling of Panther Cave destroyed a number of paintings there, and the resulting gap of six feet is so indicated here.

PLATES 24 and 25

This section of the pictographs is in the center of Panther Cave and badly overpainted, but most of the designs are quite clear and can easily be separated from the overlapping pictures.

Plate 24. Panther Cave. Copied July 10, 1937. Scale: 1/4″ to 1′

Plate 25. Panther Cave. Copied July 10, 1937. Scale: 1/4″ to 1′

for longer or shorter periods of time. But ordinarily they must have had to forage throughout their territory in small local or family groups, following a fairly regular round, and returning again and again to the same camp grounds. The nature of the refuse in the shelters and open sites, in fact, suggests just such an intermittent but long-continued occupation. Maddening to archeologists at a number of sites are churned and mixed-up cultural deposits which often do not show a clear vertical stratigraphy. Such a situation might be created if a group returned after an absence of some months and housecleaned before settling down.

Since it would be advantageous for hunters to be as intimately acquainted as possible with game trails, springs, hiding places, and other details of the territories they hunted, it is probable that after marriage a woman went to live with her husband and, consequently, the other members of his family. By remaining in his family home a hunter could continue to benefit from his accumulated knowledge of the local terrain. The less abundant the game, the greater the need for the hunter to possess such knowledge—and the lower Pecos River region was never overly endowed with game animals. Even though the number of square miles a particular family or local group exploited must have been large, a hunter who had grown up in it could have known almost every rock and prickly pear clump it supported. Patrilocal residence, then, would ensure efficient utilization of what game there was while it would not hamper the collecting activities of women, who after all could collect sotol bulbs in unfamiliar territory.

The basic social unit among the people of the lower Pecos River, if the foregoing are correct deductions, was composed of a man, his wife, unmarried daughters and sons, wives of sons, and grandchildren. Perhaps such a family group lived by itself for part of the year; probably it had close ties with one or two other similar groups, habitually hunting and foraging with them. Whether or not existence was organized specifically along these lines, in a general sense all life revolved in the orbit of kinship relationships, as it has for primitive man everywhere. To put it on an individual basis, the way in which a person behaved toward other persons was determined by how he was related to them, not by whether he worked for them or they for him, or whether they were rich and he poor, or any of the other non-kin relationships which underlie our own social structure.

Contrary to what many might at first expect, the relative scarcity of game and the probable inability to store much of a food reserve against hard times led to sharing and mutual assistance rather than individual utilization and ownership. The hard-earned deer the hunter secured was not solely, or

perhaps even mostly, utilized by him, but was shared with others of his kin and local group. With reflection it is obvious that such had to be the case, for days inevitably came, possibly they were commonplace, when the hunter's luck was bad or he was ill or injured, and he and possibly his wife could not provide for their own wants. To live with fair security under such circumstances demanded that all share; mutual assistance and dependence between members of a group of closely knit kin was a necessary part of adjustment and adaptation to this way of life.

While in such a society all were in a quite literal sense equals, some men, because of age or ability, were better hunters and providers. No doubt it was these men, or perhaps such men as had also acquired an extensive command of the anciently derived traditions, who provided the little leadership needed. Exalted rulers (kings or princes, probably not even chiefs) could not exist in such a culture, for one cannot command if he cannot control, and he cannot control if the dispersed population is in no way dependent upon him or has no need of his services. Even headmen may not have occupied a formally constituted or established position, but functioned as such only when necessity demanded. Such occasions would be during communal hunts and other times when large groups came together. The only other persons to which the title of part-time specialist might be applied would be shamans. These would be persons who had acquired special abilities or techniques for dealing with the supernatural world. We can be quite confident that, like other peoples, those of the lower Pecos River attempted to control and comprehend by more than natural means the crucial things of life they could not control through their own efforts or understand by their own factual knowledge. And it was the shamans who dealt with this phase of existence.

The harsh environment of the lower Pecos River region posed serious subsistence problems for its Archaic occupants. But by developing a diverse subsistence pattern with a relatively full utilization of available wild food resources and maintaining a pattern of consumption in which all shared equally, a small and dispersed population was able to exist here for many millennia. The threat of starvation must have been a familiar, chronic problem and one that strongly colored man's conception of the world and himself. Yet this ancient way of life proved a successful one, and its precepts, forms, and shibboleths must have been carefully nurtured, guarded, and handed down to oncoming generations. These Pecos River folk must have realized, too, that though strong in mutual assistance they were weak in numbers, and that their simple tools and techniques were useless when the game had vanished and drought had wizened the prickly pear. They must have known that there was much they could not influence or control by practical, pragmatic means however adept the hunter or industrious his wife. They must have realized that death perpetually stalked them all in the guise of disease, starvation, or through the enmity of other men. Though they were helpless or impotent in a practical sense in the face of these things, they need not have believed themselves so. For as other men, they believed that in their world more than natural forces were abroad which could be entreated or commanded, cajoled or enticed to come to their aid. And there is good cause to believe that in part through their pictographic art they sought to affect the supernatural world, and by the same token it is through their rock paintings that we know something of this aspect of their culture.

An Interpretation of the Meaning of the Pecos River Style Pictographs

This reconstruction of the culture of the people who painted the Pecos River style pictographs is too sketchy and problematical to be wholly satisfactory. But perhaps it does provide enough of the cultural framework within which its artists worked so that a meaningful basis for understanding this pictographic art has been established. It should be pointed out at the outset, as Kirkland has done (1938:16), that the immense effort involved in painting these murals

is proof enough of their serious purpose. . . . The pictures in almost every cave in Val Verde County, extend far above the reach of a man standing on the floor of the cave, so a ladder of some kind must have been required for their painting. In a few cases they were painted flat on the ceiling more than ten feet above the floor. This work would certainly have required some type of scaffolding. Grinding, mixing, and applying the paint on certain of the figures in these caves, must have required considerable labor, as they stand more than nine feet tall, are painted solid on rough surfaces, and are finished in three shades of color.

It is equally clear that the key to the meaning and purpose of the Pecos River style pictographs lies with the anthropomorphic beings, designated here as shamans. They are the focal points of virtually all paintings, dominate most by their size, and frequently overwhelm the viewer by sheer numbers. But just what these anthropomorphic beings represent is open to several interpretations. Kirkland (1938:24) thought that at least some of them (Plate 28, Nos. 1, 2) "picture a god-of-the-chase surrounded by animals pierced with arrows." Equally plausible is the possibility that they are meant to depict ordinary men masked and robed as gods or mythical beings. Actually the distinction between these categories may be minor since a

man decked out in imitation of a deity could temporarily be that deity in the eyes of the people.

The hypothesis favored here is that the anthropomorphic beings are shamans or perhaps members of medicine or dance societies, in which case they may or may not have been shamans in a narrow technical sense. But in rituals their purposes would scarcely differ from those of shamans, so that the term is used here in a broad sense. There are several reasons for favoring this sort of hypothesis: first, if the anthropomorphic beings were deities, it seems likely that they would have been painted in sacred and probably isolated places. But the shelters and caves in which the pictographs are found were probably occupied by the artists themselves, and though superimposition of paintings is common at some sites, their appearance in ordinary places seems to indicate that they were regarded as special and perhaps lucky in a magical sense but hardly sacred in a supernaturally dangerous or portentous way. Second, the variability of the anthropomorphic beings is very great, even among those belonging to the same period. Such variability is expectable of representations of persons in ceremonial attire or of members of shamanistic societies during ritualistic performances, but it does not seem likely that deities or even a pantheon would encompass such variation. Third, if these anthropomorphic beings were intended as deities, it does not seem likely that so many of them would be casually obscured by other paintings which often seem to have been contemporaneous with them. The fading representation of a deity is apt to be touched up but not disdained by being painted over, particularly by animals or objects which must have been of lesser conceptual importance.

These arguments, while plausible, are essentially negative, and there is another line of evidence which bears on the nature of the anthropomorphic beings. It supports in a positive and intriguing way the contention that these figures are shamans in our broad sense of the term. First proposed by T. N. Campbell (1958:159), it holds that "the chances are good" that a mescal bean cult was involved in the scenes depicted in the Pecos River style paintings. The mescal bean, as was mentioned earlier, has narcotic properties, and though its physiological effects on humans are not fully known, when ingested it can produce nausea, vomiting, delirium, long-lasting unconsciousness, and death (La Barre, 1938:126; Troike, 1962). The range of the mescal bean, or Texas mountain laurel, extends from West Texas eastward across Central Texas to the Gulf Coast and southward to include much of northeastern Mexico. The lower Pecos region is well within this range and in its steep-walled canyons the shrub grows vigorously. The incredibly hard, red seeds have been found in at least eight arche-

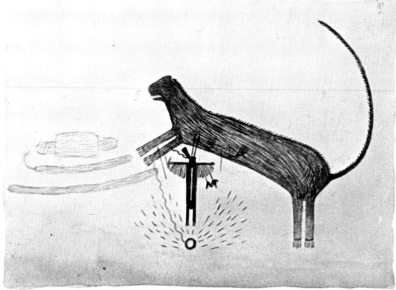

No. 1

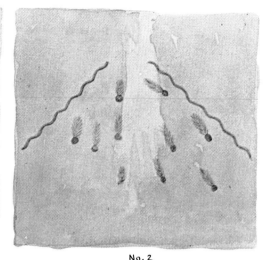

No. 2

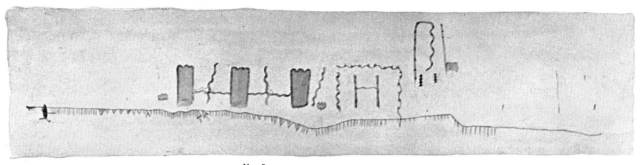

No. 3

Plate 26. Panther Cave. Copied July 10, 1937. Scale: Nos. 1-3, 1/4" to 1'

PLATE 26

No. 1. These figures complete the group of paintings under the main shelter in Panther Cave. The panther picture is still remarkably clear. If its tail were extended straight instead of curving, it would measure nineteen feet from head to tip of tail.

Nos. 2 and 3. These pictographs are poorly protected under the overhanging cliff, just to the left of the main shelter.

PLATE 27

Black Cave is in the north bank of Pressa Canyon, just above the high-water level. The cave shows signs of long occupation and its ceiling is smoked very black, hence its name. Although pictographs have been painted on most of the wall space and even on the ceiling in one place, the greater part of those in the center and at the right end are either completely indecipherable or very dim. Those at the left end are still very clear, and three of the designs (see No. 1) are still almost as brilliant as if recently painted. I believe this is due to the situation of the cave in relation to the prevailing air currents, which tend to carry dust and smoke away from this section of the wall and deposit them on the ceiling and wall to the right. Blowing rain and light have faded the group on the extreme left (No. 1). Five small drawings (A through E) which are too high to be measured are reproduced in a large scale which is only approximate.

PLATE 28

No. 1 and No. 2 are located under an overhanging cliff about one hundred yards to the left of Black Cave. They have faded badly because of their exposed location, but are copied in about their original strength of color. No. 3 is under the same overhanging cliff, but only five yards to the left of the shelter. These figures are badly faded and damaged by seep water.

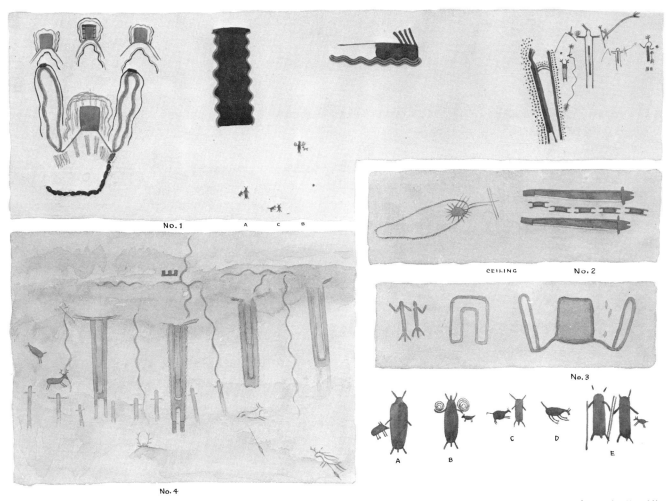

Plate 27. Black Cave. Copied July 14, 1937. Scale: Nos. 1-2, 1/4″ to 1′; No. 3, 3/8″ to 1′; No. 4, 1/4″ to 1′; Nos. a–e, about 3/16″ to 1″

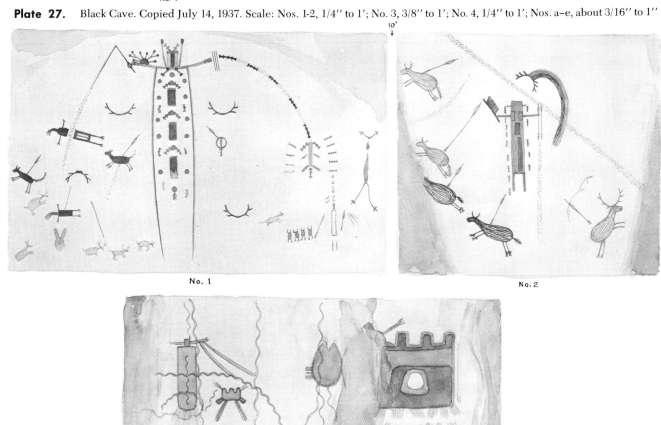

Plate 28. Black Cave. Copied July 14, 1937. Scale: Nos. 1–3, 1/4″ to 1′

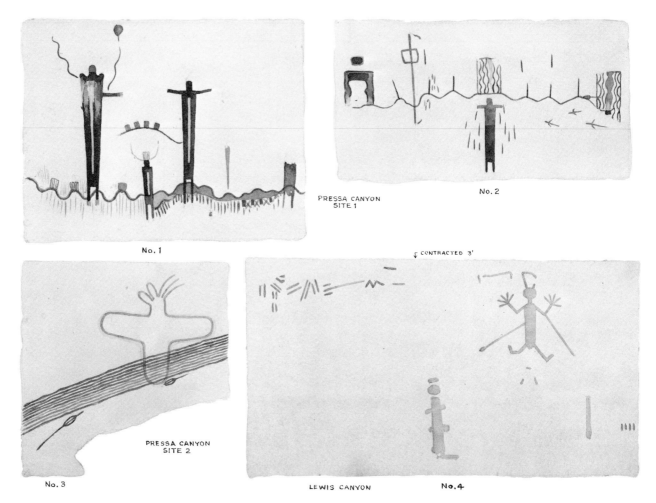

No. 1

PRESSA CANYON
SITE 1

No. 2

PRESSA CANYON
SITE 2

No. 3

LEWIS CANYON   No. 4

Plate 29. Pressa Canyon, Sites 1 and 2. Copied July 6, 1938. Scale: Nos. 1–2, 3/8″ to 1′; No. 3, 3/4″ to 1′. Lewis Canyon. Copied July 8, 1938. Scale: No. 4, 3/8″ to 1′

PLATE 29

Nos. 1 and 2, Pressa Canyon, Site 1. About seventy-five feet long, the entire back wall of this low, shallow shelter was once covered with paintings, but only a portion of the designs at each end of the shelter were still clear enough to be made out.

No. 3, Pressa Canyon, Site 2. This shelter is below Black Cave, high up in the canyon wall. Part of the wall and ceiling has weathered badly; the remaining surface is almost completely covered with a grey lichen which has destroyed the pictures that once covered the entire wall.

No. 4, Lewis Canyon. A small canyon empties over the cliff below the mouth of Lewis Canyon on the east bank of the Pecos River. Water has worn out a circular shelter, in the center of which is a round hole of fresh water about twenty feet in diameter and very deep. These few pictures were painted on the smooth wall and are still quite distinct. This site is near a large petroglyph site (Plates 56 to 63).

PLATE 30

Nos. 1, 2, 3, and 4, Pecos River, Site 3. These paintings are in a small shallow shelter high up the east cliff of the Pecos River almost directly across from Site 2. There were five groups of pictures along the back wall, all of them rather dim. The last group on the right consisted of two log-like designs and a splotch of red paint which were not worth copying.

No. 5, Pecos River, Site 4. This shelter on the east side of the Pecos River is at the mouth of a canyon where an old trail goes down the cliff. The shelter extends along the canyon wall on the left and forms a semicircle at the back, over which the water of the canyon pours. All of the pictures clear enough to copy are in the back of the shelter under the rock over which the water of the canyon above empties. Some pictures had been painted on the wall to the right of this space, but they were in such bad condition they could not be made out. The use of white on these pictures is of special interest.

PLATE 31

These pictographs are on the east end of a long shallow shelter on the west side of the Pecos River. Fully exposed to the sun and blowing rain, they are now so dim they were copied only with difficulty. No. 4 is in particularly bad condition but was copied because of the most unusual design made up of white dots over solid red.

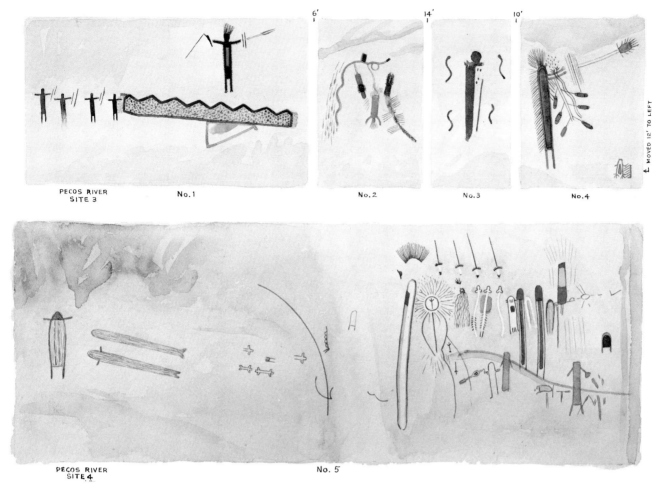

Plate 30. Pecos River, Sites 3 and 4. Copied July 11, 1938. Scale: Nos. 1–5, 1/4″ to 1′

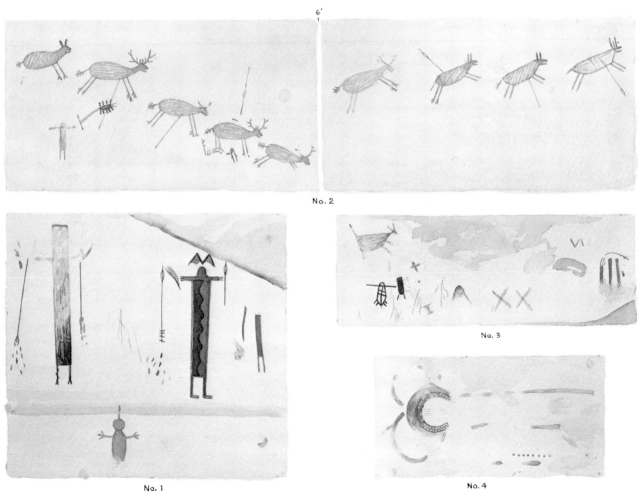

Plate 31. Pecos River, Site 8. Copied July 13, 1938. Scale: No. 1, 1/2″ to 1′; No. 2, 3/8″ to 1′; Nos. 3–4, 1/2″ to 1′

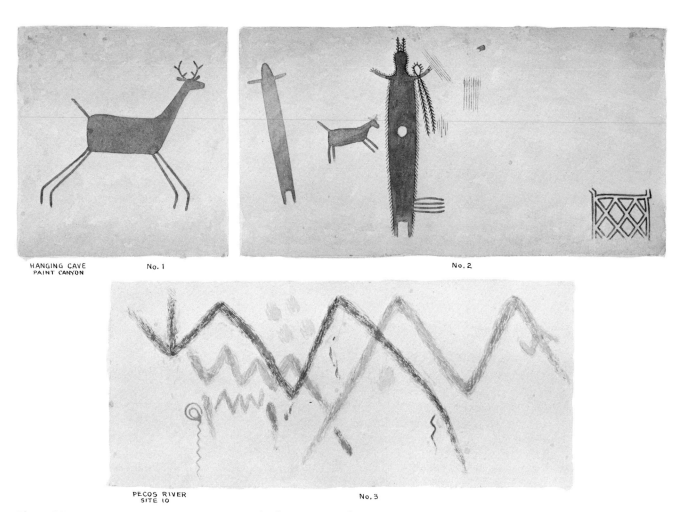

HANGING CAVE
PAINT CANYON   No. 1   No. 2

PECOS RIVER
SITE 10   No. 3

Plate 32.   Hanging Cave, Paint Canyon. Copied July 16, 1938. Scale: Nos. 1–2, 3/8″ to 1′. Pecos River, Site 10. Copied July 18, 1938. Scale: No. 3, 1/2″ to 1′

PLATE 32

Nos. 1 and 2, Hanging Cave. These dark red paintings are in a large, dry shelter high up in the cliff wall of Paint Canyon. The only way to reach the shelter is to climb a small tree that overhangs the first level of the cave, about fifteen feet above the canyon floor. Only a few pictures were painted on the wall; the deer and the largest human figure are quite clear, but the other designs were very dim.

No. 3. Pecos River, Site 10. These designs in red and yellow are in a small semicircular shelter near the top of the cliff on the west side of the Pecos River. The five dim splotches of red appear to be very poor attempts at hand-printing.

ological sites attributed to the Archaic stage and others have been recovered from sites on the Edwards Plateau (Campbell, 1958:157). At Murrah Cave the beans had been parched (Holden, 1937:70), and in a shelter near Comstock (Butler, 1948) a twined basket was found which contained about one hundred mescal beans and Mexican buckeye seeds, as well as lumps of red pigment, flint tools, eleven halves of rodent mandibles, and other objects which, as Campbell (*ibid.*) remarks, "certainly suggests ritual use of the mescal bean."

Peyote (*Lophophora williamsii*), a spineless cactus which produces vivid hallucinations and nausea when eaten, and which is well known through its modern religious usage by a number of Indian tribes, has also been recovered from several archeological sites in the lower Pecos River country (Campbell, 1958:159). Its usage by the people who painted the Pecos River style pictographs is not well established, but since the Caddo and perhaps other tribes appear to have used peyote and mescal beans interchangeably, the same possibility must be recognized for the Archaic inhabitants of the

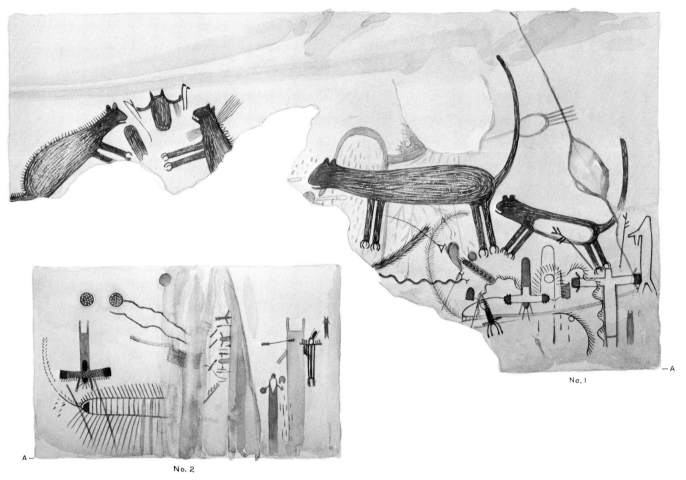

No. 1

No. 2

A—

Plate 33. Pecos River. Site 9. Copied July 17, 1938. Scale: Nos. 1–2, 1/4″ to 1′

lower Pecos River region. The usage of mescal beans (and possibly peyote) by the people responsible for the Pecos River style paintings would by itself be of little help in interpreting the anthropomorphic beings were it not that a number of historic Indian tribes used mescal beans ritually. Incredible as it may seem, many characteristic features of the pictographs are duplicated or paralleled in the mescal bean cult of these tribes!

Unfortunately the Coahuiltecans who occupied the lower Pecos River country at the beginning of historic times are poorly known, and though they apparently used the mescal bean in a ritual way, no details are known (Troike, 1962:954–955). The neighboring Tonkawas of Central Texas also seem to have used the mescal bean in a deer dance, but again no specific details are known. But the Caddo tribes of East Texas, beyond the Tonkawas and outside the natural range of the shrub, were using mescal beans ritually when first visited by Spanish missionaries, and a number of more distant tribes seem to have borrowed the mescal bean cult from this or other Texas sources (Troike, 1962:949–951;

PLATE 33

This site is a long shallow shelter more than one-hundred yards long, high on the west bank of the Pecos River. All of the back wall is soft chalk except the extreme north end. Here a part of a large group of paintings remains clear enough to copy. The picture of the cats is still quite distinct, but the bottom part of the group has completely weathered away and is two or three inches below the hard surface on which the paintings were made. The part that has weathered away is left blank on the copy. No. 2 joins No. 1 at A, and A represents the floor level. This is an unusually large group of cats.

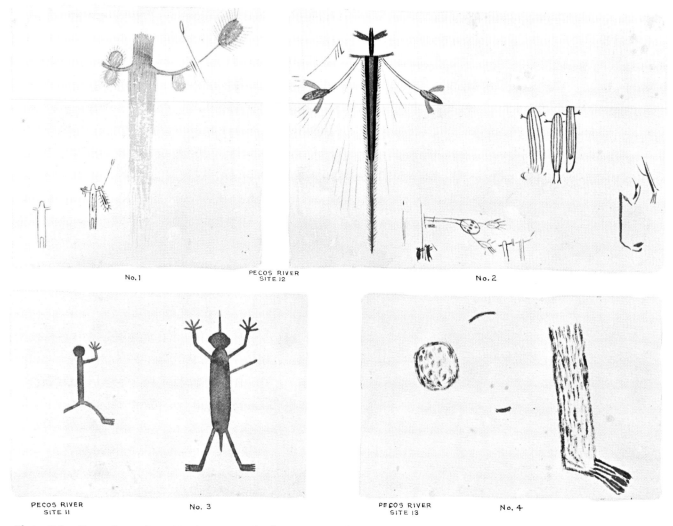

No. 1

PECOS RIVER
SITE 12

No. 2

PECOS RIVER
SITE 11

No. 3

PECOS RIVER
SITE 13

No. 4

Plate 34. Pecos River. Sites 11, 12, 13. Copied July 18, 1938. Scale: Nos. 1–2, 5/16″ to 1′; Nos. 3–4, 1/2″ to 1′

PLATE 34

Nos. 1 and 2. Pecos River, Site 12. These paintings are in a small, shallow shelter on the west bank of the Pecos River, above the mouth of Dead Man's Canyon. The pictographs were exposed to blowing rains and the east sun, so were very dim. Only about half of the original pictures could be made out.

No. 3. These red figures are in a small semicircular shelter in the east bank of the Pecos River. They could be seen clearly from the west bank of the river which is very deep at this place, so no attempt was made to reach the shelter. The designs were carefully copied through powerful binoculars, and their exact size, necessarily, had to be estimated.

No. 4. Pecos River, Site 13. These simple designs are painted on the wall of a small unoccupied shelter on the west wall of the Pecos River. The paint is still almost as bright as if newly painted and the copy shows the complete design.

PLATE 35

These paintings are in a shelter in the bottom of a canyon about one hundred yards from where it empties into the Pecos River. The pictures were well protected from the weather and from occupants of the shelter and consequently are in very good condition, except for some spalling of the rock. Every picture was copied except two or three very dim designs on rough rock.

Shelter in which were pictographs of Plate 35. View from across canyon.

No. 1

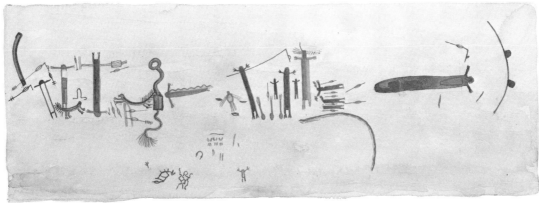

No. 2

Plate 35. Ingram Ranch. Copied July 9, 1939. Scale: Nos. 1–2, 1/4″ to 1′

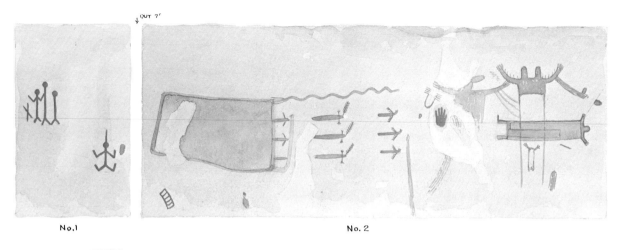

No. 1   No. 2

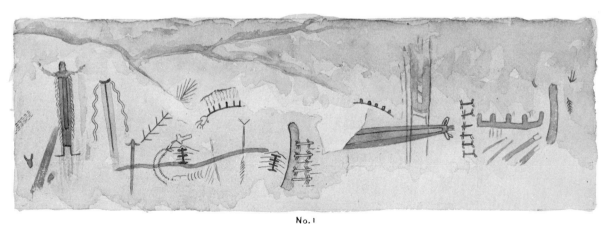

No. 3

Plate 36.   Ingram Ranch. Copied July 10, 1939. Scale: Nos. 1–3, 5/16″ to 1′

PLATE 36 and PLATE 37, No. 1

These paintings are in a low shelter which is about 150 feet long and about 20 feet deep on the east bank of the Pecos River. A narrow rock shelf runs along the back wall about 4 feet above the floor. There are many shallow mortars along this shelf and many burned rocks and cultural debris on the floor. The bottom of the pictographs begins about 4 feet above the shelf and stretch upward from 3 to 6 feet. They extend along the wall for about 60 feet, but the last 10 feet are too dim to be made out. A few later red paintings, including one handprint, are superimposed over the older Pecos River paintings.

No. 1

Plate 37.   Ingram Ranch. Copied July 10, 1939. Scale: 5/16″ to 1′

Howard, 1957). As Troike (1962:957–958) has pointed out, the Caddos must originally have acquired mescal beans, and undoubtedly their usage, from the Tonkawan and Coahuiltecan peoples to their west and south. Caddos used mescal beans, as well as other intoxicants, in several different ways. They were employed in dances, apparently by shamans, to induce visionary experiences which were subsequently described in detail to onlookers. It also appears that they used the mescal bean in their rather elaborate ceremonial preparations for war. An outstanding warrior was given a potion to drink, apparently a mescal bean preparation, and when he awoke from his stupor was able to divine the location and readiness of the enemy as well as forecast the success of the war party (Swanton, 1942:286). There were also societies or guilds of medicine men or shamans, one of which was known as a mescal bean society. This society held public initiations for its neophytes. Attired in their special regalia, shamans summoned prospective members, who were given drinks containing mescal beans. Such was the potency of the brew that the candidates passed out and remained unconscious or in pretended unconsciousness for twenty-four hours. When aroused "they related the dream experiences they had had—the journeys their souls had taken. Their experiences were cast in songs" (Newcomb, 1961:311–312).

A number of other tribes (Iowa, Kansas, Omaha, Oto, Osage, Pawnee, Wichita, and possibly the Arapaho and Ponca) had some form of mescal bean medicine society, and other tribes (Comanche, Apache), used mescal beans ritually in one way or another. Additional details about mescal bean rituals are supplied by these tribes. Hunting and deer (or elk) are often associated with the mescal bean cult by Comanche, Iowa, Omaha, Pawnee, Wichita (Howard, 1957). Among the Wichita, for example, society initiates receive power for curing through animals (G. A. Dorsey, 1904:20). Among the Pawnee the "society teaches that all animal powers were learned through the power of the mescal bean" (Murie, 1914:605). Many dancers paint their bodies in imitation of animals. Among the Omaha, for example, "some draw white lines over their limbs and bodies. Some paint as deer, putting white stripes on their limbs and bodies; others appear as bald eagles, with whitened faces" (J. O. Dorsey, 1884:350). Dancers carry a bow and arrow in their hands (Iowa, Omaha, Ponca) and gourd rattles (Iowa, Omaha, Pawnee). Among the Pawnee, dancers carry "large whistles, to symbolize the elk, and foxskins carried by the neck when dancing. A few members wear braided buffalo hide ropes into which feathers are woven and some carry wings of birds" (Murie, 1914:605). Some Omaha dancers also carry a foxskin on one arm and wear two deer tails

tied together around the neck. Among the Wichita (Newcomb, 1961:273) and Pawnee (Murie, 1914: 605), initiation into medicine societies is similar to that recorded for the Caddo, with the addition that the unconscious state of the candidate is tested by scraping the toothed jaws of a garfish over his body.

No doubt other suggestive features of historic mescal bean cults might be found, but these should suffice to demonstrate that if members of mescal bean medicine societies had been portrayed on rock surfaces they would undoubtedly look amazingly like the anthropomorphic beings depicted in the Pecos River style pictographs. Animals, particularly deer, are important to both, men dance with weapons in both, and the animal pelts, bird feathers, rattles, and other paraphernalia used in the modern cult have close counterparts in the lower Pecos pictographs. Even the purpose of rodent jaws, included with the mescal beans and other objects in a basket in a lower Pecos River archeological site, is suggested by the usage of garfish jaws in the modern cult.

Once the hypothesis that the Pecos River style pictographs are part of a mescal bean medicine society has been suggested, it is difficult not to interpret almost every element in the pictographs in these terms. Thus, the red dots associated with some Period 4 shamans (Plate 28, No. 1) become mescal beans, the feathers depicted in certain paintings (Plate 6, No. 2) almost automatically are referred to a Pawnee context in which some dancers carry ropes into which feathers are braided, and so forth. But it should be noted that the shamans of the pictographs are so varied that some of them are bound to be similar to almost any caparisoned dancers one might care to relate them to. The historic cult and the Pecos River pictographs are also separated by such an enormous span of time and distance that the connection between the two can be regarded as possible, but only that.

Whether or not the pictographs were associated with a mescal-bean medicine society, this kind of hypothesis offers a satisfactory, reasonable, and comprehensive interpretation for the Pecos River style pictographs. It accounts for both the variability and the unity of the shamans. On the one hand, we would expect that each shaman would paint and adorn himself in a unique way in accordance with the instructions he had received while in contact with supernatural forces, just as was true in the historic societies. This is precisely the nature of the vast majority of the shamans of each Period: within well-defined limits they vary from one another in a way which allows for idiosyncratic differences. On the other hand, in both Periods 2 and 3 a number of types of shamans can be discerned, as if they represented the membership of one particular shamanistic society. In Period 2, for exam-

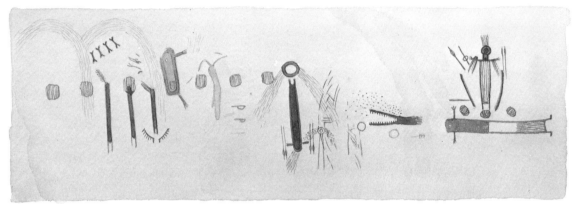

No. 1

No. 2

Plate 38.   Pecos River, Cave 1. Copied August 20, 1940. Scale: Nos. 1–2, 1/4″ to 1′

No. 1

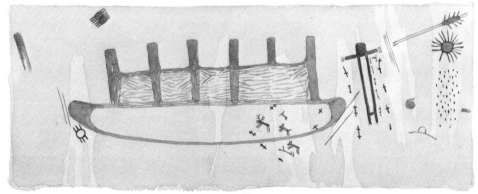

No. 2

Plate 39.   Pecos River. Cave 1. Copied August 20, 1940. Scale: 3/8″ to 1′. Cave 2, Copied August 21, 1940. Scale: 1/4″ to 1′

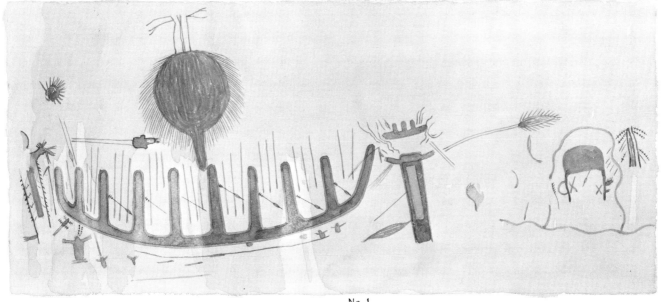

No. 1

No. 2

Plate 40. Pecos River, Cave 2. Copied August 21, 1940. Scale: No. 1, 1/4″ to 1′; No. 2, 3/8″ to 1′

PLATE 38 and PLATE 39, No. 1

This shelter is in the west bank of the Pecos River above Dead Man's Canyon. A small canyon empties over the top of the long, shallow shelter. A small spring of good water flows from a crack in the center of the shelter's back wall and has built up a large deposit of lime. The dark mass in the center of Plate 39, No. 1, represents the lime deposit. Note the red spot around the mouth of the spring and the balanced curved designs on each side. There has been considerable overpainting on the wall. There is a small midden at the south end of the shelter, and the pictographs above it have already been destroyed. Most of the paintings are to the right of the spring and are very dim.

PLATE 39, No. 2, and PLATE 40

These pictographs are in a large cave in the east cliff of the Pecos River well above the mouth of Dead's Man's Canyon. About 150 feet long and 40 feet deep, a deep midden deposit covers its floor. A wide shelf of rock several feet above the floor extends all along the back of the shelter and has protected the paintings from damage. Only about half of the wall surface is covered with pictures. There is very little overpainting and although the paint is very dim and badly streaked by seepage, most of the designs could be made out and copied. The discoloration from seepage was disregarded on the copies. All but the very bottom of the designs on Plate 40, No. 1, are too high to have been reached without a ladder. The top of the highest designs reach well out on the curved ceiling.

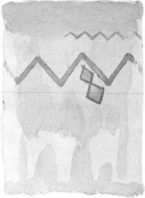

No.1　　　　　　　　　　　　　　　　　　No.2

Plate 41.　Banner Ranch. Copied July 17, 1939. Scale: Nos. 1–2, 3/8″ to 1′

PLATE 41

Nos. 1 and 2. Geddis Canyon, in Terrell County, flows into the Pecos River from the west, and high up in the canyon wall near its mouth, facing west, is a small shelter containing these pictographs. The shelter is about seventy-five feet long and fifteen feet deep, and appears to have been used for a long time. Pictographs once covered the entire back wall, which is about six feet high, but only a few at the left end of the shelter were clear enough to make out. Most of these are very dim, and are in a round recess in the wall which appears to have been used as a fireplace. A fragmentary handprint at the bottom of the recess had been made by scraping away the soot from around the hand, leaving a black print.

No.3

Plate 42.　Adams Ranch. Copied July 12, 1939. Scale: 5/8″ to 1′

PLATE 42

No. 3. These paintings are farther up Geddis Canyon under an overhanging cliff about ten feet long and eight feet above the ground. They can easily be reached by a shelf of rock below the pictures. Dim and badly flaked, they are exposed to the west sun and blowing rain.

ple, shamans depicted with the horned headdress and feathered sashes seem to represent a type. The peculiar rotund figures of Period 2 also seem to fit into this category. In Period 3 the winged shamans are very similar to one another; in fact, one wonders in some cases if they are not the work of the same artist. This possibility also fits the hypothesis, for very likely shamanistic societies performed at regular intervals in the yearly round of activities, and shamans might have duplicated their paintings on a number of occasions.

This shamanistic-society hypothesis also explains more clearly than any other the association of animals with shamans. Most other investigators who have sought the meaning of the Pecos River style pictographs have referred them to a "hunting cult" context (Kelley, 1950b; H. C. Taylor, 1949). Kirkland (1938:24) also felt that painting the pictures or viewing them in some sort of ceremonial context ensured "success in finding and killing the animals. Else, why . . . the pictures of droves of deer, each pierced with a spear, in the shelters of Val Verde County?" Gebhard (1960:43–45), apparently alone among modern investigators, has felt this was too narrow an interpretation. There is, of course, an obvious connection between some of the shamans and deer (particularly in Period 2, see Plate 23, for example), and it may be inferred that some of the ancient ceremonials were aimed at securing deer, as were some historic mescal bean medicine societies. But a hunting-cult hypothesis fails to explain the presence of cougars in the pictographs, or the fact that a majority of shamans in all periods do not have animal associations. Again, the shamanistic-society hypothesis explains these facts. Cougars (associated primarily with Period 2 shamans) are never pierced by darts nor do they seem to menace human figures. This suggests that some shamans, or perhaps members of a "cougar society" received power from this animal. Drugged perhaps by mescal beans, shamans or potential shamans may have received supernatural assistance from these beasts or their mythological counterparts. Deer, after all, are favored prey of cougars, and what would be more likely than for men to enlist the supernatural aid of such expert predators. It may well be that other animal drawings, even perhaps of deer, are intended to represent sources of supernatural power and knowledge, or guardian spirits, through which men acquired special powers. These extraordinary powers may have helped man in the chase and also in other pursuits. Shamans or shamanistic societies may have been concerned with and skilled in dealing with warfare, curing the sick, influencing the weather, and general welfare, in addition to success in the hunt. If such was the case, shamans may not have acquired power for these matters through animals

and so did not draw any. But other than hunting, the only clear and obvious concern of shamans depicted in the pictographs is warfare. The prone human figure rent apart by the forces from a shaman's dart (Plate 28, No. 1) is a good example.

This shamanistic-society hypothesis also accounts for the fact that there is a surprising amount of overpainting of Pecos River style pictographs, particularly in Period 3. Since the pictographs were presumably painted as a way of illustrating supernatural experiences and the powers gained by them, they may well have had significance only on one occasion. Other, later shamans, perhaps members of other societies and deriving power from their own particular spiritual helpers, would feel no compunction about obliterating the representations an old shaman or shamans had made. But at the same time it would be logical for shamanistic societies to hold their rituals at the old traditional places where their forerunners had been in successful communication with the supernaturals. Hence, a considerable number of pictographs could have been overpainted.

It seems likely that the painting of murals, or ceremonies utilizing those painted previously, took place at regular seasonal intervals, most likely when considerable numbers of people could congregate. This may have been during the coldest weeks of winter when the shelters would have afforded welcome protection from northers, but it may have been at a time of communal hunting or at the harvest time of various wild plant foods. Whichever the case, it would have been the time to perform the ancient rituals, the occasion for medicine societies to hold their great ceremonies—initiating new members, demonstrating their powers, renewing contacts with the supernatural world. Perhaps there were other social and religious events at such gatherings, but among the most dramatic and impressive of all must have been those of the shamanistic societies. The world of the spirits would come alive at such times, perhaps more real, more vivid than the ordinary world itself. For in brilliant colors on those harsh rock walls the shamans portrayed themselves in the attire dictated by the supernaturals, and near them they drew the miraculous animals, men, and forces with which they dealt. Indeed, these rituals must have impressed and exalted the people, and given them faith and courage to face the dangers of their rude existence. Forgotten at such times was the empty belly, the dead child, the drudgery, the brief life; the world became rich and colorful, bright with hope and lively with promise.

If the shamanistic-society hypothesis is pursued a bit further, one can readily imagine that the custom of painting shelter walls in the lower Pecos country may have originated when a shaman emerging from a trance, very possibly induced by mescal beans, attempted to visualize his hallucinations or dreams by a rude painting. Perhaps a supernatural creature instructed him to do so. The custom caught on, perhaps at first practiced only by the members of one society or fraternity of shamans, but eventually becoming a popular or even a necessary part of shamanistic rituals. It may have flourished for a considerable length of time, the shamanistic societies slowly changing, if the evolution of the pictographs is a guide. Ultimately the custom of painting shelter walls waned—perhaps new ritual practices displaced the old; possibly internal developments in the old societies made rock painting obsolete or even forbade it.

Whether or not the shamanistic-society hypothesis correctly interprets the Pecos River style pictographs, in a more general sense there can be little doubt that the paintings are religious art which was part of an Archaic culture's attempts to influence and gain assistance from supernatural powers. They were one of the devices these meagerly equipped Archaic folk possessed to survive in a harsh, demanding land. These people may even have regarded their murals, or the ceremonies of which they were a part, as of paramount importance to their survival and well-being.

When the investigators of ancient hunters and gatherers have only a relatively few stone, bone, and other tools from which to deduce the nature of that life, it is apt to seem flat and toneless, lacking relief and features. For the Archaic culture of the lower Pecos this is no longer true, for the pictographs lend a new dimension to perception. The picture of that Archaic life remains one of difficulty and hardship, but it becomes clear that it was neither drab nor dull, nor was it one of unremitting toil. The pictographs reveal an existence punctuated by exciting, colorful dramas, and a world seen through imaginative eyes.

CHAPTER 5

THE LOWER PECOS: LATER ART

The Red Monochrome Style

Less distinctive than Pecos River style pictographs but confined to the same region is a form of mural art that has been termed "Val Verde Flooded-Shelter Style" by Kirkland (1938:20) and less ponderously, "Red Monochrome" or "Red Figure" styles by others (Gebhard, 1960:10,12). It will be referred to here as the Red Monochrome style. Large panels of paintings in this style are known from only two sites and Kirkland copied Red Monochrome paintings at only twelve sites in all. Since this style has been lumped together with historic and other pictographs of the region by some earlier investigators, the total number of sites containing Red Monochrome paintings is unknown. It is certain that they are far fewer in number than Pecos River style paintings. All Red Monochrome paintings are in a single color, varying from a red or red-orange to a few figures in yellow. Kirkland did not find that any other colors had been used. Gebhard (1960:48) mentions "a few figures" in black, and Graham and Davis (1958:80) say that they "may be either red or black." The present writer has been unable to find any black pictographs which can be ascribed to this style.

The two shelters in which the bulk of the Red Monochrome paintings have been found are close together. One of them, in Seminole Canyon (Plates 43–46), is about eight miles west of Comstock, Val Verde County.

Its floor is rock and is level with the bottom of the canyon, the stream runs beneath the overhang and forms a pool under the shelter. The length of the shelter is 105 yards and the over-hang about twenty-five yards at the deepest place. The back wall is rather smooth limestone, sloping up from the floor and extending upward about fifteen feet where it rounds into the ceiling. The pictures begin about four feet above the water level and extend to a height of twelve feet in one place. The entire length of the wall has been covered with pictures. (Notes, Plate 43)

There is a burned-rock mound nearby and mortar holes in the shelter's floor. About twelve miles southwest of Comstock, just below a spring in a small canyon known as Painted Rock Canyon, is the second major site of Red Monochrome paintings (Plates 47-49):

The shelter is about 150 yards long, level with the creek, with permanent holes of water next to the back wall. It could never have been inhabited on account of this water. There is a large burned rock mound on the first level bank in front of the shelter. On top of the hill in front of the shelter are many very old hearths. There are a number of mortars in the rocks about the shelter. The entire wall is smooth and suitable for pictures and there is ample sign that at one time the entire wall and much of the ceiling was covered with Pecos River style designs. These designs, however, are almost entirely weathered off up to the ceiling, due, no doubt, to the action of the water which covers the lower part of the wall with every rise in the canyon. A few designs can still be made out at the upper end of the shelter and in places on the ceiling. (Notes, Plate 47).

It is on this weathered surface that the Red Monochrome figures were placed.

Human figures, and they make up the principal elements in the Red Monochrome paintings, are almost invariably shown full front, with animals depicted in side view. The human head is depicted as a round circle atop the shoulders, usually without any features. Ears are shown in two instances (Plate 47, No. 4) and what seems to represent a single feather or other ornament often juts upward from the top of the head, resembling nothing more than a lightning rod or aerial (Plate 44, No. 2, second figure from right; Plate 44, No. 6, second figure from right; Plate 31, No. 1, bottom; Plate 34, No. 3, right). One head (Plate 49, No. 9, far left) is circled by a band of color, giving it the appearance of a helmeted diver. Arms are normally bent at the elbows, the forearms raised, and the fingers, when present, are spread out so that they have more than a passing resemblance to persons being held up. Legs extend stiffly from the body and feet project outward from the legs at right angles to them. Since bodies are solid masses, it is difficult to determine whether or not they are clothed. In one instance (Plate 47, No. 4, second human figure from left), attire seems to consist of a simple habit or dress which extends below the knees. Male genitalia

Seminole Canyon, Shelter 1. The stream flows under the overhang. Note mortar holes in foreground. Some of the pictographs can be seen at extreme right. See Plates 43-46.

No. 1

No. 5

Plate 43. Seminole Canyon, Shelter 1. Copied July 8, 1936. Scale: Nos. 1–5, 1/4″ to 1′

No. 2

No. 6

Plate 44.   Seminole Canyon, Shelter 1. Copied July 8, 1936. Scale: Nos. 2 and 6, 1/4" to 1'

PLATES 43, 44, 45 and 46, No. 4

Seminole Canyon, Shelter 1. These copies are made so that no space is omitted between plates. If Plate 43, No. 1, is placed against Plate 44, No. 2, and No. 2 against No. 3, etc., the complete group can be reconstructed to scale, except for the two breaks noted on Plates 43 and 45. These paintings are very dim and it is impossible to say what their original shade was. It is certain, however, that some form of red ocher was used on all but two or three designs, which were painted with yellow ocher. All pictures are in one color and no animal or human figure is drawn in outline. Not only has the color faded, but water and dampness have caused the rock to flake until the paintings now appear to be rough, like crayon drawings, although they were originally painted with liquid paint. At one place (Plate 44, No. 6, three yellow figures next to farthest right figure) the red paint has almost completely flaked off, leaving a yellow stain from which the pictures can easily be made out. Evidently the oil in the color soaked into the porous limestone, resulting in this stain. A white lichen is growing down from the ceiling and has begun to cover the paintings at the lower end of the shelter.

No. 3

5'6"

No. 7

Plate 45. Seminole Canyon, Shelter 1. Copied July 8, 1936. Scale: Nos. 3 and 7, 1/4″ to 1′

are frequently indicated (Plate 43, No. 1, left center and far right, for example); whether or not women are shown is impossible to discern. The lack of male genitalia could be taken to indicate femininity, but several hunters are so depicted and it is unlikely that they are meant to represent women. In one instance (Plate 43, No. 5, center) a figure with bulging, rounded hips may represent a woman.

The Red Monochrome style has interested archeologists primarily because of the presence of bows and arrows. Simple and double-curved bows are depicted (Plate 47, No. 3, has examples of both types), and what appear to be spears or staffs are shown piercing or perhaps leaning against human figures. No arrows or spears are shown striking or penetrating animals. The only other objects associated with human figures are tassels, or perhaps pouches, suspended from the arms of some. Diverse groups of animals are depicted in these rock paintings. Gebhard (1960:50) claims that most of the quadrupeds are "undoubtedly antelope," but the present writer cannot find any paintings in which this animal is present. Only two animals are shown with antlers (Plate 43, No. 5); one is un-

questionably meant to represent a deer, and the other, whatever it is, assuredly does not possess the distinctive horns of the pronghorn. Several of the quadrupeds are excessively long of leg and all four legs are bent in an ungainly fashion (Plate 43, No. 1). They may represent crude attempts to depict animals in motion or they may represent animals that have been slain. One deer is exceptional (Plate 47, No. 4) in that what seems to be the heart or stomach is indicated as well as a line which runs toward the head; the tongue also protrudes from the mouth. The practice of depicting the "heart line" in animal representations is, incidentally, widespread in North American Indian art. Schaafsma (1963:57) has suggested "that the Athapascans brought the use of the heartline with them into the Southwest as either an Athapascan trait or one which they picked up from Plains groups." Other parallel and crosshatched lines within the body of this animal may be intended to represent other anatomical features. Rabbits are unmistakably present in these pictographs and seem to be jack rabbits rather than cottontails (Plate 44, No. 6, mid-left; Plate 47, No. 4, left). A bird with a beard (Plate 47, No. 4, far left)

No. 4   SHELTER 1

SHELTER 2

Plate 46. Seminole Canyon, Shelter 1. Copied July 8, 1936. Scale: No. 4, 1/4″ to 1′. Shelter 2. Copied July 9, 1936. Scale: 3/16″ to 1′

is a turkey, the dorsal views of fish apparently represent catfish (Plate 47, No. 4, mid-left), and a turtle or terrapin is also clearly depicted (Plate 47, No. 3). One of the quadrupeds (Plate 44, No. 2) is a cougar, others seem to be dogs or perhaps coyotes or wolves. Snakes appear to be represented by zigzag lines terminating in circular heads (Plate 43, No. 5; Plate 4, No. 1). One example is 44½ feet long (Plate 52).

Unlike the Pecos River style pictographs, most of the humans and animals are approximately the correct size in relation to one another. However, the cougar is large with respect to the human figures (Plate 44, No. 2) and the large snake (Plate 52) is of unnatural length, if the human figure touching its "head" is associated with it. But the outlined human is aberrant for this style and was almost certainly not painted at the same time. Other common elements in the Red Monochrome paintings are positive and negative handprints (Plate 43, No. 5; Plate 44, Nos. 2, 6; Plate 45, Nos. 3, 7; Plate 46, No. 4; Plate 47, No. 1; Plate 50, Nos. 1, 2; Plate 4, No. 1; Plate 37, Nos. 2, 3). For positive prints the hand was dipped in liquid paint and then

PLATE 46

Seminole Canyon, Shelter 2. This shelter is about thirty yards wide and fifteen yards deep. Water comes down a little draw and empties over the shelter and has caused the ceiling and wall to flake, damaging the pictographs on the ceiling and back wall. With the exception of one zigzag line in ocher, the complete design is painted in a dark purple red. Parts of it could not be certainly made out and were not copied. Five handprints were made in a lighter red color and are probably not a part of the original design. The five-fingered dots under the wavy line to the left are not handprints.

Painted Rock Shelter, showing shelter and burned-rock mound in foreground. See Plates 47-49.

No. 1. No. 2. No. 3.

No. 4

Plate 47. Painted Rock Shelter. Copied July 13, 1937. Scale: Nos. 1–4, 1/4″ to 1′

Plate 48. Painted Rock Shelter. Copied July 13, 1937. Scale: Nos. 5–7, 1/4″ to 1′

PLATES 47, 48, and 49

These pictographs are in Painted Rock Canyon, a small canyon which empties into the Rio Grande southwest of Comstock. About 150 yards long and level with the creek, this uninhabitable shelter has permanent holes of water next to the back wall. The entire wall is smooth and suitable for pictures, and there is ample sign that at one time the entire wall and much of the ceiling was covered with Pecos River style paintings. These designs, however, are almost entirely weathered off up to the ceiling, due no doubt to the action of the water which covers the lower part of the wall with every rise in the canyon. A few designs can still be made out at the upper end of the shelter and in places on the ceiling. The later, solid Red Monochrome figures and animals have been superimposed over the older designs.

Plate 47, No. 1. The circle and lines in black and red are remnants of Pecos River style designs over which the animals have been painted.

Plate 47, No. 4. The circle containing the cross does not belong to the animal at the extreme right. It is underneath and probably belongs to the Pecos River style designs.

Plate 49. The designs on this plate appear at the extreme upper end of the shelter and far enough away from the creek to receive some protection from flood water, and, consequently, more of the extremely dim Pecos River style designs can be made out.

Plate 49, No. 9. All of the figures to the right of the little red animal belong to the Pecos River style.

Plate 49, No. 10. Only the two solid red figures on the left belong to the more recent Red Monochrome style.

Plate 49.   Painted Rock Shelter. Copied July 13, 1937. Scale: Nos. 9–12, 1/4″ to 1′

pressed against the rock surface. For negative prints the hand was placed against the rock and paint sprayed around the hand, probably from the mouth but perhaps through a hollow reed. On the walls of an uninhabitable shelter containing a permanent pool of water are numerous positive and negative handprints of children (Plate 51, No. 3). The other pictographs in this shelter are apparently Red Monochrome style, and it is difficult not to suppose that the children of these artists, perhaps dawdling over their water-fetching chores, enjoyed themselves by decorating its walls. Two designs present in Red Monochrome murals resemble elements found in Pecos River paintings: one is a plume-like design (Plate 44, No. 2, upper right) which may well be an attempted copy of the older style; the other is a "branched design" (Plate 45, No. 3, left of center) which actually "may have been made by the Pecos River artists, who lived in other shelters no more than a quarter of a mile down the canyon" (Notes, Plate 44). A number of other geometric shapes — triangles, circles, crosses, and miscellaneous figures — may be found in various Red Monochrome paintings, but none seem to be particularly significant to their meaning or purpose.

At the two principal sites the various figures follow after one another, almost as in a procession, to form long horizontal panels of paintings. Gebhard (1960:49) remarked that "visually there is a sophistication in the way that the static verticality of the human figure is played off against the non-static angles of shafts, the "V" angles of the arms of the figures themselves, and the horizontality of the paintings of animals." None of the pictographs were placed on particularly hard-to-reach surfaces, though in several cases the tops of the paintings extend as high as twelve feet above the ground. All the Red Monochrome paintings are distinctly representational; they are attempts, albeit crude ones, to depict men and animals as they were. Our inability to determine the species of every animal is due more to the rough manner of expression than to anything else. Unlike their Pecos River precursors, these artists made absolutely no attempts to portray more than natural objects or ideas; theirs was a realistic, down-to-earth style.

The prominently shown bows and arrows in Red Monochrome pictographs establish that they were painted after this weapon was introduced, generally believed to have been sometime after A.D.

Painted Rock Shelter. See Plates 47-49.

ancient, often deep Archaic deposits. They differ from the earlier remains chiefly by the addition of arrowpoints, and pottery is also occasionally found (Johnson, 1964; Pearce and Jackson, 1933). A nomadic or seminomadic hunting-and-gathering manner of existence continued to be pursued much as it had been for many millennia. No doubt the bow and arrow were somewhat superior to the old atlatl and dart, so that hunting may have become somewhat easier and more productive, but the effects of the new weapon were not revolutionary.

Unfortunately, the later culture or cultures of the lower Pecos are not well known, and their relationships to their predecessors and to historic Indians are conjectural. The old indigenous population could have learned about and borrowed the bow and arrow from neighbors, but the new weapon could as easily have been introduced by an incursion of strangers. This is one instance in which pictographic evidence may come to the aid of traditional archeology, for the dissimilarity of the Pecos River and Red Monochrome styles suggests that the Red Monochrome artists were in fact newcomers to the area, unrelated to its former inhabitants.

In a draw emptying into the Pecos River below the crossing of the Ozona-Langtry Road is a shelter

about 100 feet long, seven feet high in front and about twenty feet deep. It has no deposit on its rock floor, but the ceiling is smoked very black. There is a deep permanent water hole in front of the shelter, beside which are a few mortars. Across the draw are several large burned rock mounds. (Notes, Plate 50)

A few red handprints are the only recognizable pictographs remaining, but

Just back from the painted pictures were small ledges on the ceiling blackened with smoke. A great deal of scratching and carving had been done on these surfaces with some sharp instrument. It appeared white on the black background, but was copied in reverse. The work was unquestionably that of the Indians because several of the arrowhead-like designs had been painted over with the same red paint used to make the handprints. (Notes, Plate 50)

One of the arrowpoints (Plate 50, No. 3, upper left) is a Perdiz point and several others may be. This arrowpoint has a widespread distribution in Texas, is found in the upper levels of archeological sites in the lower Pecos region, and dates from A.D. 1000 to the historic period (Suhm et al., 1954:504-505; Johnson, 1964). The probability seems good that these petroglyphs and handprints were executed by the artists who painted the Red Monochrome murals, which suggests that these paintings likely date from the later part of the time span established for this style. There is only one other site, in a small shelter overlooking the Pecos, which has similar petroglyphs, but this similarity may be fortuitous (Plate 51, No. 2).

600, and the absence of horses, firearms, and other European objects almost surely places them before the historic period. During which part of this time span the pictographs were painted is unknown. Two arrow points are included among the Red Monochrome pictographs in the Painted Rock Shelter (Plate 47, No. 1, No. 4); both appear to be Starr points, a type commonly found in southwestern Texas with an estimated age of A.D. 800 or 900 to A.D. 1600 (Suhm et al., 1954:506–507). Obviously they are of no help in pinpointing the age of the paintings, and the petroglyphic arrowpoints, discussed below, are too tentatively associated with the Red Monochrome style to be helpful. The fact that the relatively few Red Monochrome murals are strikingly similar to one another, undergoing no development or change, suggests that they were executed in a relatively brief span. It is as if the men who painted them visited these shelters briefly, halting long enough to sketch their rude, red pictographs, then passed on. Most archeological investigations in the lower Pecos region have revealed a veneer of cultural materials overlying the

Tardy Draw Shelter, showing artist copying paintings. See Plate 50.

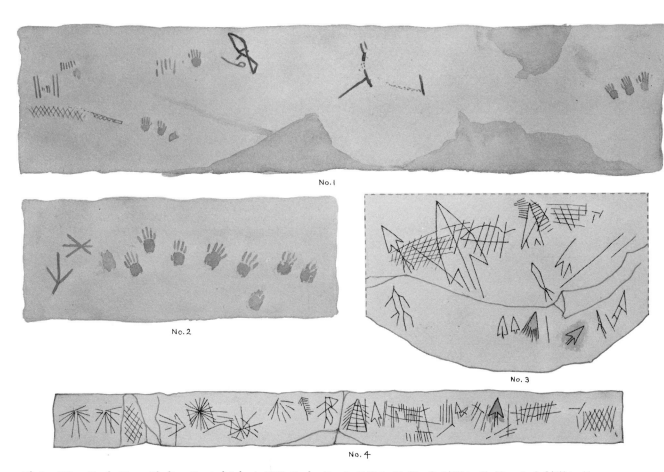

No. 1

No. 2

No. 3

No. 4

Plate 50. Tardy Draw Shelter. Copied July 4, 1938. Scale: No. 1, 1/4″ to 1′; No. 2, 1/2″ to 1′; Nos. 3–4, 3/4″ to 1′

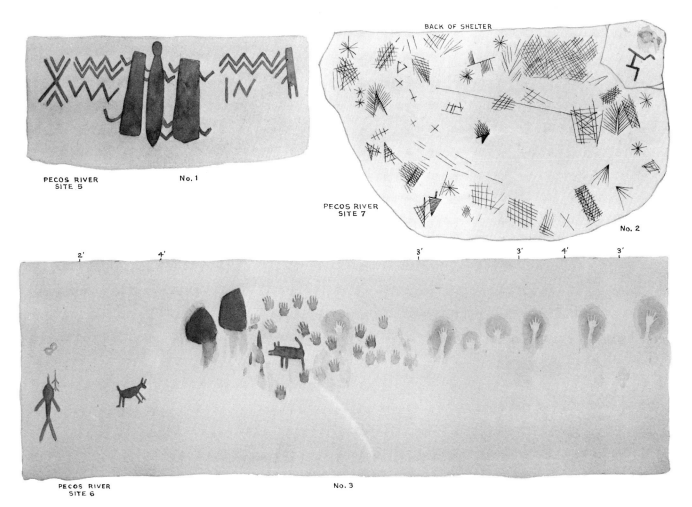

PECOS RIVER
SITE 5 No. 1

BACK OF SHELTER

PECOS RIVER
SITE 7 No. 2

PECOS RIVER
SITE 6 No. 3

Plate 51. Pecos River, Sites 5, 6, 7. Copied July 12, 1938. Scale: No. 1, 3/4″ to 1′; Nos. 2–3, 3/8″ to 1′

PLATE 51

No. 1. This small shelter high on the east cliff of the Pecos River was very difficult to reach and little evidence of occupancy was found. Large rocks from the ceiling almost completely filled the floor. This design was found on the side of one of the rocks which had fallen from the ceiling. It had been painted after the rock had fallen. One design about four feet long had been painted on the back wall, but it had almost entirely weathered away.

No. 2. Pecos River, Shelter 7. This small shelter at the base of the cliff is about fifteen feet wide by ten feet deep. It is semicircular, with a layer of ashes on the floor and a smoke-blackened ceiling. The only pictographs are a small design in red and a couple of splotches in the same color that may have been handprints. They were painted on parts of the ceiling where the soot had flaked off. The principal designs were scratched on the black ceiling with a fine-pointed tool, appearing light against the dark background. The copy shows them in reverse. Most of the designs had been smoked since they were made and now appear gray. Names and dates as early as 1881 on the same surface are still fresh and white. The nature of the scratchy designs made absolutely accurate copying impractical. Only the general effect and the approximate location of each design was attempted. No attempt was made to represent every line correctly.

No. 3. Pecos River, Site 6. This shelter, in a canyon on the east side of the Pecos River, cannot be reached from the canyon's mouth but must be approached from the top. It is a flooded shelter with a hole of fresh water in front of it. The shelter was uninhabitable but the hole of permanent water was probably used by the Indians who lived on the plain above. The pictures appear on the back wall above its very slanting rock floor. They were scattered the full length of the shelter, but for convenience were condensed as indicated on the copy. All of the handprints are small—six inches or less—and evidently are those of children.

PLATE 50

Tardy Draw Shelter. The few paintings and petroglyphs in this shelter close to the Pecos River are all on the ceiling near its front. A few splotches of color at the shelter's lower end were not included in the copy. No attempt was made to copy every scratch exactly, but the general style and shape of the designs is well represented.

Pecos River, Site 6. General view of shelter with its permanent pool of water. See Plate 51, No. 3.

The Red Monochrome paintings are unique in their preoccupation with human figures, a majority of which seem not to be engaged in any activity at all. They simply are. In Seminole Canyon, Shelter 1, for example, there are between sixty-five and seventy human figures strung out along the wall (Plates 43–46), few of whom are doing anything detectible. The possibility is immediately raised that these pictographs should be interpreted as commemorative paintings, immortalizing the visit of some group to this shelter. Pursuing this hypothesis, it takes little imagination to find all the members of a local or extended family group portrayed on these walls. Here are men, women, and children, their individualities and foibles depicted not by skillful portraiture but by those things which set people apart from one another—a person with big feet (Plate 43, No. 1, upper left), a "hippy" woman (Plate 43, No. 5, center bottom), and so forth. The numerous handprints fit this sort of explanation in the sense that they may be nonliterate signatures. But as Kirkland pointed out, "these prints have been used to make a definite design, especially on [Plate 43, No. 5]" (Notes, Plate 44), so this reasoning may be somewhat strained.

Such interpretations may be too facile, and a good case can be made for other explanations. Virtually all of the more prominent animals of this environment have found their way into the Red Monochrome paintings, for example, suggesting that the paintings may have some sort of magical, hunting cult significance. Although none of the animals are pierced by the hunter's arrows or darts,

they are positioned or oriented near hunters as if waiting to do their bidding, and in one case (Plate 46, No. 4, left) a hunter is aiming an arrow at a rabbit. Nor should it be overlooked that violence toward other men, hoped-for or already realized, may play a considerable role in these paintings. Two of the human figures in the Seminole Canyon shelter are in a prone position and one of them is pierced by four arrows or darts (Plate 44, No. 2, center top). Though depicted no differently from the other humans, they probably represent enemies. In the Painted Rock Shelter four humans appear to be wounded by darts (Plate 47, Nos. 3, 4; Plate 49, No. 9), and a Red Monochrome figure in Lewis Canyon (Plate 29, No. 4, upper right) is similarly portrayed. In short, the Red Monochrome paintings do not positively reveal through any internal evidence why they were painted on these walls. They seem best explained as commemorative art, portraying events and people, but they may have been painted for other reasons.

Miscellaneous Paintings

Near the mouth of Pressa Canyon, high on the surface of an overhanging cliff some fifty feet above the canyon floor are a group of some of the most intriguing rock paintings yet found in Texas (Plate 53). The bottom of the main panel of paintings (Plate 53, No. 1) begins about five feet above a narrow ledge and extends to such a height that scaffolding or a ladder must have been employed by the artist. No other paintings like these have been recorded, although Kirkland mentioned that

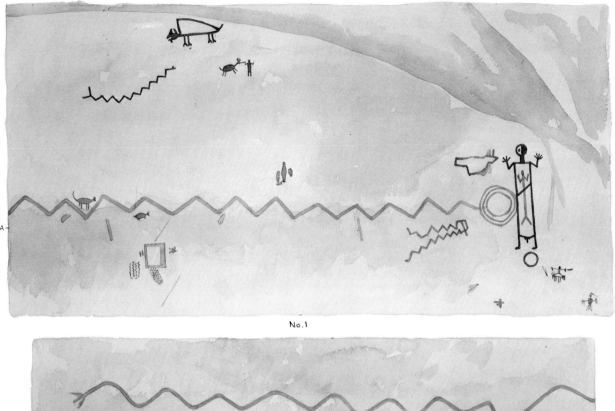

No.1

No. 2

Plate 52. Live Oak Hole, Cow Creek. Copied July 14, 1938. Scale: Nos. 1–2, 1/4″ to 1′

he had seen similar designs at "two other places" (Notes, Plate 53), Gebhard (1960:53) has entitled this style the Red Linear. In contrast to other pictographs in the lower Pecos region, or anywhere else in Texas for that matter, humans are depicted by a stick-figure technique, and almost every one gives the viewer a feeling of liveliness and motion conspicuously absent, for example, from Red Monochrome paintings. Unlike the Pecos River or Red Monochrome styles, sexuality is a prominent if not the dominant motif. This is particularly evident in one group of figures (Plate 53, No. 1, lower right), painted with strongly curved backs and legs so that many become S shaped. Perhaps reclining, possibly dancing, this group is obviously participating in an activity that can only be construed as some sort of fertility ritual. Gebhard (1960:55), who studied these particular figures many years after Kirkland, and after their disintegration had proceeded apace, said that "the artist has placed a squatting female figure balanced on each side by two additional figures which she seems to be holding." Actually, as Kirkland's painting clearly shows, it is a man "presented in a fragmented frontal pose" who is holding two women by the hands. These three figures pro-

PLATE 52

Live Oak Hole on Cow Creek near Comstock is a long low shelter just above flood water. Its ceiling is well smoked and there is a large burned-rock mound immediately in front of it. The pictographs, on the back wall near the floor, extend up until the highest figures are well up on the low ceiling. The principal design is a wavy snake-like line extending almost the full length of the shelter — forty-four feet six inches. Its extreme length made it necessary to show it in two parts.

vide the clue to the sex of the other human figures, males usually being depicted with an erect phallus, females by a circle or loop in the pelvic area. With this key in mind, a reclining woman can be discerned at the bottom of this group, and in another panel (Plate 53, No. 2, top right) two seated women can be made out. What the other humans are engaged in is not as clear, if in fact they are part of some other activity. The vertical sequence of six figures (Plate 53, No. 1, upper left) increasing in size and perhaps maturity from the top down, suggests, for the imaginative, stages in the life cycle of men, from childhood to adulthood. And it might be

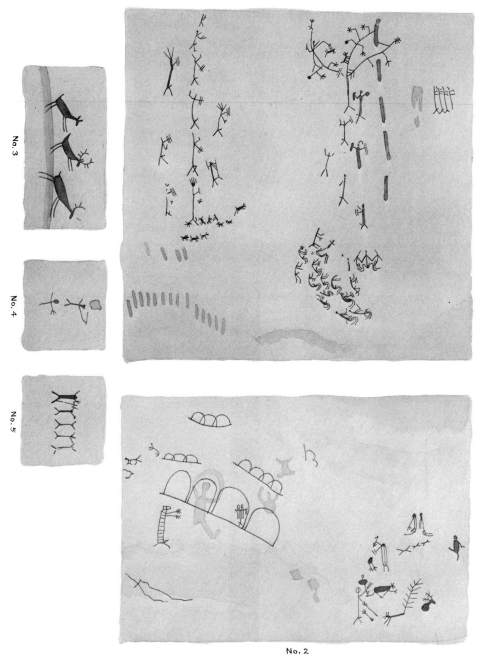

Plate 53. Pressa Canyon, Site 3. Copied July 6, 1938. Scale: Nos. 1–5, 3/4″ to 1′

guessed that the phallic equipment of these figures may well support this sort of interpretation. The other five peripheral figures, following this line of thought, might well be elders, shamans, or mythical beings who ushered men through the crucial stages of life. Many of the male figures are shown with two or three lines intersecting their arms at right angles. These lines should probably be interpreted as rabbit sticks or darts and are reminiscent of similar objects carried by the masked beings of the Pecos River paintings.

While no positive conclusions concerning the age or affiliations of these paintings are possible, several clues lead to strong presumptions. Several semicircular designs (Plate 53, No. 2) have been

PLATE 53

Pressa Canyon, Site 3. The bottom figures in No. 1 begin about five feet above the ledge on which the artist must have stood, so that a scaffolding or ladder was absolutely necessary to paint the upper figures. However, Nos. 2, 3, 4, and 5 were painted a convenient distance above the ledge.

painted over a very dim design probably of the early (Period 1) Pecos River style, and the absence of the bow and arrow and the probable presence of darts and atlatls (Plate 53, No. 2, below and to left of seated women; Plate 53, No 4, upper figure) suggests that these rock paintings date from the Archaic. The deer and other quadrupeds depicted

Black Cave, Pressa Canyon. See Plate 27. Kirkland standing on rock in center.

Pressa Canyon. Principal group of paintings are on the wall above the man's head. See Plate 53.

in these paintings are typical of Pecos River style animals. The hooves of the deer (Plate 53, No. 2, lower right) are a good example of this, and a group of three deer (Plate 53, No. 3) are also typical of the Pecos River style. The small figure (Plate 53, No. 2), referred to above as possibly wielding an atlatl, is also reminiscent of Pecos River style figures. But "the paint is in better condition than one would expect to find in Pecos River style paintings in the same exposed place" (Notes, Plate 53). In sum, although these pictographs are distinctly different from Pecos River paintings, they seem to be related to them and there is some reason to believe that they were painted at the same time as some of them. It is likely that this group of murals was drawn at a sacred spot or at one where highly important, perhaps secret ceremonies having to do with fertility and reproduction were held.

On the west bank of the Pecos River close by what is known as the Pandale Crossing (Map 1), are a few faded pictographs high above the water's edge under an overhanging bluff (Plate 54).

The overhang does not protect the pictures from the blowing rain and so they are very dim. Only three colors were used—black, and two shades of red. The handprints are in brownish-red while the other designs are in a brighter purple-red. The handprints are overpainted by the other designs and appear to be considerably older. The top designs are too high to have been painted without a short ladder. (Notes, Plate 54)

Some of the designs (Plate 54, No. 4) should probably be attributed to the Pecos River style, but the handprints and the crude designs painted above them (Plate 54, Nos. 1, 2, 3) were executed by other artists. While the handprints might be the work of Red Monochrome artists, the crude ladder-like and

Pandale Crossing. Mrs. Forrest Kirkland taking notes at this site. See Plate 54.

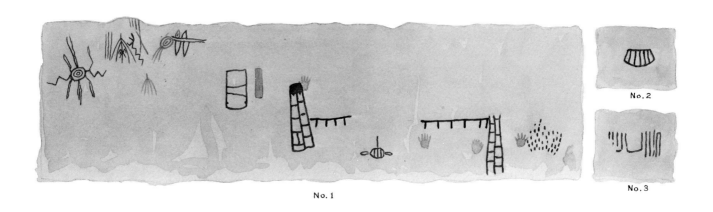

No. 1

No. 2

No. 3

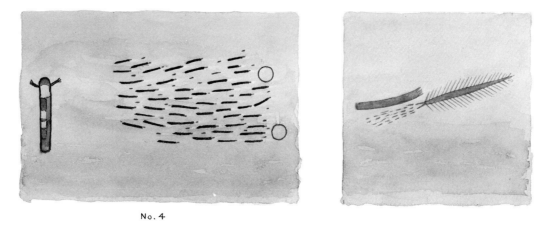

No. 4

Plate 54. Pandale Crossing. Copied July 8, 1939. Scale: Nos. 1–3, 1/4″ to 1′. Ingram Ranch, Shelter 1. Copied July 9, 1939. Scale: Nos. 4, 1/4″ to 1′

No. 2

Plate 55. Bee Cave. Copied July 4, 1938. Scale: Nos. 1–2, 1″ to 1′

PLATE 54

Nos. 1, 2, and 3. These paintings are under an overhanging bluff high above the water's edge near the Pandale Crossing of the Pecos River. There are a number of mortars under the cliff but no midden was found. The overhang does not protect the pictures from blowing rain and they are very dim. Only three colors were used — black, and two shades of red. The handprints are in brownish-red while the other designs are in a brighter purple-red. The handprints are overpainted by the other designs and appear to be considerably older. The top designs are too high to have been painted without a short ladder.

PLATE 55

These pictographs are in Bee Cave, high on the east cliff of the Pecos River. The shelter is about two hundred feet long with about a thirty-foot overhang; a three-to-four-foot midden deposit covers the floor. The general surface of the cave wall is chalky and rough, unsuited to pictographs, but a small surface about twenty feet long at the lower end of the shelter was hard and smooth, and bore these paintings. The designs in group No. 1 are all in black and resemble, somewhat, the carved designs at the mouth of Lewis Canyon, some twenty miles down the river. No. 2 is a typical Pecos River style design.

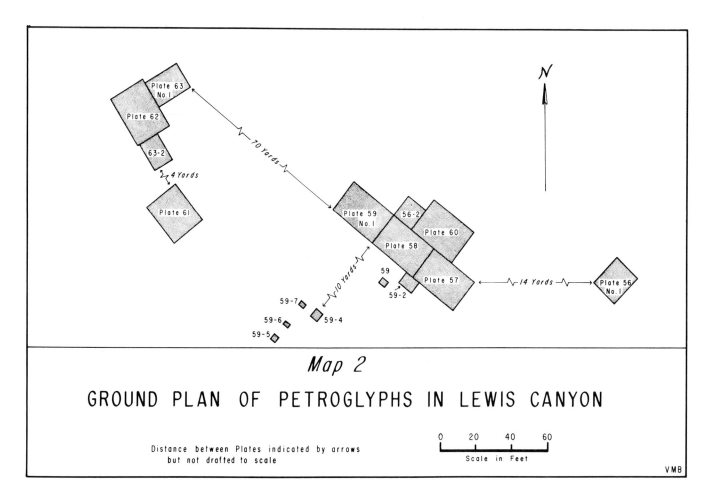

Map 2

GROUND PLAN OF PETROGLYPHS IN LEWIS CANYON

Distance between Plates indicated by arrows
but not drafted to scale

0   20   40   60
Scale in Feet

VMB

comb-like designs definitely do not belong with this style. Apparently other artists, possibly in historic times, were responsible for them.

In a shelter high on the cliff on the east side of the Pecos River, about four miles below the Ozona-Langtry Road crossing, are some unique black pictographs. The shelter is about two hundred feet long with a thirty-foot overhang, and the three to four feet of accumulated cultural debris on the floor is indicative of its long occupancy. The walls of the shelter are chalky and rough and only a limited surface, about twenty feet long at the lower end of the shelter, was suitable for painting. On it are a few designs attributable to the Pecos River style (Plate 55, No. 2); nearby is a perfect tangle of black figures (Plate 55, No. 1). Zigzag lines intersect one another, and black blobs, ticked lines, rough circles, and many other marks seem to be scattered aimlessly over each other. They have nothing in common with any other pictographs in the lower Pecos country, but, strangely, are similar to the petroglyphs in Lewis Canyon, to be discussed below. The pictographs are much more crowded, the individual elements are smaller, and none of them duplicate any of the petroglyphs exactly, yet they have the same random quality, and like most of the petroglyphs, seem not to be attempts to actually depict concrete objects or animals.

The Lewis Canyon Petroglyphs

The lower Pecos region differs from most Texas rock art regions in being almost completely devoid of petroglyphs. Only one petroglyph site has been recorded, but it in some measure makes up for the general lack by the hundreds of designs pecked into its rock. The site is on a level terrace of the Pecos River, on its east side just below Lewis Canyon (Map 2), about twenty-seven miles northwest of Comstock.

It consists of approximately ten acres of level ground, about two acres of which is smooth, flat, unbroken rock, just level with the surrounding ground. Between this rock surface and the river are several burned rock mounds and above it at the foot of the hills is much broken flint and signs of camping.

Two areas of the smooth rock surface are covered with designs carved into the rock by the Indians. The designs were made by pecking shallow trenches in the rock. These trenches now are from one-eighth to one-half inch deep and average about three-fourths of an inch wide. They were undoubtedly deeper originally, because there is evidence of considerable weathering. At present the grooves are filled with sand and a kind of dark lichen which helps make the shallow grooves more visible. Scattered round holes have weathered in the rock and were difficult to distinguish from cups made by the Indians. In some cases I am sure the Indians took advantage of these natural cups in making their designs.

The largest group of designs is at the east end of the

Lewis Canyon. The petroglyphs are on the flat rock surface in the middle distance. See Plates 56-63.

rock surface. The remainder are seventy yards west just beyond a space now covered with sand and gravel. This sand appears to have been there when the designs were made, so it is unlikely that any of the designs have been covered. (Notes, Plate 56)

The individual designs seem to be independent and unrelated to each other. Unlike the engraved petroglyphs of the Panhandle, for example, only a small minority represent recognizable, tangible objects; most are simply geometric shapes or amorphous forms. Among the recognizable objects are two hands (Plate 56, No. 2), humans (Plate 60, lower right; Plate 61, upper right of center and possibly right center), and tracks (Plate 58, center, for example). Other objects or animals may well be depicted, but are so conventionalized that it is impossible to pick them out. The most common designs are circles connected to one another by lines. There are a great many variations on this theme: the lines connecting circles may be straight or they may meander, they may connect two, three, or more circles, or a single line may wander off from a circle and connect with nothing, or several lines may interconnect several circles. The circles may have spokes which extend outward from their perimeters transforming them into suns, or there may be several circles within circles, or the circles may contain dots. There is, in fact, almost every conceivable variation on this basic line-and-circle motif.

PLATES 56-63

Lewis Canyon petroglyphs. Since almost every design was found in two groups, it seemed desirable to make the copies so that every design in each group could be shown in its true relation to all the others. By choosing a scale of ½ inch to 1 foot, a 2-inch square on the drawing equaled a 4-foot square on the rock. A complete board would accommodate a space five squares wide by seven squares long, or 20 by 28 feet. Accordingly the group of carvings was divided by means of a tight rope into 20-by-28 sections—smaller where less space would include every design. These sections were then chalked off in 4-foot squares, with corresponding sections marked off on the copying board. A plot of the different sections and their number on the copies was made, by which they could be reassembled to make up the complete group of designs. Then each square of a section was taken, the designs in it carefully traced with the end of a stick so they could be readily seen and copied in the corresponding square on the board. In this way every design was easily found and accurately copied.

A compass was placed on each separate group of designs and the correct directions recorded. This made it possible to get the correct angles of the separate groups when reassembling and enabled the artist to check the designs to see if for any reason they had been made to point in a particular direction.

The designs were accurately copied in pencil on the site and later painted in with black ink. The pencil outlines served only in fitting together the sections of a group. Only three or four unimportant designs fell outside of the area included in the copies. These were disregarded.

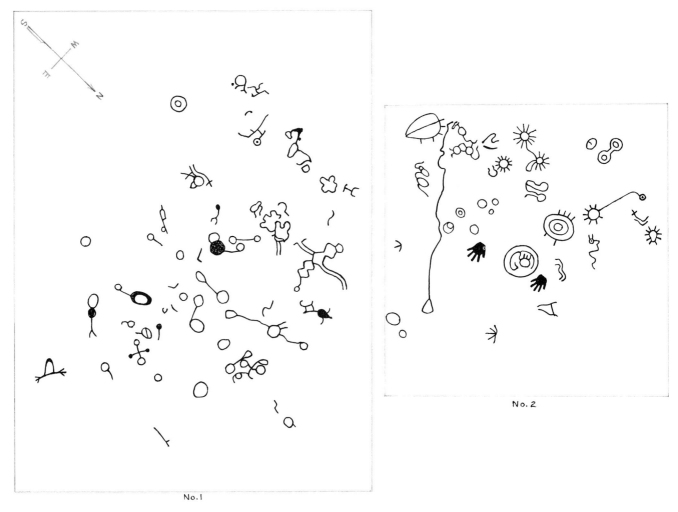

No. 1

No. 2

Plate 56. Lewis Canyon. Copied July 8, 1938. Scale: Nos. 1–2, 1/4″ to 1′

There seems to be no way of knowing whether these petroglyphs were left by any of the people who painted on the rock walls of the vicinity or whether these inscriptions were left by others. The fact that the petroglyphs are eroded to some extent suggests that they may have some antiquity, but how much cannot be determined. Jackson (1938: 450–451) mentions that

pecked figures are predominant in most of the Trans-Pecos region, while carved designs are more common farther east. The available evidence indicates that the petroglyphs pecked with a hammerstone are, as a rule, older than those carved with a sharp implement.

Historic Pictographs

Inspired by ancient example and what seems to be an old Anglo-American tradition, many pictograph sites have had new paintings and scratchings added to them in recent years. Unfortunately, names and dates have sometimes been added on top of prehistoric paintings, destroying or defacing them. Kirkland avoided copying these witless marks, but he did record the historic rock paintings he felt had been executed by Indians. The few of

these found in the lower Pecos River region bear no resemblance to their prehistoric forerunners except that positive handprints are present. Not only are other connections lacking which would link them to earlier forms of rock painting, but it is also impossible to associate them with specific historic tribes.

When Spaniards first pushed northward into the vicinity of the lower Pecos in the seventeenth century, Coahuiltecan peoples were in possession of the region (Newcomb, 1961:34ff). But this area was on the northwestern edge of their range, and these primitive hunters and gatherers were soon drawn to Spanish missions and their ranks decimated by war, slave raids, and disease. The acquisition of horses by Indians and the subsequent struggle for possession of the southern plains in the following centuries brought many tribes and fragments of tribes to and through the now empty or sparsely populated lower Pecos River country, any or all of whom may have painted and daubed on its rocks. Tribes most closely associated with this part of Texas from the eighteenth century on were Lipan Apaches and Mescalero Apaches, who were forced

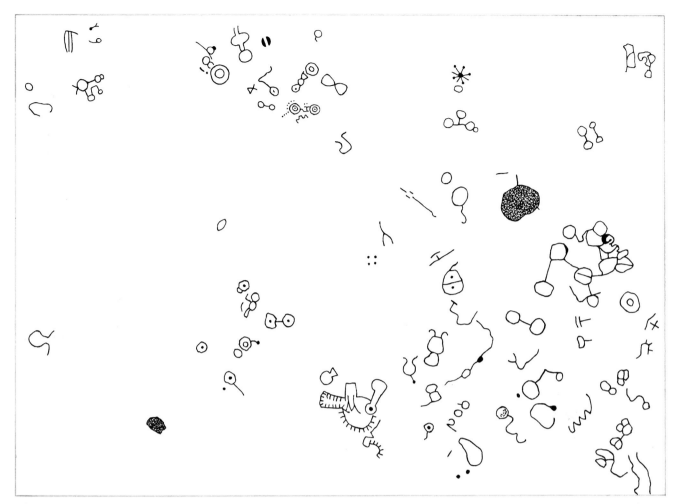

Plate 57.   Lewis Canyon. Copied July 8, 1938. Scale: 1/4″ to 1′

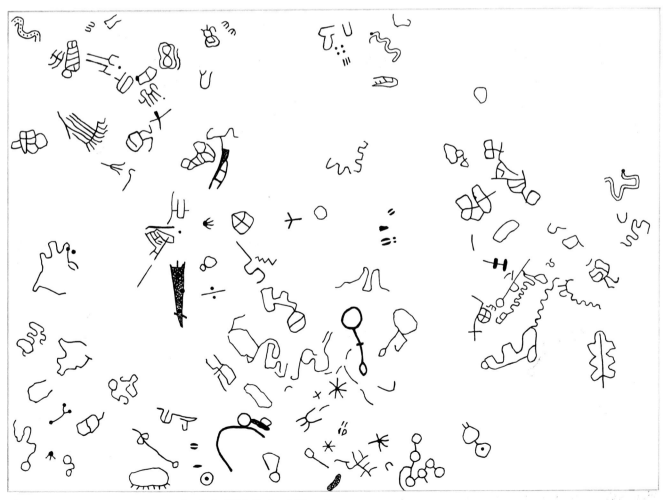

Plate 58.   Lewis Canyon. Copied July 8, 1938. Scale: 1/4″ to 1′

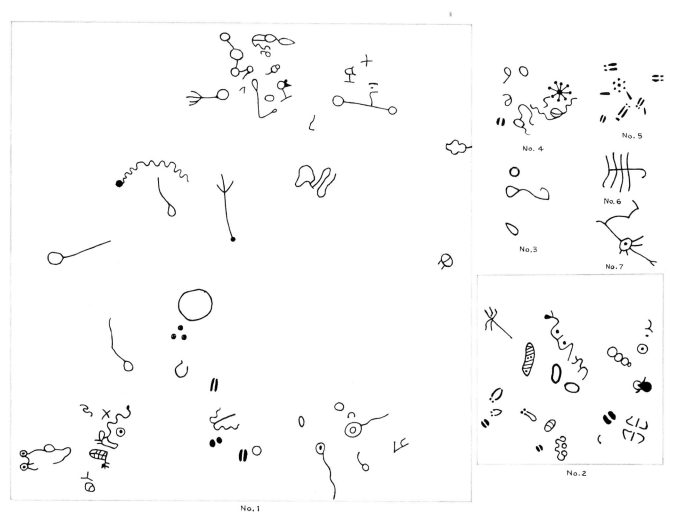

Plate 59. Lewis Canyon. Copied July 8, 1938. Scale: Nos. 1–7, 1/4″ to 1′

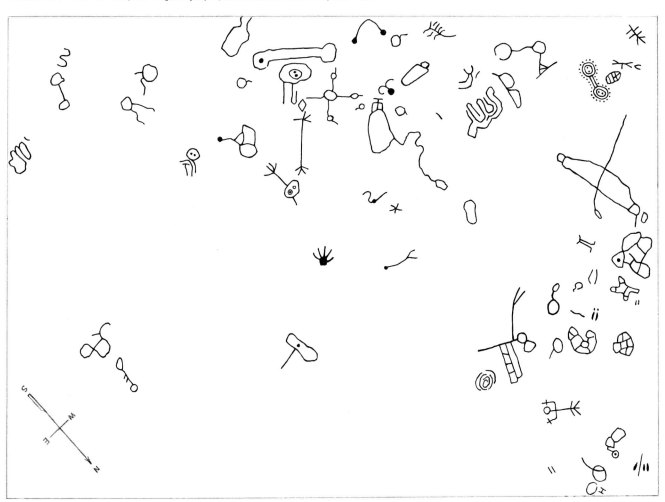

Plate 60. Lewis Canyon. Copied July 8, 1938. Scale: 1/4″ to 1′

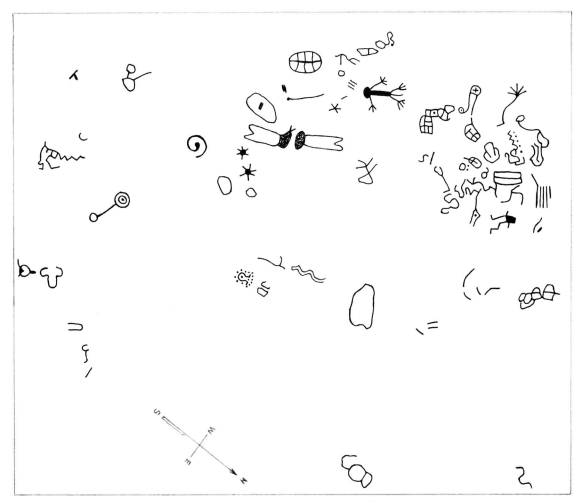

Plate 61. Lewis Canyon. Copied July 8, 1938. Scale: 1/4″ to 1′

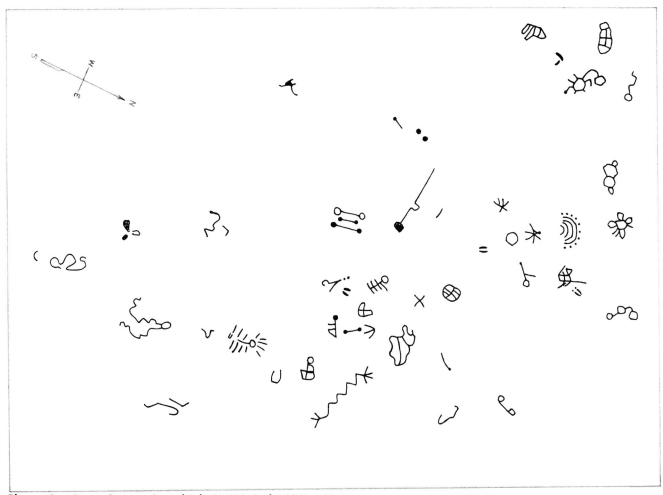

Plate 62. Lewis Canyon. Copied July 8, 1938. Scale: 1/4″ to 1′

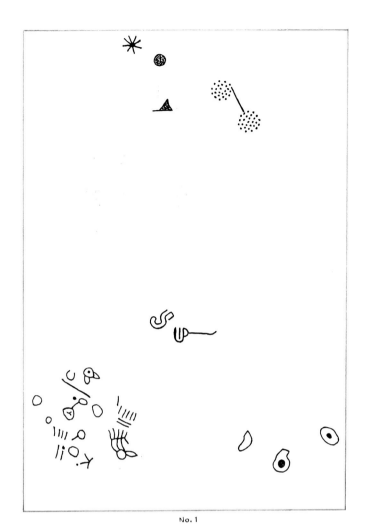

No. 1

No. 2

Plate 63.   Lewis Canyon. Copied July 8, 1938. Scale: Nos. 1–2, 1/4″ to 1′

Plate 64.   Pressa Canyon. Copied July 13, 1937. Scale: 3/8″ to 1′

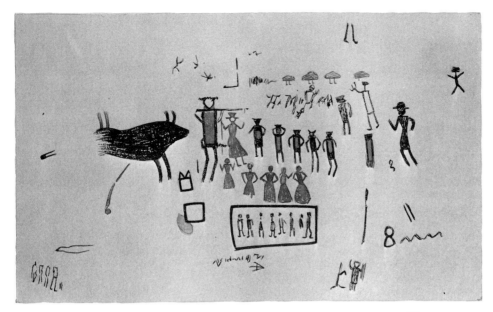

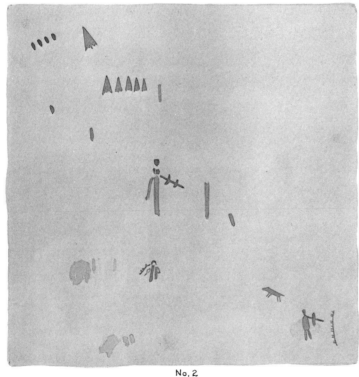

No. 2

Plate 65. Castle Canyon. Copied July 20, 1938. Scale: No. 1, 1″ to 1′; No. 2, 5/8″ to 1′

PLATE 64

These paintings are at the head of Pressa Canyon under an overhanging cliff. For about fifty yards along the cliff wall there had once been pictographs, but they were so badly weathered that only here and there could a figure be made out. Over these earlier paintings in one place was this much more recent, historic picture. The subject is so modern as to suggest that it might have been the work of cowboys, but the quality of the paint and the fact that a handprint in the same color is a part of the design makes it most probable that the work is that of Indians.

PLATE 65

These historic pictographs are at two sites: in a small shelter and on a cliff in Castle Canyon, which empties into Devils River. The pictures in the shelter proper (No. 2) are badly mixed with names, dates, and other recent work, but could readily be distinguished. The best pictures (No. 1) were found around the cliff from the main shelter, on the wall under a low overhanging part of the cliff.

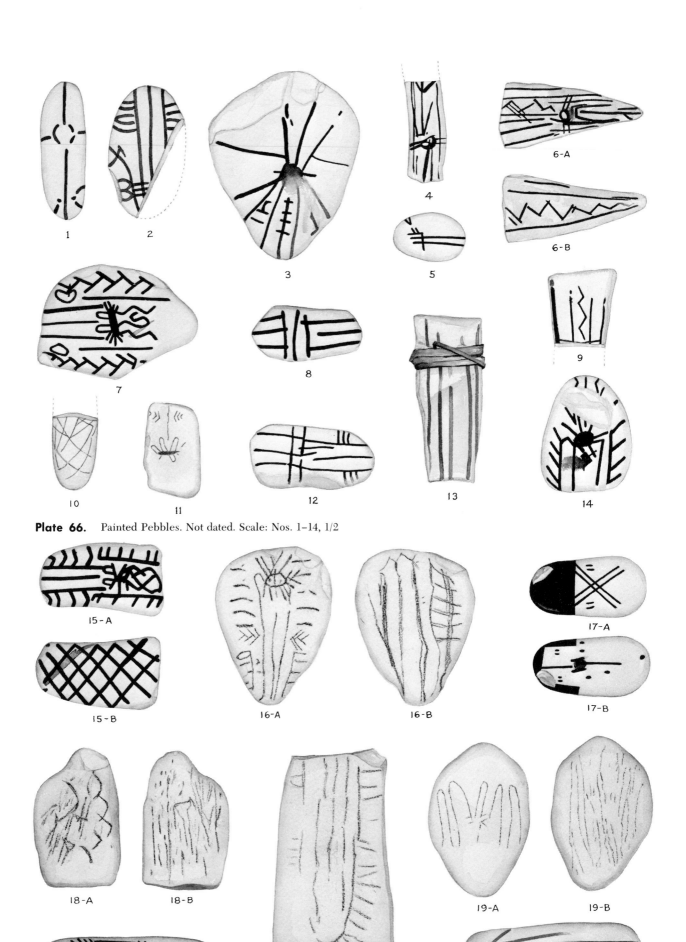

Plate 66. Painted Pebbles. Not dated. Scale: Nos. 1–14, 1/2

Plate 67. Painted Pebbles. Not dated. Scale: Nos. 15–22, 1/2

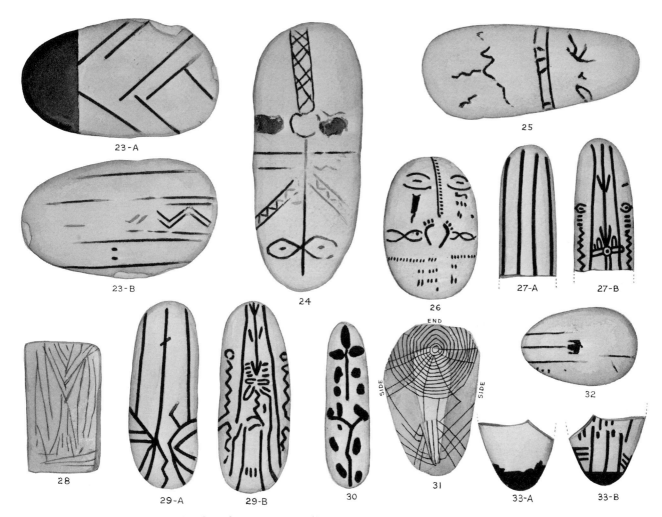

Plate 68. Painted Pebbles. Not dated. Scale: Nos. 23–33, 1/2

PLATES 66, 67, and 68

These drawings of painted pebbles are exact duplicates of pebbles from Val Verde County shelters. The outlines were traced and the picture of the pebble painted in very lightly to show the character of the rock with its cracks, chips, and other markings. No attempt has been made to express the natural color of the original rock. All tints and colors shown besides this neutral grey are Indian paints. The designs on the pebbles were carefully traced on cellophane, transferred to the drawings of the pebbles, and painted in about as strong colors as the Indian designs appeared to have been originally. Where the designs were very dim the drawing was made by aid of a strong magnifying glass. Nothing has been copied that could not be definitely made out. Through this method the copies show the designs much more clearly than they ever appeared on the originals, especially those designs on dark-colored rocks. Dotted lines show the continuation of the pebble where a part of the design has been broken off.

No. 29-B (Plate 68) is exaggerated in width to show the zigzag lines which actually appear on the sides of the pebble, joined to the design on 29-A.

southward from the better hunting grounds by Comanches and allied peoples. The Pecos River became a favorite haunt, particularly of the nineteenth-century Lipans. The Comanches, Kiowas and their associates, the Kiowa Apaches, passed through the lower Pecos country on their way to and from raiding ventures in Mexico. A surprising number of displaced and fragmented tribes from the eastern United States also occasionally crossed the region in the early years of the nineteenth century, Seminoles, Kickapoos, Cherokees, Shawnees, and Delawares being the principal ones. Portions of tribes native to eastern Texas and adjacent regions—Tonkawas, Caddos, Wichitas—who had been displaced by the westward-moving frontier may also have been acquainted with the Pecos River country.

The Indians who painted a few historic murals in the lower Pecos River country, or any historic Texas pictographs for that matter, were impressed by two aspects of European civilization: Christianity and horses. It is hardly surprising that both subjects should find their way into the rock paintings, for both had tremendous effect on the

Indians. The first extended contact most Texas Indians had with Spaniards was through missionaries, and one of the basic ways of extending Spanish influence and control was through missions and missionaries. Texas Indians in general and nomadic tribes in particular were difficult to missionize, and the Spanish missions in Texas failed, none more quickly than those established in the plains country. The Lipan Apache was the only Plains tribe in Texas to try mission life and the experience was brief. But whether friendly or hostile to the Spaniards, one of the Indians' most fixed impressions of these missionizing white men concerned their Christianity. This was not the case with the Anglo-Americans, who did not attempt to convert the Indians and who had few ministers and priests among them on the frontiers. It would seem, then, that the rock paintings which portray priests, churches, and crosses probably relate to the Spanish period and are earlier than those which lack these subjects.

Horses, a gift the Spaniards unwittingly made to the North American natives, were to revolutionize life on the plains. But in the first years of contact the Indian reaction to horses and riders was one of awe, and no doubt this strange animal and his equally exotic rider were painted and scratched on many rock surfaces for the edification of those who had not yet seen this new phenomenon. More intimate acquaintance with horses and horsemanship, particularly as gained in the seventeenth-century Spanish settlements of New Mexico, started the train of events that led to the Indians' nomadic, warring life, based on bison hunting with horses. Horses were central to the life of Plains Indians, they affected almost every aspect of life, and quite naturally were favorite subjects of those who painted and incised rock surfaces. They provide one of the chief means of identifying historic rock art but are of little aid in dating rock art within the historic period.

There are only a handful of historic pictograph sites in the lower Pecos River region, but these illustrate the importance of Christianity and horses to Indians. A case in point is a rather crude orange-red painting in Rattlesnake Canyon (Plate 3, Shelter 2) in which an arrow is shown piercing a figure. Probably intended to represent a missionary, the figure visualizes what Lipans and Mescaleros often wanted to do and occasionally did do to missionaries. Curiously, if the head were removed from the painting, the body would become a church. The handprints, horse, crosses, and oval blobs of color, together with the transfixed figure, all suggest that this painting commemorates an actual event.

Another historic painting in bright orange is in Pressa Canyon (Plate 64). Superimposed over a number of dim Pecos River style paintings of Pe-

riod 2, the church bearing three crosses suggests Spanish-Mexican influence. The dress of the bearded figure with the pipe, on the right side of the painting, would seem to indicate a late date, however. The roping scene on the left is of little use in dating the painting since longhorn cattle and vaqueros—or cowboys—might belong either to the Spanish-Mexican or to the Anglo-American period. As Kirkland (Notes, Plate 64) points out, the painting seems "intended to record some incident in the experience of the artist or tribe," and little more can be said about it.

The most enigmatic historic pictographs in the lower Pecos River region are some diminutive human figures and a strange unidentifiable animal much larger than the humans, painted in Castle Canyon (Plate 65, No. 1). These figures were

found around the cliff from the main shelter on the wall under a low overhanging part of the cliff. The wall at this place is only forty inches high so there was barely head room when sitting flat on the floor. The designs were done on a rather rough surface for so small figures, and are now in very bad condition. Work that originally was done with liquid color looks very like crayon work, so that now it is difficult to determine just how the original designs were made. . . . Never before have we found similar figures. (Notes, Plate 65).

The hat of the black figure on the right identifies the paintings as historic, and the hands-on-hips posture of several of the figures probably signifies that they are intended as white men. There is no reason to doubt Indian authorship of the paintings, but the artist's intention is moot.

Painted Pebbles

While copying the mural art of the lower Pecos River country Kirkland also carefully reproduced a number of the mysterious painted pebbles he had picked up in various caves and shelters and borrowed from several private collections (Plates 66, 67, 68). They are smooth, streamworn pebbles painted on one or both sides. Designs are usually painted in black, occasionally in red, and on one that Kirkland copied (Plate 66, 6-A, 6-B) the entire black design and pebble had been painted over with a thin red paint. Fibers are sometimes wound around pebbles, and Kirkland illustrated one example (Plate 66, 13). The design on each pebble is different from every other one, but as Davenport and Chelf (1941) have pointed out, a large proportion of the painted pebbles represent conventionalized anthropomorphic beings and all of them may do so. The features of a face are easy to pick out in some cases (Plate 68, 26, 27-B), less obvious in others (Plate 68, 24, which is upside down), and impossible to find in many (Plate 66, 8, 13, for example). What purpose the pebbles served is unknown, perhaps unknowable. An extended discus-

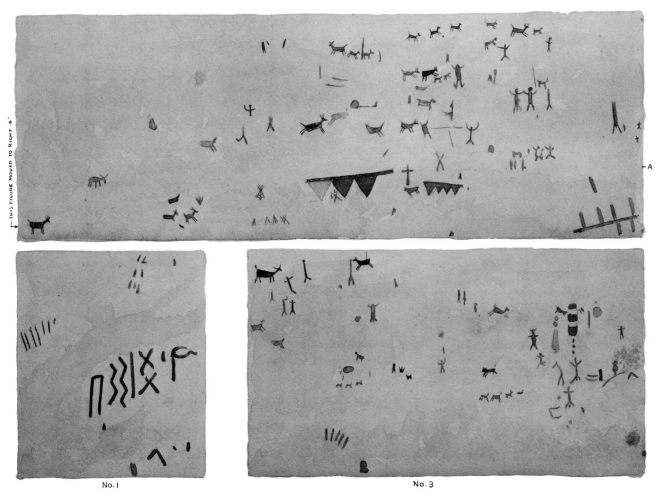

THIS FIGURE MOVED TO RIGHT 4'

No. 1

No. 3

Plate 69.   Rio Grande Cliffs. Copied July 15, 1938. Scale: Nos. 1–3, 1/4" to 1'

PLATE 69

This pictograph site is under overhanging cliffs of the Rio Grande about halfway between the mouths of Seminole and Paint canyons. The overhang is from 20 to 40 feet and there is a narrow floor of deep fine sand deposited by the overflow of the river. Mortars and a few metates remain to show that Indians once inhabited the site. Other debris has probably been removed by flood waters. The overhang extends over two hundred yards but only the upper one hundred yards has a smooth enough wall to accommodate pictures. Most of this space shows signs of paint but the pictures on only about 150 feet remain clear enough to be made out. The pictures at the upper end (Nos. 2 and 3) appear very high above the floor with too narrow a rock ledge at their base to accommodate the artist. A ladder or scaffold at least 15 feet high would have been necessary to reach the top pictures. The remainder of the designs could easily be reached from the rock shelf below them.

sion of painted pebbles is beyond the scope of this book, and these plates are included only to illustrate the fact that they cannot be associated with the Pecos River, Red Monochrome, or other styles of rock painting. Although some of the men who painted the walls of shelters also probably ornamented pebbles, the two art forms have little or nothing in common. If they had, the dating of mural art would be far easier, at least in theory, because the painted pebbles, being associated with other artifacts, can be placed in their proper cultural and temporal context.

At only one site on the Rio Grande (Plate 69, No. 1) is there even a remote resemblance between rock paintings and painted pebbles. Gebhard (1960: 45–47), who calls this a "Painted Pebble Style," though no others like it are known, says: "They appear to be less weathered than the Pecos [River] Style figures to the left and right. Tentatively they have been grouped as a separate type, which occurred some time later than the adjoining Type 1 panels" (p. 47). It should be noted, however, that the other pictographs at this site are not typical of the Pecos River style—there is not a hint of a shaman, for example—and may not be a product of Pecos River artists.

The majority of painted pebbles have been recovered from sites in the lower Pecos River region, but their distribution, as known at the present time, extends from the Big Bend (Brewster County) in the west, eastward through the lower Pecos River country, thence in a northeastward arc with sporadic finds in Edwards, Llano, Travis, and Hill counties (Martin and Woolford, 1932; Setzler, 1933; Sayles, 1935:68–69; Jackson, 1938:324–328; Davenport and Chelf, n.d.; Jelks, 1962:55–59). In the lower Pecos River country painted pebbles appear to occur throughout the long Archaic continuum (Pearce and Jackson, 1933:79–89; Johnson, 1964:70–73). But at the Kyle Site, Whitney Reservoir, in Hill County north of Waco in Central Texas, painted pebbles were found with post-Archaic, Austin Focus materials dating between A.D. 500 and A.D. 1000, and may also have been a trait of the later Toyah Focus people (Jelks, 1962:90, 96–99).

CHAPTER 6

THE BIG BEND

It seems quite proper that a region as diverse as the Big Bend country of Texas with its stark mountains, arid plains, rocky gorges, and welcome river valleys should have a variety of rock paintings. True to its surroundings, the rock art of the Big Bend is remarkably varied though less complex than that of the lower Pecos. Many different peoples through a long span of time have occupied or passed through the Big Bend; many of them have adorned its rocks with paintings. In such an arid region the chances that rock paintings will be long preserved is exceptionally good. Though Kirkland worked in the Big Bend in three separate years (1935, 1936, 1939), he recorded only a fraction of its paintings. A majority of them were copied in its northeastern half, in Terrell and Brewster counties (See Map 3), but he also visited a number of sites in the Davis Mountains. The Blue Mountain Site in Winkler County has been included with the Big Bend paintings, not because of geographical accuracy but because it did not fit elsewhere.

Archeologists subdivide trans-Pecos Texas into two divisions: a southeastern, which includes the lower Pecos River, and a western, which is sometimes further subdivided (Suhm *et al.*, 1954:27-62; Lehmer, 1958:116–119). The portions of the Big Bend in which Kirkland recorded pictographs fall wholly within the southeastern division, where the sequence and development of cultures is thought to be roughly the same as that outlined for the lower Pecos. Paleo-Indian remains are infrequently found in the Big Bend country, suggesting that this was not a favored area of these early hunters. Dr. Joe Ben Wheat of the University of Colorado Museum has discovered an extensive Paleo-Indian site, however, in the drainage system of Wild Horse Creek, near Van Horn. Preliminary investigations revealed seventy-eight partial or complete Folsom points, as well as Plainview, Milnesand, and other early projectile points, other artifacts associated with these early hunters, and evidence of subsequent occupation of the site by Archaic and later Indians. The possibility seems good that the Wild Horse Creek drainage system was part of an easy and well-traversed route into the Rio Grande country (Joe Ben Wheat, personal communication, September 9, 1964).

What may be the earliest Archaic occupation of the Big Bend is represented by the poorly known Maravillas Complex, found at the Calamity Creek Site south of Alpine in Brewster County (Kelley *et al.*, 1940:107–119; Lehmer, 1958:124). But so few artifacts were found that it is impossible to relate it, or the so-called Santiago Complex which succeeded it, to the Archaic tradition in the lower Pecos River region, or to any other. Recent investigations of Archaic sites in the lower Pecos, reinforced with radiocarbon dates, cast considerable doubt on the dating of the Maravillas Complex. But the existence of a somewhat different Archaic tradition to the west of the lower Pecos may be supported by the fact that no Pecos River style pictographs are found west of the Meyers Springs Site in Terrell County. As in the lower Pecos River drainage, the Archaic tradition came to an end sometime around A.D. 600. Subsequent peoples are poorly known, but they utilized a distinctive arrow point known as a Livermore point. Also associated with them are snub-nosed scrapers and diamond-beveled knives, both of which are skin-dressing tools characteristic of bison-hunting peoples (Lehmer, 1958:125). There is, then, a good possibility that these new people, equipped with the bow and arrow, came into the Big Bend region from the plains country to the north and northeast.

At the beginning of historic times the Big Bend was lightly occupied and seems to have served mostly as an occasional hunting ground and refuge area. Jumano hunting parties from the La Junta region (the vicinity of the juncture of the Rio Grande and Conchos), for example, hunted and crisscrossed the region, and other peoples probably did too. By the eighteenth century the Mescalero Apaches had been forced south and east and were ranging throughout the Big Bend country. Lipan Apaches in the closing decades of the eighteenth century and for many years afterward also frequented the Big Bend country. The Comanches and Kiowas, while

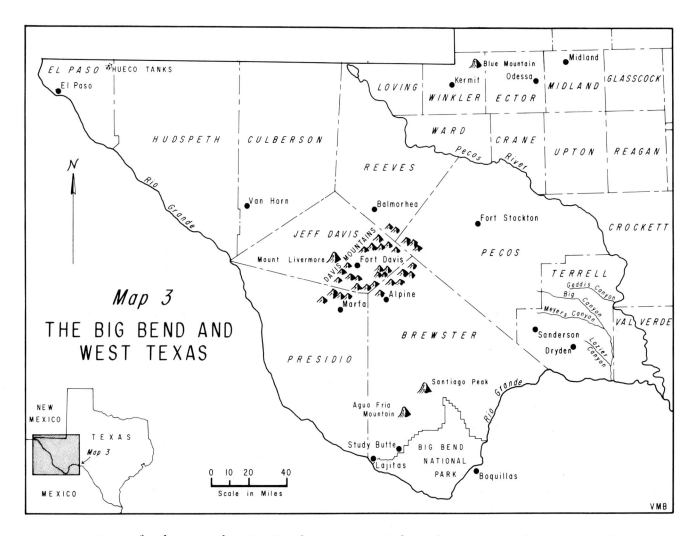

Map 3
THE BIG BEND AND
WEST TEXAS

Scale in Miles
0   10 20   40

VMB

never remaining for long in the Big Bend, repeatedly crossed the region on their forays into
Mexico, particularly in the first half of the nineteenth century. Any of these historic tribes may
have left pictographs on shelter walls and in the
canyons of the Big Bend; many of them undoubtedly did so.

Pictographs at Meyers Springs

A few miles northeast of the little crossroads
town of Dryden, in Terrell County, close to the
spectacular pictographic area of the lower Pecos
River, is a rock shelter whose walls are covered
with "one big panorama of Indian pictographs"
(Notes, Plate 70). Named Meyers Springs, for the
spring which breaks out from the cliff about thirty
yards above the shelter, this oasis has long been
used by men (Map 4; Plate 70).

The back of the shelter is one continuous buff-colored
limestone wall slightly curved but smooth to a height of
about twelve feet and protected by overhanging rock for
a distance of about seventy-five yards. . . . The stream runs
under the shelter with only a small table of rock between
it and the back wall. This table or rock contains more
than a dozen large mortar holes. On the hill in front of the
shelter are two large burned rock mounds and other
mortars. (Notes, Plate 70).

At least three periods of painting are discernible
on the walls of the shelter at Meyers Springs: an
early period whose pictographs are very similar to
if not actually Pecos River style, a middle period in
which paintings have much in common with the
Red Monochrome pictographs of the lower Pecos,
and finally, an assortment of historic paintings. The
early-period pictographs are "represented by very
large dim designs principally in the center of the
shelter. The color was a purple-red which is almost
completely gone except where it extends several
feet above the later work" (Notes, Plate 70). The
purple-red monochrome figure with the merged
head-body and outstretched arms (Plate 74, upper
right, over which is superimposed a positive,
orange handprint) is Pecos River style in conception. The lines (rabbit sticks?) which intersect the
arms are similar to those in Pecos River style paintings. If an atlatl, dart, or fringed pouch were present, there would be no hesitation in classifying it
as Period 2, Pecos River style. The fringed or rayed
figure (Plate 74, top middle) is also in the Pecos
River tradition, although nothing in the lower
Pecos is exactly like it. One shaggy figure (Plate
76, middle-right to left of rectangular design) is
strikingly like several pictographs in Panther Cave

Meyers Springs. Paintings are at the base of the cliff. See Plates 70-79.

in the lower Pecos region (Plate 24, lower right; Plate 25, right) which are associated with Period 2 paintings. Unfortunately, the Meyers Springs figure cannot be positively assigned to the early period there. Several other designs on the walls of Meyers Springs were apparently painted in the early period (Plate 75, upper left; Plate 76, upper left), but they are so dim that little can be made of them. Pecos River style pictographs were thought to be confined to the lower Pecos River and parts of the adjacent Devils River and Rio Grande. Their apparent presence at Meyers Springs extends this distribution considerably and raises the possibility that Pecos River pictographs, or paintings influenced by this style, may be discovered at other outlying sites.

Kirkland described the middle-period paintings at Meyers Springs as "generally orange-red" but dimming with age, adding that "many of the conventional figures of men were made in this period" (Notes, Plate 70). They are similar to the Red Monochrome paintings of the lower Pecos region in that the human figure is characteristically portrayed in front view with a disproportionately long body, short stiff legs, a round circle for a head, and a prominent penis (Plate 73, figures from middle to right). Positive handprints, characteristic of Red Monochrome paintings, are also present at Meyers Springs and some almost certainly date from the middle period (Plate 74, upper right). Unlike Red Monochrome paintings, arms of middle-period paintings at Meyers Springs are not usually bent, hands and feet are seldom shown, animals are not

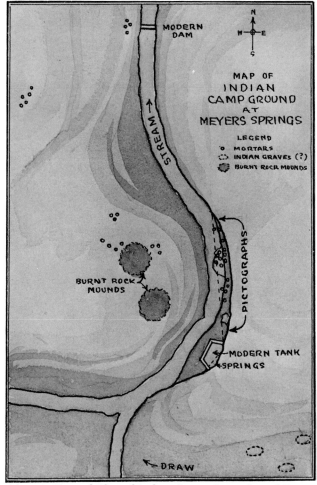

Map. 4. Ground Plan of Indian Camp Grounds and Pictographs at Meyers Springs

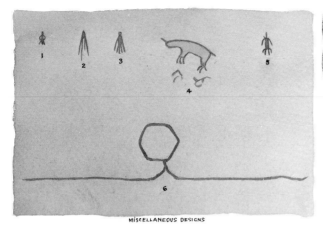

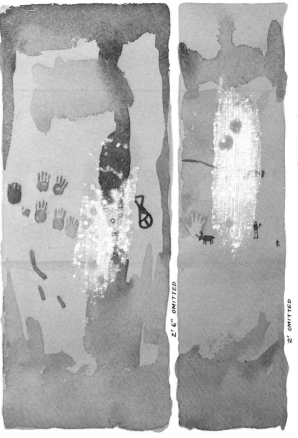

MISCELLANEOUS DESIGNS

PLATE 70

Meyers Springs is a few miles northeast of Dryden, Terrell County, near the head of a small canyon. Springs break out of the cliff about thirty yards above the shelters. The small sketch map (see Map 4) is fairly accurate and should give some idea of the camp ground at Meyers Springs where the pictographs are found.

Miscellaneous designs. These six miscellaneous designs were outside the wall covered by the continuous set of plates. Following is the location of each design: No. 1, 9 ft. 6 in. to right of Plate 79; No. 2, 2 ft. 4 in. to right of No. 1; No. 3, 2 ft. 2 in. to right of No. 2; No. 4, 6 ft. to left of spring which is about thirty yards to right of No. 3; No. 5, 8 ft. above and 3 ft. to left of deer's horns in Plate 78; No. 6, 6 ft. above sun design in Plate 74. Long lines are underneath on ceiling.

Plate 70. Meyers Springs. Copied July 24, 1935. Scale: 1/32

Plate 71. Meyers Springs. Copied July 24, 1935. Scale: 1/32

114

Plate 72. Meyers Springs. Copied July 24, 1935. Scale: 1/32

PLATE 71

Almost all of the Meyers Springs pictographs were painted with oxide of iron colors. Certain rather bright vermilion figures and handprints may have been made with cinnabar, and the few black figures, all of which are now very dim, were painted with carbon. Conditions at Meyers Springs prove the excellent quality of Indian colors, for a very small rain up the canyon will bring water over the bottom of the lowest paintings, as happened while the group was being copied. A heavy rain brings the water up to the middle of the wall, and on rare occasions the water completely covers the highest design. This inundation has been going on for a hundred or more years, yet the very bottom pictures can still be made out, while those in the center of the wall are as clear as if painted yesterday.

The colors were copied directly on the spot. Strength has been added to all colors, especially very dim designs, but the shade and relative strength has been carefully preserved. The general color of the background is correct on the copies and the more conspicuous irregularities of the rocks have been shown. The semicircles at bottom center were no doubt originally complete, the continued action of the overflowing stream having finally defaced the bottom parts. The dark streak to left is a large water stain on the rock.

PLATES 72, 73, 74, 75, 76

The wall at Meyers Springs was measured and so divided that the complete group of pictographs would go on ten drawing boards. The division lines were so chosen that all parts of a design or action picture came on the same board. Except where space has been taken out in three places, and so indicated, the plates, if placed end to end in order, represent the complete unbroken back wall of the shelter. Careful measurement was made of each design in the group as well as its distance from the center and other nearby designs. These measurements were transferred to scale on the drawing board and the smaller details carefully sketched freehand. Dim designs were copied only when they could be definitely made out. These copies are accurate in every essential detail.

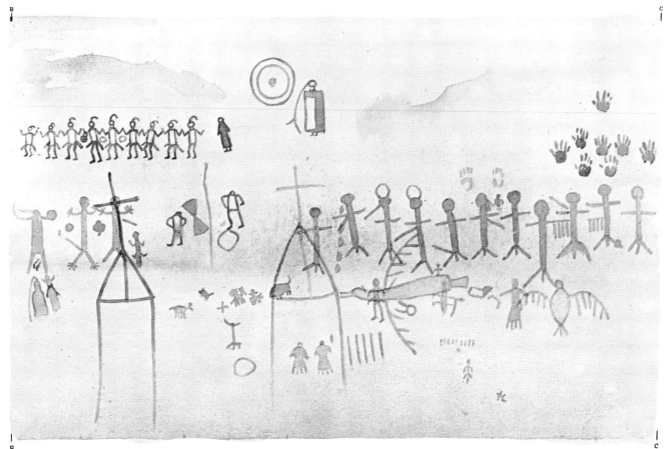

Plate 73.   Meyers Springs. Copied July 24, 1935. Scale: 1/32

THIS FIGURE MOVED
27" TO RIGHT

Plate 74.   Meyers Springs. Copied July 24, 1935. Scale: 1/32

Plate 75. Meyers Springs. Copied July 24, 1935. Scale: 1/32

Plate 76. Meyers Springs. Copied July 24, 1935. Scale: 1/32

Plate 77. Meyers Springs. Copied July 24, 1935. Scale: 1/32

Plate 78. Meyers Springs. Copied July 24, 1935. Scale: 1/32

Plate 79. Meyers Springs. Copied July 24, 1935. Scale: 1/32

PLATE 77

Seep water has run down over these paintings and dimmed them to some extent. Chemicals in the water have changed the original orange designs to a purple-red where the water has covered them (see design at right of plate, for example). The smudged figures, or thunderbirds, are examples where the Indian artist destroyed his own design.

PLATE 78

The red lines at the lower right seem to outline a very large horse, but no more could be certainly made out. The dark color at the top of the plate is a cavelike crack in the rock wall.

PLATE 79

All the designs on this plate are very dim but easily made out on close examination. The small red arrows and the crosslike figure in the dark streak are interesting because they appear to have been drawn with the sharp corner of a piece of dry color. All other work appears to be of liquid color. The yellow streak under the horse is a strata in the rock which extends entirely across the background parallel and about five feet six inches above the table of rock between the stream and the back wall. This line was used throughout the job as a measuring point, and contributed much to the accuracy of the work.

associated with human figures, and bows and arrows are not present. The hand-holding figures (Plate 73, upper left; Plate 74, right, under later "sun" symbol), apparently dancers, have no parallel in the lower Pecos region, and seem to date from the middle period at Meyers Springs. The two sets of dancing figures are not similar to one another, however, nor are they like three other typical middle-period figures with linked hands (Plate 72, middle left). Curiously, a human figure just to the right of this latter group seems to have been partly destroyed by the artist. "The smudged body of the human figure at left above cross is not the work of recent vandals. This smudge like every other smudged design at Meyers Springs seems to have been the work of the original artist" (Notes, Plate 72). The other figures blemished by their makers (Plate 77, center left) are not typical of the middle period and are not marred to the extent that this one is.

In many ways the historic pictographs at Meyers Springs are more interesting than their prehistoric forerunners because they are more skillfully executed, portray a wider variety of subjects, and are more variable. Kirkland described the third and historic period as being "represented by the church

Meyers Springs. High water almost reaches the pictographs, which can be seen on the wall in this photograph. See Plates 70-79.

towers, thunderbirds, and sun designs, which are clear and conspicuous on the wall in dark purple-red" (Notes, Plate 70). One of the churches (Plate 71) seems to represent an attempt to show both its elevation and floor plan. A human just to the right of this church, aiming an arrow at an animal, appears to be the work of the same artist, as does the four-legged animal whose tail is inside the building. The other two structures topped with crosses (Plate 73) do not have anything else obviously associated with them. Kirkland said that these

two large church towers appear to be the most recent of all the work at Meyers Springs. They were painted with a coarse stiff brush which left noticeable brush marks. By these marks it seems safe to say that not only these towers but the tower on [Plate 71] and miscellaneous designs [Plate 70, No. 6] were all made with the same brush. (Notes, Plate 73)

The two purple-red horses and riders (Plate 74, left) seem to be engaged in a bison hunt. The humans below them, apparently aiming guns at each other, were probably also purple-red but flood waters likely have dimmed them to their present rose hue. The human figure to the right of the gray turkey has an odd headdress like that of the figure near the church (Plate 71, far right), so it is probably historic. The purple-red "thunderbird" and "sun design" seem to be the work of the artists who executed the horses and riders to the left of the thunderbird. This plate "shows clearly the three periods of work: first the very dim designs above to the right, second the horned dancers overlapping these, and third, the brilliant sun design which covers the

dancers" (Notes, Plate 74). To which period the gray turkey (Plate 74) should be assigned is undetermined. If it was executed by the artists who painted the two gray thunderbirds (Plate 73), it may be fairly early, as Kirkland thought that these dim pictographs "appear to have been overpainted by the figures in red," which are middle period (Notes, Plate 73).

The three periods of painting are also in evidence on Plate 75, though the early period is represented only by the dim rectangular figure (upper left), and the middle period by the horned figure, which is in the same idiom as the dancing figures of Plate 74. The diminutive horse and rider with horned headdress and lance and the surrounding warriors, under the thunderbird, undoubtedly portray Plains Indians. This type of headdress was favored by Comanche warriors but was also worn by other Plains tribes.

The historic thunderbird of Plate 76 is very similar to the one to its left (Plate 74) and is a good example of how natural forces can obliterate pictographs and alter their colors. Kirkland said:

Note how the lower wing of the brilliant thunderbird has been dimmed by repeated action of the flooded stream. While the artist was at work a thunder shower up the canyon brought the water up on the pictographs to the bottom line of the square under the tower-like design on the right. Almost no rain at all fell at the springs. (Notes, Plate 76)

Some of the figures in the following panel (Plate 77) have also been lightened by water; Kirkland noted that "seep water has run down over the pictures on this plate and dimmed them to some extent. Chemicals in the water have changed the original orange designs to a purple-red where the water has covered them (see design, extreme right)" (Notes, Plate 77).

What the "tower-like design" (Plate 76) is intended to represent is obscure, but in any case it is the work of a historic artist. The wagon or stagecoach on the extreme left of this plate is, of course, historic and some of the other figures in this plate may be also.

A three-legged, or possibly male, figure grasping a round object (shield?) and wearing a three-pronged (feathered?) headdress is apparently but one of a number of intriguing pictures painted by a historic artist (Plate 71, center, above and right of orange tepee). The pale yellow body outlined with a reddish hue is the link which connects a number of scattered designs and anthropomorphic figures. The most obvious examples of this style are the horse and rider and the figure immediately to their right (Plate 78, to right of red deer). The outline treatment of the legs of the anthropomorphic figure explains how some small humans at first appear to be four-legged (Plate 73, lower middle and right, under thunderbird; Plate 77, to right of six-legged animal). The two peculiar figures (Plate 73, far left, lower), the thunderbird (Plate 75, left center), and the monkey-like figure adorned with miter-like hat (Plate 72, left) are also in this technique, and in fact all pictographs painted in yellow seem to be historic (Plate 71, circular designs; Plate 79, horse and tepee, right).

Kirkland declared that "only after careful study can many of the designs be correctly assigned to their period" (Notes, Plate 70), but this assumption is somewhat overoptimistic, for some of the Meyers Springs paintings defy such attempts. The five curious, purple-red upright objects in the center of Plate 75, for example, cannot positively be assigned to any of the three periods. Jackson (1938:152) suggested that they "may be conventionalized representations of atlatls," similar to some portrayed in the lower Pecos, but he also said that "they are suggestive of shinny, lacrosse or other game sticks." There are a number of other scattered figures, designs, and handprints which are unrelated or unrelatable to other Meyers Springs pictographs. The human figure (Plate 74, lower right), for example, might belong with any of the three periods or none of them. The design (Plate 77, lower left) neither represents a recognizable object nor can it be associated with other paintings. The deer and the robed figure (Plate 78) on which is superimposed a horse and rider, are among the most frustrating of the unassignable paintings, although the color and technique appear to be the same as the historic red-outlined yellow paintings. The interesting figure on the extreme left of this plate is unlike other figures at Meyers Springs, and finally, most of the pictographs in Plate 79 cannot be related to others. Kirkland noted that "the small red arrows and the cross-like figure in the dark streak are interesting because they appear to have been drawn with the sharp corner of a piece of dry color. All other work appears to be that of liquid color" (Notes, Plate 70). In sum, while most of the pictographs at Meyers Springs can be attributed to one or another of the three periods Kirkland recognized, a residue of paintings cannot be associated with them and may well have been painted by other artists at other times.

The combination of permanent water and natural shelter is not a common occurrence in the desolate reaches of the Big Bend country. Where such oases exist, as at Meyers Springs, it seems appropriate, almost inevitable, that the generations of men drawn to these havens should ornament their rock surfaces. Apart from the urge of prehistoric men to record their presence at Meyers Springs by leaving handprints, designs, and other figures, some of the artists must have had other motives. The early-period designs, whether Pecos River style or not, are hardly in the same category as casual handprints. Their size and the apparent care with which they were painted suggests that they illustrated something of considerable social concern, but they are too few and dim to know just what. The crude figures of the middle period, though far more plentiful and quite clear, are almost as difficult to fathom as the earlier ones. Handprints, some of which at least are attributable to this period, are probably in the realm of nonliterate signatures, but the human figures seem to represent other concerns. Perhaps they enumerated the individuals in a group that passed through Meyers Springs, and thus were a message for others who came that way. But if it is accurate to interpret the hand-holding figures as dancers, then the middle-period paintings likely have another meaning. Dancing may be associated with many different activities; it may be recreational, or a necessary accompaniment of puberty, marriage, or other rites, or an integral part of religious celebrations, and so forth. To which recreational or ritualistic activities these paintings belong, if any, is impossible to determine. But the probability that such an oasis would be the site for various social and ceremonial affairs is strong. That these events should be commemorated on its walls is likely.

The historic paintings seem to have been painted in part for somewhat different reasons. Some seem simply to record events — a bison hunt, for example. Others may have served to illustrate for the untutored what some had seen in the alien white world. Spanish mission buildings apparently

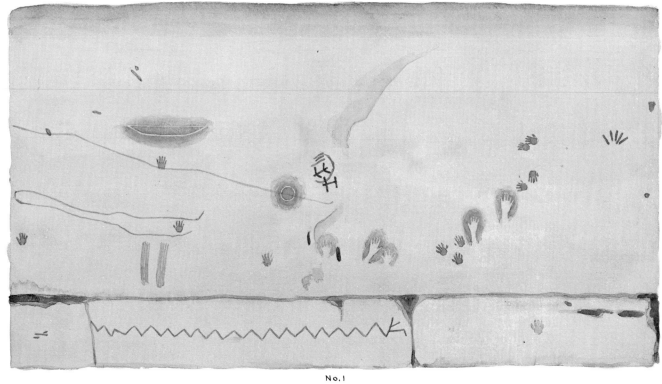

No. 1

28" out

CONTRACTED 3"

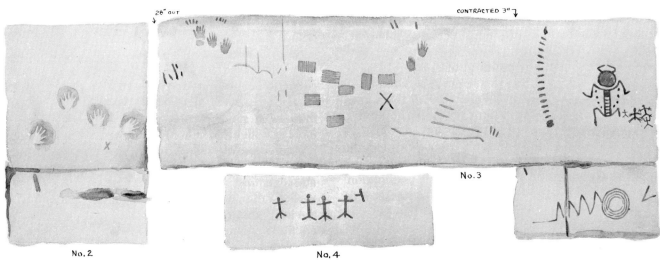

No. 2

No. 4

No. 3

Plate 80. Indian Water Hole. Copied July 11, 1939. Scale: Nos. 1–4, 1/4″ to 1′

PLATE 80

These pictographs are on the back walls and ceilings of two shelters in a small canyon about twenty miles northwest of Pumpville in Terrell County. The shelters are almost connected and directly in front of them is a hole of permanent water. On the bank above the water are two large burned-rock mounds and evidence of an extensive camp. The shelters are so low that they are flooded with each rise in the canyon.

Nos. 1 and 2. The bow and hoop prints were made by pressing the objects against the ceiling and spraying liquid color over them.

No. 3. All the paintings in the shelter are very dim except the "Devil," far right, which is still quite clear.

No. 4. This is the only design in the smaller shelter. It is on the back wall.

made a deep impression on natives familiar only with huts and tepees. As was pointed out in the preceding chapter, one of the main points of contact between Spanish-Mexican civilization and the Indian was Christianity—its appurtenances, missionary fathers, and material symbols. Drawing such buildings as churches may have served to show others what they looked like, but they also may have had magical implications. As the church—or mission—was the seat of the potent supernatural power of the Spaniard, it may have been reasoned that some of this power might be obtained by drawing such a building on the walls of a shelter. Such comments would apply as well to the cross, and there are a number of conspicuous examples at Meyers Springs (Plate 72).

Indian Water Hole

A few miles east of Dryden, Terrell County, in the same drainage system as the Meyers Springs Site, are "two small shelters in a small canyon which empties into Lozier Canyon. The shelters are almost connected and directly in front of them in the canyon is a hole of permanent water. On the bank above the water are two large burned-rock mounds and evidence of an extensive camp. . . . The shelters are so low that they flooded with each rise in the canyon" (Notes, Plate 80). Negative and positive handprints in red are scattered over the walls and ceilings (Plate 80), and a zigzag line on the wall almost fourteen feet long appears to represent a snake. The most interesting designs at this site—because they are unique—are two negative prints on the ceiling, one of a hoop, the other of a bow. These articles were pressed against the ceiling and liquid color sprayed around them with the same technique that produced negative handprints. If the liquid paint was sprayed from the mouth, as seems likely, the process of creating negative prints on the ceiling must have been a messy one for the visage of the artist. In the lower Pecos River region the custom of "handprinting," as we have seen, is associated with post-Archaic artists. The occurrence of a negative-painted bow with handprints at Indian Water Hole suggests that the custom was also relatively recent in this region.

Bee Cave Canyon and Agua Fria Mountains

In the south-central part of Brewster County, about nine miles southeast of Santiago Peak, Bee Cave Canyon opens into Chalk Draw. At the mouth of this box canyon at the foot of a high leaning cliff is a large open shelter. "The protected area is about seventy-five yards long and the overhang of the cliff is about forty feet, the cliff being two hundred or more feet high with a fairly flat wall" (Notes, Plate 81). Purple-red paintings, mostly of anthro-

pomorphic beings, are widely scattered on the back wall, all within easy reach of the floor. The shelter contained an accumulation of cultural debris, in places four feet deep, and was excavated by M. R. Harrington and E. F. Coffin. These investigations indicated that the shelter had been "occupied at different intervals and for no long time at any period" (Coffin, 1932:60). The cultural remains are referable to the Archaic tradition and are similar to those of the lower Pecos region (Suhm *et al.*, 1954:52–59).

Kirkland visited the site in 1934 and did not find all the paintings reported by Coffin, and Jackson (1938:125–127), who visited the site after Kirkland, found even fewer, so the disintegration of paintings seems to have been rapid. The most unusual pictograph in this shelter (Plate 81, No. 10) was made by tracing around a hand and arm with a crayon. Kirkland found two other handprints stamped in red paint on the walls but did not copy them. Some of the anthropomorphic beings are quite crude (No. 9, for example), but others (Nos. 3, 4) are of a unique and carefully wrought style which has not been found elsewhere. Kirkland saw a connection between those pictographs and the petroglyph "chiselled very shallowly into the rock" a foot to the left of No. 1, arguing that "it was evidently made by the same artists that produced the paintings. Note how similar its attitude is to that of the large figures in No. 4" (Notes, Plate 81).

About eight miles up Chalk Draw a number of red geometric forms have been painted under an overhang of a limestone cliff (Plate 81, Chalk Draw). The total absence of anthropomorphic or animal figures is unusual and quite unlike Bee Cave Canyon, where the reverse is true.

At the west end of the Agua Fria Mountains, in southwestern Brewster County, "the mountain terminates in an overhanging granite cliff some three hundred feet or more high, at the base of which is a large protected area covered with a deep accumulation of burned rocks and ashes. Only a few yards below this shelter is a huge spring of clear cold water, making it ideal for an Indian camp" (Notes, Plate 82). Indians who camped here painted an assortment of pictures on the granite wall. While the colors of the pictographs have remained quite strong and clear "the rock is flaking badly and it is likely that some designs have already been destroyed in this way, in fact No. 5 was discovered on the protected side of a very large block of granite at the base of the cliff. This appeared, however, to be the position of the rock when the Indian painting was made" (Notes, Plate 82). The largest painting (Plate 82, left) resembles a minotaur but this is probably accidental; it may be intended to represent a man astride an animal. (See Jackson, 1938:118, for a different interpretation.)

Bee Cave. Pictographs were found under this cliff. See Plate 81.

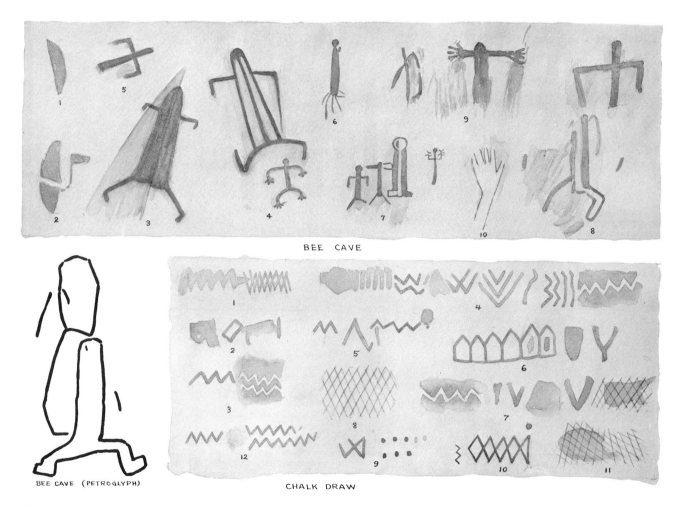

BEE CAVE

BEE CAVE (PETROGLYPH)

CHALK DRAW

Plate 81. Shuler Ranch, Bee Cave. Copied July 19, 1936. Scale: 3/4″ to 1′. Shuler Ranch, Chalk Draw. Copied July 19, 1936. Scale: 3/4″ to 1′

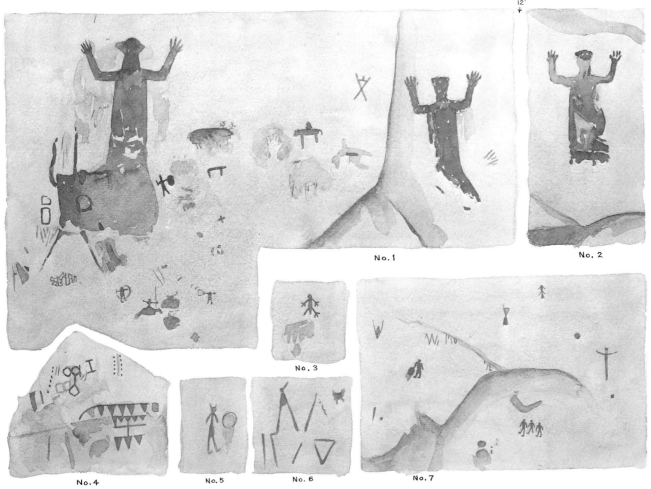

Plate 82. Agua Fria. Copied July 20, 1936. Scale: Nos. 1–7, 3/8″ to 1′

PLATE 82

Agua Fria. Only two colors were used in these paintings; most are purple-red, but the handprint (No. 1, center) and a few smaller designs are orange-yellow.

PLATE 81

Bee Cave. All the paintings at this site are within easy reach of the floor and widely scattered along the immense back wall. It was not practical to show their relation to one another more than to number them in their order along the wall from left to right. Only one color was found—purple-red. The pictures are still quite clear.

Chalk Draw. These pictographs are on a stratified limestone cliff about thirty feet high, within thirty feet of the small stream. The pictures are from four to six feet from the ground on a stratum of rock which averages about ten inches in thickness. They are protected by rocks above which overhang them about four feet. The underside of these rocks is smoked black. The creek floods the ground at the foot of the cliff but apparently seldom covers the pictographs, and they are in fair condition. Their scattered positions made it impractical to copy them in true relation on the cliff. They are numbered as nearly as possible in their order from left to right. Red was the only color used.

The other two human figures (Nos. 1, 2) are very similar to the minotaur-like figure but appear never to have been mounted on animals. A small figure with a lance, mounted on what is now a legless horse (No. 1, left bottom), dates it as the work of historic Indians. It may be, then, that the minotaur and the other figures, also painted in the same purple-red hue, are also historic. While most of the pictographs are purple-red, it should be pointed out that there is a negative handprint and near it two nondescript designs in an orange-yellow color (Plate 82, No. 1, center). These paintings do not display any particular features, apart from a general crudity, which would suggest connections to other pictographic sites.

Plate 83. Comanche Springs. Copied July 21, 1936. Scale: Nos. 1–14, 3/4″ to 1′

Comanche Springs and Study Butte

South of the Agua Fria Site, near Lajitas and the Rio Grande, are a few pictographs near the base of "a high stratified chalk cliff, on both sides of a small stream. Springs flow from under the rocks in the bed of the creek at this place. Very few flint flakes or other signs of Indians, other than the pictures, were found" (Notes, Plate 83). The rock paintings were scattered along the cliffs on both sides of the creek.

Nos. 1, 2, and 3 were on the north bank, the other designs being on the south. Those on the south were located about four feet above the base of the cliff which is on a narrow shelf or second bank of the creek. Flood waters never reach the pictures but blowing rains and the disintegration of the chalk rock have dimmed the designs until they could only be made out with much difficulty. Red, black, and a kind of brown color was used. Only handprints and geometrical designs and marks were found, although two slabs of rock containing crude drawings of men on horseback had been removed and are said to be built into a rock home in Alpine. No doubt many of the original drawings have either been destroyed or removed in this way. (Notes, Plate 83)

Just inside the western boundary of Big Bend National Park, two miles east of Study Butte, is a high ridge of red sandstone. Large blocks which have broken free from it lie along the bottom of the ridge.

PLATE 83

Comanche Springs. These Brewster County pictographs are near the base of a high chalk cliff.

The few pictures are found on the protected sides of a few of the large blocks of stone. The color is black, and as is usual for this color, very badly faded. The work was crude in the first place and the dimness of the color made it impossible to be very certain about certain parts of the designs. The copies as they are, however, fairly well represent the pictures as they were in the beginning. (Notes, Plate 84)

Hot Springs and Glenn Spring

A few miles up the Rio Grande from Boquillas, Mexico, and on its northern bank, a creek fed by a large cold spring empties into the river. The site would have been an attractive one to prehistoric men. The bluff along the Rio Grande at this point is about seventy-five feet high and is made up of thin layers of limestone and ocher-colored clay. Kirkland found indications of Indian occupation along the bank of the creek and at the base of the bluff. Pictographs were also painted on the bluff

on the edges of the limestone from two to eight feet above the ground. The stone is very badly cracked and much of the painting has probably fallen off and been destroyed. What still remains is dim but easily made out. The designs are very simple, mostly markings and geometrical shapes. A few designs may have been intended for the human figure. No handprints were found. The usual red,

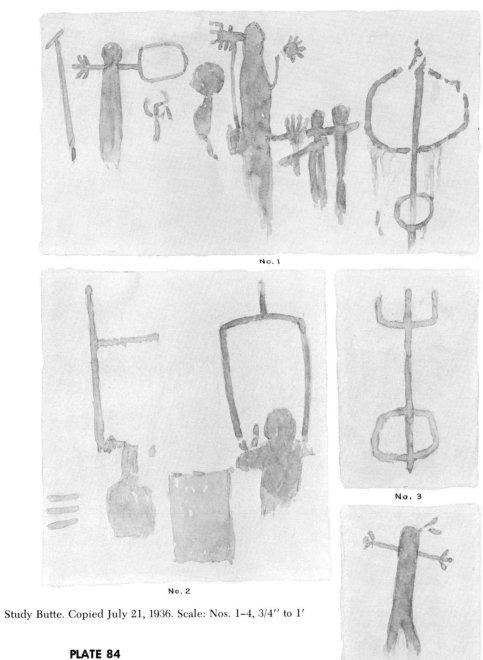

No. 1

No. 2

No. 3

No. 4

Plate 84. Study Butte. Copied July 21, 1936. Scale: Nos. 1–4, 3/4″ to 1′

PLATE 84

Study Butte. These dim black pictographs near Study Butte are on the protected faces of large blocks of red sandstone.

yellow, and black were used. The designs made up of broad flat lines were painted with a flat brush and liquid paint. The very fine line designs appear to have been made with the point of a piece of dry color. (Notes, Plate 85)

About twelve miles west of Hot Springs up Tornillo Draw, springs break out at the base of a hill.

There was once a large camp ground up the hill from the spring. Almost at the top of the hill east of a draw, is a very large block of sandstone standing on one corner which affords a good shelter on three sides. This shelter was used by the Indians, because there are burned rocks

and ashes in abundance at its base. The few pictures at this site are on the west slope of this rock. All are in red and not very clear. (Notes, Plate 85)

Marfa Lake Shelter

Kirkland did not do extensive work in the southwestern portion of the Big Bend, visiting only one site in Presidio County (Plate 86). Jackson (1938: 99–111) reported eleven petrographic sites in this large county, and it is apparent that rock art sites are widely scattered and the art rather rudimentary. The one site Kirkland did visit is one of the most in-

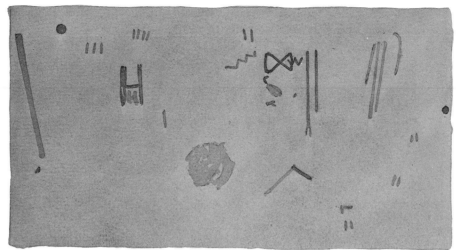

GLENN SPRING

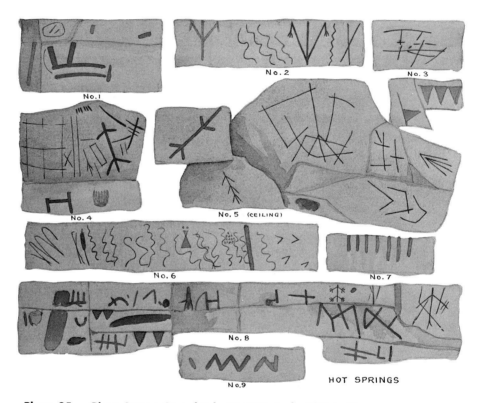

No. 1

No. 2

No. 3

No. 4

No. 5 (CEILING)

No. 6

No. 7

No. 8

No. 9

HOT SPRINGS

Plate 85. Glenn Spring. Copied July 22, 1936. Scale: 3/4″ to 1′.
Hot Springs. Copied July 23, 1936. Scale: Nos. 1–9, 3/4″ to 1′

teresting in the area and has long been known (Peabody, 1909). It is about twelve miles south of Marfa in the canyon below the dam of San Esteban Lake. The pictographs are in a shelter "under a cliff on the north wall of the canyon. A small stream including a spring empties over the top of the shelter into the canyon" (Notes, Plate 86).

Curiously, the pictographs of No. 1 and No. 2 "are at the top of a twenty-foot ledge and had to be painted from the top by reaching downward. All the other pictures are in reasonably easy reach either from the floor or from fallen rocks" (*ibid.*).

PLATE 85

Glenn Spring. These rather simple red paintings were accurately laid out in pencil, but a shower halted work before the copy could be completed and the actual color was put in later from memory. It was so simple, however, that there is little likelihood that any mistake was made.

Hot Springs. These pictographs are mostly red, but a few are yellow and black.

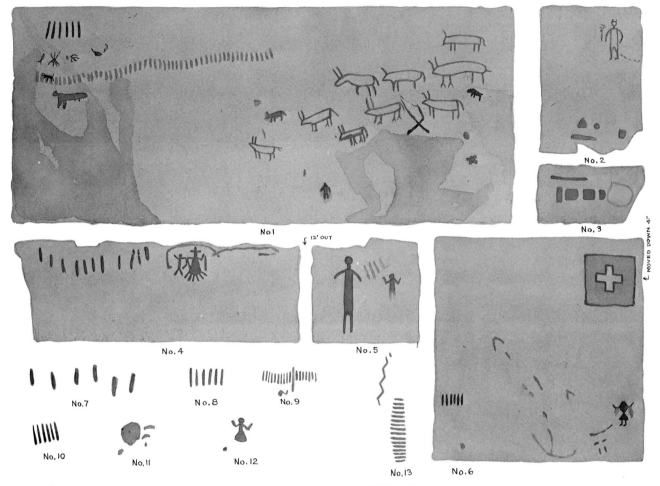

Plate 86. Marfa Lake Shelter. Copied July 15, 1939. Scale: Nos. 1–13, 3/8" to 1'

The horned animals in No. 1 appear to represent cattle, although it must be admitted that some other animal could be intended. That these are cattle — and that the pictographs executed in historic times — is strengthened by the cross outlined in red and set in a red-outlined square (No. 6, upper right). The larger figure (No. 4, top center) appears to be wearing European-style headgear and riding a horse, although it is impossible to be absolutely sure. In sum, the weight of the evidence strongly suggests that these pictographs are historic. Peabody, the first investigator to describe these rock paintings, said of them:

They include a set of figures, human and not human, in black; an outlined Greek cross in red; a headless human figure eight inches long; many parallel lines in red; six black marks over a small recess; a scalp-shaped figure in black and lines in red, a rude arrow in orange, nine horned animals pointing the same way, and some modern initials. (Peabody, 1909:102)

Some of these figures, such as the cross, are readily recognizable in Kirkland's copy, but others such as the scalp-shaped figure and the rude arrow in orange are not. Either they had disappeared by 1939, or Kirkland failed to find them, or we cannot

PLATE 86

Marfa Lake Shelter. These pictographs near Marfa are mostly red; a few are black. Nos. 7–13 are "check" marks and simple designs scattered about over the shelter.

identify them by Peabody's descriptions. Peabody's "headless human figure" is probably the hourglass figure (No. 6, lower right). Jackson (1938:102–103), whose rendering of this figure is distorted, says it is "an Indian representation of a white woman," but does not give a reason for this opinion.

It is tempting to interpret series of parallel lines, which are common at Marfa Lake Shelter, as some sort of tally marks. But the series in No. 1 could as easily represent a fence, and the others could of course stand for many other things. It is probably wisest to refer to them, as does Kirkland, as "check marks" and to withhold all interpretations. The Marfa Lake Shelter is near the La Junta region through which a number of early Spanish expeditions passed and in which missions were established (Newcomb, 1961:229ff). That nearby historic pictographs should show European and Christian influence is not surprising.

Davis Mountains. Kirkland is standing in front of boulder which served as a shelter and pictograph site. See Plates 87, 88, 89.

Davis Mountains Pictographs

The Davis Mountains have relatively few places where prehistoric men painted on rock surfaces and there are even fewer petroglyph sites. Their scarcity is probably a reflection of the limited usage and transient occupation of the area by Indians. Despite their rarity there are numbers of interesting pictograph sites. Unfortunately, Kirkland did not visit the most spectacular one, probably because he was unaware of it at the time he was copying rock paintings in the region. Jackson (1938:96) described it as "located in one of the most inaccessible, and yet most scenic, spots in Texas. It is high in the rugged mountains, in the northeastern part of Jeff Davis County, with an elevation of about 6,500 feet." Situated in a shelter whose roof is some sixty feet high, some of the paintings of what appear to be long-bodied men are eighteen feet tall and are painted in red, orange, brown, white, and green. Other smaller paintings in black and red seem to be the work of other artists. But none of these poorly known paintings, so far as is known, have any obvious similarity or relationship to other pictographs in the Davis Mountains.

Some fifteen miles west of Fort Davis, south of Mount Livermore,

pictographs are painted on the back wall of a small circular depression in the side of a huge granite rock which stands like several other similar rocks on the talus in front of a granite ridge. Soot on the back of the shelter indicates usage as a fireplace, but it is too small to have afforded much protection from the weather. The slope in front of the granite hill was probably an open camp since the ground is strewn with flint flakes. (Notes, Plate 87)

All of the designs are in red, but some are quite dim, suggesting that they are older than the brighter ones. The brighter designs illustrate well the many ways in which check marks may be altered so that they appear to our eyes to be anthropomorphic figures, animal tracks, and other things.

The figures and check marks are simple at this site and seem totally unrelated to pictographs found in two shelters located only three miles to the east. The shelters in which these pictographs are found (Plates 88, 89) were "formed by huge granite rocks which have tumbled into a pile at the west end of a small granite peak." They were large enough to afford good protection from bad weather "and the accumulation of debris on the floor indicates that they were used as dwellings" (Notes, Plate 88). The dominant pictograph in the south shelter is painted on a large rock in the center of the floor" (Plate 88, No. 3). It seems to represent a bizarre anthropomorphic figure, but Jackson (1938:96–97), who viewed it from a different angle, described it as "possibly a conventionalized animal." The gray deer and arrow (Plate 88, No. 2) is painted over a spot of white paint, as are the other gray-on-white figures. "The outline of the deer and arrow are unusual because they appear definitely blue. This may be color applied later by the white man but it has every appearance of being the original outline"

Plate 87.　West of Fort Davis. Copied July 29, 1935. Scale: 1/16

PLATE 87

Only one shade of red was used in these paintings west of Fort Davis. The principal parts of the design are quite clear, while dim splotches of the same red appear over most of the background.

(Notes, Plate 88). Kirkland also suggested that the other "gray spots on the white at the right may have originally been animals," as the lower figure in this group plainly is. Whether the orange and the gray figures are the work of the same artists is difficult to determine. The execution of deer seems to be about the same, and the lower gray figure has horns of the same color as the orange figures, although of course they could have been added later. This animal and a small orange one (Plate 88, left) seem to represent bison, animals infrequently found in prehistoric Texas rock paintings.

Low down on a sloping rock in the small shelter some ten yards north of the main shelter are nine deer painted in black and what appear to be four human figures (Plate 89, No. 1). "The bottom figure is only nine inches from the solid rock floor while the top figure is twenty-eight inches from it. The black figures are very dim and can only be seen distinctly after they have been dampened with water" (Notes, Plate 89). They are painted in the same manner as the two orange deer of Plate 88—all are in right profile and several of the black deer display motion in the same stiff-legged way. They appear to have been drawn by the same artist. The exaggerated ears of the three "does" suggest that the

artist was portraying mule deer rather than the white-tailed species—and mule deer are still abundant in this part of the state.

The handprints on this shelter's walls and ceiling are, with one exception (Plate 89, No. 4), those of children, and in this sense are similar to some in the lower Pecos River country attributed to the Red Monochrome style. It has been suggested that the habit of leaving handprints on rock surfaces was in many cases probably analogous to the American custom of scratching or painting initials or names on similar surfaces. The presence of children's handprints would seem to support this contention. The handprints in this shelter are of two kinds: the red and white ones were made by placing the hand which had been dipped in liquid paint against the rock. In the other, the rock was cleaned and perhaps painted white, after which a soot-smeared hand was pressed against the lighter surface.

Davis Mountains. See Plates 87, 88, 89. Handprints of Plate 89 are on ceiling above the artist's head.

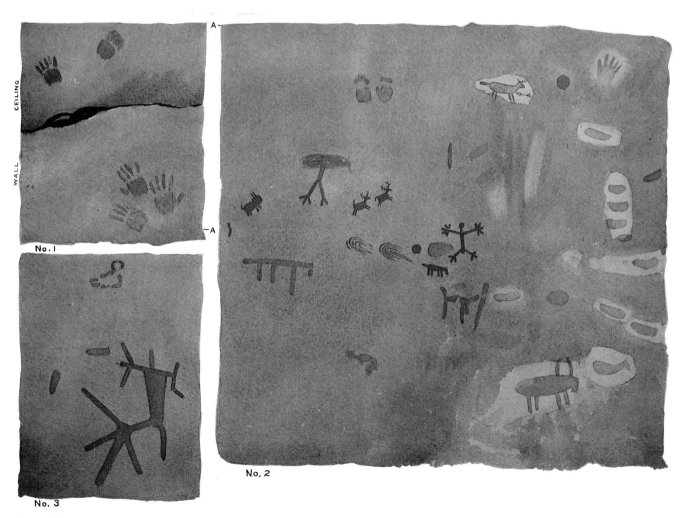

No. 1

No. 2

No. 3

Plate 88. West of Fort Davis. Copied July 29, 1935. Scale: Nos. 1–3, 1/16

No. 1

No. 2.

No 3

No. 4

Plate 89.   West of Fort Davis. Copied July 29, 1935. Scale: Nos. 1–4, 1/16

PLATE 88

Red, orange-red, white, and black were used for these pictographs.

No. 1. These red handprints are on the same wall as No. 2 and if moved up until the *A's* coincide. the painting will be in its correct position.

No. 3. This odd red figure is painted on a large rock in the center of the shelter.

PLATE 89

No. 1. These black animal pictographs are in a small shelter about ten yards north of the main shelter.

No. 2. This red figure is on one side of the rock which blocks the center of the shelter.

No. 3. These black prints are at the top of the side wall where it joins ceiling, No. 4 at *A-B*. The print to the right is evidently that of a foot. A flat rock about three feet below would make it easily possible to place the foot in that position.

No. 4. The placement of these handprints is only approximately correct. They are on the smoke-blackened ceiling, and every print except one is of the hands of children.

Under a huge rock about a quarter of a mile west of "Handprint Rock" are two other shelters which also contain pictographs.

Both of these shelters are very low and the pictographs are very near the present floor level. The lowest picture in No. 1 is eleven inches from the floor and the highest thirty-three inches. In No. 2 the lowest picture is only six inches above the floor while the highest is thirteen inches. The floor is dirt and ashes and may at one time have been somewhat below its present level. Both shelters are very small and could never have served for more than fireplaces. The slanting backs on which the pictures are painted are covered with smoke. (Notes, Plate 90)

Most of the drawings are undoubtedly of deer but other animals also may be represented. They are all similar to the deer of the nearby shelters and as Kirkland pointed out (Notes, Plate 90), "they were more than likely the work of the same Indians." Since it could not have been an easy task to paint so many animals in such cramped quarters, it is reasonable to assume that these paintings were executed for good reason. An outline drawing of an anthropomorphic being around whom are gathered

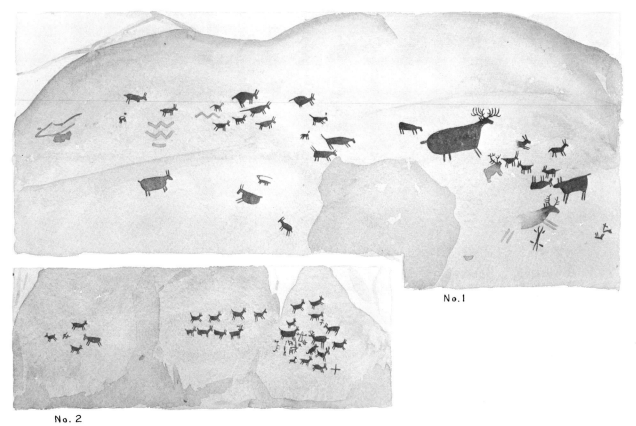

No. 1

No. 2

Plate 90.   West of Fort Davis. Copied July 30, 1935. Scale: Nos. 1–2, 1/16

PLATE 90

These animal drawings are in two shelters under a large rock a short distance west of the shelters at which the drawings in Plates 25 and 26 appear. The pictographs of No. 1 are in the largest shelter on the southwest side of the rock. The pictographs of No. 2 are in the small shelter about twenty feet east of the large shelter. They were made with black liquid paint applied with a very small brush. On No. 1 are a few very dim red designs which apparently have no relation to the animal pictures. The animal drawings are now almost completely covered with gray dust so that they cannot possibly be seen completely without being treated with water. Since color is only secondary and the action and spirit of the drawings all-important, a full black has been used in making the copies. They probably appear just as they were when first painted. More than usual care was taken in making these copies to get all measurements accurate and to reproduce faithfully the spirit of the drawings.

many deer (Plate 90, No. 2) suggests that this particular painting is part of some sort of hunting magic, or perhaps illustrates a myth concerning deer. A partially dimmed figure in the other panel (Plate 90, No. 1, to right and below largest deer) strongly suggests a man disguised in an antler head-dress. To the right of this figure an animal on its back, apparently slain, reinforces the hunting-magic interpretation.

In the valley just north of Sawtooth Mountain, thirty-seven miles northwest of Fort Davis, are four shelters under two gigantic rock piles. "On the back wall of a small shelter on the east side of the south rock pile" (Notes, Plate 91) are a number of pictographs which seem to have been drawn at several different times. Five black deer (Plate 91, No. 1, left) "appear to be much older than those in red. They cannot be seen until they are treated with water" (*ibid.*). The red deer were drawn in the same technique as those in the shelters to the south of Mount Livermore and must be the work of artists with the same cultural and artistic traditions. In this shelter, however, a human figure with a bow and arrow is depicted aiming at a deer (Plate 91, No. 1, right). Jackson (1938:90) compared the manner of indicating the arm bent across the body of this figure to one at Paint Rock (Plate 105, No. 5), but the similarity of the two seems to be fortuitous.

Rock Pile Ranch, Davis Mountains. These massive outcrops provided good surfaces for paintings.
See Plate 91.

The presence of the bow and arrow narrows the dating of this pictograph, and presumably all the deer pictographs of the Davis Mountains region, to some time after A.D. 600, when this weapon was probably introduced into Texas.

The other designs on the wall of this shelter seem to have more in common with designs in the other nearby shelters than they do with either the red or black deer. The use of a broader line, a yellow hue, and the emphasis on geometric shapes and figures are points of similarity. Pictographs of this sort, in red, yellow, white, and black (Plate 91, No. 2) are "on the ceiling of a small shelter on the south side of the north rock pile. The floor of the shelter is rock and the space between floor and ceiling is so small that one can only sit in a cramped position. The floor is about three feet above the ground outside the shelter so that the pictographs can easily be seen by one standing in front of the shelter" (Notes, Plate 91). The colors used in these designs, but not the shapes themselves, are repeated in the "so-called blanket design" which "completely covers a large leaning rock on the west side of the south rock pile. An overhead rock forms a roof which protects the painting from the weather. The rock is completely splotched with many colors, but only in places can definite designs be distinguished" (Notes, Plate 92).

In another small shelter under a large granite rock at the southeast end of the south rock pile are several other designs (Plate 92, No. 2). "The design on the right is dim but easily made out but the one on the left is not clear enough to be very certain about. Parts in question have not been copied" (Notes, Plate 92). It is easier to understand the pur-

pose of representational paintings, such as those of the deer, than those of geometrical figures. Because of their location these polychrome paintings must have represented more than idle daubing, but to go further in interpretation would be unwarranted conjecture.

Balmorhea

About eighteen miles east of Balmorhea, Reeves County, a number of mesas jut up several hundred feet from the surrounding plain. In the rimrock of these mesas are a number of shelters, many of which bear traces of human occupation, and a few contain pictographs. On one of the small mesas standing alone in the plain with a dry creek at its base near which was a large burned-rock hearth, Kirkland found a pictograph shelter. The shelter floor contained ashes and its ceiling was smoked black. Most of the designs were black, a few red, and none had any resemblance to those of the Davis Mountain shelters to the south" (Plates 93, 94, 95). "Liquid color was used in most cases and a very small, well-shaped brush must have been used. The designs were so small and intricate that a very large scale 3/16 inch to one inch was found necessary to copy them accurately. No handprints were discovered" (Notes, Plate 93). Peabody first described the pictographs in this shelter in 1909, and Jackson (1938:80–82) also mentions them. Apart from a few anthropomorphic figures and animals, the designs do not seem to represent objects of the natural world, but seem rather to be visual and symbolic illustrations of beliefs or events. As such they are probably not amenable to rational explanation.

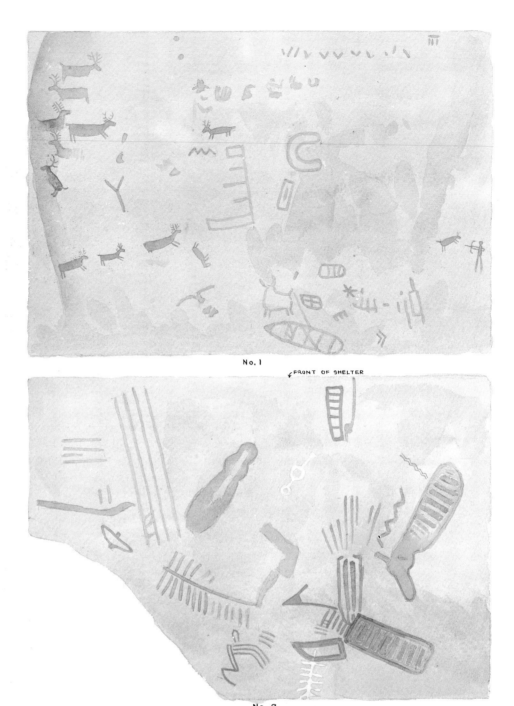

No. 1

FRONT OF SHELTER

No. 2

Plate 91. Rock Pile Ranch. Copied July 31, 1935. Scale: Nos. 1–2, 1/16

PLATE 91

Rock Pile Ranch. Black, white, red, orange, and yellow colors were used in these paintings. Splotches of color, mostly red, are also present, but it does not appear that many of them were ever designs.

No. 1. These pictographs are on the back wall of a small shelter on the east side of the south rock pile. The animals drawn in black (upper left) appear to be much older than those in red, and cannot be seen until treated with water.

No. 2. These paintings are on the ceiling of a small shelter on the south side of the north rock pile. The floor of the shelter is rock and the space between floor and ceiling is so small that one can sit only in a cramped position. But the floor is about three feet above the ground so that the pictographs can easily be seen from the front of the shelter.

PLATE 92

No. 1. On the west side of the south rock pile, Rock Pile Ranch, a so-called blanket design in the same colors as Plate 91, No. 1, covers a large leaning boulder. Only in places can definite designs be distinguished. An effort was made to reproduce the general color-effect observed and such fragments of designs as could be clearly made out were copied.

No. 2. These red pictographs are in a small shelter under a large granite rock at the southeast end of the south rock pile. The design on the right is dim but easily made out, whereas the one on the left is not clear enough to be certain about. Parts in question were not copied.

Rock Pile Ranch, Davis Mountains. The so-called blanket design is on the wall of this small shelter. See Plate 92.

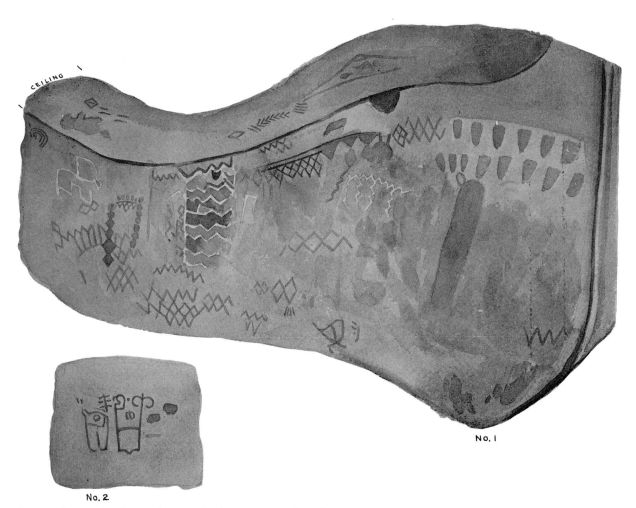

No. 1

No. 2

Plate 92.   Rock Pile Ranch. Copied July 31, 1935. Scale: 1/32

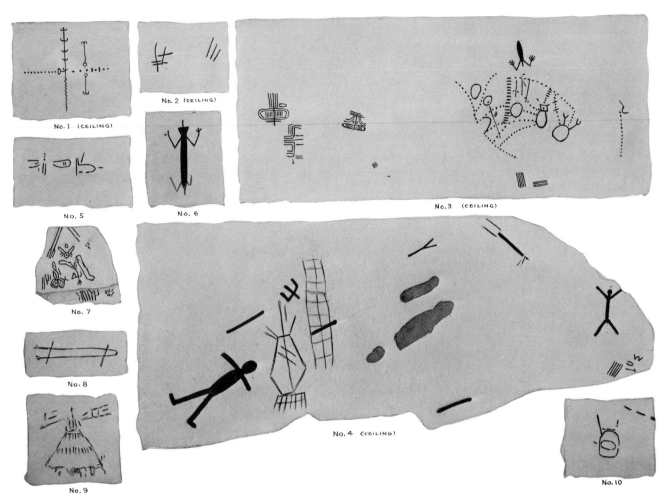

Plate 93. Balmorhea, Shelter 1. Copied July 25, 1936. Scale: Nos. 1–10, 3/32″ to 1″

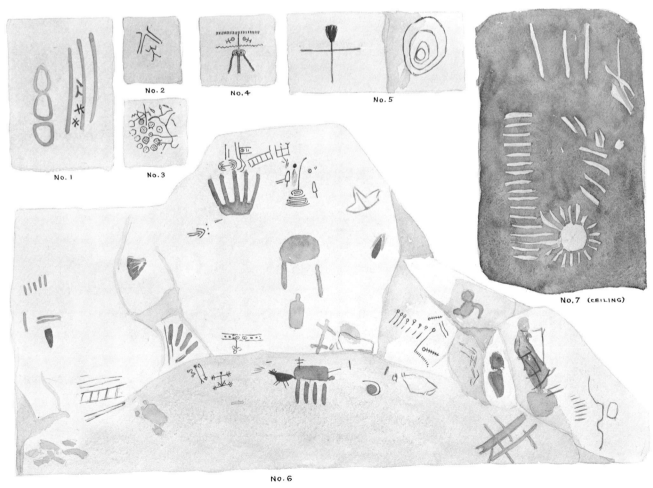

Plate 94. Balmorhea, Shelter 1. Copied July 24, 1936. Scale: Nos. 1–7, 3/32″ to 1″

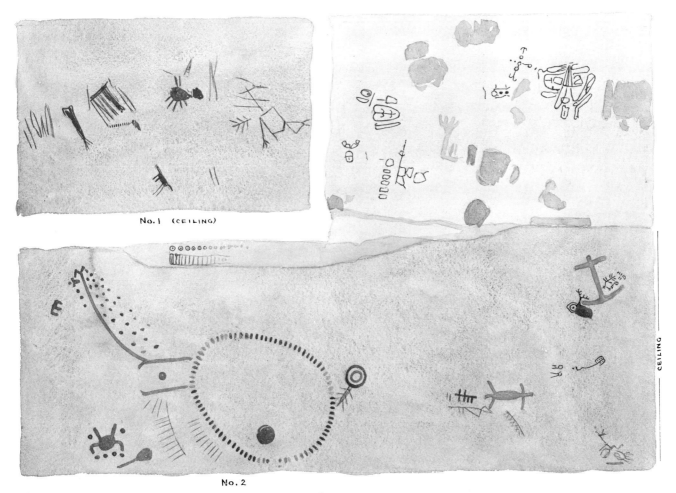

No. 1 (CEILING)

No. 2

CEILING

Plate 95. Balmorhea, Shelter 1. Copied July 24, 1936. Scale: Nos. 1–2, 3/32″ to 1″

PLATE 93

Balmorhea, Shelter 1. The pictographs in this plate are all black. Nos. 1, 2, 3, and 4 are underneath overhanging rocks outside the main shelter. Nos. 8 and 9, and fine line designs at left of No. 4 were made with dry brush or charcoal crayon.

PLATE 94

Balmorhea, Shelter 1. All of these red designs are on the left wall of the shelter, except No. 7, which is underneath a protruding rock. No. 7 is unusual in that the rock is black from smoke and the design is painted over the soot with a yellow mud paste.

PLATE 95

The mostly black designs on this plate are on the right side of the shelter. No. 1 and the lower part of No. 2 are painted over soot-covered ceilings and had to be wet before the designs could be seen at all. The top part of No. 2 is on the side wall about four feet high, which turns into the ceiling of a low extension of the cave. This ceiling is only about three feet above the floor, and it is necessary to be flat on one's back in the ashes to see the lower part of No. 2.

Every investigator seems to see something different in these intricate little designs. Peabody, for example, described a group of designs on the left wall of the shelter (Plate 94, No. 3) as "a combination of curved lines and circles with dots in black, suggesting a grotesque cactus" (1909:213). J. Charles Kelley, in a letter to Jackson (1938:82), thought part of the figure showed "a marked resemblance to a conventionalized horse and rider." (It should be noted that the Jackson and Kirkland copies of this pictograph are at variance with one another, Jackson's appearing much more horselike.) To Jackson (1938:82) "at least four of the circles enclosing dots seem to represent human heads. The connected circles containing dots are of the same class as certain petroglyphs at Site No. 81, Val Verde County."

The design of Plate 94, No. 4, also on the left wall of the shelter, was described by Jackson (1938: 82) as

of particular interest because of the combination of such diverse elements. They include two small human figures, or "twins"; a line of 29 numeration dots on one side and 28 on the other; a vertical line or "back-bone"; a zigzag line; three concentric quadrants; two so-called discs,

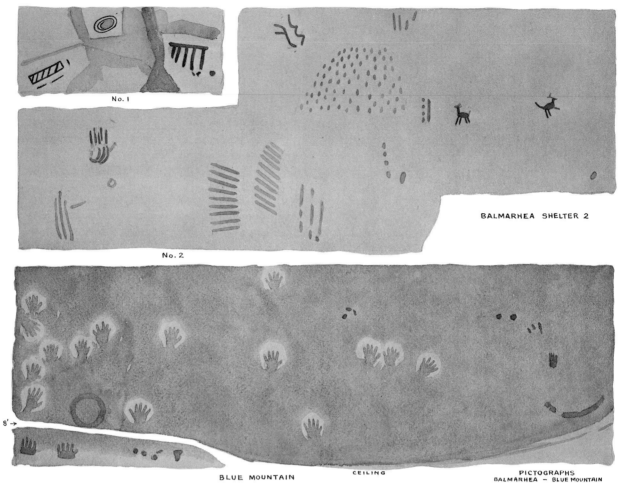

No. 1

No. 2

BALMARHEA SHELTER 2

8' →

BLUE MOUNTAIN

CEILING

PICTOGRAPHS
BALMARHEA — BLUE MOUNTAIN

Plate 96. Balmorhea, Shelter 2. Copied July 24, 1936. Scale: Nos. 1–2, 3/4″ to 1′. Balmorhea, Blue Mountain. Copied July 29, 1936. Scale: 3/8″ to 1″

with an open space between; a chain of nine connected circles suspended from one side and 11 from the other; and, in the lower center, a ladder containing 22 rungs. This may be a fertility symbol.

It might also be a picture of the road to the other world, or any of a number of other things, including a meaningless doodle. But some of the pictographs in this shelter are in such low, awkward places (Plate 95, No. 2, for example) that it seems unlikely that they were placed there as an idle pastime. It is unlikely that such intricate designs had no forerunners or counterparts. But until other related paintings are discovered these must remain enigmatic mysteries — undated, unrelated, and isolated.

Scattered along a bluff about one and one-half miles west across the valley are many small shelters with walls suitable for pictographs. But only one contains a few pictures, some of which are very dim. The rather simple red pictures (Plate 96, Nos. 1, 2) show no kinship to the ones across the valley. "The hand, printed from a design painted in the palm, is the second example of this technique I have observed" (Notes, Plate 96).

PLATE 96

Balmorhea, Shelter 2. These mostly red pictographs are in a small shelter in a bluff across the valley west from Balmorhea, Shelter 1.

Blue Mountain. These handprints, which have not been copied accurately, are in a small shelter in Blue Mountain, about forty miles west of Odessa.

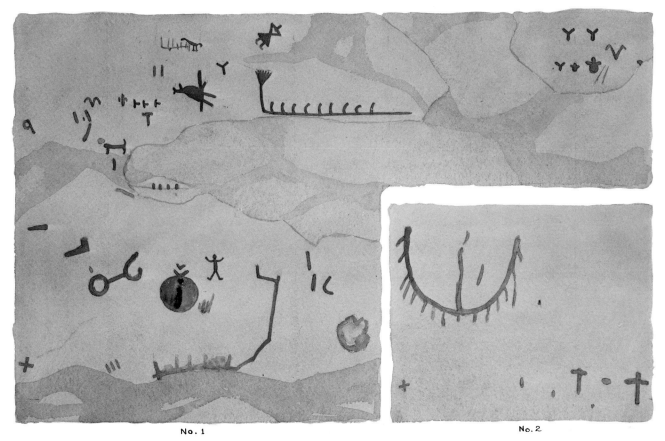

No. 1

No. 2

Plate 97. Blue Mountain. Copied July 29, 1936. Scale: Nos. 1–2, 3/8″ to 1′

PLATE 97

Blue Mountain. These pictographs are in a shelter next to the one whose handprints are reproduced in Plate 96. They are red except for a little black used in one circular design near the bottom of No. 1. In the rock above the shelter are more than one hundred mortars, most of which are of the oval type.

Blue Mountain

Just under the cap rock of Blue Mountain, about forty miles northwest of Odessa in eastern Winkler County, are two small shelters side by side. One has a smoked ceiling and a quantity of ashes and burned rock on the floor. Its

designs consist largely of very dim handprints which have not been copied at all accurately. Only their position is approximately correct. The chief interest in this shelter is in the way the handprints were made. The open hand was pressed against the soot-covered rock, while wet mud was daubed around it leaving a negative handprint when the hand was removed. Only a small part of the mud, however, clung to the rough surface of the rock, thus resulting in very poor prints. (Notes, Plate 96)

The other shelter also has a smoke-blackened ceiling, "but because water pours in from above with each rain, no refuse has accumulated on the floor." The rough limestone walls are spalling badly and "no doubt many of the original pictures have already fallen away and those remaining will also go soon" (Notes, Plate 97). The likelihood, then, is that the pictographs have no great age, and though Kirkland did not recognize any white man's influence, Jackson (1938:141-145) interpreted one design (Plate 97, No. 1, upper left) as a horse tethered to a fence, and noted the presence of "a white woman." He does not indicate which figure he means, but the one with the hourglass shape was probably meant. This manner of representing the human figure is common in the southwest and is not necessarily confined to the historic period.

R. Henderson Shuffler (1934) first reported this site, and took Jim Cook, a former Comanche captive, to it in hopes that he could throw some light on the meaning of the paintings. The former captive recognized the site as one the Comanches had visited, saying:

It was after the raids down in the white man's country, though, that the Comanches did most of their paintings. . . . The Indians took a soft red rock and burnt it until it was ready to crumble, then crushed it to a powder and mixed it with water to make a red pasty paint. Then, with a stick or twig feathered out on the end for a brush, they painted whatever came into their minds. The kids were always fooling around with the paint, practicing, and the older fellows did the same thing. When a warrior came back from a raid he always made a long harangue about what he had seen and done in the white man's country, and he would often draw a picture on the cliff to illustrate what he told. . . . The Comanches didn't go in for signs much, just as signs. They usually tried to paint the things they were thinking about in full. (Shuffler, 1934)

Cook also explained that the horse and fence indicated the surrounding country contained many horses which were easy to steal. The angular figure (Plate 97, No. 1, below and to right of hourglass figure) on which there are nine vertical bars, Cook interpreted as "a water hole sign." It was, he said, "nine days' travel" to a waterhole north of where Lamesa is now. Something is apparently wrong with this interpretation as Lamesa is less than one hundred miles away, scarcely more than a good days' ride for a Comanche in a hurry. Cook also interpreted the two circular elements joined in Kirkland's copy with a bar (Plate 97, No. 1, lower left) as a water sign. Some of the other remarks Cook made, such as the Comanche method of chipping flint, are probably false, so his statements cannot be taken at face value. The likelihood seems good, however, that these pictographs are of Comanche origin, though Cook's interpretation of them cannot be regarded as entirely reliable.

CHAPTER 7

CENTRAL TEXAS—THE EASTERN PERIPHERY

Thinly scattered throughout Central Texas are a number of places where native peoples painted and incised rock surfaces. Jackson (1938:239–299) listed fifty-seven such localities but he and his co-workers visited only twenty-seven of them. Kirkland copied the rock art at only twelve sites, seven of which had pictographs, but the ones he did copy appear to be representative of the region. The Paint Rock Site is one of the major pictograph localities of the state, and it is unique so far as Central Texas is concerned. If Kirkland had first seen pictographs at any other Central Texas site, it is hard to imagine that he would have been inspired to embark on a career of copying them.

Central Texas is set apart here as a separate rock art province because it is almost isolated geographically from other such areas and because its generally low-key and rudimentary art does not seem to be closely related to that of other regions. The Balcones Escarpment (see Map 5) serves as a boundary on the south and east beyond which there are only a few petroglyph and fewer pictograph sites (Jackson, 1938:2–3). North and northwest of the Clear Fork of the Brazos is a broad swath of country lacking rock art. The upper tributaries of the Colorado west of San Angelo are similarly barren. Only to the southwest of Central Texas is the occurrence of sites relatively continuous. Rock art sites are also more numerous in the southwestern part of Central Texas, particularly along the headwaters of the Nueces and Frio rivers quite close to the lower Pecos region. This occurrence suggests that the pictographs and petroglyphs of Central Texas are somehow related to those of the lower Pecos, perhaps in a peripheral and derivative way. But there are few similarities between the pictographs and petroglyphs of the two regions. Climatic factors affecting the preservation of pictographs and the lack of suitable rock surfaces in adjacent areas may also make the near isolation of Central Texas rock art and its connection with the lower Pecos region more apparent than real. Until more exhaustive studies can be made, it is probably best to regard the rock art of Central Texas as an indigenous de-

velopment or developments, possibly derived from the lower Pecos region, but never elaborated by the peoples who practiced it.

Central Texas has been occupied by men for many millennia and it is impossible to pinpoint precisely just which prehistoric people or peoples or which historic tribes painted and engraved the area's rocks. The earliest known occupation of the region was in late Pleistocene times, about twelve thousand years ago. A habitation site dating from this Paleo-Indian stage, the Kincaid Shelter in Uvalde County (Map 5), has been excavated by the Texas Memorial Museum and The University of Texas Field School in Archeology. This investigation revealed that the Paleo-American contemporaries of Pleistocene horses, bison, and mammoths paved the shelter's muddy floor with large, smooth stones. But there is no indication that these or any later occupants painted or otherwise ornamented its rock walls (Suhm *et al.*, 1954:101–102; Suhm, 1958:72–73). The Levi Shelter in the Pedernales River drainage system west of Austin (Blanco County, see Map 5) also served as a dwelling place of Paleo-Indian hunters as well as later peoples, but its rock surfaces are also barren of paintings and drawings (Alexander, 1963). Paleo-Indians left other scattered indications of their presence in Central Texas, but there is no evidence of any sort that they practiced the petrographic arts.

By about 5000 B.C. the Paleo-Indian cultures of Central Texas had disappeared and had been replaced by Archaic cultures. The mammoths, mastodons, giant bison, and other large game animals upon which these hunters depended had become extinct. If men were to continue to thrive in Central Texas, new sources of food, new adjustments to nature had to be made. In Central Texas the solution of the Archaic peoples was to broaden the range of items used for food. Hunting remained an important activity and perhaps game animals supplied the bulk of the food supply, but considerable usage was now made of wild plant foods—roots, seeds, fruits, tubers, and the like. So far as archeologists can tell, deer were the most important game

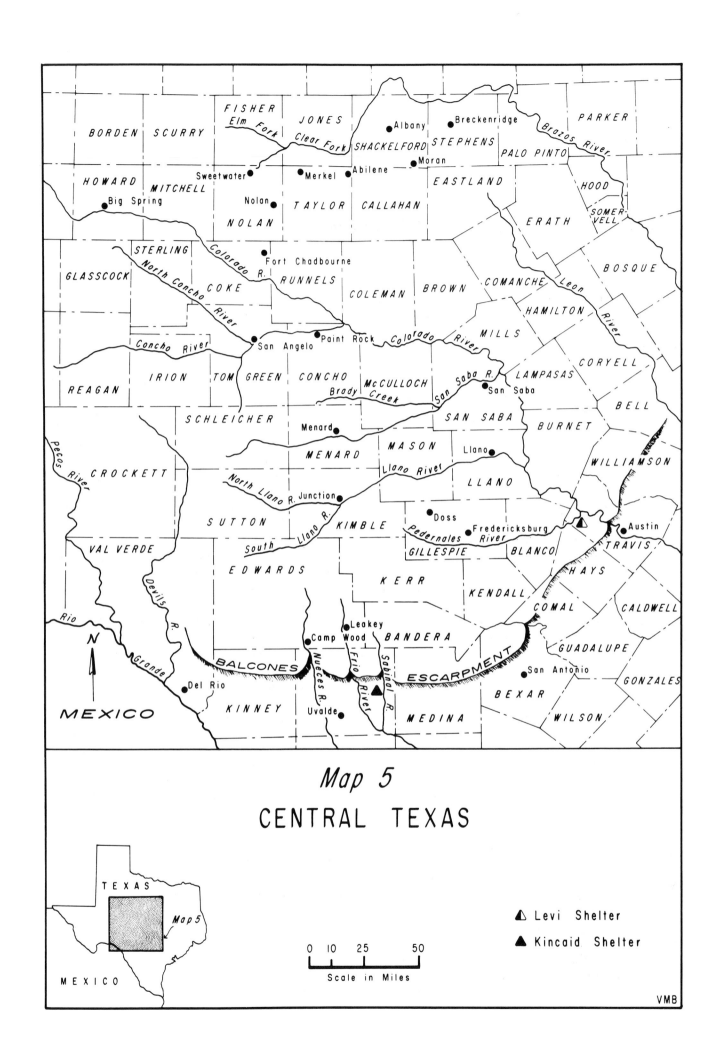

Map 5
CENTRAL TEXAS

▲ Levi Shelter
▲ Kincaid Shelter

0 10 25   50
Scale in Miles

TEXAS

Map 5

MEXICO

VMB

animals. Bison were hunted, but they appear not to have been plentiful, and many smaller animals were taken. Though much is unknown, perhaps unknowable, about the subsistence habits and general way of life of Archaic peoples, it is clear that this new cultural type was a successful one. The Archaic apparently lasted about as long as the Paleo-Indian tradition in Central Texas, but the population, if judged by the tremendous number of Archaic sites and the scarcity of Paleo-Indian sites, must have increased greatly. It may be argued that the earlier hunters had fewer tools and other objects to discard or lose, and that fewer of these remains have survived the vicissitudes of the longer span of years; nevertheless, a considerable growth in population seems certain.

The most conspicuous Archaic sites in Central Texas are burned-rock middens located along permanent watercourses. Composed of burned and fire-cracked hearthstones and much other camp refuse, middens may cover as much as an acre and attain a depth of six feet or more (Suhm, 1958:68). These large, accidental accumulations of refuse seem to have resulted from the returning again and again to favored campsites by many generations of people. Although population had increased, the hunting-and-gathering mode of existence must have severely limited and dispersed the population. It is probably best, in the present state of knowledge, to think of the Archaic population as being divided and subdivided into a large number of small, essentially independent units—bands or tribelets. Each of these probably occupied a fairly well-defined range of country and, like similar peoples of historic times, followed a fairly regular seasonal round, dependent upon the availability and harvest time of various wild foods.

Such Archaic cultures persisted in Central Texas until about A.D. 600 (Jelks, 1962), changing but little through the millennia. The Central Texas Archaic is now generally subdivided into three sequential stages, recognized by changes in types of projectile points. The Early Archaic was characterized by the use of straight-stemmed dart points (*Nolan, Travis, Bulverde*), which were succeeded in the Middle Archaic by a *Pedernales* point, a straight-stemmed form with a concave base. Finally, in the Late Archaic, dart points with expanding stems (*Ensor, Montell, Frio, Marcos*) replaced earlier types (Johnson, 1964:100-102.). The significance of such changes is not entirely clear; they may reflect alterations in the way dart points were hafted, or perhaps they were merely alterations for the sake of change; but they could also be indications of the movement or influence of other peoples, or reflect changes in hunting techniques or in the game hunted. The same general sequence of Archaic point types has been noted in the lower

Pecos region, but not until the Late Archaic are both areas characterized by essentially the same types of projectile points. If, then, the lower Pecos and Central Texas had essentially a common culture in Late Archaic times, it would seem to indicate that Pecos River style pictographs were not painted during this interlude, since there are only a few petroglyphs in Central Texas which could possibly be related to the mural art of the lower Pecos.

None of the pictographs or petroglyphs of Central Texas can be positively attributed to the Archaic. The only hint that the Archaic peoples may have ornamented rock surfaces there comes from the fact that burned-rock middens are often found near places where there is some form of rock art. While Archaic peoples were chiefly responsible for these middens, later peoples also camped on them, so mere propinquity does not prove association. And, since rock art sites are often found along streams where good rock surfaces are common, they are apt to be near burned-rock middens which are also located on or near streams. Hence, even indirectly there is no solid evidence of an Archaic age for Central Texas rock art. It is of course true that the more humid climate of Central Texas, in comparison to that of West and Southwest Texas, would shorten the span of existence of pictographs, so much so that Archaic pictographs may not have survived. There are, in fact, a number of places in Central Texas where a few blobs and patches of pigment on rock surfaces indicate the former existence of pictographs, but there is no way of determining their age. In sum, there is now no positive evidence which demonstrates that the Archaic population of Central Texas painted or incised rock surfaces. Undoubted cultural affiliations with the artists of the lower Pecos and nearness to that major pictographic area make the possibility attractive but purely speculative.

By about A.D. 600 (Jelks, 1962:98) the bow and arrow, as indicated by diminutive arrowpoints, appeared in Central Texas, marking the end of the Archaic and the beginning of the Neo-American phase of prehistory. The terminology may be somewhat misleading, however, for there seem to have been no basic changes or abrupt break in the way of life of the Central Texas Indians. The hunting-and-gathering subsistence pattern of Archaic times continued, in all probability carried on by descendants of the ancient population (Suhm *et al.*, 1954:112-117; Suhm, 1958:85; Jelks, 1962:91). The arrow propelled by the bow was more efficient than the dart launched from the old spear thrower (atlatl), but it seems not to have made a radical difference in the productivity of the hunter. The earliest Neo-American occupation in Central Texas (the Austin Focus) is characterized by the usage of *Scallorn* arrowpoints. Other flint implements—knives, scrapers, and the like—are, much like those of earlier times, reduced somewhat in size. By about A.D. 1000 (Jelks, 1962:98) the *Perdiz* arrowpoint type had become characteristic of what is now referred to as the Toyah Focus, and locally made pottery (*Leon Plain*) had also made its appearance.

Most of the petroglyphs and pictographs of the region seem to have been executed during the Neo-American phase of Central Texas prehistory (see Suhm, 1958:72-73). This opinion is based on the depiction of bows in some rock paintings, and little else. Unfortunately, many of the Central Texas pictographs are confined to geometric figures which reveal little about the nature or affiliations of those who painted them. It is also impossible to find stylistic similarities in Central Texas pictographic sites. Most paintings are in red, but the geometric designs and occasional human figures are so crude that more meaningful connections cannot be found. At most sites, as we shall see, the paintings show no sign of being part of any important or particularly significant tradition. In some cases the pictographs seem to be the by-products of something akin to play or what in our society would be described as doodling. In other pictographs, particularly where there are series of parallel lines, the paintings could well be tallies—perhaps messages referring to the numbers in a party that passed by, perhaps counts of animals seen or slain, or other things. Still other paintings seem quite clearly to recount events, either actual or mythical. In sum, as there is no common or shared style of rock painting in Central Texas, there seems to be no common motive for the paintings.

A number of the pictographs in Central Texas were painted by Indians in historic times, but determining the tribal groups responsible for them is almost as difficult as for those of the prehistoric era. At the opening of the historic period, bands of Tonkawa Indians occupied most of Central Texas. They appear to have spoken a Coahuiltecan language (Swanton, 1915, 1940), with others of the same tongue occupying southern Texas and much territory in northeastern Mexico. The autonomous Tonkawa bands lived by hunting deer, bison, and other animals, and utilized considerable wild-plant food; they seem not to have practiced any agriculture. They are but poorly known in the sixteenth and seventeenth centuries, and in later years have been described as a peripheral southern Plains tribe (Newcomb, 1961:Chapter 6). The Tonkawas seem to be the historic descendants of the indigenous occupants of Central Texas. True, no sites of the Toyah Focus contain historic artifacts that might link them to the Tonkawas, and no known Tonkawa sites have been excavated, but the Toyah Focus exactly fits what the archeological remains of the

Tonkawa would be like, and until some sort of concrete evidence to the contrary can be found, it would seem reasonable to assume this connection (see Jelks, 1962:99, for a contrary view).

By the mid-eighteenth century the Tonkawas were much decimated by disease and war, and seem to have offered little if any resistance to the Plains Apaches, primarily Lipans, who were then being forced into Central Texas by Comanches. The Apaches were much more numerous than the Tonkawas, were well equipped with horses, and well acquainted with the Spaniards and Spanish missions. The likelihood that some of the historic Central Texas pictographs were painted by Lipans or other Apaches is very great. The Lipans in turn were dispersed and much reduced in numbers by their European and Indian adversaries. Southern Comanche bands came to range throughout Central Texas from the second half of the eighteenth century until their ultimate expulsion by Texans in the following century. Comanches likely also added their pictographs to the assortment in Central Texas.

The Paint Rock Pictographs

The most outstanding pictograph site in Central Texas is along a limestone bluff on the north side of the Concho River, about a mile northwest of the town of Paint Rock in Concho County. The bluff rises about seventy feet above the valley floor some 150 to 200 yards from the river. Pictographs extend along the bluff for a little over a thousand feet and are easily accessible "on the broken edges of the rocks that form the back of the shelters or on the ends of rocks protected by overhanging ledges" (Notes, Plate 98; also see Sherfesee, 1963). A wide range of colors was employed by the artists: "purple-red, red, orange, yellow, black, and white. The reds are most likely oxides of iron, the orange and yellow are ochres, [also oxides of iron], the white is chalk, and the black, carbon. All of these materials are to be found in the vicinity of the cliff" (Notes, Plate 98). Geometric, animal, and human figures were painted singly and in groups, and the individ-

PLATE 98

The paintings copied at Paint Rock run from left to right along the cliff. Individual designs are shown only approximately as they appear on the cliff; oftentimes they were shifted one or two spaces to help even them out. The number of the design in this copy, therefore, does not necessarily indicate its order on the cliff. The face of the rock in each case was measured and sketched and the principal divisions of the designs were measured, but in general the work was done freehand and no claim of complete accuracy is made. In some cases space was taken out between figures on the same rock and no note made of it, but the relative size and position of each part of the design is reasonably well preserved.

The cliff at Paint Rock. See Plates 98-110.

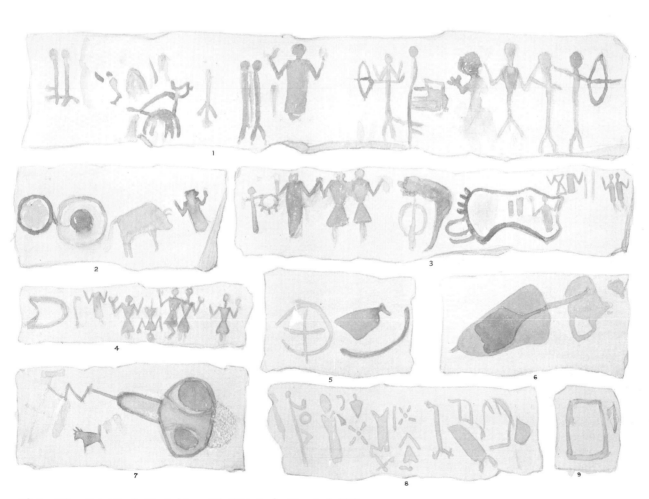

Plate 98. Paint Rock. Copied June 21, 1934. Scale: Nos. 1–8, 1/16

Paint Rock. See plates 98-110. Names and initials have been painted over many of the pictographs at this site.

ual figures are all quite small, most being less than a foot high. But the size of the limestone blocks rather than anything else appear to have dictated the dimensions of the paintings.

There are several distinct types of painting, some overpainting, and considerable variability in the amount of weathering the pictographs have undergone, all of which make it abundantly clear that they accumulated over a substantial period of time and were probably executed by artists of at least several different cultures. Kirkland (Notes, Plate 108) thought "the fact that red designs are painted over dim black designs in so many places would seem to indicate that the very oldest designs on the rocks were painted in black" (Plate 104, Nos. 6, 12; Plate 107, No. 3; Plate 108, No. 7). Some dim black figures are recent enough to be historic, however, as one such panel depicts horses and riders (Plate 100, No. 7), and the dimness of the black carbon paint cannot be taken as being indicative of relatively great age, because it has less permanency than the red paints derived from oxides of iron (Notes, Plate 108). There are also a few dim red designs over which are superimposed other figures (Plate 108, No. 8, left; possibly Plate 100, No. 3, lower right) and these apparently belong with the black paintings. These dim black and red paintings when taken together do not constitute a distinctive type of pictograph. They consist of "check lines" or "tally marks" (Plate 108, Nos. 7, 8), crude portrayals of animals (Plate 104, No. 12), and undecipherable figures (Plate 104, No. 6; Plate 107, No. 3). The chances seem good that these represent the first attempts at rupestrian art at this site.

PLATE 99

Colors for each design were mixed at the site of the original painting and care was taken to approximate that of the Indian artist. In most cases, especially the very dim designs, the color has been forced and the whole effect is stronger than it actually appears on the rocks. Buff was used for backgrounds since that is the general color of the cliff, and no attempt was made to show individual rock colors or imperfections. This evenness of background tends to make the designs stand out more clearly than the originals even when the color is not forced.

In 1935 every design was checked against the original and corrections made. These copies now vary from the originals in no essential way.

PLATE 100

No. 6. This beautiful design has been badly mutilated. The black leaf shapes very likely alternated originally with the red around the circles, but now they are dimly seen in only three places.

No. 7. [In the following note Kirkland freely criticizes his own work.] This strip is in such bad condition that it cannot definitely be made out and should not have been copied. Some of the figures are just as definite as shown but others may be the result of a good imagination. Imagination is the one thing the artist must fight when copying very dim pictographs and this is the outstanding example in this set of plates, where the artist has allowed it too free a hand.

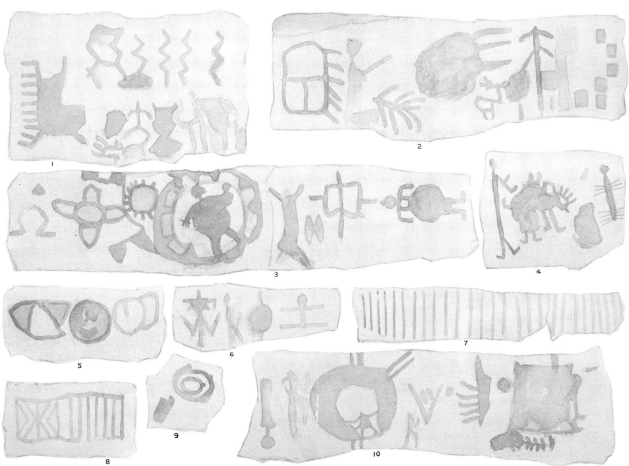

Plate 99. Paint Rock. Copied June 21, 1934. Scale: Nos. 1–10, 1/16

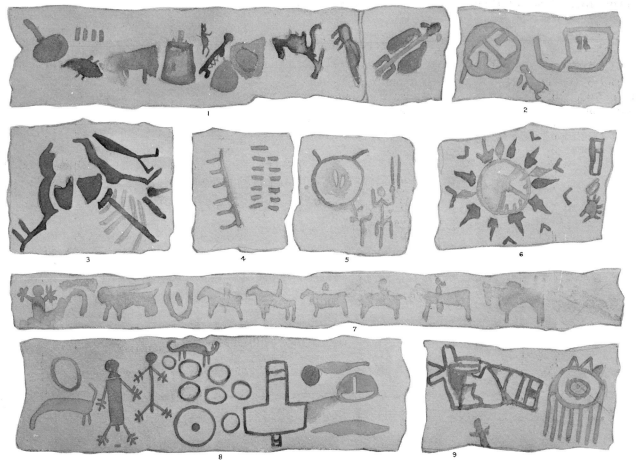

Plate 100. Paint Rock. Copied June 21, 1934. Scale: Nos. 1–9, 1/16

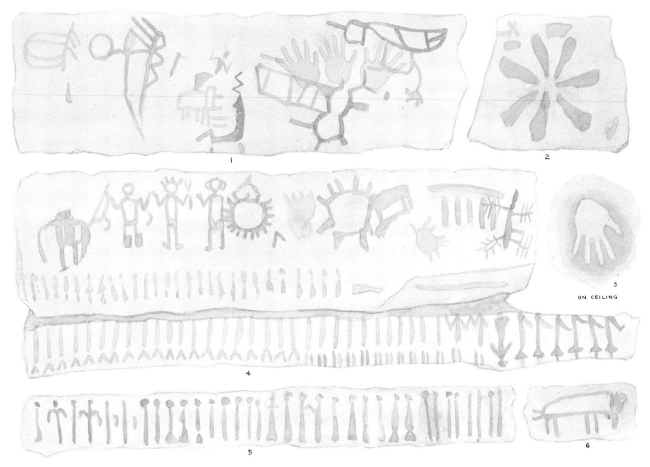

Plate 101. Paint Rock. Copied June 21, 1934. Scale: Nos. 1–6, 1/16

PLATE 101

This plate contains the two types of handprints found at Paint Rock. On No. 1, the commonest form, the hands were dipped in color and plastered on the rock while still wet. No. 3 was made by placing the hand against the rock and spraying color over and around it, thus leaving the handprint the natural color of the rock. Spatters can still be seen around the edge of the sprayed paint. Likely as not the liquid color was blown directly from the mouth.

No. 5. This design is immediately below and slightly to the right of No. 4 and seems to be a continuation of the design above. This may have been a tabulation of people.

PLATE 102

No. 4. The left part of this group is badly blurred in the center so that nothing definite can be made out. The reclining figure with bow and arrow is very clear and distinct, and appears to have been drawn with the sharp edge of a dry piece of color.

No. 5 and 6, along with Plate 101, No. 3, are the only designs at Paint Rock painted on the undersurface of the rocks.

PLATE 103

No. 6. This buffalo, like the turkey on Plate 102, No. 9, is high up on the rocks and can easily be seen from the road below the cliff. These pictographs are gradually being destroyed by bullets from the guns of hunters who choose them as targets.

Note the horses in Nos. 9, 11, and 12. The horse in No. 9 is drawn over another design which may be much older.

Plate 102. Paint Rock. Copied June 22, 1934. Scale: Nos. 1–9, 1/16

Plate 103. Paint Rock. Copied June 22, 1934. Scale: Nos. 1–12, 1/16

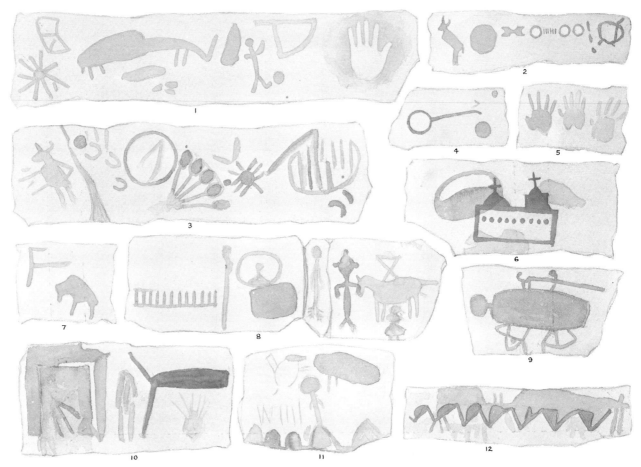

Plate 104. Paint Rock. Copied June 22, 1934. Scale: Nos. 1–12, 1/16

PLATE 104

No. 6. This picture of a church over an older design is still very bright and must be one of the last designs drawn on the cliff.

There are a number of other examples of over-painting, but they are not helpful in establishing a sequence of styles. In one case a rambling red design is superimposed over three faint orange-red handprints (Plate 101, No. 1); in another a black design is partly painted over a dim orange-red comb-like design (Plate 101, No. 4). A horse and rider in orange has been painted over a darker human figure and footprint, or track (Plate 103, No. 9), an anthropomorphic figure in black is superimposed over a horse (Plate 103, No. 12), and other examples may be found. It is also entirely possible that later artists "improved" upon earlier work (possibly Plate 109, No. 9), though this practice is impossible to verify.

The most distinctive drawings of humans at Paint Rock are in an angular red style characterized by arms sharply bent at the elbows and bi-triangular bodies, the apexes of the triangles meeting to form wasp-waisted figures (Plate 98, Nos. 1, 2, 3, 4). If the design on the back of a horse (Plate 104, No. 8, right) was intended to be or once was a human in this style, it would indicate that all these paintings are historic. A few wasp-waisted humans are depicted at Hueco Tanks (Plate 134, 14-B) but they are not similar to one another in other respects. Several other ways were used to depict the human figure at Paint Rock, and it is probably fair to assume that each was the work of different artists from different tribal or cultural groups. They range from exceptionally crude stick-figure humans with short straight legs, long bodies, straight arms, and round circles for heads (Plate 105, No. 3, for example) to outlined humans (Plate 101, No. 4, upper left) in which interest is focused on weapons and ornaments. There are also a number of distinctive human figures which cannot readily be grouped with others (Plate 99, No. 4, central figure; Plate 102, No. 4, prone figure; Plate 107, No. 14; Plate 109, No. 8, prone figure). Animals are often portrayed on isolated rocks and none of them seem characteristically to accompany the various kinds of human figures. Apart from easily identifiable horses and two birds (Plate 102, No. 9; Plate 110, No. 3), the paintings of quadrupeds are so crude that the species can seldom be positively identified, al-

Plate 105. Paint Rock. Copied June 22, 1934. Scale: Nos. 1–8, 1/16

though one is almost certainly a bison (Plate 103, No. 6) and another is probably a deer (Plate 102, No. 4). The bulk of the Paint Rock pictographs are geometric shapes which may or may not represent actual objects. In any case, they do not seem to fall into stylistic or temporal groups.

Who the first men were to paint on the boulders at Paint Rock is unknown. Several of the shelters in the irregular cliff face contained refuse and debris of people who were probably responsible for some of the paintings, and there are several burned-rock middens in the vicinity of the bluff (Jackson, 1938:267; Notes, Plate 98). But no controlled excavations have been conducted at these sites. The discovery of a *Leon Plain* potsherd in association with small pieces of hematite at the base of the bluff, however, is good evidence that pictographs were painted as early as Toyah Focus times, perhaps a thousand years ago.[1] Depictions of the bow and arrow are present in some pictographs (Plate 98, No. 1; Plate 101, No. 4; Plate 102, No. 4; Plate 105, No. 5), and also indicate a Neo-American or

[1] Fred R. Campbell, on February 16, 1964, sent the potsherd and hematite in question to the Texas Memorial Museum, where Curtis Tunnell confirmed their identity. Other *Leon Plain* sherds have been reported from Paint Rock.

PLATE 105

No. 5. The man and especially the animal in this group are very dim but distinct enough to be accurately copied.

No. 6. Note the stalk of corn with the fully developed ear in the center of this group.

later date for these particular paintings. There is virtually no evidence indicating that any of the pictographs date back to some earlier era. There are, it is true, some comb-like figures (Plate 100, No. 4; Plate 104, No. 8; Plate 106, No. 6; Plate 108, No. 8) vaguely similar to those found in the lower Pecos region, where they date from the Archaic. But even if they are intended to represent the same object or idea, there is no assurance that they are of the same age.

Only a few of the Paint Rock pictographs can be positively ascribed to the historic period, although the probabilities are high that others also date from the last few centuries. It is impossible to determine positively which tribe or tribes were responsible for the historic drawings. The paintings of a church or mission with two cross-bearing towers (Plate 104, No. 6) and the obvious devil (Plate 107, No. 9) suggest, however, that Lipan Apaches have the best

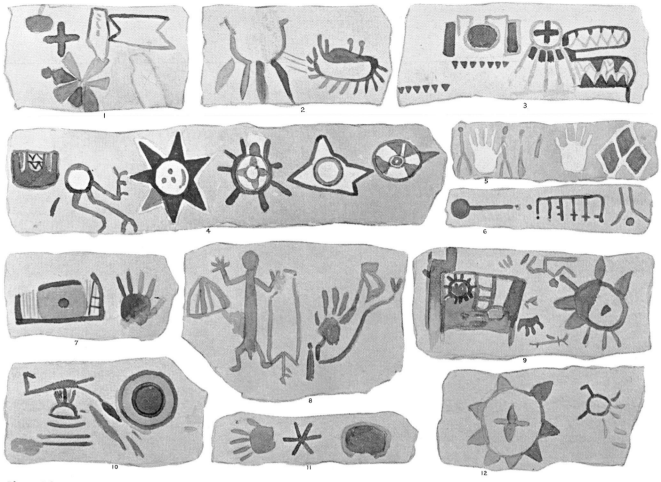

Plate 106. Paint Rock. Copied June 23, 1934. Scale: Nos. 1–12, 1/16

Plate 107. Paint Rock. Copied June 23, 1934. Scale: Nos. 1–14, 1/16

Plate 108. Paint Rock. Copied June 23, 1934. Scale: Nos. 1-9, 1/16

PLATE 106

White, sparingly used at Paint Rock, is limited almost entirely to two rocks under the same shelter. These are Nos. 4 and 5, where the white appears to have been put on first and other colors painted over it.

PLATE 107

No. 3. This rock is covered with many dim and uncertain designs. The very clear outline drawings of the inverted man and the conventionalized animal head were probably painted over much older drawings.

No. 13. This design was copied entirely for the handprints. All handprints definite enough to be clearly determined are included in these copies.

PLATE 108

No. 7. Note the very dim design on black over which the red design has been painted.

claim to their authorship. They were the only tribe in this part of Texas to come under heavy mission influence, and it is probable that a band of Lipans, led by a Chief Bigotes (Mustaches) camped at Paint Rock (Loma Pinta) in 1763 and perhaps in other years (Castañeda 1939: 189-190). The San Saba Mission was established in 1758 for the Lipans near the present Menard, only about forty miles south of Paint Rock. In the following year the Mission was destroyed by a combined force of Comanche, Wichita, and other Indians. The presidio, located a few miles away from the mission, was finally abandoned in 1768, the garrison retreating to the Mission of San Lorenzo de la Santa Cruz on the upper Nueces, at the present Camp Wood, some one hundred miles farther south. The Lipans were also familiar with the San Antonio missions and those along the Rio Grande, but their acquaintance with them was primarily as hostile raiders. It is entirely possible that a Comanche or other Indian, having no familiarity with Christianity might have been sufficiently impressed with the sight of a church or mission subsequently to paint a picture of it on a boulder. But it is highly improbable that such a person could create a visual image of a basic belief of that church — the devil.

Plate 109. Paint Rock. Copied June 23, 1934. Scale: Nos. 1–10, 1/16

This does not mean to say that all the historic pictographs must have been the work of Lipans. A fierce struggle took place, particularly in the latter half of the eighteenth century, between the Lipans and Comanches in this part of Texas. It is reasonable to suppose that the Comanche victors likely asserted their occupancy of Paint Rock by adding to, painting over, and possibly obliterating the paintings of former occupants. It is entirely possible too that any of the Indians who passed by Paint Rock in later years could have painted these pictographs—Shawnees, Delawares, Cherokees, and Kickapoos, to mention a few.

Painting and incising the rocks did not cease with the expulsion and extermination of the Indians, for many names and dates (the earliest being 1856) have been added to the older paintings, unfortunately often defacing them. Kirkland (Notes, Plate 98), much irritated by this thoughtless practice, remarked that

the greatest damage to the paintings has been done by curious sightseers, who have written, painted, or carved their names all over the cliff, a favorite place being across the face of the best pictographs. Fires at the base of the shelters have destroyed many of the lower designs, and bullets from rifles have worked havoc on many of the de-

PLATE 109

No. 3. This design is so dim and uncertain that it should not have been copied. [Again Kirkland criticizes himself.]

No. 9. This intricate design is at ground level and would certainly have been destroyed had it not been in an isolated place.

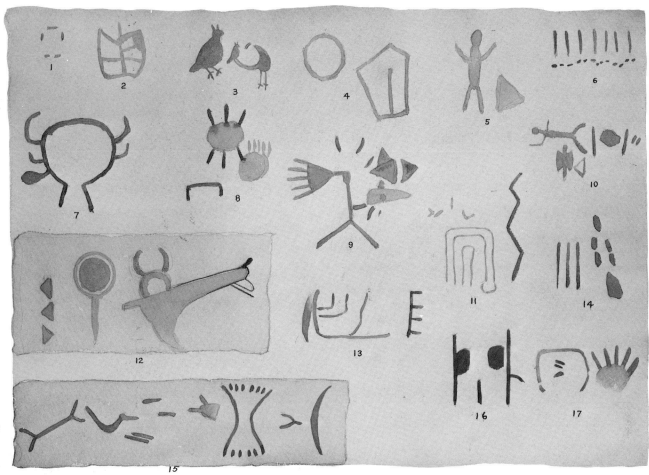

Plate 110. Paint Rock. Copied July 22, 1935. Scale: Nos. 1–17, 1/16

PLATE 110

This copy was made in 1935 and consists entirely of designs overlooked by the artist in 1934.

No. 3. This design was omitted in 1934 because it was thought to be recent [and not authentic Indian] work; but a careful study of the color indicated that it is genuine Indian work.

No. 7. This design was omitted for the same reason as was No. 3, but the color is certainly Indian color. The design must have been one of the very last to be painted on the cliff by Indians.

The designs on this plate are taken from all parts of the cliff. The following list will give their location: No. 1 follows No. 2, Plate 98; No. 2 follows No. 5, Plate 98; No. 3 follows No. 6, Plate 98; No. 4 follows No. 8, Plate 99; No. 5 follows No. 5, Plate 100; No. 6 follows No. 6, Plate 100; No. 7 follows No. 7, Plate 100; No. 8 follows No. 5, Plate 102; No. 9 follows No. 4, Plate 101; No. 10 follows No. 12, Plate 103; No. 11 follows No. 10, Plate 107; No. 12 follows No. 8, Plate 108; No. 13 follows No. 7, Plate 109; No. 14 follows No. 7, Plate 109; No. 15 follows No. 7, Plate 109; No. 16 follows No. 7, Plate 109; No. 17 follows No. 7, Plate 109.

signs high up on the cliff. Sixty-one single designs and forty-one complete groups have been destroyed beyond recognition—about one-fourth of the original pictographs at the location.

The most perplexing aspect of the Paint Rock pictographs has been why this particular bluff should be the site of such a concentrated and assorted group of paintings. There are many other cliffs and rock shelters in Central Texas situated in what appear to be equally advantageous locations. But they are completely barren of rock art. A reasonable explanation for this curious situation, however, can be summed up succinctly as imitation. The ancient Indian who, for whatever reason, first painted a figure on the limestone of Paint Rock bequeathed to generations of later occupants and visitors the idea that men could, and had, decorated its rocks. That other men should try their hand at ornamenting the same rocks and adjacent vacant surfaces is not surprising. The more paintings that accumulated, the stronger the stimulus for other people to add their quota. The presence of a considerable number of negative and positive handprints also fits this explanation, for the handprint of a nonliterate person is probably as personal a signature to him as a written name or initial is to a literate

The Lehmann Rock Shelter. See Plates 111-112.

one. It must be admitted, however, that many motives may lie behind the common practice of handprinting rock surfaces, from play to magic to all sorts of symbolism. As the Paint Rock pictographs served to stimulate fresh generations of Indians to painting, so too did they stimulate more recent Americans, for if there had been no Indian paintings at Paint Rock there surely would have been few names and dates scratched and painted on the bluff. But there are a great number there despite the efforts of recent landowners to discourage the practice.

This hypothesis implies that the Paint Rock pictographs had relatively little meaning to the artists, that they were casual creations with as little social and aesthetic significance as the names and dates carved and painted there in recent years. While such an explanation seems reasonable for a majority of the Paint Rock pictographs, some of them probably had a deeper meaning. As Kirkland noted, series of parallel lines present on several rocks could well be tallies of some sort, perhaps enumerating the members of a group that passed that way. The hand-holding figures (Plate 98; Plate 101, No. 4) may be dancers, perhaps engaged in some ceremonial activity. This conjecture in turn raises the possibility that Paint Rock may have been used by some Indian groups for ceremonial activities, and that it could have been regarded as a special, perhaps sacred place. Some of the paintings may also be commemorative in the sense that they illustrated events which were still fresh in the artist's mind.

Lehmann Rock Shelter

On a small tributary of the Llano River, about twenty miles northwest of Fredericksburg and a few miles north of the small town of Doss, is a large shelter which contains some unusual pictographs (Plates 111, 112). Kirkland described the shelter as

a huge crevice weathered into a seventy-five foot sandstone bluff, on the north bank of the creek. It measures about seventy-five yards long and has a twenty-five yard overhang at its deepest place. The level floor is filled with a deep deposit of ashes and refuse from Indian camp fires. The back of the shelter is almost perpendicular, reasonably smooth, and from six to twelve feet high. At one time the back wall contained many pictographs, but unfortunately a white lichen has spread over the back of the shelter, completely covering many and doing great damage to all but a very few of these pictographs. A misfortune just as great has befallen most of the designs that have escaped the ravages of the lichen. Someone, through ignorance or disregard, has recently painted over the best of them with some kind of oil, evidently in an effort to get photographs. This oil has since spread over the rock and collected dust and dirt from the floor of the shelter until only a dirty yellow spot remains. The Indian color can only be seen now after the design has been soaked with water. In a few more years this, with the ever-spreading lichens, will completely efface this interesting group of pictographs. (Notes, Plate 111)

Kirkland termed the shelter Lange's Mill, for the old mill located a mile or so upstream, but it is better known as the Lehmann Rock Shelter, after the landowner who permitted A. M. Woolsey of the Department of Anthropology, The University of Texas, to excavate there in January, 1936. The excavations revealed that the shelter was occupied

No. 1

No. 3

No. 2

Plate 111. Lehmann Rock Shelter. Copied July 5, 1936. Scale: Nos. 1-3, ¼″ to 1′

PLATE 111

Lehmann Rock Shelter. The principal color used at this site was red ocher, although two designs and a few lines were made with black, and four human figures and one design on the ceiling were painted with some form of white. The sections copied from the wall are numbered on Plates 111 and 112 as they appear from left to right. Human figures, animals, and geometrical designs were carefully measured, drawn to scale, and placed in their exact relation to each other. The many simple marks and dashes (Plate 111, Nos. 1 and 2) were not measured individually and are only approximately accurate in number and proportion.

No. 2. If the animal at the bottom of this group is a horse, these paintings are historic. But since it has no rider, it would seem better to class it a nondescript.

No. 3. The crooked line in this group had been traced in oil much farther along the wall and originally must have reached a length of twenty feet or more, but only the eight feet copied contained enough original color to show its exact shape.

over a long span of time, from Archaic to late prehistoric times (Kelley, 1947), but there appears to be no way of determining which, if any, of its occupants painted its walls.

The Lehmann Rock Shelter is the only one in Central Texas in which some of the pictographs quite clearly record a narrative of some sort (Plate 112, No. 6). Some highly imaginative interpretations have been made (Estill, 1925), but as Jackson (1938:255) has pointed out, "There is no way of knowing what that story may have been." Nevertheless, he conjectures *(ibid.)* that

The story possibly pertains to adventures that befell a hunting or a war party. Some 15 feet of zigzag line, generally taken to represent skyline or distance traveled, marks the beginning of the record. A projectile, enclosed on one side by a double row of dots and on the other by a single row of numeration marks (a total of 109), may have referred to a number of animals or enemies encountered.

Near the center of the group is a reclining human figure, located on the line or trail being traveled. Immediately beneath are seven human forms. The situation may symbolize a night attack of the enemy, made while the party slept. A disc a short distance above the line might be interpreted as recording the fact that the party fled and was a considerable distance away when the sun came

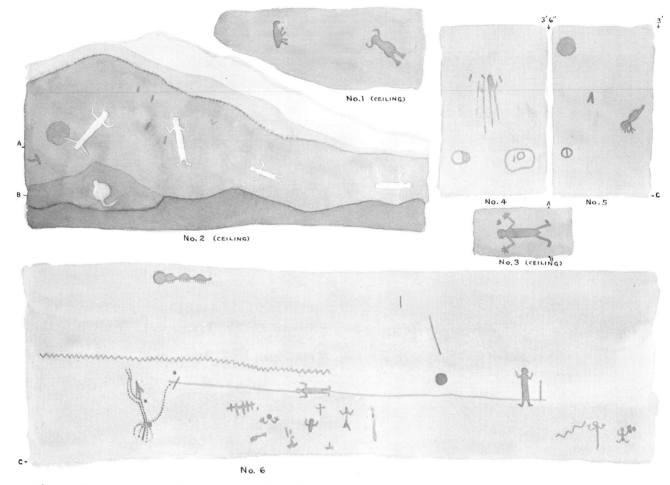

No.1 (CEILING)

No.2 (CEILING)

No.4   No.5

No.3 (CEILING)

No. 6

Plate 112. Lehmann Rock Shelter. Copied July 5, 1936. Scale: Nos. 1-6, ¼″ to 1′

up next morning. At night, suggested by a star, the party was out of danger and changed the course (as shown by the line) to return by a devious route to their camp.

Kirkland noted that one of the animals (Plate 111, No. 2, lower middle) might be intended to portray a horse, but added that "since there is no rider it would seem better to class it as nondescript." None of the other figures on the walls of the Lehmann Rock Shelter indicate a historic date, so they are generally assigned to the prehistoric era.

Frio Canyon

At the head of Frio Canyon, fourteen miles north of Leakey, are some large springs protected by a rugged bluff. A long shallow shelter under the bluff was evidently used by Indians although no cultural debris remains on the floor. "A few pictographs in black are still dimly visible on the back of the shelter. Only two marks and three crosses are in red. A few other pictures may have once been on the cliff, but now are only dim black splotches of color" (Notes, Plate 15). The figure in an overcoat or frock coat with a high hat and gun (Plate 15, No. 4) has become known as the "fighting parson" (Jackson,

PLATE 112

Nos. 1, 2, and 3. These designs are painted on the ceiling about six feet above the present floor level. The white designs are quite clear but the red can only be seen with favorable reflected light. No. 3 rightly is a part of No. 2 at *A-B*, but became visible only in the late afternoon light, after No. 2 had been copied.

No. 6. The parts of this design seem to hold some relation to each other. Perhaps it is one of the few pictographs that actually record a narrative.

Paint Rock Springs. See Plates 113, 114. Kirkland shown copying petroglyph of Plate 113, No. 2.

1938:247). Kirkland remarked that "it is said to be the picture of a priest who was killed by the Indians, and whose grave can still be seen a few hundred yards below the spring." No verification of this tale has been found. The red crosses (Plate 15, No. 3) also seem to be the work of historic Indians, and since the other figures are executed with black paint indistinguishable from that used for the "fighting parson" it seems likely that all the paintings are of historic vintage.

Paint Rock Springs and Fort Sterrett

About eighteen miles southwest of Junction (Map 5) a rocky bluff on the southeast side of the South Llano River bears traces of pictographs and has a number of petroglyphs carved into the boulders at its foot (Plates 113, 114). Two small canyons empty into the river at this point; there is a good spring at the mouth of one of them and a deep hole of permanent water is near one of the two small shelters which lie at the base of the cliff. Because high water periodically scours out the shelters, they contain no cultural remains other than petroglyphs and about two dozen shallow mortar holes in the bedrock. Upriver from the shelters on the hillsides are many burned-rock middens. There were at one time

a good many pictographs in the shelter above the waterhole, but almost every design has flaked off. At present [1937] only three or four bits of paint remain, and only one design can be clearly made out [Plate 113, No. 3]. It is a sun emblem in orange. Three check lines are in red. (Notes, Plate 114)

A number of designs have been scratched on the large rocks which have tumbled from the bluff and lie at its base. Though wind and water have not been able to obliterate them, recent visitors have scratched over old designs and painted over some in black paint (Jackson, 1938:251–254) so that it is extremely difficult to distinguish ancient figures from more recent ones. In addition "the nature of the Indian's work made accuracy [in copying them] very difficult. The lines are merely scratches in most places, as if they had been made with one stroke of a sharp flint. The designs, in general, are very sketchy, and consequently no attempt was made to duplicate each line exactly" (Notes, Plate 114).

In a cave high in a bluff overlooking the North Llano River, about one-half mile above the ruins of old Fort Sterrett, Sutton County, are a few pictographs and petroglyphs (Plate 123, Nos. 2, 3).

The cave is smoked black and contains some ashes and other refuse, and in the bedrock along the river in front of the cave are about twenty-five round mortars. The pictures are of two kinds: a few marks, dots, and simple designs in red paint, and scratches on the black smoked ceiling. The scratches appear white on black and were made with a fine pointed tool. They do not appear to be merely abrading marks. (Notes, Plate 123)

They have no particular similarity to those on the South Llano, and are chiefly of interest because they combine painting and incising.

Nolan, Coke, and Taylor County Petroglyphs

Unlike many regions in western United States, pictographs are apparently more common in Texas than are petroglyphs. But north of San Angelo and

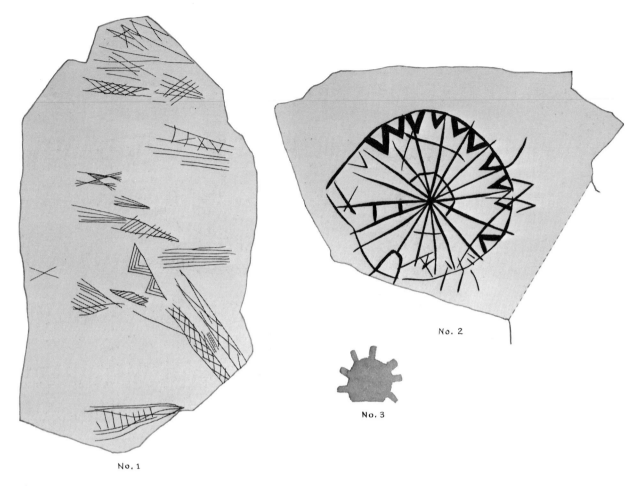

No. 1

No. 2

No. 3

Plate 113. Paint Rock Springs. Copied July 4, 1937. Scale: Nos. 1–3, 1/8″ to 1″

Plate 114. Paint Rock Springs. Copied July 4, 1937. Scale: 1/8″ to 1″

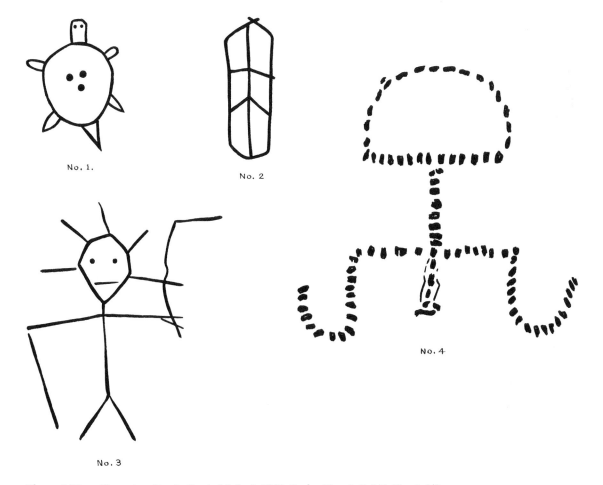

No. 1.

No. 2

No. 4

No. 3

Plate 115. Champion Creek. Copied July 6, 1935. Scale: Nos. 1–3, 1/4; No. 4, 1/6

PLATE 113

Paint Rock Springs. No. 1. These petroglyphs closely resemble those of Plate 114, but no recognizable animals or humans could be made out.

No. 2. This petroglyph is on a large rock near the water's edge at the base of the cliff on which the pictographs were painted. The grooves are much deeper than on other petroglyphs at the site, the deepest being over one-quarter of an inch. There were indications that white men had added depth to the grooves by retracing them with pocket knives, but undoubtedly the design was originally Indian.

No. 3. This is the only pictograph remaining of the original group at this site, with the exception of three very dim check lines in red. This design is orange.

PLATE 114

These petroglyphs are lightly scratched into the large rocks of hard chalk which have fallen from the cliff at Paint Rock Springs and are piled along its base. Most of them are still quite clear but are difficult to separate from the names, dates, and drawings of the white man.

PLATE 115

These Champion Creek petroglyphs were carefully copied to actual size in pencil at the site, later reduced and traced with ink. The placement on this plate does not represent their relative positions on the rocks; although Nos. 1, 2, and 3 are on the same rock, they are from three to six feet apart.

Nos. 1, 2, and 3 are scraped into the flat rock, level with the ground, only a few yards south of the road on the east bank of the creek. The grooves are about one-sixteenth-inch deep. The dots appear to have been made with a drill.

No. 4. This petroglyph is on a rock level with the ground and was found about one mile south of the other petroglyphs. The design was made by chiseling rough holes slightly more than one-sixteenth-inch deep into the rock.

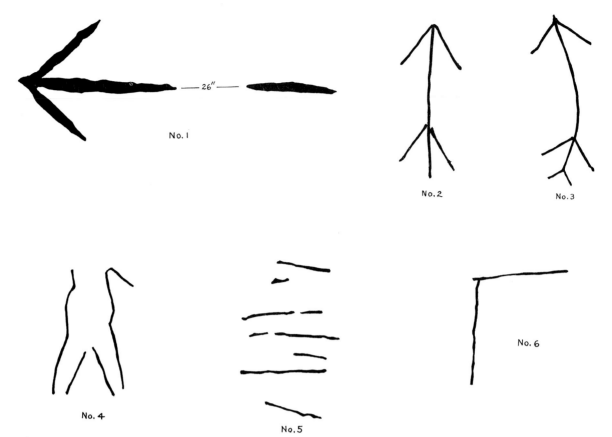

Plate 116. Champion Creek. Copied October 27, 1940. Scale: Nos. 1–6, 1/4

west of Abilene in Nolan and Coke counties are a number of sites where petroglyphs predominate and only a few pictographs are to be found. On the bank of Champion Creek, about eleven miles southwest of Roscoe in Nolan County, for example, a number of figures have been ground and pecked into the sandstone outcrop of the valley floor. There are also dozens of deep, round and oval mortar holes scattered along the creek for more than a mile. One anthropomorphic figure (Plate 115, No. 3) seems to be holding a spear thrower with a dart in place, but it is so crudely done that this interpretation cannot be regarded as positive. If it is a spear thrower, this petroglyph probably has considerable antiquity. Another petroglyph appears to represent a turtle (Plate 115, No. 1), several seem to be arrows or darts (Plate 116, Nos. 1, 2, 3), and one is a partially completed human figure (Plate 116, No. 4). The balanced design (Plate 115, No. 4) is undeciphered, as are a rectangular design (Plate 115, No. 2) and several lines (Plate 116, Nos. 5, 6).

In the eastern part of the county, about five miles east of the town of Nolan, a small rock shelter under a limestone bluff overlooking a creek contains a few small petroglyphs and seven negative red-orange handprints, only one of which Kirkland copied (Plate 117, No. 2). Most of the petroglyphs

PLATE 116

Champion Creek Petroglyphs. These designs are scattered over the rock and were overlooked earlier when other designs here (Plate 115) were copied. Nos. 1, 2, and 3 are on rocks near Plate 115, Nos. 1, 2, and 3. Nos. 4, 5, and 3, rubbed into a rock two hundred yards east, are all very dim.

were incised on a rock above the end of the shelter, which was easily reached from the floor; the handprints were scattered at random over the back wall of the shelter. Unfortunately, the petroglyphs and pictographs "were all in a very bad state of preservation. Hundreds of names and designs had been carved over them by vandals in recent years. It was necessary to consult a photograph taken ten years before to positively make out the Indian designs" (Notes, Plate 117). Intriguing and possibly of great significance is the similarity between all three of the anthropomorphic figures in this shelter and anthropomorphic creatures of the Pecos River style. If these petroglyphs had been found in the lower Pecos region there would be little hesitation in associating them with the Pecos River style paintings. The angular shape of the petroglyphs, the fringed object in the hand of one (Plate 117, No. 1), the crossed darts penetrating this figure, and

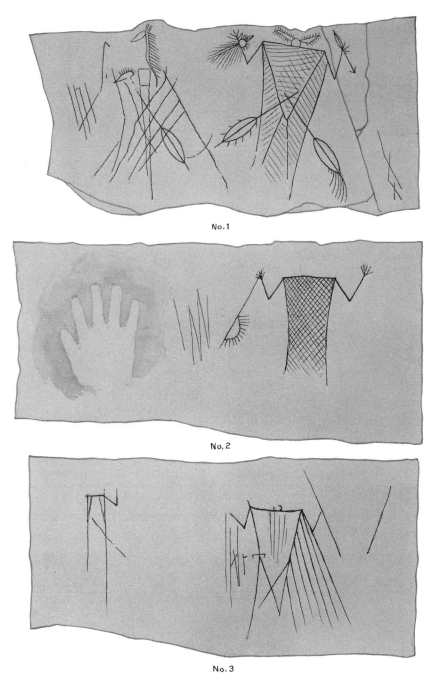

No. 1

No. 2

No. 3

Plate 117. Brownfield Ranch. Copied July 3, 1939. Scale: Nos. 1–3, 3/16″ to 1″

PLATE 117

Brownfield Ranch Petroglyphs. These small petroglyphs were scratched into the rather soft limestone of this cliff. Most of the designs were on a rock above the end of the shelter, easily reached from the floor. Seven negative handprints in red-orange were also scattered over the shelter's back wall. Only one (No. 2, left) was copied.

Rock shelter near Fort Chadbourne. See Plate 118.

its headdress are all found in Pecos River style pictographs. The dart on the left of this figure, apparently penetrating a fringed oval object, is also common in Pecos River style paintings. What might be interpreted as an atlatl with attached atlatl weight (Plate 117, No. 2) and the fringed attire of the other figure (Plate 117, No. 3) are also strongly reminiscent of the Pecos River style. On the other hand, these petroglyphs are two hundred miles northeast of the lower Pecos River and there are no known intervening sites containing Pecos River style pictographs or petroglyphs. The sharply bent stick-figure arms of the petroglyphs have no parallel in the lower Pecos, and of course, there are no petroglyphs of Pecos River style in the Pecos River country. Handprints are not part of the Pecos River tradition either, but there is no way of knowing whether the negative handprints in the Nolan County shelter were placed there by the people who inscribed the petroglyphs.

While Kirkland was copying the petroglyphs in this small shelter the partial skeleton of a child was discovered. Also found with the burial, between the shelter's back wall and a large boulder, were a flint knife, seven straws cut at each end and measuring from four to six inches long, and a coiled basket from whose edge a semicircular piece had been cut (Notes, Plate 117; Ray, 1939:244–249). Cyrus N. Ray subsequently sank some test pits in the shelter's floor and found

three different strata of ashes, each of which is separated by a sterile layer. The top layer is separated by a sterile layer which is only a few inches deep, but the sterile stratum between the second and third layers of ash is broad. One of the deeper layers of ashes extends under

the huge fallen rock below the hand pictographs and petroglyph. (Ray, 1939:246)

The age and interrelationships of the cultural material found in these various layers is not clear, and none of it must necessarily be associated with the petroglyphs or handprints. The diagonal cross-hatching employed in two of the Nolan County petroglyphs (Plate 117, Nos. 1, 2) is similar to that used in the figures at Paint Rock Springs (Plate 114) on the Llano River. In general, however, the Paint Rock Springs petroglyphs are cruder or at least more hastily done, and are less like Pecos River style pictographs, though this site is much nearer to the lower Pecos region. In sum, a good case can be made for some sort of connection between the Nolan County petroglyphs and Pecos River style pictographs, but to draw any hard and fast conclusions from such skimpy evidence is unwarranted.

Very different petroglyphs are found in some shallow shelters and on a few boulders below the south rim of a small mesa about two miles west of old Fort Chadbourne in Coke County (Plates 118, 119). Most of the petroglyphs were carved into the back walls of the sandstone shelters three to five feet above the floor, but they are exposed to blowing sand and rain from the south and are being obliterated. Though the shelters do not appear to have been inhabited, midden debris is scattered over the top of the mesa and extends all around it, so undoubtedly it was a favored campsite. According to Kirkland (Notes, Plate 118):

Rocks have been blasted from the cliff near the petroglyphs, presumably in search of treasure; but no noticeable damage was done to the designs. There is said to be

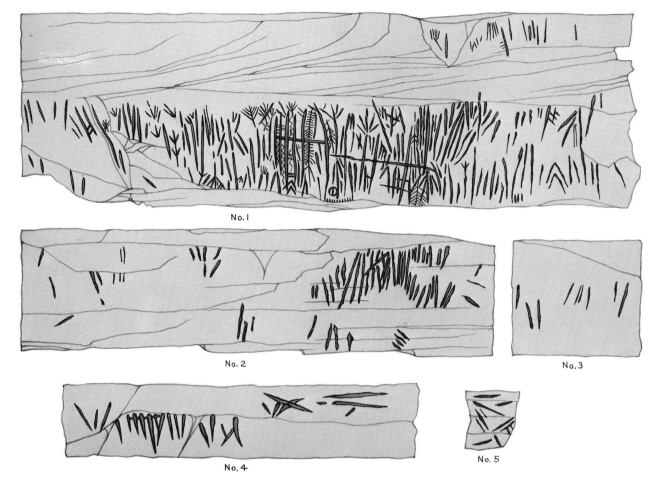

No. 1

No. 2

No. 3

No. 4

No. 5

Plate 118. Fort Chadbourne. Copied April 6, 1941. Scale: Nos. 1–5, 1/2″ to 1′

a legend about a lost mine in the district marked by two lizards. The two crude human figures on [Plate 119, No. 2] on the ceiling of the largest shelter were mistaken by the amateur prospectors for the two lizards, which accounts for the blasting which was done ten feet from the pictures.

Kirkland recognized two kinds of petroglyphs in these shelters: older and more numerous ones which he called the "Fort Chadbourne Type," and a few he thought were historic. The older type consisted

of many almost straight, more or less parallel grooves, perpendicular to the floor. These grooves are ornamented with connecting straight or zigzag lines which distinguish the petroglyphs from so-called abrading marks. The width of the grooves varies from one-fourth to one inch wide; the depth reaches one inch in a few cases. Most of the grooves have round, smooth bottoms as if they had been rubbed into the rock with some round pointed object. (Notes, Plate 118)

The other type, confined to the ceiling of the deepest shelter (Plate 119, Nos. 1, 2) were "only lightly scratched into the rock and appear little older than recent names on the rock near them, but they are definitely the work of Indians, probably historic nomads" (*ibid.*). Nearby Fort Chadbourne, estab-

PLATE 118

Fort Chadbourne Petroglyphs. These petroglyphs, except those in Nos. 4 and 5, were carved into the back walls of shallow shelters along the south rim of a small mesa west of Fort Chadbourne. Nos. 4 and 5 are located on the back wall of a small shelter near the top of the north side of Blowout Mountain in Taylor County.

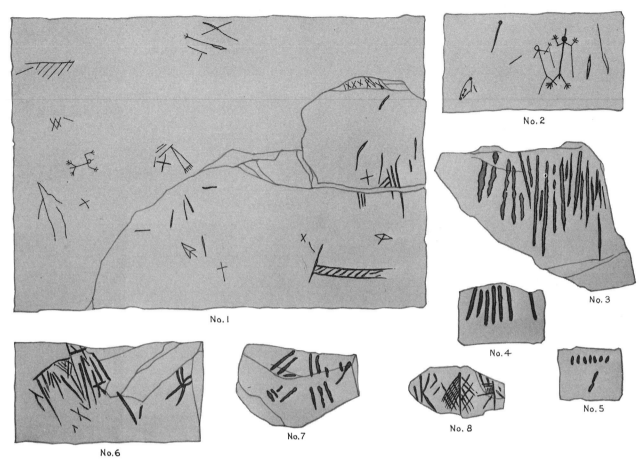

Plate 119. Fort Chadbourne. Copied April 6, 1941. Scale: Nos. 1–8, 1/2″ to 1′

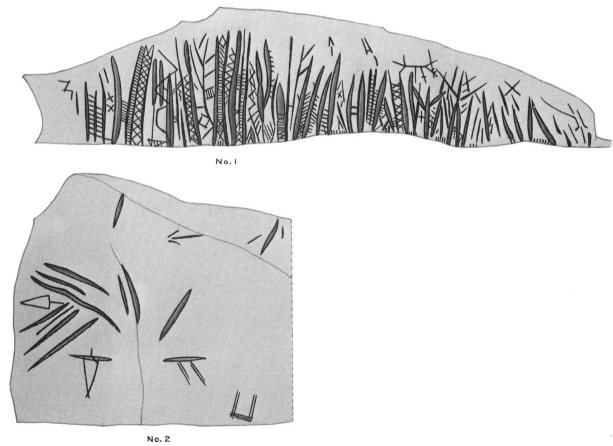

Plate 120. Fort Chadbourne. Copied July 25, 1941. Scale: Nos. 1–2, 1/16″ to 1″

Petroglyphs and graffiti near Breckenridge. See Plate 121.

PLATE 119

Fort Chadbourne Petroglyphs. Nos. 1 and 2. These designs are on the ceiling of the deepest shelter. The square at the end of No. 1, marked by an arrow, had fallen from the ceiling and was lying on the shelter floor. No. 3 is to the right of No. 1 in an exposed position and is very badly weathered. No. 5 is on the cliff nearby.

No. 6 is on the side of a large boulder at the base of the cliff. No. 7 is on a loose rock a few feet away. No. 4 is on top of another boulder at the base of the mountain.

No. 8, which had been chopped from a fallen rock half-way down the talus, was copied in Abilene at the home of Dr. Cyrus N. Ray, where it had been taken for exhibition purposes.

PLATE 120

Fort Chadbourne Shelter, on Oak Creek, Coke County, near Fort Chadbourne.

lished as one of a chain of frontier posts in 1852 and abandoned fifteen years later, attracted many Indians and any of them might have been responsible for these petroglyphs.

E. B. Sayles and Carl Chelf (Sayles, 1930) excavated a small rock shelter on Oak Creek, also in Coke County near Fort Chadbourne, where there were other "Fort Chadbourne type" petroglyphs. Plate 120, No. 1, which Kirkland copied at this site,

is a particularly good example of how the round-bottomed perpendicular grooves are joined by narrower, horizontal, diagonal, and zigzag lines. The excavations turned up no definitive artifacts, but the discovery of three separate hearth levels plus part of a glass bottle suggested that the shelter could have been occupied over a long span of time. Petroglyphs of the same type (Plate 118, Nos. 4, 5) were found by Kirkland "on the back wall of a small shelter near the top of the north side of Blowout Mountain in Taylor County, about six miles south of Merkel. They are well protected from the weather but appear to be badly weathered" (Notes, Plate 118). The significance of these highly distinctive "Fort Chadbourne type" petroglyphs is unknown, as is their distribution.

Other Central Texas Sites

South of the Clear Fork of the Brazos in Shackleford and Stephens counties are several rock art sites. The pictographs at each of them are crude, and few if any similarities can be found which would connect them with rock paintings in other parts of Texas. They are geographically peripheral so far as Central Texas is concerned, and their crudity also suggests that they are in a fringe area of rock painting. A few miles southeast of Breckenridge, Stephens County, is a sandstone cliff overlooking a level valley to the east. In the eroded cliff are a series of shallow shelters and overhangs which were occasionally utilized by men, as indicated by the cultural debris and pictographs Kirkland found in them (Plate 121). Unfortunately, no archeological

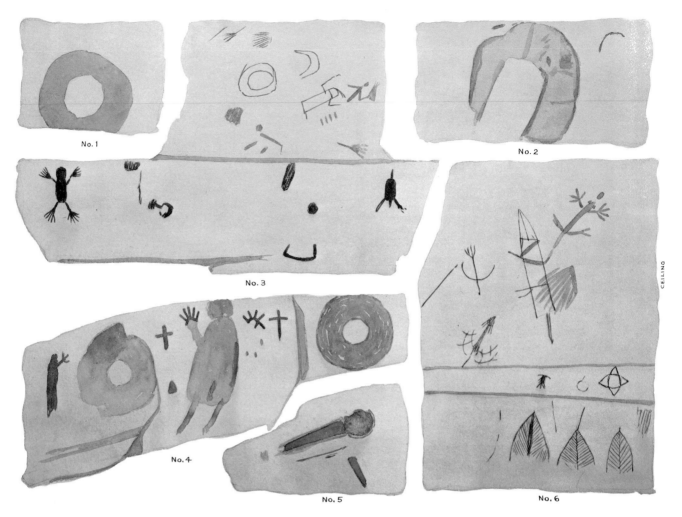

CEILING

No. 1

No. 2

No. 3

No. 4

No. 5

No. 6

Plate 121. Breckenridge. Copied October 28, 1938. Scale: Nos. 1–6, 1/2″ to 1′

investigations have been made there, so who the occupants were is unknown. According to Kirkland:

Two or three sections of the rock under the overhang are almost covered with abrading marks. These vary from light to half-inch deep scratches. No petroglyphs could be positively identified, the nearest being turkey track-like designs resulting from three or more grooves radiating from the same point. Pictographs had been painted on the back walls and ceilings of three of the shelters. They were very dim and in some instances, badly confused by recent names and designs painted over them. More than the usual amount of vandalism was found at the site due no doubt to the nearby oil field. An active well is within a quarter of a mile. Several of the designs were too dim to be copied. One or two others could not definitely be identified as Indian and were not included in the copies. The use of a dull blue [No. 5] on one design was the most unusual thing at the site. The blue appeared to have resulted from a mixture of white ashes and soot. This color is the most definite blue we have yet found in Texas. (Notes, Plate 121)

About twenty miles southwest of this site, northeast of Moran, Kirkland found another small shelter near the top of a bluff overlooking a small creek, which contained pictographs (Plate 122, No. 1). There was no cultural debris in the shelter, but

PLATE 121

Breckenridge. These predominantly red pictographs are on the walls and ceilings of three shallow shelters. The lower figures in No. 3 are in black. No. 5 is red and blue.

PLATE 122

Moran Shelter and Brady Creek. All of these pictographs are executed in an orange-red hue.

signs of an Indian camp were noticed along the nearby creek.

All of the pictures in orange-red are on the back wall of the shelter. They were evidently painted with thick wet paint which ran badly so that the bottom portions of the pictures are not very distinct. The shelter does not protect the pictures very well. Seep water has run down over most of the designs, and a deposit of lime has dimmed or covered a few of them. (Notes, Plate 122)

Ray (1942:155–156), who studied these pictographs a decade after Kirkland, believed "it must have required a very long period of time to form the stalagmitic deposit" over the paintings.

Brady Creek. Kirkland shown copying rock paintings in this small shelter. See Plate 122.

No. 1   MORAN SHELTER

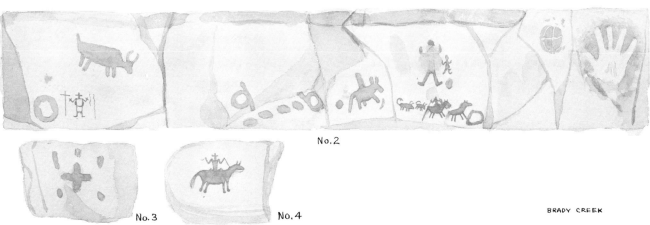

No. 2

No. 3   No. 4   BRADY CREEK

Plate 122.   Moran Shelter. Copied July 5, 1939. Scale: No. 1, 3/4″ to 1′. Brady Creek. Copied July 6, 1939. Scale: Nos. 2–4, 1″ to 1′

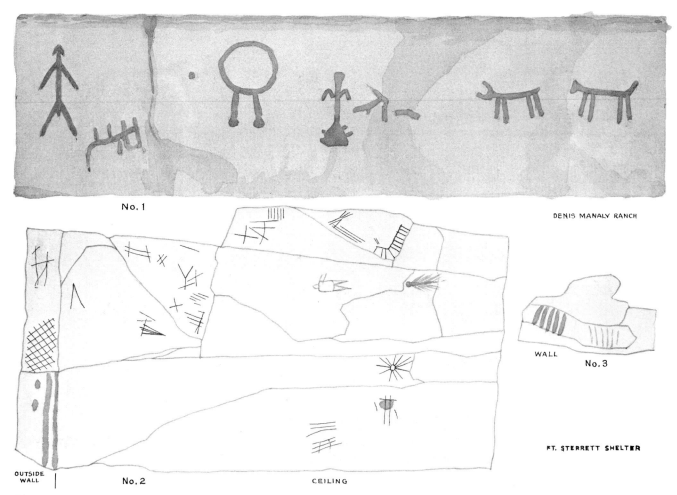

No. 1

DENIS MANALY RANCH

WALL   No. 3

FT. STERRETT SHELTER

OUTSIDE WALL

No. 2

CEILING

Plate 123.   Denis Manaly Ranch. Copied July 5, 1939. Scale: No. 1, 1″ to 1′. Fort Sterrett Shelter. Copied July 7, 1939. Scale: Nos. 2–3, 3/4″ to 1′

Another twenty miles to the west, under a sandstone ledge on the east bank of a creek, about fifteen miles northeast of Abilene, Kirkland found a few more animal and anthropomorphic figures painted in red (Plate 123, No. 1). In good condition, they appear to be relatively recent. They evince no obvious similarities to the other, almost as sketchy, rock paintings of the region.

Farther south, in a small shelter on the bank of Brady Creek about one mile above where it flows into the San Saba, are a few pictographs painted in red (Plate 122, Nos. 2, 3, 4). About one hundred yards downstream is a large burned-rock midden in which the Kirklands found several flint artifacts and a potsherd. But that any of the paintings are prehistoric is questionable since the riders on horseback (Nos. 2, 4) and the man in the hat (No. 2, left) are definitely attributable to the historic period.

In a fair state of preservation, the pictures are on a rock ledge in the back of the shelter about three feet from the floor. A negative handprint was found on the ceiling of a nearby shelter, and seven very dim negative handprints were found under an overhanging cliff in a small canyon opposite the shelter. All of the handprints were in red; none of them were copied. (Notes, Plate 122)

PLATE 123

No. 1. These red pictographs are under a protective ledge of sandstone in Shackleford County.

Nos. 2 and 3. These simple red paintings and petroglyphs are in a narrow, deep cave at the upper end of a high bluff on the North Llano River above old Fort Sterrett, in Sutton County.

CHAPTER 8

HUECO TANKS AND THE PANHANDLE

In far West Texas, a short distance northeast of El Paso, three massive outcrops of granite, each half a mile or more long and almost as wide, thrust upward several hundred feet above the level desert floor (see Map 6). Tremendous boulders and jumbled masses of rock are strewn over these ponderous hills, deep canyons cut into them at several points, and where there are pockets of soil a few stunted oaks and other vegetation struggle for life. Natural crevices and depressions in the rocks near ground level — known as tanks — catch and hold water from occasional rains. In a land where water is scarce — the nearest natural supply is the Rio Grande — and where it is usually heavily laden with minerals, the cool, sweet water of the Hueco Tanks has long been famous. Indians have known and used these natural cisterns for hundreds, perhaps thousands of years; Spanish explorers and priests, American pioneers, ranchers, and modern picnickers have continued to use them. The chaotically piled rocks, overhanging cliffs, crevices, and pockets weathered into the rock form many natural shelters suitable for human occupation, and those near tanks usually show signs of having been inhabited by Indians. Ceilings are smoked black from innumerable fires, mortar holes are often worn deep in the rock near them, cultural debris is scattered about, and back walls and ceilings are ornamented with thousands of paintings.

A few pictures have been damaged by smoke and a few others in exposed places have been dimmed by rain or blowing sand. But in many well protected shelters the pictures are remarkably clear. Less than one per cent of the designs were too dim to be easily copied. Although thousands of names and dates had been placed on the rocks about the tanks, hardly a single Indian design had been seriously damaged by vandals. Practically all damage observed resulted from age or exposure. Very little flaking of the rock was noticed. (Notes, Plate 126)

These pictographs have virtually nothing in common with those found in the Big Bend, lower Pecos River country, or Central Texas. For the most part they belong to the distinctively different artistic traditions of the Southwest, an area which witnessed the development of one of North America's great cultural centers. Far to the north of Hueco Tanks in the Canadian River Valley in the Texas Panhandle, at Rocky Dell, are a few pictographs whose affiliations also lie with the Southwest. There are also a few scattered prehistoric petroglyphs in the Panhandle attributable to a Southwestern influenced people. For this reason the rock art of Hueco Tanks and the Texas Panhandle, though widely separated in space, are discussed in the same chapter. There are also a number of petroglyph sites in the Panhandle left by one or another of the historic Plains Indian tribes which hunted and fought over this land. They are included here with their Southwestern-inspired neighbors as the remarkably accomplished and chronologically final petrographic art of Texas Indians.

Hueco Tanks

The earliest known occupants of the El Paso region were an Archaic people who were similar to and shared many traits with Archaic inhabitants of the Big Bend and lower Pecos River country. Most remains of this occupation, known as the Hueco Phase, have been found in caves and shelters. Unlike the Archaic peoples farther east, those in the El Paso region were relatively near the developing Puebloan civilization of the Southwest and were greatly influenced by it. Puebloan is used here in a loose sense to apply to the general, overall culture of the Southwest. Actually, it was a variant of this civilization, the Mogollon, and a peripheral version of it, the Jornada Branch, which was primarily responsible for the cultural development in the El Paso-Hueco Tanks vicinity. Another variant, known to archeologists as the Anasazi, was ancestral to modern Pueblo peoples and had little direct influence at Hueco Tanks (Lehmer, 1958; Wheat, 1955). Pottery and the cultivation of corn, squash, and perhaps other crops, spread from the Southwestern centers of development to this region so that by about A.D. 900 a Neo-American culture known as the Mesillo Phase had been established. Depending

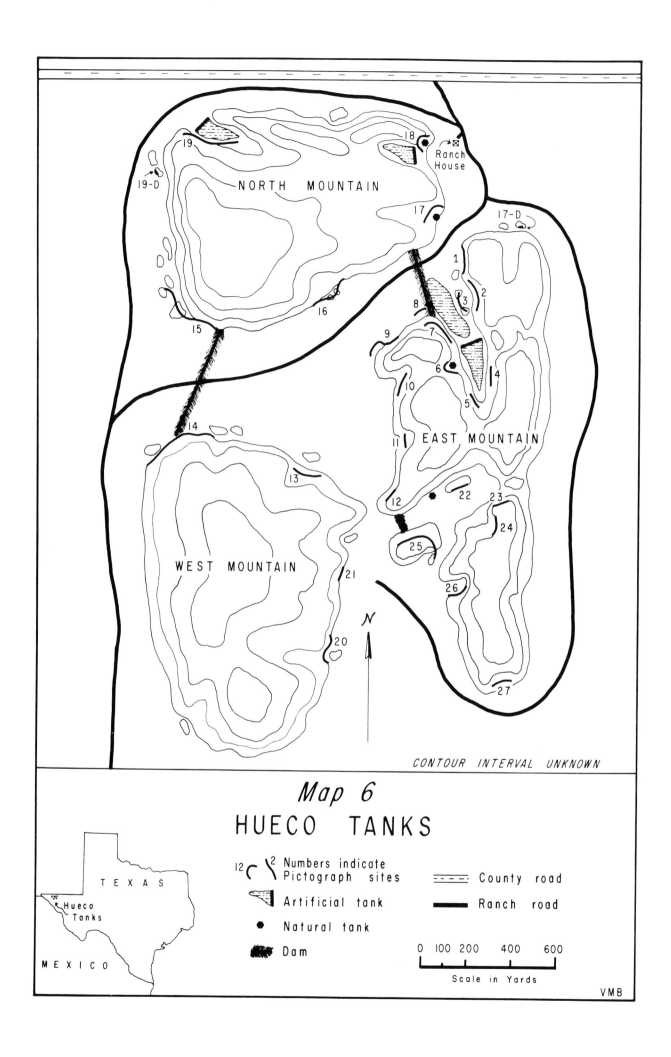

VMB

19

19-D

NORTH MOUNTAIN

18

Ranch House

17

17-D

1

16

2

15

8

3

9

7

6

4

10

5

EAST MOUNTAIN

14

11

13

12

22

23

WEST MOUNTAIN

25

24

21

26

N

20

27

CONTOUR INTERVAL UNKNOWN

Map 6
HUECO TANKS

TEXAS

Hueco Tanks

MEXICO

12 ⌒ ⌍2 Numbers indicate Pictograph sites

▽ Artificial tank

● Natural tank

▧ Dam

‒ ‒ ‒ County road

━━━ Ranch road

0 100 200   400   600

Scale in Yards

VMB

primarily upon agriculture, these people lived in permanent villages of both round and rectangular pit houses. Several hundred years later, presumably following the infusion of new ideas or perhaps an influx of peoples from the centers of Puebloan development, the pit houses were replaced by multi-roomed adobe pueblos during a short-lived Doña Ana Phase. A number of population movements in the Southwest during the twelfth and thirteenth centuries appear to have been responsible for a final flowering of this peripheral Puebloan civilization. Pueblos of this El Paso Phase were larger and encompassed a greater area. Influences from the El Paso Phase were felt, for example, as far down the Rio Grande as the La Junta (Presidio) region. But rather suddenly in the fifteenth century this complex waned (Lehmer, 1948; 1958:127–128; Suhm et al., 1954:31–45). That some of these prehistoric peoples knew of and occasionally camped at the Hueco Tanks seems likely. That they contributed some of the pictographs found there is highly probable.

Although many Spaniards—explorers, soldiers, and missionaries—visited the El Paso region in the sixteenth and seventeenth centuries, distressingly little is known about the natives who then inhabited the region. In the vicinity of El Paso and northward along the Rio Grande were a people termed Mansos by the Spaniards. They practiced some agriculture and seem to have had strong ties with Puebloan peoples farther north. It is likely that they were the impoverished descendants of the prehistoric peoples whose cultural remains are known to archeologists as the El Paso Phase. Below El Paso and extending to the La Junta region were a people known as the Suma. The probabilities are good that they were the same people as the Jumanos of the La Junta region (Newcomb, 1961, Chapter 9). Somewhat less influenced by the Puebloan civilization than were the Mansos, they also practiced agriculture whenever possible. As early as the seventeenth century Apache raiders were making life miserable for both the Mansos and Sumas, and their cultures soon disintegrated through such strife, introduced diseases, and the other debilitating effects of an expanding Spanish colonial empire.

In 1680 the scattered and exploited Pueblo Indians of New Mexico joined forces to drive out their Spanish conquerers. It was a temporarily successful revolt, but one of its by-products was the forced migration of some Tigua Indians from Isleta Pueblo to a new settlement and mission a few miles below El Paso on the Rio Grande. Governor Otermin had surprised and captured Isleta, located in 1681 about twelve miles south of Albuquerque. He took 519 captives south with him, 115 of whom escaped (Hodge, 1907, Part 1:623). Otermin and a Franciscan, Fray Francisco Ayeta, subsequently founded the mission of Isleta del Sur for these people on the northeast bank of the Rio Grande. The name and location of the settlement changed several times through the years, and the descendants of these Pueblo refugees have disappeared, absorbed into the local populace. It is barely possible that some of these displaced Pueblo Indians visited Hueco Tanks sometime after 1682 and were responsible for some of its paintings.

The Apaches who attacked the Indians native to the Hueco Tanks vicinity and for many years harried Spaniards, Mexicans, and Americans were principally Mescaleros. One of the southern Athapascan tribes, they belong linguistically with the western division of Apaches (the others include the Navaho, San Carlos, and Chiricahua tribes). Fronting on the plains, in some respects they were more similar to the eastern Apaches (Lipan, Jicarilla, and Kiowa Apache) than to their western brethren. All these Apache peoples were late-comers to the Southwest, and though their time of arrival has not been precisely pinpointed, it must have been within relatively recent centuries. The Hueco Tanks were within the range of the Mescaleros by the eighteenth century and they may have known them in earlier centuries, though there is little reason to suppose that they used them to any extent. The surrounding country held little game and the Hueco Tanks could never be regularly or permanently inhabited. In fact, the lack of any deep cultural deposits suggests that no people ever regularly occupied the Tanks. They were simply a way station, an oasis which provided water and a temporary haven for travelers and war parties. In the eighteenth and nineteenth centuries, by which time the Mescaleros were well supplied with horses and much more mobile than in earlier years, there must have been increased usage of Hueco Tanks. It was a convenient stopping point for parties raiding in the El Paso vicinity, as well as for those bound for or returning from more distant adventures in Mexico. It also served as a temporary refuge when they were hard pressed by Spaniards, Mexicans, and Americans.

The first specific references this writer has found to Mescalero utilization of Hueco Tanks date from the last quarter of the eighteenth century. In 1775, after suffering much from Apache raids, the Spaniards organized a major campaign, raising two thousand men in southern New Mexico and marching into Apache country in a three-pronged pincers movement (Thomas, 1932:11–12; Sonnichsen, 1958: 47–48). The Apaches were badly defeated, and the following year another campaign drove the Mescaleros as far as the Colorado River of Texas, where they encountered Comanches who also administered a drubbing. By 1777 the Mescaleros were suing for peace at El Paso, with one band then hid-

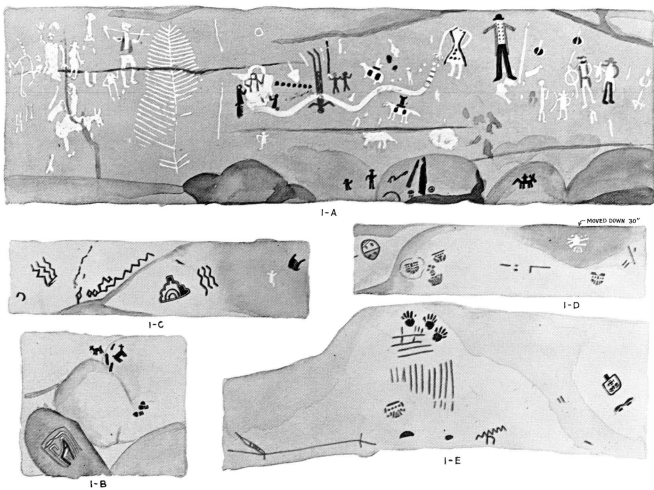

Plate 124.   Hueco Tanks, Site 1. Copied July 17–25, 1939. Scale: No. 1a, 1/4″ to 1″; Nos. 1b–1e, 3/8″ to 1′

Hueco Tanks, Site 1. The main group of paintings can be seen over the artist's head. See Plate 124.

I-F

2-A

2-B   12' OUT   2-C   12' OUT   2-D

Plate 125.   Hueco Tanks, Sites 1 and 2. Copied July 17–25, 1939. Scale: Nos. 1f, 2a-2d, 3/8″ to 1′

PLATE 124

Hueco Tanks, Site 1. *1-A.* This group of paintings is on a protected vertical rock wall overlooking the entrance to the main tank.

1-D and *1-E.* These designs are on the back walls of two low shelters on the second level to the right of *1-A.* The yellow designs were carefully painted with very thin color which looks like a stain on the rock. They appeared at first to have been stenciled. The face on *1-E* and the center design on *1-C* were also carefully done with thin paint.

PLATE 125

Hueco Tanks, Sites 1 and 2. *2-A.* This mask drawing appeared to have been originally blue and white, but the blue had faded to a blue-gray. It is located on a ceiling about three feet high.

2-B. This design is on an exposed wall above a high rock and is almost too dim to copy.

2-C is high on a poorly protected wall which can be reached only from a high rock. The yellow as well as the white appeared to be a kind of clay paint.

2-D. This red pictograph is below and to the right of *2-C.* It is badly exposed to the weather but because of the better quality of its pigment is still quite clear.

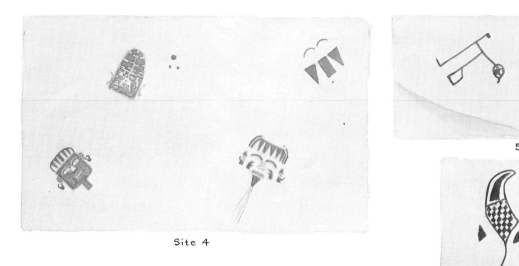

Site 4

5-A

5-B

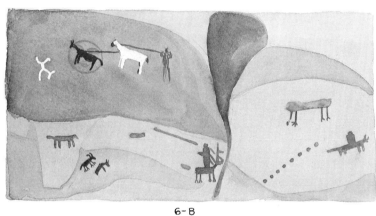

6-B

6-A

Plate 126. Hueco Tanks, Sites 4, 5, 6. Copied July 17–25, 1939. Scale: Nos. 4, 5a–b, 6b, 3/4″ to 1′; No. 6a, 3/8″ to 1′

PLATE 126

Hueco Tanks, Sites 4, 5, 6. Site 4. These masks were painted in red and blue. *5-A* and *5-B*. These dim black designs are at the end of a long shelter very near the ground.

6-B. These mostly black pictographs are painted on the walls of the dark hole in *6-D*. Due to the uneven surfaces of the hole the relative positions of the pictures are not exactly accurate in the copy.

PLATE 127

Hueco Tanks, Site 6. The white paintings are very clear, but those in blue (*6-D*, lower center) and black (*6-C*, extreme right) are very dim.

PLATE 128

Hueco Tanks, Sites 3 and 6. *6-E*. The position of these paintings with respect to those of Plate 127: *6-D* is indicated by common point *B*.

3-A and *3-B*. These red pictographs are under small shelters or pockets in two large boulders between Sites 1 and 2. The paint is very dim and a few designs could not be made out.

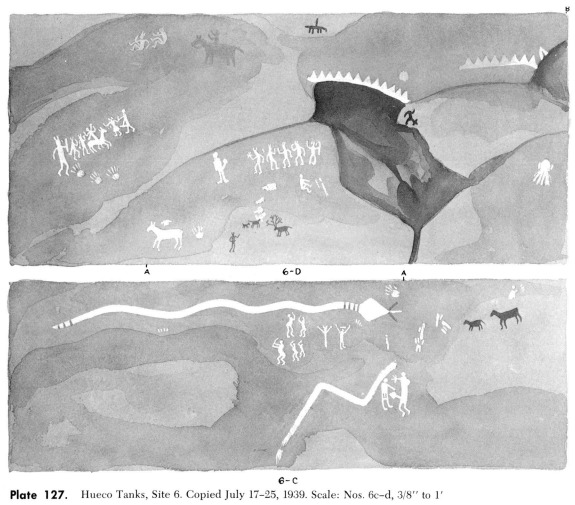

Plate 127. Hueco Tanks, Site 6. Copied July 17–25, 1939. Scale: Nos. 6c–d, 3/8″ to 1′

Plate 128. Hueco Tanks, Sites 3 and 6. Copied July 17–25, 1939. Scale: Nos. 3a–b, 6e, 1/4″ to 1′

A typical scene at Hueco Tanks. Sites 7, 8, 9, left to right, are at the base of this rock mass.
See Plates 129, 130.

ing near the village of San Elizario and another having taken refuge at the Hueco Tanks (Thomas, 1941:17; Sonnichsen, 1958:48). For the remainder of the century and until Mexico became independent in 1824, relations between the Mescaleros and Spaniards were relatively peaceful. But after 1824, with few organized defenses and a chaotic political situation in Mexico, the Mescaleros went on a rampage. Before 1840 all the livestock of the El Paso region had been appropriated by Mescaleros and other Indian raiders, and in the forties a military force of eight hundred men had to be organized to defend El Paso (Sonnichsen, 1958:54). It may have been this force to which Captain John Pope (1855:53–54) referred in 1854 when he wrote:

about 14 years ago these Arabs of New Mexico, the Apaches, having made a desperate foray upon the Mexicans, retreated with their plunder to these mountains. The Mexicans surprised and surrounded them, hemming them up in the rocky ravine forming the eastern Tank. Here an engagement took place, in which the Indians were totally defeated and nearly exterminated, only two or three escaping. It is said that upwards of one hundred of them were killed.

John Russell Bartlett, chief of the American Boundary Commission, also alluded to this massacre at Hueco Tanks, his account differing somewhat from Pope's:

the hills expand, forming an amphitheatre, which is celebrated from its being the place where the Apaches used formerly to hold their councils, and the scene of a contest between them and the Mexicans. The Indians had been committing some depredations and murders in the settlements, and, being pursued, were traced to the Waco Mountains. A party set off from El Paso, and surprised them in the narrow space or amphitheatre alluded to. The besieged retreated as far as possible; and finding no chance to escape, they built a wall across the entrance, which is about one hundred feet from one perpendicular mass of rock to the other. Here they were kept several days, when they were finally overcome, and all, to the number of a hundred and fifty, put to death. (Bartlett, 1854:174)

Both the Pope and Bartlett accounts are probably erroneous in many essentials, since the Kiowas remembered the details of a raid in 1839 in which their warriors were penned up by a Mexican force at Hueco Tanks. It is unlikely that two different groups of Indians were surrounded at the same place in the same year by the same force. The Kiowas were far-ranging raiders from the southern plains who often crossed into Mexico at El Paso, but they were not Apaches. The Kiowas recounted the incident to James Mooney (1898:302–305) in the latter part of the century, still remembering the leader and the names of several members of the raiding party. About twenty Kiowa warriors had set out to raid El Paso, they told Mooney, but for some reason—probably the newly created military force there—did not dare attack, and turned back, camping at a "rock house cave." "None of the Kiowa can define its exact location, but they describe it as a deep rock well with a large basin of water and on one side of it a cave running under the rock from the water's edge" (*ibid.*, 302). This could only have been the cave Kirkland refers to as Comanche Cave, Site 6, at Hueco Tanks. While camped there

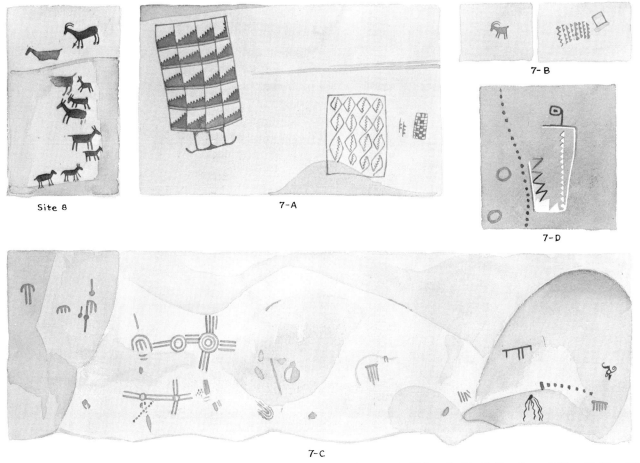

Site 8   7-A   7-B

7-D

7-C

Plate 129. Hueco Tanks, Sites 7 and 8. Copied July 17–25, 1939. Scale: Site 8, 3/4″ to 1′; Site 7, Nos. 7a–c, 3/8″ to 1′; Nos. 7d, 3/4″ to 1′

PLATE 129

Hueco Tanks, Sites 7 and 8. 7-A. These dim red designs are low on the wall of a very narrow deep crack in the cliff.

7-B and 7-C. These predominantly red pictographs are in small shelters a few yards to the right of 7-A.

7-D. This black and white design is under an overhang on the second level above Site 8. The two circles are red. Poorly protected, these paintings are in very poor condition.

Site 8. These dim black animals are in a small shelter at ground level in front of the main cliff.

the Mexican force surrounded them and killed several of their horses. Taking refuge in the cave, the Kiowas soon found themselves in a serious plight, for the dead horses became too putrid to eat and the Mexicans covered the tank with their guns so that even getting a drink was a hazardous business, one of the warriors being shot in the leg while attempting to do so. After ten days of suffering and mounting desperation the Kiowas decided to make an attempt to escape. One by one that night they

silently climbed a tree growing in a crevice and gained the top of the cliff without being discovered by the soldiers. But the warrior wounded in the leg could not climb and had to be left behind to a bitter fate. Another warrior, Koñate, was seriously wounded during the escape when a sentry fired blindly at an inadvertent sound the Kiowas had made. The story of Koñate's abandonment by his comrades and ultimate rescue by Comanches is harrowing and ethnographically revealing, but it has no place here. That the Kiowas had any inclination to adorn the walls of their temporary prison is doubtful, and virtually all the Indian paintings on the walls of Comanche Cave apparently should be attributed to the Mescaleros. But it does illustrate the point that many varied Indians paused long enough at Hueco Tanks to contribute their bit to the rock art which covers its walls. Comanches must have known and used the Tanks, and many other Indians probably visited there during the nineteenth century.

The Mescaleros are probably best described as originally a marginal Plains people who became a peripheral Southwestern tribe after they were forced from their ancestral hunting grounds by

Hueco Tanks. Entrance to Comanche Cave where Kiowas were trapped. Note sign reading "Watter Hear."

Hueco Tanks. Looking north from Site 14. See Plate 134.

Comanches and other northern tribes.[1] Before the advent of Europeans and the adoption of horses, most if not all Mescalero bands depended upon a combination of bison hunting, gardening, and the gathering of wild plant foods. They planted their gardens in late April or May, most if not all people remaining nearby until August when the crops were harvested. Soon afterward they went bison hunting, utilizing the skin-covered tepee and travois, and pursuing vagrant hunters' lives until the following spring and the new planting season (Thomas, 1935: 81, gives a good example of this subsistence pattern.) After they acquired horses and became more nomadic, gardening declined drastically in impor-

[1] This characterization is contrary to the established belief which has it that "the Mescalero relatively recently detached themselves from the Chiricahua to live east of the Rio Grande" (Kroeber, 1947:37, footnote). Documentary studies reveal that the old tradition, based on historical reconstruction from ethnographic data, is wrong, and that the opposite is more in accord with the facts (Forbes, 1960).

PLATE 130

Hueco Tanks, Sites 9 and 10. 9-A and 9-B. These red designs are in small pockets in the cliff about four feet from the ground.

9-C. These predominantly red designs are on the ceiling of a small, deep shelter under a very large boulder. The ceiling and walls of the shelter had been smoked black and the paintings are not very clear.

9-D and 9-E. These red, and red and yellow paintings are under two open shelters exposed to moisture and blowing sand. They are very dim.

10-C. This red and green mask design is on the ceiling of a small overhang about nine feet above the ground and is in a very good state of preservation.

PLATE 131

12-A. This design is on the ceiling of a large rock pocket above a shallow, exposed shelter on the second level. A small shelf of rock below the pocket gave footing for the artist. Part of the designs were in very bad condition and could not be made out.

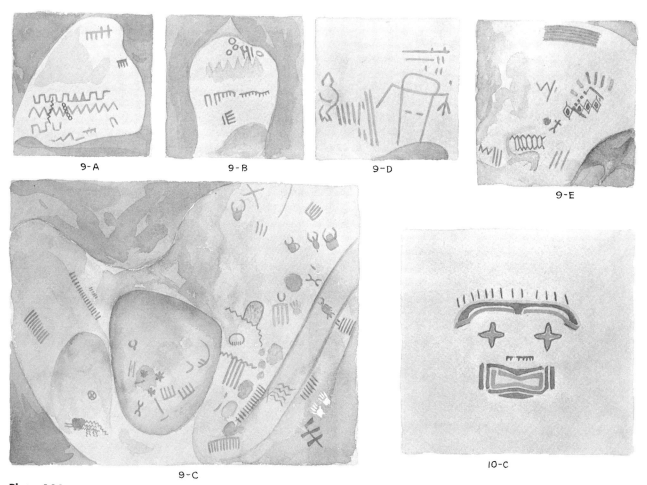

Plate 130. Hueco Tanks, Sites 9 and 10. Copied July 17–25, 1939. Scale: Nos. 9a–e, 3/8″ to 1′; Nos. 10c, 1/8″ to 1′

Plate 131. Hueco Tanks, Site 12. Copied July 17–25, 1939. Scale: 3/4″ to 1′

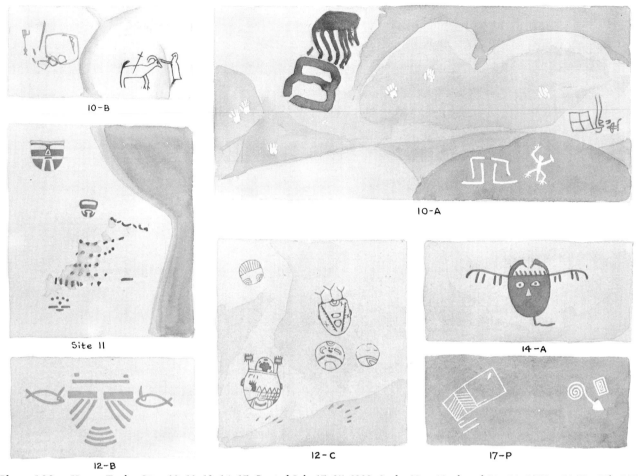

Plate 132. Hueco Tanks, Sites 10, 11, 12, 14, 17. Copied July 17–25, 1939. Scale: Nos. 10a–b and Site 11, 3/8″ to 1′; No. 12b, 1/8″ to 1″; No. 12c, 3/4″ to 1′; No. 14a, 1/8″ to 1″; No. 17p, 3/8″ to 1′

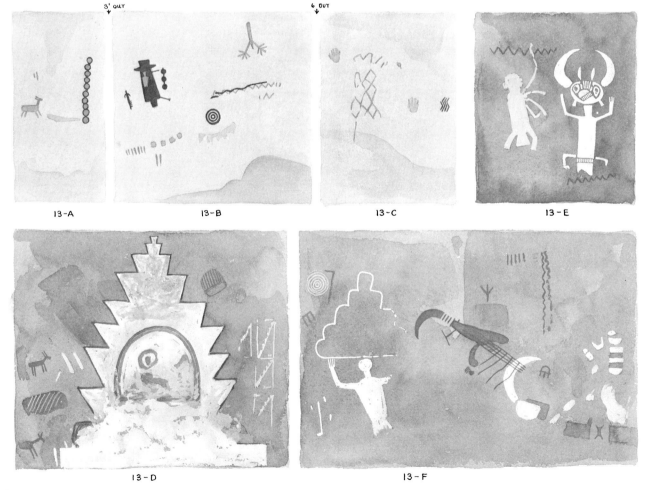

Plate 133. Hueco Tanks, Site 13. Copied July 17–25, 1939. Scale: Nos. 13a–f, 3/8″ to 1′

14-B

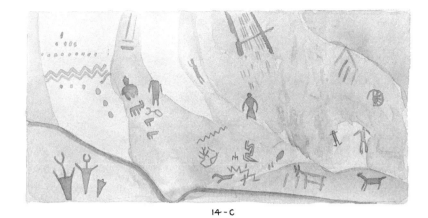

14-C

14-C

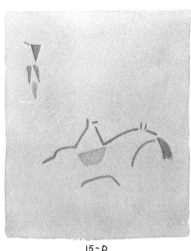

15-D

15-E

17-F

Plate 134. Hueco Tanks, Sites 14, 15, and 17. Copied July 17–25, 1939. Scale: Nos. 14b-d, 15d-e, 17f, 3/8″ to 1′

PLATE 132

Hueco Tanks, Sites 10, 11, 12, 14, 17. *10-A.* These black and white paintings are under a small shelter high up a small canyon to the left of *10-B.* There were small water holes in front of the shelter.

10-B. These figures are on a hard-to-reach shelf of rock just behind the red and green mask of *10-C.*

Site 11. These designs are low on a wall in a large rock crevice. Nearby is a very large shelter smoked so black that the design in it could not be accurately copied. The masks are in red; the other designs are black.

12-B. This yellow mask drawing is on the rock just below the pocket containing *12-A.*

12-C. These red designs, badly exposed and very dim, are low down to the right of *12-B.*

14-A. This red painting is alone under a huge boulder about fifty yards to the left of *14-B.*

17-P. These white designs are on the ceiling of a horizontal rock crack barely large enough to permit entry. They are just to the left of *17-G.*

PLATE 133

Hueco Tanks, Site 13. *13-A, B, C.* These dim paintings are on the back wall of a small open shelter on the second level and are badly exposed to blowing sand. Most of the paintings are red but the connected circles in *13-A* are also outlined in black; the three designs on the left in

13-B, the target in *13-B,* and the zigzag lines of *13-C* are also black.

13-D, E, F. These paintings are in a small shelter at ground level and are badly smoked. *13-D* is very dim and had to be reconstructed to some extent; the bottom part had been smeared badly and the top smoked black. The left figure of *13-E* is very dim but the right figure is perfectly clear. All of the designs of *13-F* are in bad condition. *13-E* fits between *13-D* and *13-F* only a foot or so was omitted on either side in the copy.

PLATE 134

Hueco Tanks, Sites 14, 15, 17. *14-B* and *C.* These pictographs are on the back wall of a high overhanging cliff just above the ground. This spot was used as a shelter by the Indians. An unusual, very dim yellow color was used for *14-B.*

14-C. These red designs are under a leaning boulder about thirty yards to the right of *14-B.*

15-D and *E.* These pictographs are on the ceiling of a small shelter at the end of the levee at Site 15. A few other designs in the shelter were too dim to copy. *15-D* is red, the animal to the left in *15-E* is white, the lines and animal to the right are black.

17-F. These red paintings are in a high rock pocket just below *17-E.* The bird's head is almost destroyed.

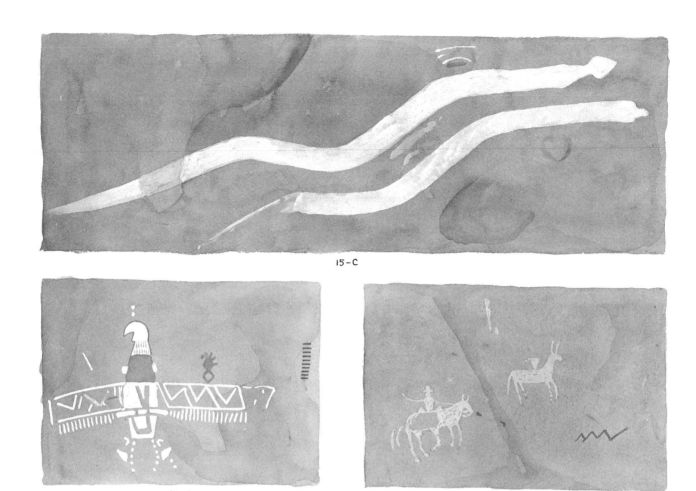

Plate 135. Hueco Tanks, Sites 15 and 16. Copied July 17–25, 1939. Scale: No. 15c, 1/4″ to 1′; Nos. 16a and d, 3/8″ to 1′

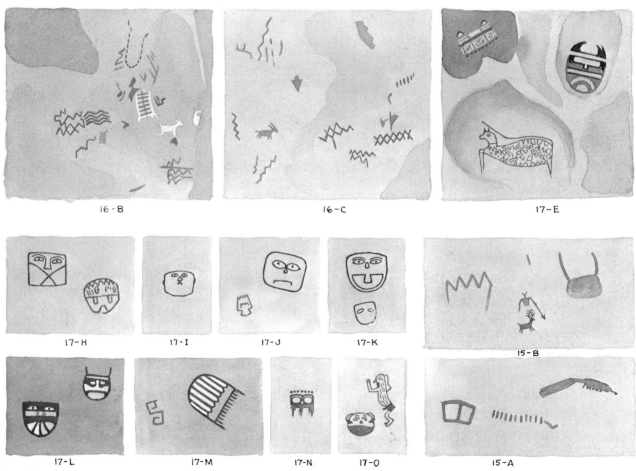

Plate 136. Hueco Tanks, Sites 15, 16, 17. Copied July 17–25, 1939. Scale: Nos. 15 a–b, 3/4″ to 1′; Nos. 16b–c and 17e, 3/8″ to 1′; Nos. 17h–o, 3/4″ to 1″

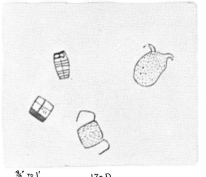

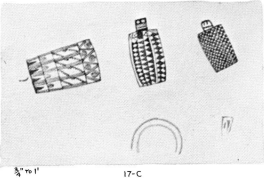

¾" TO 1'   17-G

¾" TO 1'   17-D

¾" TO 1'   17-C

¼" TO 1"   18-E

Plate 137. Hueco Tanks, Sites 17 and 18. Copied July 17–25, 1939. Scale: Nos. 17g,d,c, 3/8″ to 1′; No. 18e, 1/8″ to 1″

PLATE 135

Hueco Tanks, Sites 15 and 16. *15-C*. These snake designs are on the ceiling of a very large shelter at the point of the cliff. The ceiling is smoked and smeared with color, and the earlier designs have been destroyed. It appears that the snakes were never outlined as they were in other shelters.

16-A. This red and white design is on a low wall behind a large rock in a small unused shelter. It is so dim that it could be copied only with difficulty.

16-D. This painting is on the wall of a high shelter. It was painted with gray mud or clay.

PLATE 136

Hueco Tanks, Sites 15, 16, 17. *16-B* and *C*. These mostly red designs are under two large boulders in front of the cliff.

17-E. These red, black, and white paintings are in a small rock pocket high up the cliff and are very difficult to reach. Rather than risk a fall they were copied from some eight feet away, so they are only approximations.

17-H, I, J, K. These black outlined faces are on the rock at various places below *17-E*.

17-L, M, N, are under boulders high up to the left of *17-E*.

17-O. This little red painting does not properly belong to Site 17. It was found in a well-used shelter under a huge boulder in front of the hill about three hundred yards west of Site 17. No other paintings were in the shelter.

15-A and *B* are under boulders a few yards north of *15-C*.

PLATE 137

Hueco Tanks, Sites 17 and 18. *17-G*. These pictographs are on the wall and ceiling of a large well-used shelter at the base of the cliff. There is a tank of permanent water at this site, and on the smoked wall are hundreds of names. The pictures have been damaged by rough usage. The snake is accurately copied except that the color has been strengthened and restored.

17-D and *C*. These red designs are under large rocks no more than four feet above the rock floor. They are quite dim, but distinct in good light.

18-E. These small red masks, here shown in detail, are just above the black figure shown in Plate 139, *18-A*.

Hueco Tanks. View from top of cliff above Site 17. See Plates 137, 138.

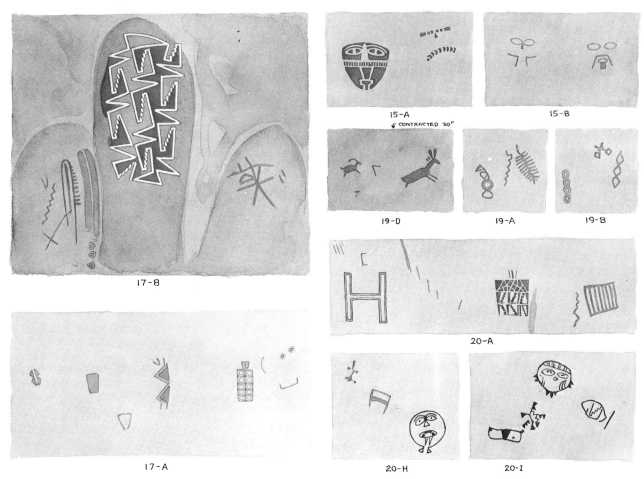

Plate 138. Hueco Tanks, Sites 15, 17, 19, 20. Copied July 17-25, 1939. Scale: Nos. 15a-b, 3/4″ to 1′; Nos. 17a-b, 3/8″ to 1′; Nos. 19a,b,d, 3/8″ to 1′; Nos. 20a, 5/8″ to 1′; Nos. 20h-i, 3/4″ to 1′

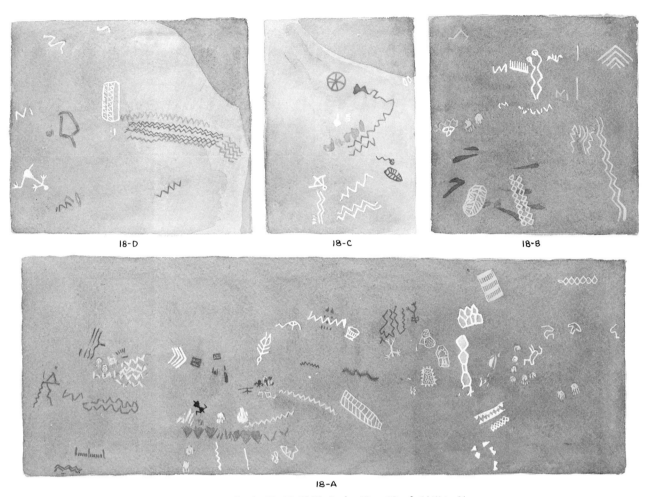

Plate 139. Hueco Tanks, Site 18. Copied July 17–25, 1939. Scale: Nos. 18a–d, 1/4″ to 1′

PLATE 138

Hueco Tanks, Sites 15, 17, 19, 20. *17-B*. These designs are under a large rock on top of the cliff back of *17-C* and are in excellent condition.

17-A. These red figures are on the wall of a shelter up the cliff from *17-B*.

15-A and *B*. These red pictographs are in very small shelters just north of *15-C*.

19-D. These red designs are on a smoked ceiling of a large shelter under a huge boulder in front of the cliff.

19-A and *B* are in red on protected rocks in the little canyon at Site 19.

20-A. These red designs are in a large rock crevice in the cliff.

20-H and *I* are black and in small rock pockets near the floor of the low shelter at Site 20.

PLATE 139

Hueco Tanks, Site 18. These red, yellow, white, blue, and black designs are on the ceiling of a large cave containing one of the natural water tanks, which furnishes water for the nearby ranch. The ranch house is only a few yards away, and part of the cave is used as a cow barn. Most of the pictures are still quite distinct. The small red squares above the black figure in *18-A* (left of center) are masks drawn on a larger scale in Plate 137, *18-E*.

tance. The invasion of the southern plains by Comanches early in the eighteenth century also denied the Mescaleros some of their best hunting grounds. Raiding compensated somewhat for these losses and greater reliance must have been placed on wild plant foods, but increasing impoverishment was the general lot of the Mescaleros during their last century of freedom, an excellent preparation, one might suppose, for the care they were to receive from the United States government during the early years of the reservation period.

The Mescaleros were in intimate contact with the settled Puebloan peoples along the Rio Grande. In the early days relations between them seem to have been largely peaceful, the Mescaleros and other Apaches journeying to the Pueblos in fall and winter to trade bison hides and meat for agricultural products and other things. In later years many Mescalero bands became chronic enemies of the Pueblos and their Spanish overlords but, of more importance here, they learned much from their Pueblo neighbors. Their knowledge of agriculture and many cosmological and mythological beliefs and practices, perhaps including their visual expression in pictographs and petroglyphs, were

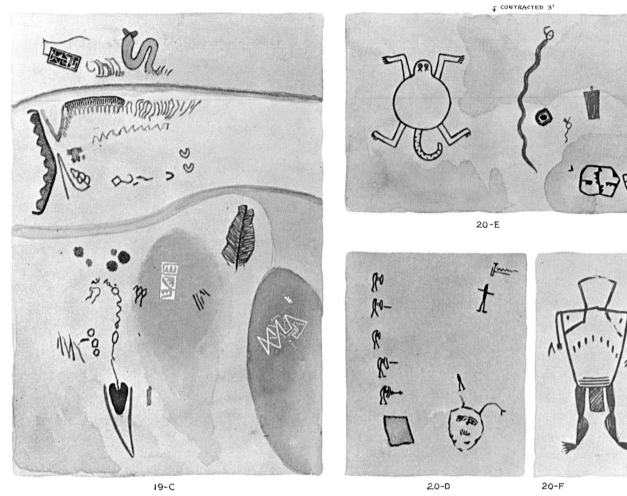

CONTRACTED 3'

20-E

19-C

20-D   20-F

Plate 140. Hueco Tanks, Sites 19 and 20. Copied July 17–25, 1939. Scale: Nos. 19c, 20d–f, 3/8″ to 1′

probably borrowed from or heavily influenced by the Pueblos.

The basic social unit in Mescalero life was the matrilocal extended family, a stable group composed of several nuclear families related through females. (For a detailed description of Mescalero kinship system and comparison with other Apache tribes, see Opler, 1936; Bellah, 1952). A number of these extended families were joined together in a local group under a leader. Composition of local groups was fluid, their stability depending upon the success and abilities of their leaders. A number of local groups were linked together in a band, the most outstanding local group leader being recognized as band chief. There was no tribe in a political sense above the band level, the Mescaleros being a unit in that they shared a common language and culture.

At the apex of Mescalero religious belief was a vaguely conceived creator god, Yusn. But more importantly and directly involved in Mescalero affairs were White Painted Woman and her son, Child of the Water. Even more intimately known were Mountain Spirits (Gahe) who lived inside sacred

PLATE 140

Hueco Tanks, Sites 19 and 20. *19-C.* These designs are under a large rock which forms a small shelter at the entrance to a small draw extending into the rock mass. They are very carefully drawn with thin paint.

20-D and *E.* These designs are on opposite walls of a tunnel-like shelter about ten feet from the entrance near the floor. *20-D* is very dim.

20-F is on the same wall as *20-E* but nearer the entrance.

PLATE 141

Hueco Tanks, Site 20. *20-C.* These pictographs are in a large rock crack above and to the left of the main shelter. The designs in blue-gray are very dim and are on the ceiling only about three feet above the bottom of the crevice.

20-G is on the ceiling at the entrance to a deep tunnel-like shelter. It is quite clear except on the right corner.

20-L is just outside a small shelter about forty feet above and to the right of the tunnel-like shelter. The designs are exposed to blowing rain and are so dim they could hardly be copied.

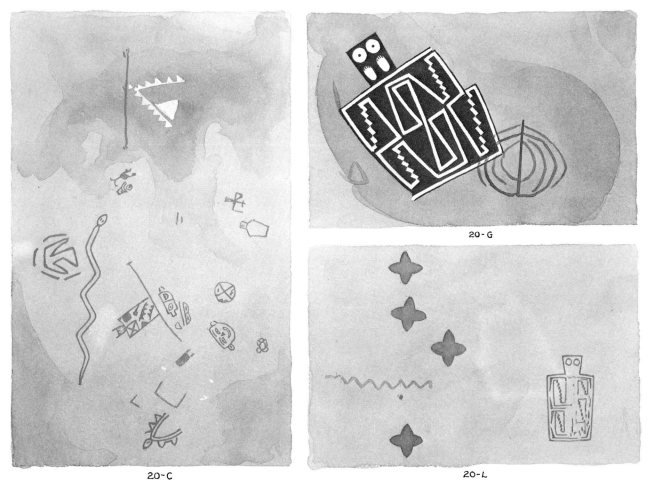

20-C

20-G

20-L

Plate 141. Hueco Tanks, Site 20. Copied July 17–25, 1939. Scale: Nos. 20c and g, 3/4″ to 1′; No. 20l, 1/2″ to 1′

Hueco Tanks. The main shelter at Site 23. The pictographs of Plate 144 are on the wall in front of the artist.

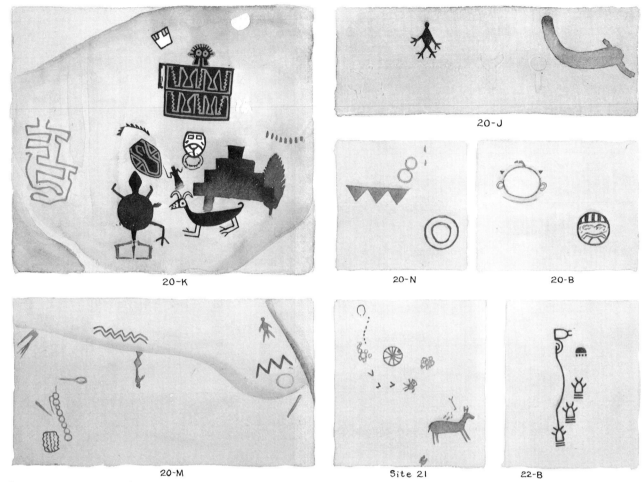

Plate 142. Hueco Tanks, Sites 20, 21, 22. Copied July 17–25, 1939. Scale: Nos. 20m–n, 3/8″ to 1′; Nos. 20k, b, 3/4″ to 1′; No. 20j, 1/2″ to 1′; Site 21, 3/8″ to 1′; No. 22b, 1/8″ to 1′

PLATE 142

Hueco Tanks, Sites 20, 21, 22. *20-J* is in the same shelter and a few yards to the left of *20-K*. The two upper figures are black, the others yellow.

20-K. These pictures, in a small shelter high up the cliff, are quite clean. Black, red, white, and yellow were employed to paint them.

20-M and *N*. These red designs are on a wall near the ground below *20-K*.

20-B is in a small low shelter in front of the cliff.

Site 21. These red paintings are low on the cliff about two hundred yards east of Site 20.

22-B is a large-scale copy of the small design on *22-A*.

PLATE 143

Hueco Tanks, Sites 22, 23, 24. Site 22 is on the side of a large rock standing in front of the main rock mass. The designs were very dim.

23-A and *B* are on the ceiling of the largest cave at Site 23.

23-D and *E* are on a large rock and the back wall, respectively, low in the same cave.

23-F is in a small shelter below and to the right of the big cave at Site 23.

24-A-1, 2, 3, 4, 5 are on the ceiling of a very small shelter on the level above Site 23. The shelter is too low to allow one to sit up comfortably. The designs are sharp but the red color is weak.

24-I is in the large shelter with *24-H* (Plate 147).

PLATE 144

Hueco Tanks, Site 23. *23-C* is the main design on the back wall of this large cave. It is above a wide shelf about five feet high in the back of the cave. Most of the designs are very dim. A few, directly in front of the bird, may have been destroyed.

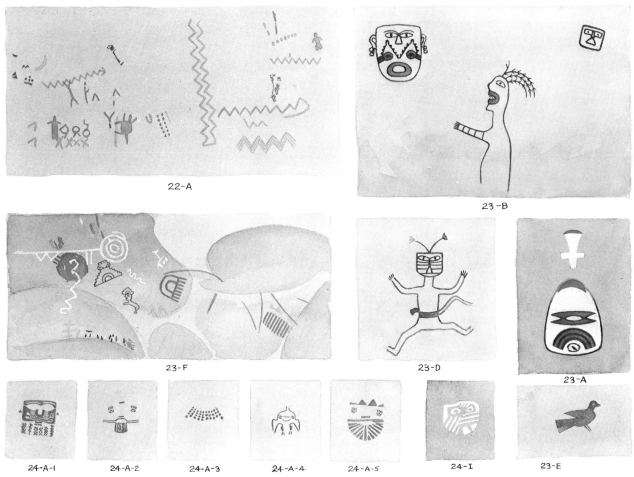

Plate 143. Hueco Tanks, Sites 22, 23, 24. Copied July 17–25, 1939. Scale: Nos. 22a and 23f, 3/8″ to 1′; Nos. 23b, d, a, e, 3/4″ to 1′; Nos. 24a¹ –a⁵ and i, 3/4″ to 1′

Plate 144. Hueco Tanks, Site 23. Copied July 17–25, 1939. Scale: No. 23c, 9/16″ to 1′

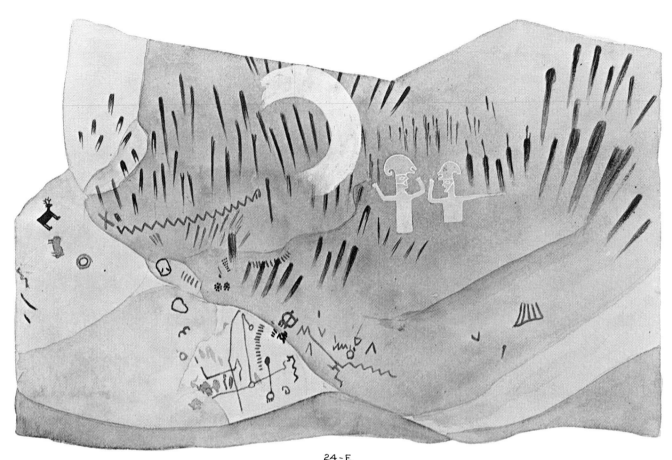

24-E

Plate 145. Hueco Tanks, Site 24. Copied July 17–25, 1939. Scale: No. 24e, 3/8″ to 1′

mountains and sometimes revealed themselves to people in visions. At important ceremonials men donned masks and costumes to impersonate the Mountain Spirits. Basic to the religious customs of the Mescaleros was the belief that there were many sources of supernatural power. Such power could reside in animals, plants, natural forces, and mythological beings such as the Mountain Spirits. During a dream or visionary experience, one of these creatures or forces revealed itself to a person. Then, usually assuming human form, it explained the nature of the power it was offering, and if it was acceptable, the person was taught the songs, prayers, and ritual that went with such power. Supernatural power so acquired varied, in its power, the spheres of life it affected, and so forth (Opler, 1935, 1938, 1946).

Since many of the old ceremonies were abandoned before the present century, knowledge of them has been lost. Surviving is an elaborate four-day puberty ceremony for girls in which masked dancers play an important part. Representations of the Mescalero masked dancers as they are known today do not appear in the pictographs at Hueco Tanks (Nicholas, 1939). There were also rites to heal the sick, and apparently rather elaborate war

PLATE 145

Hueco Tanks, Site 24. *24-E* is the principal design on the back wall of the main shelter. This shelter is two levels above and to the right of Site 23 and overlooks the whole valley to the west. A small trace of midden could be seen against the cliff. A large rectangular rock stands a few feet in front of the wall and about five feet high. The splashes of red were probably made by striking the wall with a large color-soaked brush on the end of a stick while standing on this rock.

and victory dances. Among the Chiricahuas, whose ritual life was almost identical to that of the Mescaleros, there was some loosening of conventional sexual behavior during victory celebrations, if not outright license, raising the possibility that the Mescaleros practiced the same customs (Castetter and Opler, 1936:9; Opler, 1941:353–354). This knowledge may help in interpreting some of the pictographs attributed to the Mescaleros. In any event, it is clear that the mythological and ritual life of the Mescalero Apaches was rich and varied, and it is likely that they visualized it in pictographs at places which may well have been regarded as homes of Mountain Spirits, such as Hueco Tanks.

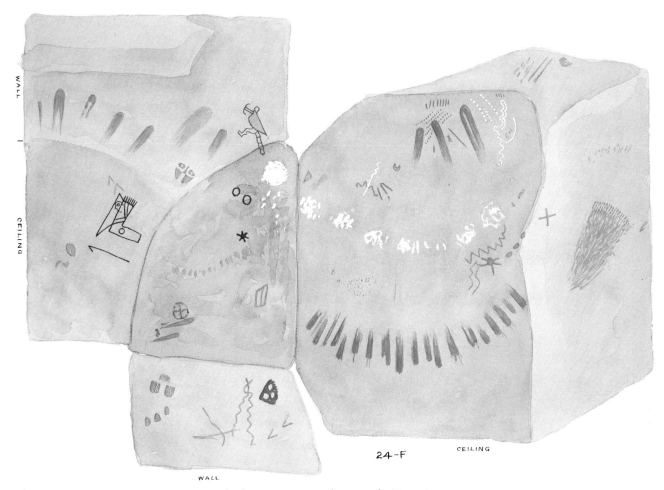

Plate 146. Hueco Tanks, Site 24. Copied July 17–25, 1939. Scale: No. 24f, 3/8″ to 1′

PLATE 146

Hueco Tanks, Site 24. *24-F* is the ceiling of the shelter above the large rock on the floor in front of *24-E*. The white splotches were in easy reach of a man standing on the highest part of the rock. The red crescent of strokes was made by striking the ceiling with a long brush from a position at the top of this rock.

At an oasis to which men of many cultures over many years have been drawn by the common need for water, the presence of pictographs of distinctly different styles, executed by varying techniques and painted for an assortment of reasons, is expectable. Such is the case at Hueco Tanks: two major styles of painting authored by men of different cultures are clearly recognizable, at least one other style is present though represented by fewer paintings, and there are possibly several others. Kirkland (Notes, Plate 126) felt that "the condition of the pictures does not point to extreme age," and no evidence to the contrary has been discovered. The paintings themselves do not depict any objects, such as atlatls, which would indicate con-

siderable antiquity. There is very little aboriginal overpainting and such as there is does not suggest that the underlying paintings are ancient. There have been no controlled excavations of archeological sites at Hueco Tanks, and it is not known whether there was an Archaic or earlier occupation, much less whether such people, if present, practiced the rupestrian art.

The most numerous pictographs at Hueco Tanks, designated here as Puebloan style and by Kirkland (1940:10) as "Type Two," are evidently prehistoric as none show any sign of white contact. The style is termed Puebloan because many of these paintings are almost identical to paintings or decorative elements found on kiva walls, pottery, and petroglyphs of prehistoric and historic Pueblos. The people whose remains are known to archeologists as the El Paso Phase would seem to have the best claim to being the artists. But it should be recognized that there is considerable variability within the Puebloan style of paintings, perhaps an expression of time depth or a reflection of visits to Hueco Tanks by several different Pueblo tribes. Rock paintings, similar to these, have been found at a

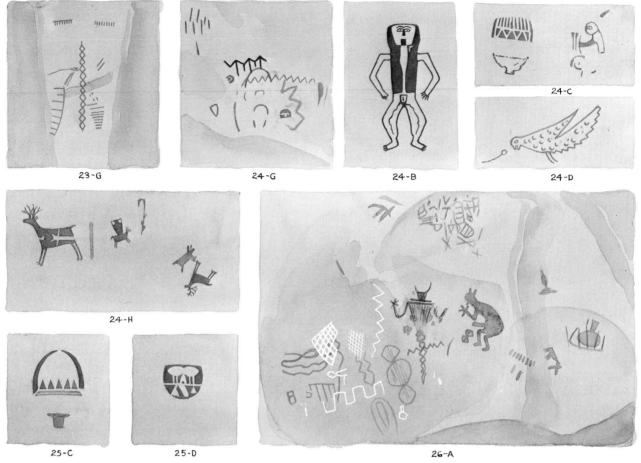

Plate 147. Hueco Tanks, Sites 23, 24, 25, 26. Copied July 17–25, 1939. Scale: No. 23g, 3/8″ to 1′; Nos. 24b, c, d, h, 3/4″ to 1′; No. 24g, 3/8″ to 1′; Nos. 25c–d, 3/4″ to 1′; No. 26a, 1/4″ to 1′

number of other widely scattered Puebloan sites in the Southwest (Cosgrove, 1947:155–160).

The Puebloan pictographs at Hueco Tanks are skillfully drawn and include

mountain sheep, deer, serpents, birds, kachina-like figures, masked heads, blanket-like designs, and other objects too highly conventionalized to be easily identified. These pictures are in a wide range of colors — red, black, white, yellow, brown, gray, blue, and green. They are found in large numbers at all parts of the site. (Kirkland, 1940:10)

These paintings are typically isolated single drawings; several masks or other designs may be found near one another on the walls of a single shelter, but each figure or design usually stands alone as an independent painting, unrelated to others. It is a static, placid style, partly because paintings of masks and geometric designs can hardly be dynamic and action-packed. But even in those few instances in which the full human figure is portrayed or in the animal drawings, in only one case (Plate 143, 23-D) has the artist indicated action.

The most common Puebloan pictographs are masks of many shapes and varieties. Some were not completed (Plate 126, Site 4, upper right) and others

PLATE 147

Hueco Tanks, Sites 24, 25, 26. 23-G is in the small shelter with 23-F.

24-B, C, D, G are low along the wall and on the base of the big rock in the main shelter.

24-H is low down on the bottom of a large leaning rock at ground level in front of the large shelter.

26-A is dim and crudely done under a shelter near ground level at Site 26.

are so conventionalized that it is occasionally difficult to distinguish a mask from a design (Plate 138, 15-A, right; Plate 147, 25-D). There are fundamentally two types of masks; the more common — there are fifty-one of them — is an outlined form. The exterior margins of the mask are always depicted and the salient features of the face are usually shown (Plate 131, 12-A; Plate 136, 17-H through 17-L, for example). "Forty-six of the outline masks are painted either in red or black or a combination of the two; three in gray; one in white; and one in gray and white" (Kirkland, 1940:14). Some are quite simple and perhaps should be described as simple faces rather than masks (Plate 136, 17-J, for example). Others bear quite intricate designs (Plate 131, lower right center; Plate 132, 12-C) or headdresses (Plate 144, 23-C; Plate 132, 12-C, 14-A). The other form of mask emphasizes facial features and ornamentation, and the outline of the mask may be absent (Plate 126, Site 4, lower right; Plate 130, 10-C; Plate 132, 12-B). They often appear to be much more masklike than the outlined form (Plate 136, 17-E, upper right, for example), but they are also easier to confuse with geometric designs which may or may not be masks (Plate 143, 24-A-1, A-2, 24-A-5; Plate 132, 12-B, for example).

The workmanship of the outline masks is generally much cruder than that of the solid type. The paint in most cases is thicker and less expertly applied and the designs are less artistic. Nearly all of the solid masks were painted with thin liquid color that seemed to have soaked into the rock like dye. Each individual block in the masks is sharp and distinct; and the designs themselves reflect considerable artistic ability. . . . Most of the solid masks are either red, black or white; three are in brown; two are in red and yellow; three in red and blue; and one in red and green—the only green we have found, so far, in Texas. Thus, the outline masks appear in only four colors while the solid masks are in eight. (Kirkland, 1940: 14)

Closely related to the mask paintings and also divisible into outlined and solid subtypes are drawings of the full human figure. A good example of the outlined type is painted on the smoke-blackened walls of Site 1 (see Map 6; Plate 125, 1-F). The central figure in yellow is a clear depiction of a warrior or kachina dancer with a short, tasseled kilt. The three lines below the eye, or eyehole if a mask was intended, are symbolic of rain among the Zuni and other Pueblos. The smaller yellow figure to the right, also clad in a checkered kilt, was probably painted by the same artist. Most of the other outlined humans, also apparently representing kachina dancers, are black (Plate 131, 12-A; Plate 143, 23-B, 23-D; Plate 144, 23-C), but there is one in red (Plate 136, 17-0), and near the entrance to a tunnel-like shelter is a human figure in a distinctive blue-gray color (Plate 140, 20-F). It has little in common with these others, but in a large rock crack nearby are a number of Puebloan designs painted in the same distinctive color (Plate 141, 20-C). A black-outlined figure of a woman (Plate 147, 24-B) is cruder and more hastily painted than other outlined humans and is only tentatively grouped with them.

Only a few human figures are depicted in the solid style, but some may be so conventionalized that they have not been recognized for what they are. One figure in white (Plate 133, 13-E), for example, may or may not represent a masked human. Jackson (1938:12) said that it is "known locally as a vinegaroon or whip scorpion"; Kirkland (1940:19) included it with other kachina-like figures, describing it as having "large horns and an elaborate face

in the solid mask style." Two other figures with truncated bodies are painted in solid gray outlined in white (Plate 145). Kirkland (1940:19) felt they were "of interest because their head dress represents highly conventionalized animal heads." The thinness of the paint, precision and deftness of execution, and being drawn in profile place them within the solid subtype of Puebloan paintings.

Another group of carefully, sometimes meticulously, executed paintings which Kirkland refers to as blanket-like designs are also attributable to the Puebloan style. They consist of "united series of geometrical patterns similar to certain textile designs, usually in a rectangular shape. When the pattern is enclosed by a border, as it sometimes is, the design resembles an Indian blanket" (Kirkland, 1940:20). At Site 7 (Plate 129, 7-A), for example, low down on the wall of a very narrow deep crack in the cliff are two such designs in red. They are quite dim as are those near a tank of permanent water at Site 17 (Plate 137, 17-C). The checkerboard pattern and shape of one of these (17-C, upper right) is reminiscent of a basketry container. But the mask-like object which adorns it and the one to its left gives them the appearance of weird, armless and legless anthropomorphic beings. The practice of adorning geometric designs with face-like elements is found elsewhere at Hueco Tanks. On the ceiling near the entrance to a deep tunnel-like shelter is a black and white example in which the face-like element contains a pair of eyes and feet (Plate 141, 20-G). About forty feet above this tunnel, outside a small shelter, is another very similar figure (20-1), but it has been exposed to blowing rain and was so dim that Kirkland had difficulty in copying it (Notes, Plate 141). Very high on the cliff in black and yellow is another example (Plate 142, 20-K, center top), and at Site 17 there seems to be still another in red (Plate 138, 17-A, right).

Some of the geometric designs are reminiscent of decorative elements on Pueblo pottery and may be derived from it. Under a large rock on top of the cliff at Site 17 (Plate 138, 17-B), for example, is such a design composed of stepped elements and abrupt angles in red and white. At Site 27 (Plate 149) are a number of random geometric figures in white, as well as one grotesque animal, which are also similar to those found on Pueblo ceramics. At Site 18 (Plate 139) similar designs in blue, yellow, red, and white are found "on the ceiling of a large cave containing one of the natural water tanks" (Notes, Plate 139). Some animal paintings are ascribed to the Puebloan style because of the care with which they are drawn and their static quality. Cases in point are the long-tailed birds (Plate 134, 17-F; Plate 143, 23-E; Plate 147, 24-D; Plate 144, 23-C, left) all of which are at rest and have the appearance of decorative designs rather than real birds. Because of propinquity to some outlined masks, a a simple black-outlined mountain sheep (Plate 131, 12-A, lower right) is classed as Puebloan, and several others may be (Plate 134, 15-E; Plate 132, 10-B; Plate 129, 7-B; Plate 129, Site 8; Plate 148, 26-B; Plate 138, 19-D). A group of three mountain sheep (Plate 144, 23-C, center top) and a snake above them, are executed in the same technique as some nearby masks. Only two other snakes (Plate 140, 20-E; Plate 141, 20-C) can safely be ascribed to the Puebloan style. A few grotesque animal pictographs also appear to have been drawn by Puebloan artists. On a low wall behind a large rock in a small uninhabited shelter is a dim painting of what was apparently a thunderbird (Plate 135, 16-A); there are no others remotely resembling it. In a small shelter high on a cliff at Site 20 (Plate 142, 20-K) are two black animals, apparently drawn by the artists who painted the other pictographs in this shelter. The round figure may be a turtle; the quadruped to its right seems to be a mountain sheep. At Site 20-E (Plate 140) is a carefully executed, rotund, symmetrical figure which is Puebloan in conception, though it too is a unique design at Hueco Tanks.

The raincloud altar (Plate 124, 1-C, center) is a typical and popular Pueblo device (Dutton, 1963: 58, 77), and the nearby zigzag lines undoubtedly represent lightning. The terraced motif has been borrowed from the Pueblos by other Southwestern tribes such as the Navaho, so that its usage does not necessarily indicate Puebloan authorship. But at Hueco Tanks it appears that all of the stepped pyramids, terraces, and altars should be attributed to the Puebloan style (Plate 133, 13-D, 13-F; Plate 142, 20-K; Plate 143, 23-F). The kiva murals at Kuaua, on the Rio Grande near Bernalillo, New Mexico, portrayed a terraced altar on top of which was a pottery vessel (Dutton, 1963:77). At Site 23 (Plate 143, 23-F, left center) there is a simplified version of the same device. Just below and to the right of it is a human wearing a tableta headdress, another typical item of Pueblo ceremonial attire. The parallel semicircular lines ornamenting these altars apparently represent rainbows (see also Plate 124, 1-C, center), and sometimes are used as isolated designs. To the right of the tableta-crowned figure, for example (Plate 143, 23-F), is a mustard-colored rainbow design from the bottom of which extend a series of lines, no doubt indicating rain. At the end of a long shelter very near the ground are some very dim, black designs (Plate 126, 5-A, 5-B). The terraced design is at least Pueblo-derived, and the checkerboard design is reminiscent of the kilt patterns in Plate 125, 1-F, but the paintings are so slipshod and crude that they are very hesitatingly grouped with the Puebloan style.

There are a number of isolated and for the most part geometric designs scattered among the shelters at Hueco Tanks. Many are difficult to assign to one or another style of painting, but those which are rather precisely drawn in thin colors or which seem to be traditional Pueblo designs have been tentatively assigned to the Puebloan style. The carefully rendered circular design in white and black on an exposed wall above a high rock at Site 2 (Plate 125, 2-B), for example, almost certainly should be associated with the nearby outlined mask painted on a ceiling about three feet high (2-A). The mask "appeared to have been originally in blue and white, but the blue had faded to a blue-gray" (Notes, Plate 125). The isolated design under a boulder high up on the cliff at Site 17 seems to be a very carefully painted conventionalized rainbow and rain symbol, and probably was done by the Puebloan artists who drew the masks at this site. "On the back wall of a small open shelter on the second level, badly exposed to blowing sand" (Notes, Plate 133) are several pictographs, one of which is quite curious. It is a black figure with a yellow inset design (Plate 133, 13-B), but whether it represents an anthropomorphic figure of some sort or something else is impossible to determine. The three solid black circles joined to one another with a black line next to this figure, and the black-outlined red circles also on the wall of this shelter, are unique to Hueco Tanks. Conventionalized and precisely executed, these designs seem best attributed to the Puebloan style.

The geometric designs on the ceiling of a small but deep shelter under a tremendous boulder at Site 9 and the nearby pictographs, are attributed to the Puebloan style (Plate 130, 9-A to 9-C; also Plate 129, 7-C, 7-D). Series of parallel lines, parallel zigzag lines, rake- or comb-like elements, and other more or less angular designs predominate. In terms of Pueblo symbolism, the comb-like and zigzag lines would be interpreted within the context of rain and lightning figures. "Under a large rock which forms a small shelter at the entrance to a small draw extending into the rock mass" (Notes, Plate 140) are another series of geometric designs which are not so readily interpreted, but because "they are very carefully drawn with thin paint" (Notes, Plate 140) they are assigned to the Puebloan style. The carefully drawn though now dim "stars" (Plate 141, 20-L) above a tunnel-like shelter may also be seen in Pueblo Kachina masks, occasionally as eyes, (Kirkland, 1934:24) and are therefore ascribed to the Puebloan style. The small, very precise design (Plate 142, 22-B) near some zigzag lines in what may be another style, are almost certainly the work of the artists who painted the terraced altar and the tableta headdress in a nearby cave (Plate 143, 23-F).

A second style of painting is much less common than the Puebloan but equally distinctive. These

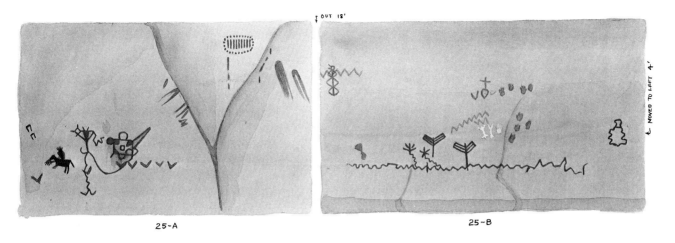

25-A   25-B

26-B

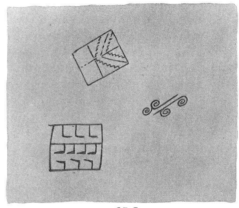

25-E

Plate 148. Hueco Tanks, Sites 25 and 26. Copied July 17–25, 1939. Scale: Nos. 25a–b, 1/4″ to 1′; Nos. 25e and 26b, 3/8″ to 1′

PLATE 148

Hueco Tanks, Sites 25, 26. 25-A and B are the main designs in a shallow, poorly protected shelter. Most of the red color is still very bright and probably not very old.

25-E is one of several very dim "blanket" designs under a small shelter near 25-A. Only these were judged clear enough to copy.

26-B is in a deep cave high up the cliff at Site 26.

pictographs are historic, white is the most frequently used color, humans and animals are depicted with solid bodies rather than being outlined, and scenes are portrayed in which humans and animals are related to one another in what appears to be storytelling form. They also differ from Puebloan paintings by being much more dynamic. Human figures are in motion — they dance, make love, cavort. Since the Mescalero Apaches were the principal tribe to frequent the Hueco Tanks in historic times, and because some of the elements in these pictographs are derivatively Puebloan, these paintings have been tentatively ascribed to the Mescaleros. But it should be understood that this terminology is a matter of convenience and probability, not established fact. These paintings have

virtually nothing in common with some presumably Mescalero paintings found northwest of Ruidoso, New Mexico, in the Sierra Blanca Mountains (Gebhard, 1957; also see Gebhard, 1958). The Sierra Blanca pictographs appear to date from the nineteenth century as do some of those at Hueco Tanks, so that a time differential cannot be invoked to account for the differences.

On a protected, vertical rock wall overlooking the entrance to the main tank (see Map 6) are a number of Mescalero style paintings (Plate 124, 1-A). The top of the pictures is about ten feet from the ground and a ladder or long-handled brush must have been used to paint them. "The white is quite thick and roughly applied. The yellow is also coarse. The black is so badly faded that in places it could hardly be detected. The red is the usual oxide of iron" (Notes, Plate 124). The sinuous white line in the central part of the panel, though lacking a head, has rattles and is undoubtedly meant to represent a rattlesnake. It is painted over the chest area of an upside down human figure. Whether this yellow figure and the two smaller ones to its right were painted by the same or other, earlier, artists is not clear. The attire of the man with the yellow coat, black trousers, and what appears to be a polka-dot shirt or vest (Plate 124, 1-A, middle right, upper) dates it as a product of the nineteenth century. If it is true, as some have said, that Europeans and Americans are often portrayed by Indians with hands on hips, then most of the other figures on this rock are intended to represent white men. This manner of painting white men derives from the fact that the hands on hips posture was and is one of their common bodily habits, but it was rare or absent among Indian tribes. The artist had only to show posture to convey the identity of the subject.

"High on a poorly protected wall which can only be reached from a high rock" (Notes, Plate 125) are a series of yellow, white, and black figures in some sort of clay paint (Plate 125, 2-C). They are very similar to those of shelter 1-A and are also historic, as the figure on horseback indicates. They probably are the work of the same artists. Below and to the right of these pictographs, exposed to the weather, is a red horse (Plate 125, 2-D). It is as crude as the white and yellow figures, but its size and color suggest that it may have been painted by other artists.

The most intriguing Mescalero paintings are at Site 6, locally known as "Comanche Cave" at the largest of the tanks. It

is about forty feet back in the narrow cave and is almost completely covered by a huge flat rock. It is said to have never gone dry. The water is cold, clear, and sweet. On the walls of the cave are many names bearing dates of 1849 and later. Most of the pictures in the cave appear to be historic. One set of conspicuous pictures was not copied, although they look somewhat primitive, because they were over-painted by some of the names. They pictured men wearing chaps with swords, riding horses, and were probably the work of white men. (Notes, Plate 127)

The liberal use of a heavy white paint, the way in which human figures are portrayed, and the manner of depicting snakes are similar to the paintings at Site 1. More care was taken by the artists at Comanche Cave, perhaps because they were portraying Indians on what was probably a ceremonial occasion, but the paintings at the two locations are undoubtedly the work of artists with a common artistic tradition. A circular design near the front of the cave (Plate 126, 6-A) is apparently in the Mescalero style since it was done with heavy white paint. In a dark recess (indicated on Plate 127, 6-D, as an irregular black spot) are several horses (Plate 126, 6-B) in the same style as the paintings on the cave's more accessible surfaces. A black horse (upper left) is superimposed over a face outlined in blue, which may be prehistoric and the work of other artists. One of the white figures (Plate 127, 6-D, left) is astride a horse, and a yellow horse and rider (Plate 127, 6-D, upper center) are also portrayed.

The human figures, all in heavy white paint save one which is blue (6-D, lower center), mostly wearing headdresses which look like rabbit's ears, are unlike most other paintings at Hueco Tanks in that

sexuality is the dominant motif. One of these Mescalero style figures (Plate 127, 6-C, lower right) represents the Humpbacked Flute Player, an ancient and widespread deity of the Southwest. The ultimate origin of this deity seems to be southern, apparently having diffused northward with other cultural traits to the Anasazi and other prehistoric southwesterners (Lambert, 1957:103). In turn, other people who came in contact with the Pueblos, such as the Navahos, borrowed the concept. Besides pictographs and petroglyphs, representations of this deity have turned up on pottery effigy vessels, in pottery designs, on stone statuettes, and in the kiva mural art of the Pueblos. The Flute Player is usually shown playing this instrument and in some kind of erotic pose. Sometimes he is playing his flute for animals, sometimes for a girl or girls, and occasionally he is portrayed making love, as he is in this pictograph. Petroglyphs of the humpbacked figure in north-central New Mexico are adorned with ear-like headdresses, and a stone humpbacked statuette from Pecos had attached rabbit ears at one time (Lambert, 1957:104–105). In the Navaho Reservoir District of northern New Mexico and southern Colorado, Pueblo petroglyphs of the humpbacked deity lack headdresses, but other human figures wear them (Schaafsma, 1963:34–35). The ear-like headdresses of the dancing figures in Comanche Cave are, then, proper and appropriate for paintings which feature a Humpbacked Flute Player. As is to be expected with an age-old concept which has spread to a number of different peoples, the nature and role of the Humpbacked Flute Player have come to be quite variable. His obvious associations are with fertility and reproduction, but some tribes also seem to associate him with rainfall, game, hunting, and tracking. Possibly significant is the fact that the phallus of the Flute Player in Comanche Cave is depicted in the same manner as the head of the large white and blue rattlesnake above him. Two groups of dancing figures, mostly attired in the same type of headdress (Plate 127, 6-D, left and center) also contain males with erect phalli, but they cannot be identified as Humpbacked Flute Players.

Kirkland thought that "the circular-bodied men" in Comanche Cave (Plate 128, 6-E) were not painted by the artist who was responsible for the cave's other paintings. But several of these rotund figures are executed in the same thick white paint and two have rabbit ears very similar to those of the white figures, so that they probably should be credited to the same source. Pictographs of what are designated as shield-bearing warriors are frequently found in central Montana (Conner, 1962: 30, 35; Mulloy, 1958:120ff; Secrist, 1960:7ff) and also in Utah (Wormington, 1955). They are virtually identical to the rotund figures in Comanche Cave

Plate 149. Hueco Tanks, Site 27. Copied July 17–25, 1939. Scale: 1/4″ to 1′

PLATE 149

Hueco Tanks, Site 27. These paintings are in a large deep shelter level with the ground at the extreme southern point of the south mountain. The ceiling is smoked black and the designs in white are very dim on the black surface. They can easily be reached while standing on the floor of the shelter.

and without question stem from the same artistic tradition. This is not to say that artists of a single tribe must have painted all the shield-bearing warriors. It seems much more likely that these particular figures were part of some unknown but popular trait complex which diffused over a wide area in historic times. These shield-bearing warriors obviously pose an intriguing problem in terms of distribution, origin, and meaning, but one which cannot be pursued here.

At Site 17, a large shelter at the base of a cliff, there is a tank of water utilized by many early travelers. Hundreds of names have been scratched on the smoked wall, to some extent damaging the paintings (Plate 137, 17-G). A large white rattlesnake dominates the paintings and is similar to the rattlesnakes which accompany other Mescalero-

style paintings (Plate 124, 1-A; Plate 127, 6-C). This identification is confirmed by two white rabbit-eared figures, differing from those in Comanche Cave only by being slightly larger. One figure is quite obviously male, the other female. The warrior (17-G, center) mounted on a white horse, carrying a round red, white, and black shield seems to confirm the identification of the "round-bodied" figures as shield-bearing warriors. He would closely resemble them if he had been depicted afoot.

There are several other places at Hueco Tanks where there seem to be Mescalero-style paintings. In a very large shelter at Site 15 there were once many pictographs, but Kirkland was able to make out only two white snakes (Plate 135, 15-C). Although these snakes seem to have never been finished, they are similar to the one at Site 17 (Plate 137, 17-G) and so are ascribed to this style. Under a shelter high up in a small canyon, in front of which are some water holes, are a few pictographs (Plate 132, 10-A). The positive white handprints, the angular design, and the anthropomorphic figure are apparently in the Mescalero tradition. A pictograph of a red horse on the saddle of which is a cross (Plate 125, 2-D), and two horses painted with mud or clay (Plate 135, 16-D) also seem to be the work of Mescalero artists.

Just above the ground under a high overhanging cliff at Site 14 are a few very dim but distinctive pictographs in an unusual brownish-yellow color representing another style of painting (Plate 134, 14-B). Two of the anthropomorphic figures are painted with an hourglass shape, a rare way of depicting the human body at Hueco Tanks. The only other instance of this style is at Site 17 (Plate 137, 17-G, left). These figures seem three-legged at first glance, but the male sex is probably intended. Three of the anthropomorphic figures wear headdresses with two horns or ears and resemble those of the Mescalero style. At least two of the animals are mountain sheep and perhaps all four are intended as such. Under a boulder at Site 15 (Plate 136, 15-B, center) is the upper part of a body grasping a spear or arrow below which is a deer—undoubtedly the work of these same artists.

A very sketchy, incomplete, red-outline drawing of what is apparently a horse (Plate 134, 15-D) is unlike other horses at Hueco Tanks attributed to the Mescaleros and probably is the work of other artists. On one of the walls of a tunnel-like shelter are a series of five diminutive archers outlined sketchily in black and engaged in shooting arrows at two black figures (Plate 140, 20-D). What appears to be a black-outlined mask and a rough parallelogram complete the paintings on this wall. Paintings on the shelter's opposite wall and on nearby rocks are of Puebloan style, but this similarity is hardly sufficient justification for so classifying these simple, equivocal little figures.

The cultural affiliations of many of the pictographs at Hueco Tanks are better known than those at most sites; consequently the reasons why they were painted are also better understood. This is particularly true of the numerous and varied Puebloan paintings. As Kirkland (1940:19) pointed out, seventy of the eighty-nine mask paintings

were found in small niches, crevices or shelters too small or otherwise unsuited for habitation; but adjoining or near very large well used shelters. Some of the mask paintings were reached with difficulty, and were copied while lying flat on the back, there being hardly room to sit erect under the rocks on which they were painted. Others were in small recesses, difficult to reach, immediately above the main shelter in plain view of the living quarters.

Historic Pueblo peoples frequently established shrines in small caves and depressions near their villages (Fewkes, 1924:378, 379, 382; Cosgrove, 1947:168; Kirkland, 1940:24). These contained pictures, dolls, idols, prayer sticks, and other sacred objects. The mask paintings in secret niches and high crevices at Hueco Tanks undoubtedly represent the remains of similar shrines. It seems unlikely that Hueco Tanks was ever more than a temporary residence of Puebloan peoples. But because plenty of cool life-sustaining water could always be found there it may have been regarded as a sacred or special place to which pilgrimages were made from Puebloan villages along the Rio Grande. Or, perhaps hunters or travelers periodically camped at Hueco Tanks. In either case it is likely that these Puebloans set up shrines, and by their prayers and rituals promoted rainfall, fertility, health, or other things, or in the case of travelers, guaranteed the safety and success of their journey.

Such surmise does not mean that all the Puebloan paintings at Hueco Tanks had as serious or as important a motivation as the mask paintings. Possibly Indians returning from visits to kinsmen in the north commemorated the designs they had seen or the deeply moving experiences they had just had by painting the rocks of Hueco Tanks. Perhaps some of the mask paintings and masked dancers, particularly those not in niches and crevices, may have been instructional, painted to teach children the nature of supernatural beings, just as kachina dolls serve to instruct Pueblo children. Perhaps some of the Puebloan pictographs were designed to serve as magical aids to hunters and warriors who passed this way. There may be other, equally plausible explanations. Whatever other purposes may be suggested for the Puebloan rupestrian art at Hueco Tanks, it should be taken into account that most of it is carefully drawn and that a considerable expenditure of time and effort went into its execution, so that little if any of it would seem to fall into the category of idle scribbling or doodling.

The historic Indian pictographs at Hueco Tanks, the bulk of which have been ascribed to the Mescalero Apaches, are somewhat more difficult to interpret than the prehistoric paintings. It cannot be positively established that they are of Mescalero origin, and they cannot be fully explained by what is known about the socio-religious customs and beliefs of the Mescaleros. The Mescalero-style paintings which portray white men (Plate 124, 1-A) should probably be accounted for within the context of explanatory devices. They visually depict, perhaps for those not familiar with white men, their dress, bodily posture, and perhaps some of their activities. It is difficult to find any other explanation for these paintings, but the fact that they are high on a wall out of reach of a person standing on the ground strikes a discordant note for such an interpretation.

The main body of Mescalero-style paintings, painted on the dark, secluded walls of Comanche Cave (Plate 127; Plate 128, 6-E), are much clearer in meaning. The presence of the Humpbacked Flute Player demonstrates that there is a connection between these pictographs and mythical, supernatural beings and with the belief system in general. In a more specific sense, the paintings are

Rocky Dell. See Plates 150, 151, 152.

concerned with procreation, and hence with reproduction and fertility, certainly with that of humans and perhaps with that of other animals. Assuming that the identification of the artists as Mescaleros is correct, it should be recalled that one of the sources of supernatural power resides in Mountain Spirits (Gahe) who live in caves in mountains. In short, Comanche Cave may well have been an abode of supernatural beings, a sacred place to the Mescaleros.

Rocky Dell and the Panhandle

On a tributary of the Canadian River in the Texas Panhandle, a few miles northwest of Adrian in Oldham County, is a long-known group of rock paintings and petroglyphs. This rock shelter, known as Rocky Dell, was first reported in 1853 by members of a government party surveying possible routes for a railroad to California (Whipple et al., 1856); it was mentioned by Mallery (1886) in his pioneering work on pictographs and by later investigators (Studer, 1931; Jackson, 1938). Lieutenant Whipple of the original survey party remarked:

The first of the Indian hieroglyphics discovered upon our route were at Rocky Dell creek, between the edge of the Llano Estacado and the Canadian. The stream flows through a gorge, upon one side of which a shelving sandstone rock forms a sort of cave. The roof is covered with paintings, some evidently ancient, and beneath are innumerable carvings of footprints, animals, and symmetrical lines. (Whipple et al., 1856:36–37)

Many of the rock paintings were copied for the Whipple report and a comparison of them with those Kirkland made in 1941 reveals that some have been completely obliterated, others are much disintegrated, and some are little changed. Whipple, for example, reproduced what appeared to be an alligator that had been drawn immediately under a distinctive human figure (Plate 150, No. 2, at left) but Kirkland failed to find a trace of it. On the other hand, the "plumed serpent" (Plate 150, No. 1), a drawing of an animal over thirteen feet long, was depicted very similarly by the two men. A human figure, which Kirkland could reproduce only as undistinguished blobs of red (Plate 150, No. 2, center), Whipple copied as unquestionably a human, noting that it "is much defaced, and appears to be very old. It occupies a conspicuous part of the rock. The figure is naked, and to the head are appended circles, as if to represent enormous ears. In one hand is a huge club, and in the other a sword. The colors used are red, black, and white" (Whipple et al., 1856:37). Jackson (1938:311) took exception to this interpretation, arguing:

One can easily understand why an army lieutenant might interpret the curved line as a sword; but the present writer doubts if it was intended as such. If it represents a sword, then the other object might well be a gun, rather than a club. A seemingly significant point overlooked by him is that the hairdress, which he describes as "appended circles," is strikingly like the whorls worn by Hopi girls on reaching the marriageable age.

Some of the Rocky Dell paintings are historic, for horsemen are portrayed in Kirkland's work (Plate 150, No. 3, right), and Whipple noted others, now obliterated, the sketches of which were also

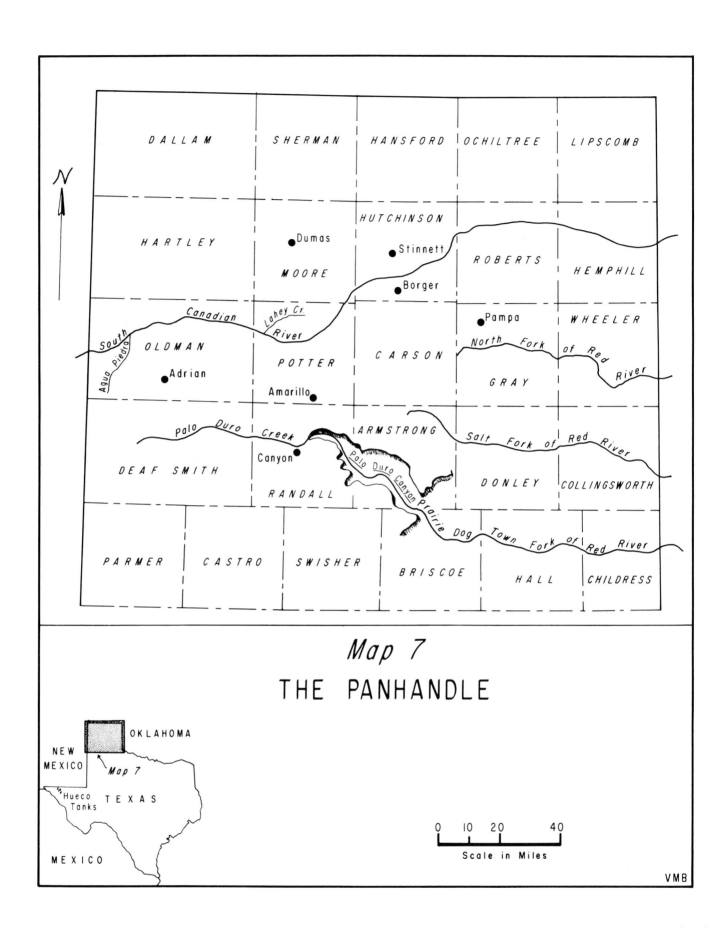

Map 7
THE PANHANDLE

lost. He said of these, however (Whipple *et al.*, 1856:37–38):

This series, more than the others, seems to represent a chain of historical events, being embraced by serpentine lines. First is a rude sketch resembling a ship, with sails; then comes a horse, with gay trappings, a man with a long speaking-trumpet being mounted upon him, while a little bare-legged Indian stands in wonder behind. Below this group are several singular looking figures: men, with the horns of an ox, with arms, hands, and fingers extended as if in astonishment, and with clawed feet. Following the curved line, we come to the circle, enclosing a Spanish caballero, who extends his hands in amity to the naked Indian standing without. Next appears a group with an officer and a priest bearing the emblem of Christianity.

Some of the paintings of animals, because of the curvature of the horns, seem to be longhorn cattle rather than bison (Plate 150, No. 3, left of center; Plate 151, No. 1, No. 2, left), and the hands-on-hips posture of one human and the long skirt of an adjacent one (Plate 150, No. 2, center) all suggest historic dates for these paintings. Other Rocky Dell pictographs and petroglyphs are probably prehistoric though it is impossible to demonstrate it conclusively for any specific painting. But that any of them are of great age seems unlikely. Kirkland remarked that "some antiquity has been claimed for these pictographs, but it should be noted that one of the dimmest groups at the site shows a buffalo hunt with a man riding a horse" (Plate 150, No. 3, right).

Though not of large size, the shelter at Rocky Dell contains a considerable variety of paintings, probably painted by several different peoples. The Canadian River Valley was a convenient highway into and from the plains, and places such as Rocky Dell must have seen the ebb and flow of many tribes through many centuries.

The outstanding picture at the site is that of a strange animal 13 ft. long, with horns, a vicious mouth, and a forked tail. It faces a smaller animal with long ears and tail and what appears to be an anthropomorphic man 4 ft. tall [Plate 150, No. 1, No. 2]. This strange animal is said to represent the plumed serpent, guardian of the water—a myth of the Pueblos, who were in New Mexico a little more than a hundred miles to the west. This may be true since Pueblo potsherds have been found at the site, but the writer has found no proof of the claim. (Kirkland, 1942:10–13)

While Lieutenant Whipple and his party were at Rocky Dell they were visited by Pueblo Indians. Querying them Whipple learned that "this place was once a favorite buffalo range, and here their fathers hunted, feasted, and danced, and then, sitting by the waterside, recorded their thoughts and deeds upon the rocks" (Whipple *et al.*, 1856:38). The large human figures (Plate 150, No. 2), Whipple was told, were "representations of Montezuma,

placed there to sanctify the spot, and secure a perpetual supply of water" (*ibid.*, p. 38). The plumed serpent, they told him, was "the great watersnake, created by Montezuma to give rain, and preserve the lives of those who should pray to him. They described it as being as large around as a man's body, and of exceeding great length, slowly gliding upon the water, with long wavy folds, reminding one of the accounts of the Nahant sea-serpent" (*ibid.*). Snakes are ritually and mythologically important to a number of Pueblo tribes, often being associated with rain and water, so there is no reason to doubt the essential accuracy of the traditional interpretation of this pictograph. And rock paintings of the plumed serpent have been found at other places in the Southwest (Cosgrove, 1947:155).

How many of the other pictographs at Rocky Dell were the work of these Pueblo hunters is difficult to determine. The style, technique, and colors of the plumed serpent and the two associated human figures are not so distinctive that they are readily distinguished from other paintings. However, their rather crude rendering and heroic proportions in relation to other paintings are two qualities which seem to indicate that other peoples also left pictographs on the walls of this shelter. This suspicion is reinforced by the diversity of ways in which human bodies are drawn. The lines of red figures, each adorned with a distinctive type of headdress (Plate 150, No. 3, left), for example, differ markedly from the solid red humans on the ceiling (Plate 151, No. 3) and from all the other scattered human representations. These red figures with the drooping headdresses are, incidentally, strikingly similar to some of the dancers found on the walls of Meyers Springs far to the south (Plate 73). The probabilities seem good, then, that at least several different tribes were responsible for the Rocky Dell pictographs.

There are also many petroglyphs at Rocky Dell, either sharply incised into or lightly scratched on the shelter wall or floor and in poor state of preservation. They consist of many aimless lines, simple geometrical designs [Plate 151, Nos. 12, 14: Plate 152, Nos. 1, 2], and human and animal representations [Plate 151, Nos. 8, 9, 12, 15; Plate 152, Nos. 3, 4, 5, 6]. The dozen or more outlines of sandals on the shelter floor are unique [Plate 151, No. 15]. No other such designs were found in the Panhandle, nor have we found similar designs anywhere else in Texas. Pictures of tepees were only found at this site [Plate 151, No. 11, No. 16]. The horse-back rider and the church date the work as historic [Plate 152, No. 5]. (Kirkland, 1942:13)

Although the medium of expression may effect their dissimilarity to the pictographs, Kirkland seems to have been quite right in remarking that "no similarity between the pictographs and petroglyphs at the site could be recognized that even

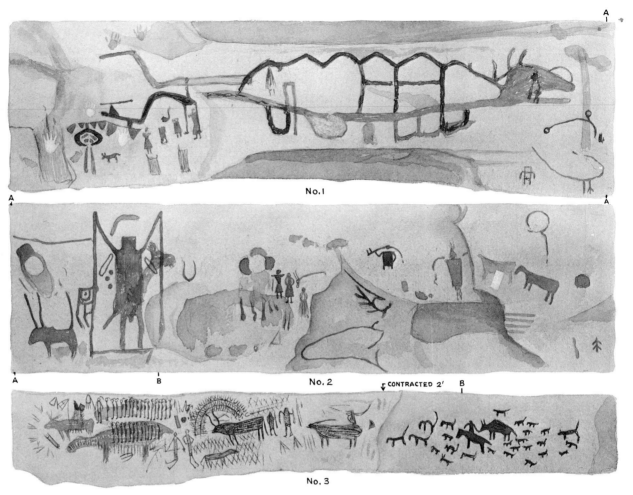

No. 1

No. 2

r CONTRACTED 2'   B

No. 3

Plate 150.   Rocky Dell. Copied July 14, 1941. Scale: Nos. 1–3, 3/8″ to 1′

PLATE 150

Rocky Dell. Nos. 1 and 2 are continuous on the back wall of this shelter and No. 3 is under them, its position indicated by *B*. The colors used were red, black, yellow, and white. Unfortunately, the principal designs have been chalked so heavily that it was difficult to make accurate copies.

PLATE 151

Rocky Dell. Nos. 1, 2, 3 are pictographs on the ceiling of the main shelter. No. 4 is on the ceiling of a small overhang to the right of the main shelter. No. 5 is on the ceiling of the small secondary shelter and Nos. 6 and 7 are on the wall at the extreme right of the main shelter. All of the petroglyphs (Nos. 8–16) were rubbed or carved into the soft sandstone. Some of the lines were originally fairly deep but now most of them are shallow and hard to see. Many of the lines were doubtless abrading marks made with little or no thought of design. No. 8 is on a ceiling less than two feet from the floor in a small recess to the left of the shelter. No. 12 is on the left side of the shelter. The lower part is on the ceiling of a recess so low that one must lie on his back to reach the designs. Nos. 11 and 14 are on the flat surface of tables at the left end of the shelter. Nos. 13, 15, and 16 are on the floor of the main shelter.

PLATE 152

Rocky Dell, Nos. 1–6. No. 1 is on a table of rock in the center of the main shelter floor. No. 5 is on a shelf of rock extending out under the right end of the main shelter. This rock is about seven feet above the edge of the cliff so that a ladder must have been necessary to reach the right end of it. Nos. 4 and 6 are on rocks about two hundred yards down the creek from the shelter on the east side.

Castle Rock, No. 7. These petroglyphs are on a conspicuously white rock formation on the banks of a small dry creek about half a mile from its juncture with Agua Piedra Creek, not very far from the Canadian River. The petroglyphs are deeply carved into the soft sandstone and look no older than the names and cattle brands carved by cowboys. It was almost impossible to determine exactly which lines were carved by Indians.

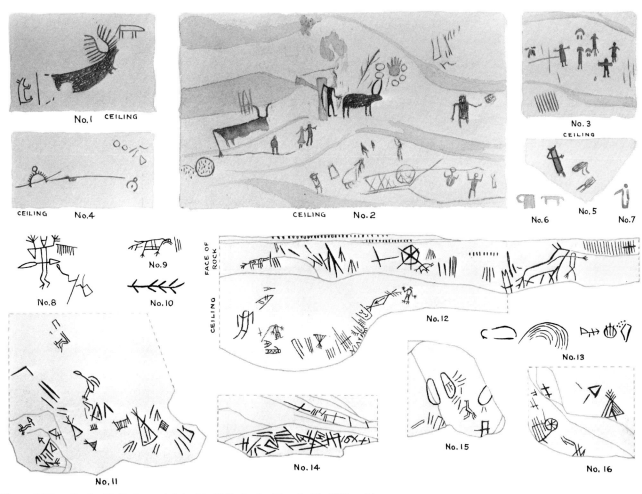

Plate 151. Rocky Dell. Copied July 14, 1941. Scale: Nos. 1–16, 3/8″ to 1′

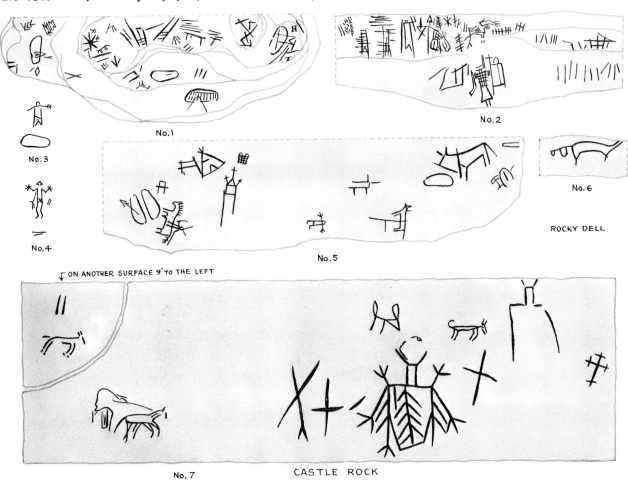

Plate 152. Rocky Dell. Copied July 14, 1941. Scale: Nos. 1-6, 3/8″ to 1′. Castle Rock. Copied July 17, 1941. Scale: No. 7, 5/8″ to 1′

Mujares Creek. See Plates 154, 158.

suggested that they were made by the same Indians. The fact that similar petroglyphs were found at seven other sites nearby containing no pictographs leads to the conclusion that they were not made by the same Indians" (*ibid.*).

About fifteen miles west of Rocky Dell on Mujares Creek, another southern tributary of the Canadian, are some of the state's most fascinating historic petroglyphs (Plates 153, 154). They are inscribed from five to twelve feet above the ground, scattered out for a distance of about fifty feet on the cliff bordering the creek. A narrow shelf between the protecting cliff and the creek provided an adequate camp ground. Of rare occurrence in Texas, surfaces within the outlined pictures had been smoothed in a number of instances (indicated on the plates as a gray, shaded area), and in two cases smaller petroglyphs were subsequently carved on this smooth surface (Plate 154, center). In another case "a deeply carved picture of a man about nine inches high wearing a robe of some sort" (Kirkland, 1942:19) had been painted red (Plate 153, No. 1, right of center). The petroglyphs are obviously historic since horses and firearms are frequently portrayed. Although Kirkland referred to the horned animals as bison, the size and curvature of the horns of some suggests that longhorn cattle were intended. If such is the case the petroglyphs probably date to post-Civil War days when cattle were first brought into this region. The group of carefully wrought weapons, consisting of three bows, thirteen arrows, three war clubs, and one gun, most of which are decorated with feathers or other ornaments, is unique (Plate 154, top). They are chiseled into the cliff above the other petroglyphs more than ten feet above the ground. The gun seems to be of the percussion type, which would date the petroglyphs no earlier than the 1820's. The other firearms (Plate 153, No. 13; Plate 154, far right), on the other hand, seem to be older flintlocks since they appear to be equipped with conspicuous frizzens.

PLATES 153 and 154

Mujares Creek. All of these petroglyphs were carved or scratched into the soft sandstone. The lowest design is about five feet above the present floor of the shelf, and at one place the petroglyphs extend fourteen feet above the floor. Plate 153, No. 1, is on the left end of the cliff. Plate 154 is a continuation of it, and is in correct position when the A's overlap. Plate 153, No. 8, joins Plate 154 on the right at *B*. Plate 153, Nos. 2 to 6, are to the left of the main group; Nos. 7, and 9 to 13 are to the right. Some of the petroglyphs were made with deep grooves while others were barely scratched into the surface of the rock. The thickness of the lines on the copies will indicate the depth of the grooves. Several designs were scraped smooth and slightly depressed into the rock. This is indicated on the copies by gray shading. One picture on the main panel (Plate 153, No. 1) directly above No. 11 is unusual in that it had been carved into the rock about one-eighth of an inch deep and then painted red. Many names and dates had been carved into the cliff, the earliest date noted being 1876. The Indian designs looked little older than the names and dates.

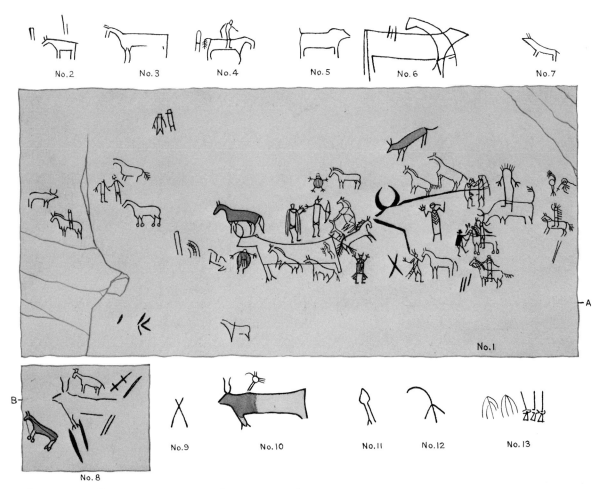

No.2 No.3 No.4 No.5 No.6 No.7

No.8 No.9 No.10 No.11 No.12 No.13

Plate 153. Mujares Creek. Copied July 19, 1941. Scale: Nos. 1–13, 3/8″ to 1′

Plate 154. Mujares Creek. Copied July 19, 1941. Scale: 3/8″ to 1′

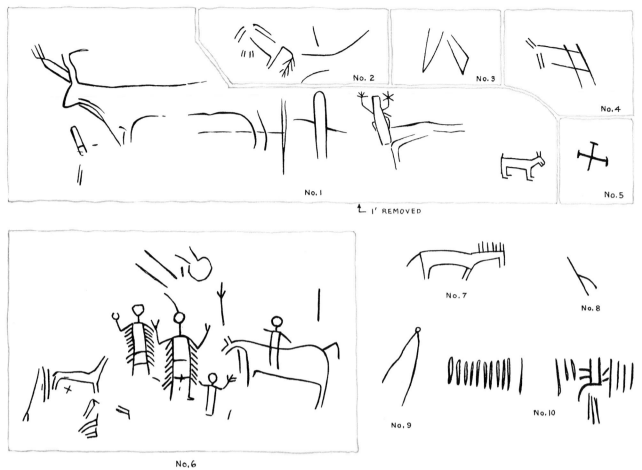

No. 2

No. 3

No. 4

No. 1

No. 5

⌐ 1' REMOVED

No. 6

No. 7

No. 8

No. 9

No. 10

Plate 155. Brown's Camp. Copied July 18, 1941. Scale: Nos. 1-10, 1/16″ to 1″

A few miles west of the Mujares Creek site are a few other historic petroglyphs "on rocks at the end of a small mesa in front of the ranch house at Brown's Camp on the Matador Ranch. . . . A good spring. . . . runs from beneath the mesa cap rock" (Kirkland, 1942:19). The petroglyphs had been deeply carved, but being in an exposed location they have weathered badly and are quite dim (Plate 155). On a red sandstone bluff on Agua Piedra Creek, into which Mujares Creek flows, are a few other petroglyphs. There are "several deep cut designs including two buffalo pictures more than five feet long [Plate 156, Nos. 15, 16], and a few small lightly scratched pictures of men and horses. The pictures are similar to those at Mujares Creek but more crudely executed" (*ibid.*, p. 19). Near the mouth of the creek on an isolated mass of gray sandstone are a few more petroglyphs. Unfortunately, "the few deeply cut Indian pictures can hardly be distinguished from names, dates, and cattle brands carved on the same surface by cow hands" (*ibid.*).

On the north rim of Palo Duro Canyon in the drainage of the Red River, southeast of the Oldham County petroglyphs, Kirkland found several other historic petroglyphs. "The designs are carved and

PLATE 155

Brown's Camp. These petroglyphs are on three of the boulders which have broken off the escarpment and are scattered out at the end of a mesa. The petroglyphs were carved fairly deep in the sandstone but now are so weathered that they can hardly be made out. No. 6 is on the exposed side of a boulder; the others are under protective overhangs.

PLATE 156

Agua Piedra Creek. These petroglyphs are on a red sandstone bluff on the west bank of this creek a few miles above its mouth. The designs of No. 1 were carved quite deeply into the rock. All the other designs were lightly scratched into the very weak sandstone and now can be made out only with difficulty.

Brown's Camp. See Plate 155.

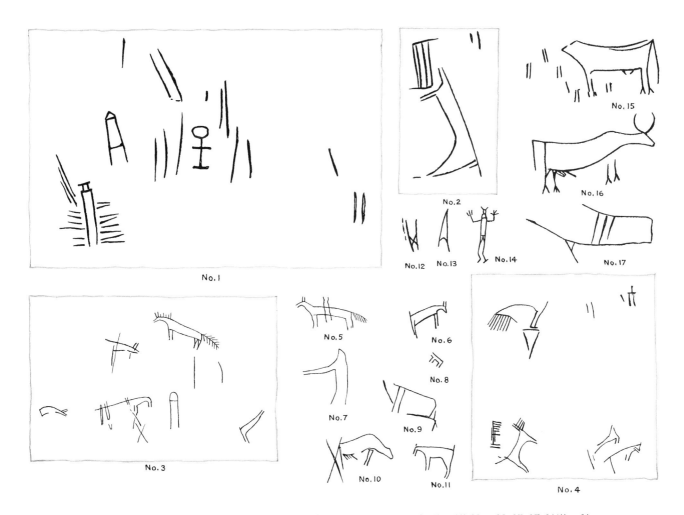

No. 1

No. 2

No. 15

No. 16

No. 12 No. 13 No. 14 No. 17

No. 3

No. 5

No. 6

No. 7

No. 8

No. 9

No. 10

No. 11

No. 4

Plate 156. Agua Piedra Creek. Copied July 18, 1941. Scale: Nos. 1–9, 11–14, 1/16″ to 1″; Nos. 10, 15–17, 1/4″ to 1′

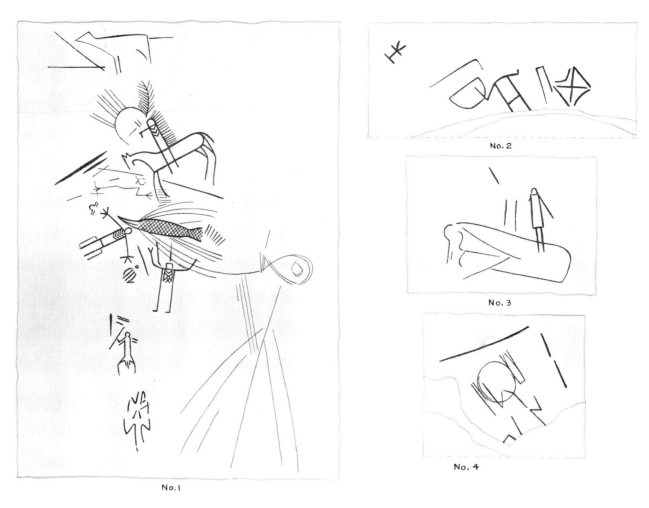

No. 1

No. 2

No. 3

No. 4

Plate 157.   Newton Harrall Ranch. Copied July 16, 1941. Scale: Nos. 1–4, 1″ to 1′

PLATE 157

Colonel Goodnight located his first camp on the rim of Palo Duro Canyon in 1877, and a stone fence Goodnight built still can be seen from the shelter in which these petroglyphs are located. The petroglyphs were scratched and carved into the soft sandstone floor of this small shelter. The scratched designs have almost completely weathered away.

scratched on the floor of a small shelter in the bank of a spring creek. The decorations on the men's clothing are of more than ordinary interest and the 'thunder bird' reminds one of the prominent painted birds at Meyers Springs in Terrell County [Plate 157]" (*ibid.*, pp. 20-23). The clothing decoration (Plate 157, No. 1, middle left) of one figure is identical to one at Mujares Creek (Plate 153, middle right); they probably represent hair-pipe breastplates, a popular ornament of Plains warriors. The similarity between the thunderbird (Plate 157, No. 1, crosshatched figure) and those at Meyers Springs seems strained, however.

Two petroglyph sites on the north side of the Canadian River also seem to date from the historic period. Near the mouth of Lahey Creek, northeast of Amarillo in Potter County, on the side of a small mesa are "both scratched and carved pictures of animals and men. The projectile point pictures at this site are similar to those found at many other late sites in various parts of Texas" (*ibid.*, p. 20) (Plate 158, Nos. 3-10). Several miles west of this site, at Chimney Rock, near some masonry ruins of the Antelope Creek Focus, are another group of

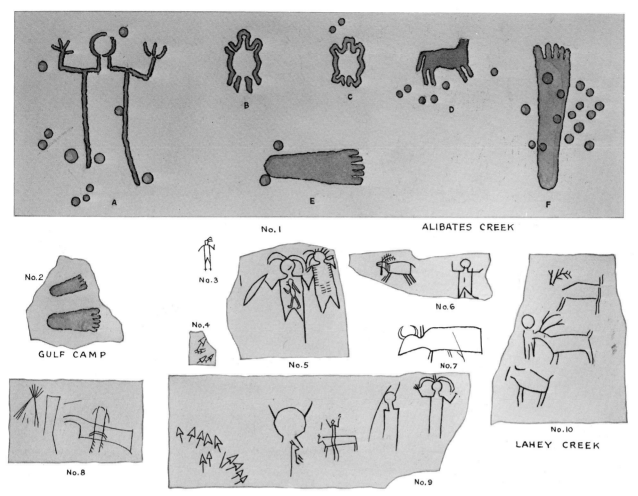

No.1

ALIBATES CREEK

No.2

GULF CAMP

No.3

No.4

No.5

No.6

No.7

No.8

No.9

No.10

LAHEY CREEK

Plate 158.   Alibates Creek. Copied July 17, 1941. Scale: Nos. 1a-f, 1/16″ to 1″. Gulf Camp. Copied July 21, 1941. Scale: No. 2, 1/16″ to 1″. Lahey Creek. Copied July 22, 1941. Scale: Nos. 3-10, 3/8″ to 1″

dim, badly weathered petroglyphs (Plate 159). Kirkland (*ibid.*, p. 19) believed that it was not "likely that even deep carved lines in the soft sandstone could have survived the six or seven centuries necessary to connect them with the ruins at the foot of the cliff." The petroglyphs also seem to be in the same style as other historic petroglyphs in the Panhandle, although there are no horses, guns, or other evidence of white contact.

A few of the pictures at this site show more realistic human forms than is usual for petroglyphs [Plate 159, Nos. 14, 15]. They resemble the designs painted on historic buffalo robes and on historic pictographic records like the autobiographies of Sitting Bull. One of these figures has its surface scraped away like the designs at Mujares Creek, suggesting a similar date for the work. Two or three other pictures of men at the site which we judged to be the work of white men may actually have been made by these very late Indians. (*ibid.*, pp. 19–20)

All of these historic petroglyphs in the Panhandle are quite similar to one another and are almost surely the work of one of the Plains Indian tribes which ranged this area. The preoccupation of these petroglyphs with horses, bison (and/or cattle),

PLATE 158

No. 1. Alibates Creek. These petroglyphs were pecked into hard limestone boulders along the escarpment about one hundred yards west of the Alibates Creek House ruins. The designs are very shallow and rough, and are difficult to see. The circles represent smooth shallow cups ground into the boulders; other boulders nearby also contained similar cups.

No. 2. Gulf Camp. The petroglyphs at this site southeast of Stinnett had been removed and only these footprints were located. There were originally about eight tracks, it was said, and several people who had seen the tracks reported that one showed the great toe at right angles to the foot.

Nos. 3 to 10. Lahey Creek. This Potter County site on the east bank of the creek about a mile north of the Canadian River, contains only petroglyphs, lightly scratched or carved into the very weak sandstone at the end of the bluff. Most of the designs are very dim.

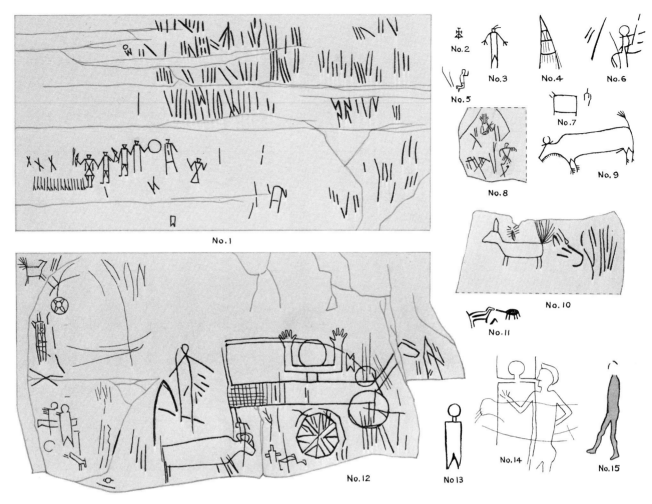

Plate 159. Chimney Rock. Copied July 22, 1941. Scale: Nos. 1–15, 3/8″ to 1′

PLATE 159

Chimney Rock. These petroglyphs had been scratched or lightly carved into the soft sandstone of Chimney Rock and the bluff at the end of the mesa. Nos. 1, 2, and 3 are on the east side of Chimney Rock. Only the bottom row of petroglyphs on No. 1 can be reached now without the aid of a ladder. Nos. 8, 10, and 12 are on the point of the mesa directly across from Chimney Rock. The other designs are scattered along the bluff for about one hundred yards west of the point. Nos. 14 and 15 seemed to be different from the other designs but looked like Indian work. Two or three other lightly scratched designs similar to No. 14 looked so modern that they were attributed to the white man and were not copied. No. 15 was scraped smooth like the buffalo designs at Mujares Creek, Plate 154.

weapons, and warriors reflects the major concerns of such tribes as the Kiowas, their Kiowa Apache confederates, and the Comanches. Any of these peoples could have inscribed these petroglyphs, probably during the last half of the nineteenth century.

At another site three miles from the Canadian on Alibates Creek at the Alibates Creek house ruin, a few miles west of Borger in Hutchinson County, are some very different petroglyphs (Plate 158, No. 1). The rocks are hard enough so that petroglyphs would last many centuries, and they are not like historic petroglyphs in the Panhandle. They may well be the work of the people who inhabited the ruins, though there is no direct evidence linking them together. These ruins belong to an archeological complex known as the Antelope Creek Focus, and are those of a people who lived in masonry buildings, practiced agriculture, and engaged in some hunting. Apparently originating in the Great Plains to the north, the Antelope Creek people had acquired a number of Puebloan traits. The discovery of several types of Puebloan potsherds at Antelope Creek sites dates the complex between

No. 2

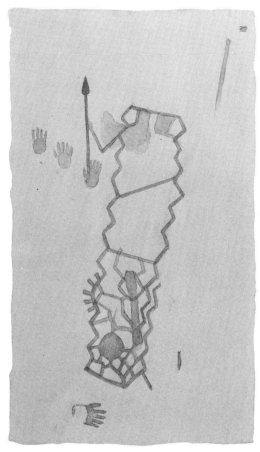

No. 1

Plate 160. Tulia Canyon. Copied July 23, 1941. Scale: Nos. 1–2, 5/8″ to 1′

PLATE 160

Tulia Canyon. These pictographs are painted in red on a chalk bluff on the west side of Tulia Canyon, Swisher County. No. 1 is protected by a slight overhang and is still quite clear. Its base is about four feet from the ground. No. 1 is about fifty yards to the right of No. 2, which is exposed to the weather and is now so dim that only a part of the design could be made out. Burned rock hearths and other signs of an extensive Indian camp were observed in the canyon below the pictographs.

A.D. 1300 and 1450. (A summary of what is known about the Antelope Creek Focus may be found in Krieger, 1946.) The petroglyphs at the Alibates Creek ruin

were roughly pecked into the top surfaces of hard limestone boulders. They consisted of a man, two turtles, a headless animal, and two exaggerated human tracks. On the same boulders and on others nearby were numerous small cup-shaped depressions, apparently small mortars not related to the pictures in any way. The largest track measures 24 in. long. The designs are now so badly weathered that they are not easily made out. (Kirkland, 1942:23)

At Gulf Camp, five miles south of Stinnett, Hutchinson County, there were once some petroglyphs of human footprints, much like those at Alibates Creek (Plate 158, No. 2). But someone had removed them and Kirkland was able to find only "one of the rocks which contained two tracks. The stone and workmanship was similar to that at Alibates Creek. However, the tracks—one adult and one child—were actual size and so realistically done that one can readily understand why they

were first reported as fossil human tracks" (*ibid.,* p. 23).

In south-central Oklahoma in Grady County, more than two hundred miles east of the Alibates Creek site, three pairs of human footprints as well as other petroglyphic tracks have been pecked on a rock outcrop. They are very similar in appearance and apparently in technique of execution to those in the Texas Panhandle (Lawton, 1962:191, 193). The distribution, significance, and relationships of such petroglyphic footprints are unknown; the Alibates Creek and Gulf Camp sites are the only ones in Texas where pecked footprints of this type are found.

The reasons why the walls and ceiling of the Rocky Dell shelter were painted may well be as diverse as the tribes that paused there. The plumed serpent, guardian of springs and streams, was almost certainly placed there out of concern for the ever-present problem in that land—water. But the other pictographs, perhaps painted by Plains Indians, may not have been the result of such a serious concern. Some may well be the products of idle hunters waiting out a summer's storm, spurred to leave their mark by the curious paintings already adorning the shelter. And almost the entire range of motivations ordinarily invoked to account for rock art can be found in one or another of these pictographs, from tally marks and personal signatures as represented in handprints, to hunt magic and the commemoration of ceremonial dances.

Oddly, Rocky Dell is the only major pictograph site in the Panhandle. Why paintings should be found here and not elsewhere is an enigma. There are many places in the area as suitable for rock paintings, and the presence of petroglyphs indicates that men were interested in decorating rock surfaces. But the only other known pictograph site in the Panhandle is in Tulia Canyon, in northwestern Briscoe County, where there are only several faint red paintings. Kirkland (1942:10) described them as "a highly conventionalized representation of a man, five feet high, holding a spear in his right hand, and four positive hand prints, all in dim red paint. . . . Faint indications of another man holding a bow could be made out on an exposed wall of the cliff" (Plate 160). They bear no similarity to those at Rocky Dell, or to any other pictographs for that matter.

Some of the historic Panhandle petroglyphs, particularly those at Mujares Creek, quite clearly record events of various sorts. The mounted warrior struggling with the black-hatted man over a spear (Plate 153, No. 1, right) is a good example, and there are many others. They are strongly reminiscent of Kiowa calendar histories—yearly records of tribal history painted on buckskin (Mooney, 1898). There are, incidentally, no close stylistic connections between the historic Panhandle petroglyphs and these calendars. Plains Indian warriors also recounted their exploits—the horses they had stolen, the coups they had counted—to their fellows at various social gatherings to enhance their personal standing. It is likely that some of these petroglyphs are part of this tradition, enduring records of personal achievements. But many of these petroglyphs cannot be interpreted within this context. The pictures of bison (or cattle) seem rather to express concern with a vital food source, and one which, so far as bison are concerned, was diminishing through much of the nineteenth century. There is no overt indication of hunting magic of the sort that is concerned with actually killing game, but there was no need for any if these petroglyphs date from the late half of the century. Mounted on swift ponies and equipped with excellent weapons, the Indians' problem then was not one of killing but of finding the bison. The need was to have an assured supply of these beasts, and these petroglyphs may well be portrayals of this wish, this necessity, which increasingly could not come true. A few of the historic petroglyphs seem best explained within the realm of tally marks (Plate 159, No. 1, lower left, for example); others may not have been this purposeful, and any explanation for some is mostly guesswork. Why an arsenal of weapons should be carefully carved high on the cliff at Mujares Creek, for example, is a puzzle. These faithful representations of weapons may have figured in some event, but this cannot be demonstrated in any way, and further conjecture seems pointless.

CHAPTER 9

A SUMMING UP

Hundreds, perhaps thousands, of distinct tribal groups have existed in Texas during the last hundred and more centuries. Some of them for one reason or another incised or painted rock surfaces. How much of this art has been destroyed is, of course, unknown although it seems reasonable to suppose that a majority of pictographs and a lesser number of petroglyphs have been obliterated. In any case, thousands of petroglyphs and pictographs have survived at more than two hundred sites and undoubtedly others will be discovered in the future. It seems safe, then, to conclude that engraving and painting rock surfaces was a fairly common practice of prehistoric and historic Texas Indians. But nowhere, so far as present evidence indicates, did the art of incising petroglyphs become a carefully nurtured habit, and in only a few regions was the painting of rocks a well-established, long-followed tradition.

The most distinctive, probably the earliest and longest continued tradition of rock painting in Texas, and perhaps in the New World, centered in a localized area around the junction of the Pecos River with the Rio Grande. This Pecos River style of painting seems to have been a purely indigenous growth, originating, developing, maturing, and dying in this relatively small area, neither receiving stimuli from foreign sources nor influencing to any great extent the pictographic art of adjacent areas. It was, it would seem, the product of a remote, isolated people. A far different kind of pictographic art is found in far West Texas, at Hueco Tanks and to a limited extent in the Panhandle. Consisting mostly of mask paintings, it was a product of prehistoric Puebloan people. This distinctive artistic style was expressed in several media, in ceramics and on kiva walls for example, so that these pictographs are part of a larger, relatively well known artistic heritage. The beginnings of Puebloan culture and this artistic tradition are ancient, and it has a long history, for in a general sense it continues to be produced by surviving Puebloan peoples. But the Puebloan pictographs in Texas were not painted throughout this long continuum; they seem rather to have been sporadically executed, probably at various times between A.D. 900 and about 1500. Though they are quite varied, these paintings do not evince any sort of stylistic development. They are also peripheral in that they are the easternmost representatives of this form of painting. The Puebloan civilization was a relatively influential one artistically, with many of its motifs being adopted by other artists. The pictographs at Hueco Tanks which have been ascribed to the Mescaleros, for example, apparently owe much to the Puebloan source.

Other than for the Pecos River and the Puebloan style pictographs, there seem to be no well-established, developed traditions of rock painting anywhere in the state. Numerous peoples at different places and times painted rock surfaces, but their pictographs do not suggest that they practiced the art frequently or consistently, or had benefited from any particularly strong heritage of rock painting. At one site, Paint Rock in Central Texas, a variety of peoples painted a profusion of pictographs, probably over a considerable period of time. This suggests that viewing pictographs is apt to stimulate other artists or would-be artists into trying their hand at this form of expression, and that as pictographs accumulate, the stimulus to paint is heightened. Perhaps this also accounts in part for some of the more recent pictographs in the lower Pecos River region. Undoubtedly the people who were responsible for the Red Monochrome paintings, and probably all the other peoples who left pictographs there, were aware of the ancient Pecos River style paintings which adorned the walls of so many rock shelters. There is, of course, no way of knowing precisely what sort of impact these pictographs had on later occupants of the region, but the fact that they also quite frequently painted its rock surfaces, while paintings are much less common in nearby regions, suggests that the earlier art may well have stimulated them too.

The rock art of Texas is remarkably varied, a fact which reflects the considerable extent of territory throughout which it is found, the many centuries during which it was produced, and the many different cultural groups responsible for creating it. Many pictographs, particularly in the Big Bend and Central Texas, are crude stick figures or simple outlines in single colors. Most of these are attempts to portray animals or men, but there are also many geometric forms, amorphous figures, "tally marks," and handprints. Most of the cruder figures are entities in themselves and do not seem to be intentionally grouped or related to other figures. Not all the scattered pictographs at the many small sites in these regions are necessarily rough and crude. The strange paintings at the Rock Pile Ranch (Plate 91), for example, were executed in several colors, the simple red figures at the Lehmann Rock Shelter (Plate 112) are surely an intentional composition, and the herd of diminutive black deer from a site west of Fort Davis (Plate 90) are anything but crude.

Standing in marked contrast to the many crude pictographs in the state are the complex and sophisticated paintings of the Pecos River style. This form of painting underwent considerable development, as has been demonstrated, and though shading, foreshortening, and other devices were never discovered by these artists, their art became refined and polished, and utterly unique. It can unhesitatingly be placed alongside the other great rock art of the world.

Between these extremes of roughness and polish are many varied paintings. The stiff and static pictographs of the Puebloan style, for example, represent another highly distinctive and far from crude type of pictographic art. Though it often seems ill-adapted to rock surfaces, yet it too is an impressive form of rock art. Finally, the petroglyphs seem almost as varied as the pictographs. The most complex petroglyphs Kirkland recorded, in Lewis Canyon in the lower Pecos River region (Plates 56–63), required a prodigious amount of labor to complete, whatever else may be said about them. They are quite different from the simple incised and pecked figures found at so many sites, and have little in common with the skillfully rendered men, horses, and other animals executed by historic Plains tribes at several sites in the Panhandle.

As the form of Texas rock art was varied, so too were the reasons for its execution. Though it is ordinarily impossible to be absolutely positive about why any particular petroglyph or pictograph was made, and the part it played in the social life of a people is apt to be obscure, often a surprising amount of evidence is available to be brought to bear on the problem. As a result, there is little doubt that the Pecos River style pictographs, for example, were painted for magico-religious reasons and were probably part of ceremonial or cult activities of the artists. Pictographs in other areas

were religiously motivated too—the Puebloan style paintings, for example; others seem to have been executed for a wide variety of reasons. Some of the paintings at Paint Rock appear to be tallies, perhaps enumerating the members of a group that passed that way. Such paintings may have served as messages for others, but they may not have been even this purposeful. Other incised and painted tally marks may be game counts or may represent any of a number of other things. The widely scattered, varied handprints may represent something akin to pre-literate signatures, or they may be simply the result of play; or possibly some have a deeper, magical, or other significance. Other rock art seems to commemorate various happenings, and many paintings and petroglyphs probably illustrate myths and tales; others, particularly historic paintings, seem simply to be illustrations of things observed in encounters with an alien white world. And some rock art, the petroglyphs in Lewis Canyon, for example, have as yet no adequate explanation. In short, the rock art of Texas seems to have been executed for a diversity of reasons, perhaps as varied as those which inspire a house painter, a small boy, a sign painter, and a Picasso in our own society.

Over a span of eight years Forrest Kirkland labored to capture on paper and so preserve for other generations the exact likeness of the Indian paintings and engravings he found throughout the western half of Texas. It was a prodigious task, as it turned out, and had it not been a self-imposed labor of love, could hardly have been accomplished. Certainly it would never have been done so skillfully. It was a task, too, that demanded multiple but scarce abilities and skills. It required a talented and experienced artist who could subordinate his own creative impulse to faithful copying of the work of others; it called for an ability to work rapidly under uncomfortable and trying circumstances, a fierce determination to persevere, a love of the outdoors, and a keen interest in the people who were responsible for this rock art. The paintings reproduced in this book are witness to the fact that in Forrest Kirkland these attributes were combined in a most felicitous way.

Although Kirkland succeeded in recording a tremendous amount of rock art in superb fashion, and apparently also obtained a representative sample of the kinds of pictographs and petroglyphs to be found in Texas, he copied only a fraction of the state's rock art, much of which still has not been adequately recorded. Until this basic task has been accomplished, understanding of the relationships between the rock art of various regions, its development through time, and its function in prehistoric cultures will remain fragmentary and tentative. Even in relatively well-known regions, such as the lower Pecos River country, it can be claimed only that a beginning has been made. There, because Kirkland amassed a quantity of data, it has been possible to trace the development of a pictographic style and, with the utilization of other archeological knowledge, to suggest the part that this art played in an Archaic culture. Yet, it should be obvious that much remains to be learned about Pecos River style pictographs. Their distribution, particularly on the Mexican side of the Rio Grande, is poorly known, the beginnings of the style are obscure, its association with an Archaic cultural complex can be demonstrated only in a general way, and the nature and characteristics of Pecos River style periods can probably be refined.

Kirkland, as it has been pointed out, was incensed that ignorant and thoughtless Americans were destroying rock art, and distressed that over the passage of centuries all rock art was slowly being obliterated. Consequently he felt that his task was of great urgency. The task is even more urgent today. In the lower Pecos River region, for example, water impounded in the Amistad Reservoir will in a few years inundate some pictograph sites and make many others much more accessible to vandals. Those pictographs which have not been recorded must be soon, or they will be irretrievably lost. Efforts must also be made to preserve those ancient paintings which soon will be more vulnerable to the fisherman's campfire, the hunter's bullet, and the idiot's pocket knife and paintbrush. The same statement and exhortation could be made about the rock art in many other parts of Texas.

Finally, petroglyphs and pictographs, whether rough scratches or complex polychrome paintings, are relatively rare and absolutely irreplaceable human documents. They can often reveal much about the ways of ancient men, including aspects of life which otherwise would forever go unrecorded, for they may illustrate how a vanished, nameless people perceived of themselves and their world, their relation to God and to each other, and their fantasies and fears. They are, then, a treasure to be valued and a heritage to be preserved.

APPENDIX

Because Forrest Kirkland numbered his copies of pictographs and petroglyphs chronologically, it was necessary to assign new numbers to the reproductions in this book, where they are geographically ordered. The concordance below is supplied for those who may wish to use or refer to the paintings by their original designations. Kirkland's paintings are deposited in the Texas Memorial Museum, The University of Texas, where they bear the numbers Kirkland assigned them.

New Plate Number	Original Kirkland Number
Chapter 1	
Frontispiece	61
1	43
2	44
3	45
Chapter 2	
4	88
5	89
6	90
Chapter 3	
7	101
8	102
Chapter 4	
9	30
10	31
11	38
12	39
13	40
14	41
15	57
16	42
17	96
18	97
19	46
20	58
21	59
22	60
23	62
24	63
25	64
26	65
27	70

New Number	Kirkland No.
28	71
29	78
30	91
31	93
32	98
33	99
34	100
35	108
36	109
37	110, No. 1
38	140
39	141
40	142
41	112, Nos. 1, 2
42	112, No. 3
Chapter 5	
43	34
44	35
45	36
46	37
47	66
48	67
49	68
50	77
51	92
52	94
53	79
54	107
55	76
56	80
57	81
58	82
59	83
60	84
61	85
62	86
63	87
64	69
65	103
66	P-1
67	P-2
68	P-3
69	95

New Number	Kirkland No.	New Number	Kirkland No.
Chapter 6		115	72
70	14	116	143
71	15	117	104
72	16	118	144
73	17	119	145
74	18	120	157
75	19	121	75
76	20	122	106
77	21	123	105
78	22	**Chapter 8**	
79	23	124	114
80	110, Nos. 2, 3, 4	125	115
	111	126	116
81	47	127	117
82	48	128	118
83	49	129	119
84	50	130	120
85	51	131	121
86	113	132	122
87	24	133	123
88	25	134	124
89	26	135	125
90	27	136	126
91	28	137	127
92	29	138	128
93	52	139	129
94	53	140	130
95	54	141	131
96	55	142	132
97	56	143	133
Chapter 7		144	134
98	1	145	135
99	2	146	136
100	3	147	137
101	4	148	138
102	5	149	139
103	6	150	146
104	7	151	147
105	8	152	148
106	9	153	152
107	10	154	153
108	11	155	151
109	12	156	150
110	13	157	149
111	32	158	154
112	33	159	155
113	73	160	156
114	74		

BIBLIOGRAPHY

Alexander, Herbert L.
1963   The Levi Site: A Paleo-Indian Campsite in Central Texas, *American Antiquity*, 28:510–528.

Anati, Emmanuel
1961   *Camonica Valley*. Translated from French by Linda Asher. Alfred A. Knopf, New York.

Bandi, Hans-Georg, and Johannes Maringer
1952   *L'art Préhistorique, les Cavernes le Levant Espagnol, les Régions Arctiques*. Charles Massin & Cie, Paris.

Bartlett, John R.
1854   *Personal Narratives of Explorations and Incidents in Texas, New Mexico, California, Sonora, and Chihuahua*. 2 vols. United States-Mexican Boundary Commission, 1850–1853, New York.

Baumhoff, M. A., R. F. Heizer, and A. B. Elsasser
1958   *Lagomarsino Petroglyph Site, Storey County, Nevada*, University of California Archaeological Survey Report, No. 43, Part II. Berkeley.

Bégoüen, Count [Henri]
1929   The Magic Origin of Prehistoric Art, *Antiquity*, 3:5–19.

Bégoüen, Henri, and L' Abbé H. Breuil
1958   *Les Cavernes du Volp, Trois Frères-Tuc D'Audoubert, Montesquieu-Avantès (Ariège)*. Travaux de l'Institut de Paleontologie Humaine, Arts et Metiers Graphiques, Paris.

Bellah, Robert N.
1952   *Apache Kinship Systems*. Harvard University Press, Cambridge.

Berndt, Ronald M. (ed.)
1964   *Australian Aboriginal Art*. With chapters by R. M. Berndt, A. P. Elkin, F. D. McCarthy, C. P. Mountford, T. G. H. Strehlow, and J. A. Tuckson. Collier-Macmillan Ltd., London.

Blair, W. Frank
1950   The Biotic Provinces of Texas, *The Texas Journal of Science*, 2:93–115.

Bleek, D. F., and G. W. Stow
1930   *Rock Paintings of South Africa*. Methuen, London.

Bleek, D. F., and J. and M. Van der Riet
1940   *More Rock Paintings in South Africa*. Methuen, London.

Boman, Éric
1908   *Antiqutés – de la Région Andine de la République Argentine et du Désert d'Atacama*. 2 vols. Imprimerie, Paris.

Breuil, Abbé Henri
1934   Peintures rupestres préhistoriques du Harar (Abyssinie), *L'Anthropologie*, 44:473–483.
1952   *Four Hundred Centuries of Cave Art*. Translated by Mary E. Boyle. Paris.

1955a   *The Rock Paintings of Southern Africa*. Trianon Press, London.
1955b   *The White Lady of the Brandberg*. With the collaboration of Mary Boyle and E. R. Scherz. Trianon Press, London.

Burkitt, M. C.
1928   *South Africa's Past in Stone and Paint*. Cambridge University Press, London.

Butler, Charles T., Jr.
1948   "A West Texas Rock Shelter." Unpublished M. A. thesis, The University of Texas, Austin.

Cain, Harvey T.
1950   *Petroglyphs of Central Washington*. University of Washington Press, Seattle.

Campbell, T. N.
1958   Origin of the Mescal Bean Cult, *American Anthropologist*, 60:156–160.

Carpenter, Rhys
1942   The Basis of Artistic Creation in the Fine Arts, in *The Bases of Artistic Creation*, by Maxwell Anderson, Rhys Carpenter, and Roy Harris. Rutgers University Press, New Brunswick.

Cartailhac, Émile, et L'Abbé Henri Breuil
1906   *La Caverene d'Altamira á Santillane près Santander (Espagne)*. Imprimerie de Monaco, Monte Carlo.

Castañeda, Carlos E.
1939   *Our Catholic Heritage in Texas, 1519–1936*. Vol. IV, *The Mission Era: The Passing of the Missions, 1762–1782*. Von Boeckmann-Jones Company, Austin.

Caster, Kenneth E.
1945   A New Jellyfish (*Kirklandia Texana Caster*) from the Lower Cretaceous of Texas, *Palaeontographica Americana*, III, No. 18 (March 15, 1945). Palaeontological Research Institution, Ithaca, New York.

Castetter, E. F., and M. E. Opler
1936   *The Ethnobiology of the Chiricahua and Mescalero Apache*, University of New Mexico Bulletin, Biological Series, Vol. 4. Albuquerque.

Childe, V. Gordon
1951   *Man Makes Himself*. Mentor Books, New York.

Christensen, Erwin O.
1955   *Primitive Art*. The Studio Publications, Inc., New York.

Clark, J. Desmond
1954   *The Prehistoric Cultures of the Horn of Africa*. Cambridge University Press, London.
1959   *The Prehistory of Southern Africa*. Penguin Books, London.
– – – (ed.)
1957   *Third Pan-African Congress on Prehistory* (Livingstone, 1955). Chatto & Windus, London.

Coffin, Edwin F.
1932 *Archaeological Exploration of a Rock Shelter in Brewster County, Texas,* Indian Notes and Monographs, No. 48. Museum of the American Indian, Heye Foundation, New York.

Cole, Sonia
1965 *The Prehistory of East Africa.* Mentor Books, New York.

Colton, Mary-Russell, and Harold Sellers Colton
1931 Petroglyphs, the Record of a Great Adventure, *American Anthropologist,* n.s., 33:32–37.

Conner, Stuart W.
1962 The Fish Creek, Owl Canyon and Grinnvoll Rock Shelter Pictograph Sites in Montana, *Plains Anthropologist,* 7:24-25.

Cooke, C. K.
1957 The Prehistoric Artist of Southern Matabeleland: His Materials and Technique as a Basis for Dating, pp. 282–294 in *Third Pan-African Congress on Prehistory* (Livingstone, 1955). Edited by J. Desmond Clark. Chatto and Windus, London.

Cosgrove, C. B.
1947 Caves of the Upper Gila and Hueco Areas in New Mexico and Texas. *Papers of the Peabody Museum of American Archaeology and Ethnology.* Vol. 24, No. 2. Harvard University, Cambridge.

Davenport, J. Walker
1938 *Archaeological Exploration of Eagle Cave, Langtry, Texas.* Witte Memorial Museum Bulletin, No. 4. San Antonio.

Davenport, J. Walker, and Carl Chelf
[1941] *Painted Pebbles from the Lower Pecos and Big Bend Regions of Texas.* Witte Memorial Museum Bulletin, No. 5, San Antonio.

Davidson, Daniel S.
1936 Aboriginal Australian and Tasmanian Rock Carvings and Paintings, *Memoirs of the American Philosophical Society,* Vol. 5. Philadelphia.

Delabarre, Edmund B.
1928 *Dighton Rock: A Study of the Written Rocks of New England.* Walter Neale, New York.

Dewdney, Selwyn, and Kenneth E. Kidd.
1962 *Indian Rock Paintings of the Great Lakes.* University of Toronto Press, Toronto.

Dibble, David S.
1965 *Bonfire Shelter: A Stratified Bison-Kill Site in the Amistad Reservoir Area, Val Verde County, Texas.* Miscellaneous Papers, No. 5, Texas Archeological Salvage Project. Austin.

Dorsey, George A.
1904 *The Mythology of the Wichita.* Carnegie Institution of Washington Publication No. 21. Washington, D.C.

Dorsey, J. O.
1884 *Omaha Sociology.* Third Annual Report, Bureau of American Ethnology. Washington, D.C.

Dutton, Bertha P.
1963 *Sun Father's Way, The Kiva Murals of Kuaua.* The University of New Mexico Press, Albuquerque.

Elkin, A. P.
1949 The Origin and Interpretation of Petroglyphs in Southeast Australia, *Oceania,* 20:119–157.

Elkin, A. P., and Catherine and Ronald Berndt
1950 *Art in Arnhem Land.* University of Chicago Press, Chicago.

Emmons, George T.
1908 Petroglyphs of Southeastern Alaska, *American Anthropologist,* 10:221–230.

Epstein, Jeremiah F.
1963 Centipede and Damp Caves: Excavations in Val Verde County, Texas, 1958, *Bulletin of the Texas Archeological Society,* 33:1–129.

Estill, Julia
1925 Indian Pictographs Near Lange's Mill, Gillespie County, Texas, *Publications of the Texas Folk-Lore Society,* 4:103–114.

Fewkes, J. Walter
1903 Prehistoric Porto Rican Pictographs, *American Anthropologist,* 5:441-467.

1907 *The Aborigines of Porto Rico and Neighboring Islands.* Twenty-fifth Annual Report, Bureau of American Ethnology, pp. 1–220.

1924 *The Use of Idols in Hopi Worship,* Annual Report, Smithsonian Institution, 1922. Washington, D.C.

Forbes, Jack D.
1960 *Apache, Navaho and Spaniard.* University of Oklahoma Press, Norman.

Forde-Johnston, James L.
1959 *Neolithic Cultures of North Africa.* Liverpool University Press, Liverpool.

Frasetto, Monica F.
1960 A Preliminary Report on Petroglyphs in Puerto Rico, *American Antiquity,* 25:381-391.

Friendly, Alfred
1963 Africa's Bushman Art Treasures, *National Geographic Magazine,* 123:848–865.

Frobenius, Leo, and Douglas C. Fox
1937 *Prehistoric Rock Pictures in Europe and Africa.* The Museum of Modern Art, New York.

Gebhard, David S.
1951 The Petroglyphs of Wyoming: A Preliminary Paper, *El Palacio,* 58:67–81.

1957 Pictographs in the Sierra Blanca Mountains, *El Palacio,* 64:215–221.

1958 Hidden Lake Pictographs, *El Palacio,* 65:146–149.

1960 *Prehistoric Paintings of the Diablo Region—A Preliminary Report,* Publications in Art and Science, No. 3. Roswell Museum and Art Center, Roswell, New Mexico.

Gebhard, David S., H. A. Cahn
1950 The Petroglyphs of Dinwoody, Wyoming, *American Antiquity,* 25:219–228.

Graham, John, and William A. Davis
1958 *Appraisal of the Archeological Resources of Diablo Reservoir, Val Verde County, Texas.* Archeological Salvage Program Field Office, Austin, Texas.

Graziosi, P.
1961 *Paleolithic Art.* McGraw-Hill Book Company, Inc., New York.

Grieder, Terence
1965 *Report on a Study of the Pictographs in Satan Canyon, Val Verde County, Texas.* Miscellaneous Papers, No. 2, Texas Archeological Salvage Project. Austin.

Haag, William G.
1960 The Artist as a Reflection of His Culture, pp. 216–230 in *Essays in the Science of Culture.* Edited by Gertrude E. Dole and Robert L. Carneiro. Thomas Y. Crowell Co., New York.

Heizer, Robert F.
1947 Petroglyphs from Southwestern Kodiak Island, Alaska, *Proceedings of the American Philosophical Society,* 9:284–293.

Heizer, Robert F., and Martin A. Baumhoff
1962 *Prehistoric Rock Art of Nevada and Eastern California.* University of California Press, Berkeley.

Hicks, F. N.
1959 *Archaeological Sites in the Jamau-Jaquijel Region, Baja, California: A Preliminary Report.* Annual Re-

port, Archaeological Survey, Department of Anthropology-Sociology, University of California, Los Angeles.

Hodge, Frederick Webb. (ed.)
1907 *Handbook of American Indians North of Mexico.* Bureau of American Ethnology, Bulletin 30, Parts 1 and 2. Washington, D.C.

Holden, W. C.
1937 Excavation of Murrah Cave, *Bulletin of the Texas Archeological and Paleontological Society,* 9:48–73.

Holmes, William H.
1888 *Ancient Art of the Province of Chiriqui.* Sixth Annual Report, Bureau of American Ethnology, pp. 5–194. Washington, D.C.

Howard, James A.
1957 The Mescal Bean Cult of the Central and Southern Plains: An Ancestor of the Peyote Cult? *American Anthropologist,* 59:75–87.

Jackson, A. T.
1938 *Picture-Writing of Texas Indians.* The University of Texas Publication No. 3809. Austin.

Jelks, Edward B.
1962 *The Kyle Site, A Stratified Central-Texas Aspect Site in Hill County, Texas,* Archaeology Series, No. 5, The University of Texas, Austin.

Jennings, Jesse D., and Edward Norbeck (eds.)
1964 *Prehistoric Man in the New World.* University of Chicago Press, Chicago.

Johnson, LeRoy, Jr.
1964 *The Devil's Mouth Site, A Stratified Campsite at Amistad Reservoir, Val Verde County, Texas,* Archaeology Series, No. 6, The University of Texas, Austin.

Keithahn, E. L.
1940 The Petroglyphs of Southeastern Alaska, *American Antiquity,* 6:123–132.

Kelley, J. Charles, T. N. Campbell, and Donald J. Lehmer
1940 The Association of Archaeological Materials with Geological Deposits in the Big Bend Region of Texas, *Sul Ross State Teachers College Bulletin,* 21, No. 3. Alpine, Texas.

Kelley, J. Charles
1947 The Lehmann Rock Shelter: A Stratified Site of the Toyah, Uvalde, and Round Rock Foci, *Bulletin of the Texas Archeological and Paleontological Society,* 18:115–128.
1950a The Livermore Focus: A Clarification, *El Palacio,* 64:42–52.
1950b Atlatls, Bows and Arrows, Pictographs, and the Pecos River Focus, *American Antiquity,* 16:71–74.

Kirkland, Forrest
1934 Archeological Notes. Typescript on file, Texas Memorial Museum, Austin.
1937a A Comparison of Texas Indian Pictographs with Paleolithic Paintings in Europe, *Central Texas Archeologist,* No. 3:9–26.
1937b A Study of Indian Pictures in Texas, *Bulletin of the Texas Archeological and Paleontological Society,* 9:89–119.
1938a An Archeological Survey of the Cranfills Gap Area, *Central Texas Archeologist,* No. 4:71–84.
1938b A Description of Texas Pictographs, *Bulletin of the Texas Archeological and Paleontological Society,* 10:11–39.
1939 Indian Pictures in the Dry Shelters of Val Verde County, Texas, *Bulletin of the Texas Archeological and Paleontological Society,* 11:47–76.
1940a Pictographs of Indian Masks at Hueco Tanks, *Bulletin of the Texas Archeological and Paleontological Society,* 12:9–29.
1940b An Interesting Indian Workshop in Coryell County, Texas, *The Record,* Vol. 2, No. 3:15–17.
1941 Petroglyphs of the Abilene District, *Bulletin of the Texas Archeological and Paleontological Society,* 13:63–76.
1942a Historic Material from Fielder Canyon Cave, *Bulletin of the Texas Archeological and Paleontological Society,* 14:61–71.
1942b Indian Pictographs and Petroglyphs in the Panhandle Region of Texas, *Bulletin of the Texas Archeological and Paleontological Society,* 14:9–25.
1942c The Series of Non-Pottery Sites in Dallas County, Texas, *The Record,* Vol. 3, No. 6:32–38.

Kirkland, Forrest, and Lula Kirkland
1941 Clear Fork Culture Artifacts from an Extensive Workshop in Nolan County, Texas, *The Record,* Vol. 3, No. 2:6–11.

Kirkland, Forrest, and R. K. Harris
1941 Two Burials below the White Rock Lake Spillway, *The Record,* Vol. 2, No. 10:49–53.

Kirkland, Forrest, R. K. Harris, and Robert Hatzenbuehler
1949 Refuse Pits Excavated in Site 27A-1-2, *The Record,* Vol. 7, No. 5:17–19.

Kirkland, Lula
1934-1939, 1941
Diary. Typescript on file, Texas Memorial Museum, Austin.
1940 A Pictograph Print of a Prehistoric Indian Bow, *The Record,* Vol. 1:23–25.

Krieger, Alex D.
1946 *Culture Complexes and Chronology in Northern Texas.* The University of Texas Publication No. 4640, Austin.

Kroeber, A. L.
1947 *Cultural and Natural Areas of Native North America.* University of California Press, Berkeley.
1948 *Anthropology.* Harcourt, Brace and Company, New York.

Kühn, Herbert
1956 *The Rock Pictures of Europe.* Translated from German by Alan Houghton Brodrick. Sidgwick and Jackson, London.

LaBarre, Weston
1938 *The Peyote Cult.* Yale University Press, New Haven.

Lambert, Marjorie
1957 A Rare Stone Humpbacked Figurine from Pecos Pueblo, New Mexico, *El Palacio,* 64:93–108.

Lawton, Sherman P.
1962 Petroglyphs and Pictographs in Oklahoma: An Introduction, *Plains Anthropologist,* 7:189–193.

Leakey, L. S. B.
1936 *Stone Age Africa, An Outline of Prehistory in Africa.* Oxford University Press, London.

Lehmer, Donald J.
1948 The Jornada Branch of the Mogollon, *University of Arizona Bulletin,* Vol. 19, No. 2.
1958 A Review of Trans-Pecos Texas Archeology, *Bulletin of the Texas Archeological Society,* 29:109–144.

Lhote, Henri
1959 *The Search for the Tassili Frescoes: The Story of the Prehistoric Rock Paintings of the Sahara.* Translated by A. H. Brodrick. E. P. Dutton & Company, London.

Mallery, Garrick
1886 *Pictographs of the North American Indian,* Fourth Annual Report of the Bureau of American Ethnology. Washington, D.C.
1893 *Picture-Writing of the American Indians,* Tenth Annual Report, Bureau of American Ethnology. Washington, D.C.

Maringer, Johannes
1960　*The Gods of Prehistoric Man.* Knopf, New York.
Maringer, Johannes, and Hans-Georg Bandi
1953　*Art in the Ice Age, Spanish Levant Art, Arctic Art.* In execution of a plan by Hugo Obermaier. Translated by Robert Allen. Frederick A. Praeger, New York.
Martin, George C.
1933　Archaeological Exploration of the Shumla Caves, *Big Bend Basket Maker Papers,* No. 3. Witte Memorial Museum, San Antonio.
1935　Report on Four Shumla Cave Packets, *Bulletin of the Texas Archeological and Paleontological Society,* 7:115-117.
n.d.　The Big Bend Basket Maker, *Big Bend Basket Maker Papers, No. 1.* Witte Memorial Museum, San Antonio.
Martin, George C., and Samuel Woolford
1932　Painted Pebbles of the Texas Big Bend, *Bulletin of the Texas Archeological and Paleontological Society,* 4:20-24.
McBurney, Charles B. M.
1960　*The Stone Age of Northern Africa.* Penguin Books, London.
Merwin, Bruce W.
1937　Rock Carvings in Southern Illinois, *American Antiquity,* 3:179-182.
Mooney, James
1898　*Calendar History of the Kiowa Indians.* Seventeenth Annual Report, Bureau of American Ethnology. Part I. Washington, D.C.
Mountford, Charles P.
1954　*Australia, Aboriginal Paintings Arnhem Land,* UNESCO World Art Series, Published by the New York Graphic Society, New York.
1961　The Artist and His Art in Australian Aboriginal Society, *The Artist in Tribal Society.* Edited by Marian Smith. Glencoe Free Press, Glencoe, New York.
Mulloy, William T.
1958　*A Preliminary Historical Outline for the Northwestern Plains.* University of Wyoming Press, Laramie.
Munro, Thomas
1963　*Evolution in the Arts, and Other Theories of Culture History.* The Cleveland Museum of Art, Cleveland, Ohio.
Murie, James
1914　Pawnee Societies, *Anthropological Papers of the American Museum of Natural History,* Vol. 11. New York.
Newcomb, W. W., Jr.
1961　*The Indians of Texas, from Prehistoric to Modern Times.* University of Texas Press, Austin.
Nicholas, Dan
1939　Mescalero Puberty Ceremony, *El Palacio,* 46:193-204.
Obermaier, Hugo
1931　L' Age de l' Art Rupestre Nord-Africain, *L' Anthropologie,* 41:65-74.
Opler, Morris E.
1935　The Concept of Supernatural Power among the Chiricahua and Mescalero Apaches, *American Anthropologist,* 37:65-70.
1936　The Kinship Systems of the Southern Athabascan-Speaking Tribes, *American Anthropologist,* 38:620-633.
1938　The Sacred Clowns of the Chiricahua and Mescalero Indians, *El Palacio,* 44:75-79.
1941　*An Apache Life-Way: The Economic, Social, and Religious Institutions of the Chiricahua Indians.* University of Chicago Press, Chicago.
1946　The Creative Role of Shamanism in Mescalero Apache Mythology, *Journal of American Folklore,* Vol. 59, No. 233.
Peabody, Charles
1909　A Reconnaissance Trip in Western Texas, *American Anthropologist,* 11:202-216.
Pearce, James E., and A. T. Jackson
1933　A Prehistoric Rock Shelter in Val Verde County, Texas, *Anthropological Papers,* Vol. 1, No. 3. The University of Texas Publication No. 3327, Austin.
Pérez de Barradas, José
1941　*El arte rupestre en Colombia.* Consejo superior de investigaciones científica, Publicaciones del Instituto Bernardino Sahagún, Ser. A, Num. I. Madrid.
Pope, John
1855　*Report of Exploration of a Route for the Pacific Railroad from the Red River to the Rio Grande,* 33rd Congress, 2nd Session, House Executive Document No. 91, pp. 53-54. Government Printing Office, Washington, D.C.
Ray, Cyrus N.
1939　Some Unusual Abilene Region Burials, *Bulletin of the Texas Archeological and Paleontological Society,* 11:226-250.
1942　Prehistoric Paintings Covered with Stalagmitic Deposit, *Bulletin of the Texas Archeological and Paleontological Society,* 14:49-56.
Reed, Erik K.
1952　The Myth of Montezuma's Bison and the Type Locality of the Species, *Journal of Mammalogy,* 33:390-392.
1955　Bison Beyond the Pecos, *The Texas Journal of Science,* 7:130-135.
Renaud, Etienne Bernardeau
1936　*Pictographs and Petroglyphs of the High Western Plains,* The Archaeological Survey of the High Western Plains, Eighth Report. Department of Anthropology, University of Denver, Denver.
1939　Indian Petroglyphs from the Western Plains, pp. 295-310 in *So Live the Works of Men,* Edited by Donald D. Brand and Fred E. Harvey. University of New Mexico and the School of American Research. Albuquerque, New Mexico.
Rhotert, Hans
1952　*Libysche Felsbilder.* Ergebnisse der XI und XII, Deutschen Inner-Afrikanischen Forshungs-Expedition (Diafe) 1933/1934/1935. L. C. Wittich Verlag, Darmstadt.
Rosenthal, Eric, and A. J. H. Goodwin
1953　*Cave Artists of South Africa.* A. A. Balkema, Capetown.
Rouse, I.
1949　*Petroglyphs. In Handbook of South American Indians.* Bureau of American Ethnology Bulletin 143. Washington, D.C.
Sayles, E. B.
1930　A Rock Shelter in Coke County, *Bulletin of the Texas Archeological and Paleontological Society,* 2:33-40.
1935　An Archaeological Survey of Texas, *Medallion Papers,* No. 17. Gila Pueblo, Globe, Arizona.
Schaafsma, Polly
1963　*Rock Art in the Navajo Reservoir District,* Museum of New Mexico Papers in Anthropology, No. 7. Santa Fe.
Schuetz, Mardith K.
1956　An Analysis of Val Verde County Cave Material,

Bulletin of the Texas Archeological Society, 27:129–160.

1961 An Analysis of Val Verde County Cave Material: Part II, *Bulletin of the Texas Archaeological Society,* 31:167–205.

Secrist, Kenneth G.
1960 *Pictographs in Central Montana* (Part I: Fergus County), Anthropology and Sociology Papers No. 20. Montana State University, Missoula.

Setzler, F. M.
1933 *Prehistoric Cave Dwellers of Texas, Explorations and Fieldwork of the Smithsonian Institution in 1932.* Washington, D.C.

Sherfessee, Charles Moseley
1963 The Paint Rock Pictographs. Unpublished thesis, Midwestern University, Wichita Falls, Texas.

Shuffler, R. Henderson
1934 Blue Mountain Caves in Indian Days Described by Captain Cook, *Odessa News-Times,* December 7, 1934.

Simpson, Colin
1953 *Adam in Ochre.* Frederick Praeger, New York.

Solecki, Ralph S.
1952 A Petroglyph in Northern Alaska, *American Antiquity,* 18:63–64.

Sonnichsen, Charles L.
1958 *The Mescalero Apaches.* University of Oklahoma Press, Norman.

Spencer, Baldwin, and F. J. Gillen
1899 *The Native Tribes of Central Australia.* MacMillan, London.
1904 *The Northern Tribes of Central Australia.* MacMillan, London.

Stanton, M. S.
1947 Pictographs from Tramping Lake, Manitoba, *American Antiquity,* 13:180–181.

Steward, Julian H.
1929 Petroglyphs of California and Adjoining States, *University of California Publications in American Archaeology and Ethnology,* 24:47–438. Berkeley.
1937 *Petroglyphs of the United States.* Annual Report of the Board of Regents of the Smithsonian Institution, 1936. Washington, D.C.

Studer, Floyd V.
1931 Archaelogical Survey of the North Panhandle of Texas. *Texas Archaeological and Paleontological Society,* 3:73-75.

Suhm, Dee Ann
1958 A Review of Central Texas Archeology, *Bulletin of the Texas Archaeological Society,* 29:63–107.
1959 The Williams Site and Central Texas Archeology, *The Texas Journal of Science,* 11:218–250.
1961 The Beidleman Ranch Site: An Early-Man Kill Site in Stonewall County, Texas, *Bulletin of the Texas Archaeological Society,* 31:207–212.

Suhm, Dee Ann, and Alex D. Krieger, with the Collaboration of Edward B. Jelks.
1954 An Introductory Handbook of Texas Archeology, *Bulletin of the Texas Archaeological Society,* Vol. 25.

Swanton, John R.
1915 Linguistic Position of the Tribes of Southern Texas and Northeastern Mexico, *American Anthropologist,* 17:17–40.
1940 *Linguistic Material from the Tribes of Southern Texas and Northeastern Mexico.* Bureau of American Ethnology Bulletin 127. Washington, D.C.
1942 *Source Material on the History and Ethnology of the Caddo Indians.* Bureau of American Ethnology Bulletin 132. Washington, D.C.

Tatum, R. M.
1946 Distribution and Bibliography of the Petroglyphs of the United States, *American Antiquity,* 12:122–125

Taylor, Herbert C., Jr.
1948 An Archaeological Reconnaissance in Northern Coahuila, *Bulletin of the Texas Archaeological and Paleontological Society,* 19:74–87.
1949 A Tentative Cultural Sequence for the Area about the Mouth of the Pecos, *Bulletin of the Texas Archeological and Paleontological Society,* 20:73–88.

Taylor, Walter W.
1956 Some Implications of the Carbon-14 Dates from a Cave in Coahuila, Mexico, *Bulletin of the Texas Archaeological Society,* 27:215–234.

Taylor, Walter W., and Francisco González Rul
1961 An Archeological Reconnaissance behind the Diablo Dam, Coahuila, Mexico, *Bulletin of the Texas Archeological Society,* 31:153–165.

Thomas, Alfred B.
1932 *Forgotten Frontiers, A Study of the Spanish Indian Policy of Don Juan Bautista de Anza, Governor of New Mexico, 1777-1778.* University of Oklahoma Press, Norman.
1935 *After Coronado: Spanish Exploration Northeast of New Mexico, 1696-1727.* University of Oklahoma Press, Norman.
1941 (tr. and ed.). *Theodoro de Croix and the Northern Frontier of New Spain, 1776-1783.* From the original document in the Archives of the Indies, Seville. University of Oklahoma Press, Norman.

Troike, Rudolph C.
1962 The Origins of Plains Mescalism, *American Anthropologist,* 64:946–963.

True, D. L.
1954 Pictographs of the San Luis Rey Basin, California, *American Antiquity,* 20:68–72.

Uhle, Max
1924 Explorations at Chincha, *University of California Publications, American Archeology and Ethnology,* 21:57–94.

Walton, James
1957 The Rock Paintings of Basutoland, pp. 277–281 in *Third Pan-African Congress on Prehistory* (Livingstone, 1955). Edited by J. Desmond Clark. Chatto & Windus, London.

Wedel, Waldo
1959 *An Introduction to Kansas Archeology.* Bureau of American Ethnology Bulletin 174. Washington, D.C.
1961 *Prehistoric Man on the Great Plains.* University of Oklahoma Press, Norman.

Wheat, Joe Ben
1955 *Mogollon Culture Prior to* A.D. 1000, American Anthropological Association, Memoir No. 82.

Whipple, A. W., Thomas Eubank, and William W. Turner
1856 *Report upon the Indian Tribes,* in *Reports of Explorations and Surveys To Ascertain the Most Practicable and Economical Route for a Railroad from the Mississippi River to the Pacific Ocean.* 33rd Congress, 2nd Session, Senate Ex. Doc. No. 78, 1856, Vol. III; Also House of Representatives, Ex. Doc. No. 91, Vol. III. Government Printing Office, Washington, D.C.

White, Leslie A.
1947 Evolutionary Stages, Progress, and the Evaluation of Cultures, *Southwestern Journal of Anthropology,* 3:165-192

1959   *The Evolution of Culture: The Development of Civilization to the Fall of Rome.* McGraw-Hill Book Company, Inc., New York.

Willcox, A. R.

1956   *Rock Paintings of the Drakensberg.* Max Parrish, London.

1963   *The Rock Art of South Africa.* Thomas Nelson & Sons, Johannesburg.

Windels, Fernand

1950   *The Lascaux Cave Paintings.* The Viking Press, New York.

Wormington, H. M.

1955   *A Reappraisal of the Fremont Culture.* Denver Museum of Natural History, Denver.

INDEX

Abilene, Texas: petroglyphs near, 164, 172

abrading marks: at Fort Sterrett, 161; Fort Chadbourne type, 167; at Breckenridge, 170; at Rocky Dell, 206

abstraction: at Altamira, 26; in Australian art, 32; in Pecos River style, 48, 57-58; Red Monochrome style, 88; in Lewis Canyon art, 99; of painted pebbles, 108; in Meyers Springs art, 121; in Fort Davis art, 130; in Balmorhea art, 135, 139; in Hueco Tanks art, 196, 197, 198

Adams Ranch: pictographs at, 78

Africa: Pleistocene fauna in, 28; rock art of, 16, 23, 28-31, 36

agriculture: of Basket Makers, 34-35; lack of, in lower Pecos, 60; lack of, among Tonkawas, 146; as Puebloan influence, 173, 189; of Mescaleros, 182, 189; of Antelope Creek Focus, 214

Agua Fria: rock art of, 10, 126

Agua Piedra Creek: rock art near, 206, 210

Alaska: rock art of, 32, 33, 34

Alberta, Canada: rock art in, 35

Algeria: rock art of, compared to Levantine, 28; Tassili n'Ajjer in, 29

Alibates Creek: petroglyphs at, 213, 214-215; house ruin at, 214

alligator: depicted at Rocky Dell, 203

Alpine, Texas: Victor Smith at, 10; near rock shelters, 40; Calamity Creek site near, 111; removal of rock art to, 126; mentioned, 7, 13

altar, raincloud: as Puebloan style, Hueco Tanks, 198

Amarillo, Texas: petroglyph site near, 212

Amazon River: rock art in area of, 33

America, rock art of: compared to Arctic, 27; general discussion of, 33-36. SEE ALSO petroglyphs; pictographs; rock art

Armistad Reservoir: Pecos River-style sites in, 37, 219

Anasazis: influence of, in Hueco Tanks region, 173; and diffusion of Flute Player deity, 200

anatomical features: of Pecos River-style shamans, 58; of Red Monochrome figures, 81, 84; of Red Monochrome animals, 84; of figures at Meyers Springs, 113; of figures at Rocky Dell, 205. SEE ALSO human figures; genitalia, male

Ando-Peruvian region: rock art of, 32-33

Anglo-Americans: and Texas Indians, 108; as painted by Indians, 200. SEE ALSO figures in rock art, human; hands-on-hips posture; white men

Angola: petroglyphs in, 30

animals: use of hides, 23, 30, 61, 75; game, 38, 39-40, 60-61, 62, 64-65, 143, 145, 146, 175, 200, 218; and mescal bean cults, 75; tracks of, at Fort Davis, 130; tallies kept of, 146, 218; associated with Flute Player, 200. SEE ALSO animals in rock art; hunting; hunting and gathering cultures; hunting cult; hunting grounds; hunting peoples

— in rock art: in Africa, 29; development of style, in Europe, 26; of Bushman, 30; in South America, 33; in Colombian-Vene-

zuelan region, 33; in Brazilian region, 33; of Texas plains, 35; of Canadian Shield, 33-34; in Canada, 33-34; at Mile Canyon, 39; in Pecos River style, 46, 52, 54, 57, 58, 65; associated with shamans, 46, 52, 54, 57, 65, 79; as source of supernatural power, 79; in Red Monochrome style, 81, 84-85, 87, 92; at Pressa Canyon, 94-95, 108; at Meyers Springs, 113, 119, 120; absence of, at Chalk Draw, 123; at Marfa Lake Shelter, 129; at Fort Davis, 130, 134; at Balmorhea, 135; at Rock Pile Ranch, 136; at Paint Rock, 146, 148, 152-153; at Lehmann Rock Shelter, 159; at Manaly Ranch, 172; at Hueco Tanks, 181, 185, 196, 197, 198, 199, 202; and Flute Player deity, 200; at Rocky Dell, 203, 205; in Lahey Creek petroglyphs, 212; in Alibates Creek petroglyphs, 215; in Panhandle, 218

antelope: Pecos River style, 60; Red Monochrome style, 84

Antelope Creek Focus: masonry ruins of, 212; Alibates Creek house ruin, 215; Puebloan traits of, 214-215; date of, 214-215

anthropomorphic figures: in Australian rock art, 31-32; in Basket Maker rock art, 35; in Pecos River style, 43, 47, 54; on painted pebbles, 108; in Bee Cave art, 123; absence of, at Chalk Draw, 123; in art west of Fort Davis, 130, 133-134; at Balmorhea Shelter 1, 135; at Paint Rock, 152; at Champion Creek, 164; at Brownfield Ranch, 164, 166; at Manaly Ranch, 172; at Hueco Tanks, 197, 198, 201, 202; at Rocky Dell, 205. SEE ALSO shaman

antlers. SEE horns

Apaches: rock art of, 34; use of mescal bean by, 75; Plains Apaches in Central Texas, 146; raids of, 175; at Hueco Tanks, 175; relation of, to Mescaleros, 175; trade with Puebloans, 189. SEE ALSO Kiowas; Lipan Apaches; Mescalero Apaches

Arapahos: use of mescal bean by, 75

archeology: Kirkland's interest in, 3, 4, 5, 6; rock art as related to, 17, 23, 32, 84, 89, 219

archeological sites: Archaic, weapons from, 41; artifacts from, related to shamans, 49; lower Pecos Archaic, 60, 64, 65, 70; mescal beans in, 60, 65; *Perdiz* point in, 89; at Kincaid Shelter, 143; Central Texas Archaic, 143, 145; Tonkawa Indian, Central Texas, 146; at Brownfield Ranch, 166; Breckenridge site, 169-170; Hueco Tanks, 195

— excavations: lack of, at Paint Rock, 153; at Lehmann Rock Shelter, 158-159; at Oak Creek Shelter, 169

archeologists: division of trans-Pecos Texas, 111; and El Paso Phase, 175, 195; mentioned, 173

archers: at Hueco Tanks, 202. SEE ALSO arrow points; bow and arrows

Arctic: rock art of, 27-28, 33; petroglyphs near Arctic Ocean, 33

Argentina: rock art of, 32, 33

Arizona: Western Archaic sites in, 40

Arnhem Land, Australia: rock art of, 31, 32

arrowpoints: Kirkland collects, 5; at Painted Rock Shelter, 89;

catfish: in Red Monochrome style, 85; as food, 60

catsclaw: in lower Pecos, 37; beans of, as food, 61

cattle: in Tassili art, 29; in Ethiopian art, 29; in African art, 29-30; zebu, 29; longhorn, 108, 205, 208; in Marfa Lake Shelter art, 129; in Panhandle petroglyphs, 213-214, 216

Centipede Cave: 40

ceramics, Puebloan. SEE pottery

ceremonies: puberty rites, 34, 121, 194; intervals of, 79; secret, and Pressa Canyon, 95; marriage rites, 121; at Paint Rock, 158; of Mescaleros, and rock art, 194; at Comanche Cave, 200; Puebloan, at Hueco Tanks, 202; at Rocky Dell, 216; Pecos River style, 218. SEE ALSO rituals

Chalk Draw: rock art at, 10, 123, 125

Champion Creek: petroglyphs at, 163, 164

Cherokee Indians: historic, in lower Pecos, 107; at Paint Rock, 156

Chibcha civilization: 33

Chief Bigotes (Mustaches): and Lipans at Paint Rock, 155

Child of the Water: Mescalero god, 190

Chile: rock art of, 32, 33

Chimney Rock: petroglyphs at, 212-213, 214

Chiricahua Indians: 175, 182 n., 194

Chiriqui, Panama: rock art in, 33

club: grooved, Western Archaic, 40; in Pecos River style, 41; at Rocky Dell, 203. SEE ALSO rabbit stick; weapons

Coahuila, Mexico: Pecos River style in, 37

Coahuiltecans: lower Pecos Archaic, 40, 60; Western Archaic, 40; historic, 60, 71, 100; use of mescal bean by, 71, 75; in lower Pecos, 100; language of, and Tonkawas, 146

Colombian-Venezuelan region: rock art of, 33

color. SEE pictographs, colors used; pictographs, methods of applying color

Colorado: study of rock art of, 18; Western Archaic sites in, 40; Pueblo petroglyphs in, 200

Colorado Plateau: Basket Maker-type art in, 35

Colorado River: rock art near, 143; Mescaleros on, 175

Comanche Cave: rock art in, 13, 180, 200, 202-203

Comanches: use of mescal bean by, 75; and Apaches, 107; historic, in Big Bend, 111; at Blue Mountain Shelter, 142; in Central Texas, 146; and San Saba Mission, 155; at Paint Rock, 156; and Mescaleros, 175, 181-182; at Hueco Tanks, 181; on southern plains, 189; petroglyphs as reflection of, 213-214

Comanche Springs: rock art of, 10, 126

Comstock, Texas: Red Monochrome site near, 81; mescal beans in shelter near, 70; Live Oak Hole near, 93; mentioned, 98

Concho River: rock art near, 3, 146; La Junta region on, 111

Congo: petroglyphs in, 30

Cook, Jim: 142

corn: at Paint Rock site, 153; in Hueco Tanks region, 173

costumes: in Pecos River style, 46, 49, 65; of shamans, 46, 65, 75, 79; of mescal bean cult dancers, 75; in Red Monochrome style, 81; of Pressa Canyon figure, 108; of Meyers Springs figure, 121; of Frio Canyon figure, 160; in Brownfield Ranch art, 166; in Mescalero style, 199-200; on Rocky Dell figure, 205; of Mujares Creek figure, 208; of Harrall Ranch petroglyphs, 212. SEE ALSO ornaments

cougars: in Pecos River style, 40, 54; in Pecos River-style art, 71; and hunting-cult theory of Pecos River style, 79; in Red Monochrome style, 85

cowboys: at Pressa Canyon, 105, 108; in Rocky Dell petroglyphs, 206; Spanish, in Rocky Dell painting, 205; Agua Piedra petroglyphs destroyed by, 210

coyotes: as food, 60; in Red Monochrome style, 85

crayons: used to apply color, 42; used in Parida Cave, 58; used at Balmorhea, 139

Crete: Mycenaen art of, 29

cultural debris: at Pecos River, 20, 77; at La Grèze, 26; in French caves, 24; in Pecos River-style sites, 39-41, 47; of Western Ar-

chaic, lower Pecos, 40; Archaic, and Pecos River style, 41; at Mile Canyon, 41, 42; Archaic, lower Pecos, 41, 64; near Langtry, 54; at Parida Cave, 54; animal remains in, 60; at Ingram Ranch, 74; and Red Monochrome style, 89; at Bee Cave, 97, 123; at Pandale Crossing, 97; at black pictograph site, 98; at Rio Grande Cliffs, 109; at Fort Davis site, 130; of Archaic, Central Texas, 145; at Paint Rock, 153; at Paint Rock Springs, 161; at Frio Canyon, 160; at Lehmann Rock Shelter, 158; at Brownfield Ranch, 166; at Fort Chadbourne site, 166; at Breckenridge, 169; at Moran Shelter, 170; at Hueco Tanks, 173, 175, 194. SEE ALSO artifacts; burned-rock mounds

culture: effect of, on artist, 19; definition of, 14; role of aborigine rock art in, 31; patterns of, in arid N. America, 40; recent clues to, 62; of Big Bend, compared to lower Pecos, 111. SEE ALSO culture, Archaic; culture, hunting-and-gathering; hunting peoples; pastoral peoples

—, Archaic: rock art as clue to, 18, 219; in lower Pecos region, 39, 62, 64, 70-71, 79-80; Early, 40, 145; Late, 40, 145; Middle, 40; Western, 40, 41; art of, 65; archeological sites of, 89; post-Archaic, 110, 123; painted pebbles of, 110; in Maravillas Complex, 111; in Wild Horse Creek area, 111; west of lower Pecos, 111; Bee Cave remains of, 123; in Central Texas, 143, 145; at Lehmann Rock Shelter, 159; in El Paso region, 173, 175; at Hueco Tanks, 195

—, hunting-and-gathering: of Red Monochrome artists, 89; of lower Pecos Coahuiltecans, 100; of Central Texas Archaic peoples, 145

Cumberland River: rock art near, 35

cups, natural rock: at Lewis Canyon, 98; at Alibates Creek, 213. SEE ALSO mortar holes

Cupeño tribe: puberty ceremony of, 34

Damp Cave: 40

dance: Pecos River-style shamans, 57; mescal bean cult, 75; in Pressa Canyon art, 93; in Meyers Springs art, 119, 120, 121, 205; significance of, in rock art, 121; in Paint Rock art, 158; of Mescaleros, 194; in Comanche Cave art, 200; Puebloan-style masks in, 202; in Rocky Dell art, 205

Danger Cave: Western Archaic site, 40

dart points: Archaic, 40, 145; Pecos River style, 49, 54, 56, 57, 58; associated with shamans, 49, 56, 57, 79; Red Monochrome style, 89, 92; at Pressa Canyon, 94; at Meyers Springs, 112; types of, in Central Texas, 145; at Brownfield Ranch, 164; at Champion Springs, 164

Davis Mountains: rock art of, 7-8, 130-131, 132, 133-135

Dead Man's Canyon: 72, 77

deer: in Kenya art, 30; in lower Pecos, 38, 64; in Pecos River style, 40, 52-54, 57, 60; in Fate Bell Shelter, 47; in Hanging Cave art, 70; and mescal bean cults, 71, 75; and Omaha dancers, 75; in Val Verde County art, 79; as source of shamans' power, 79; in Red Monochrome style, 84; in Pressa Canyon art, 94-95; in Meyers Springs art, 114, 121; in Fort Davis art, 130, 131, 133, 218; in Rock Pile Ranch art, 134-135; in Central Texas, 143, 145, 146; in Paint Rock art, 153; in Hueco Tanks art, 196, 202

deities: in Southwestern rock art, 34; in Colorado Plateau art, 35; and shamans, 65, 79, 80; of Mescaleros, 190, 194; Flute Player, 200. SEE ALSO shamans; religion

Delawares: in lower Pecos, 107; at Paint Rock, 156

Denis Manaly Ranch: rock art at, 172

de Sautola, Maria: and Altamira, 24

de Sautola, Don Marcelino: 24

Desert Culture: of North America, 34. SEE ALSO culture, Archaic

devil: at Indian Water Hole, 122; at Paint Rock, 153, 155

Devil's Mouth Site: 40

Devils River: and Castle Canyon, 105; Pecos River style near, 37, 113; mentioned, 13

Diablo Reservoir. SEE Amistad Reservoir

studies archeology, 5; diaries kept by, 5, 9; copying of rock art, 3-13 passim; at Comanche Cave, 7. SEE ALSO Kirkland, Forrest

Kirklandia texana Caster: named for Kirkland, 5

kiva wall art: compared to Puebloan style, 195; at Kuaua, and Hueco Tanks art, 198; Flute Player in, 200; Puebloan tradition, 217

Kodiak Island: petroglyphs in, 33

Koñate: at Hueco Tanks, 181

Kuaua: kiva murals at, 198

Kyle Site: painted pebbles from, 110

ladder: possible use of, in rock art, 92, 97, 109, 199, 206; designs as, 95, 98; as fertility symbol, 140

La Grèze: rock art at, 26

Lahey Creek: petroglyphs near, 212, 213

Lajitas: Comanche Springs site near, 126

La Junta Region: Jumanos from, 111; Marfa Lake Shelter near, 129; El Paso Phase influence in, 175

La Mouthe: discovery of, 24

lance: Plains Indian type, 120

Lange's Mill. SEE Lehmann Rock Shelter

Langtry, Texas: sites near, 8, 39-40, 41, 54; cultural debris in shelter near, 41; bison bone deposits near, 60

Lascaux: cave art in, 24, 26

leaf shapes: at Paint Rock, 148

Lehmann Rock Shelter: discussion of art at, 158-160; occupation site, 158-159; mentioned, 9

leopards: in Bushman art, 30

Les Combarelles: discovery of paintings in, 24

Les Eyzies, France: mentioned, 24

Levantine rock art: 28, 31

Levi Shelter: Paleo-Indian site, 143

Lewis Canyon: petroglyphs in, 12, 98-100, 218; paintings in, 68; compared to Bee Cave, 97; meaning of rock art of, 218

Libyan Desert: rock art of, 29

Libya, Fezzan province of: petroglyphs in, 29

life-line: in rock art animals, 27

lightning: in Puebloan style, Hueco Tanks, 198

line-and-circle motif. SEE rock art, geometric designs of

lines, parallel: SEE rock art, geometric designs of

lions: in Bushman art, 30

Lipan Apaches: historic, in Texas, 100, 107, 111; and missions, 108; 155; in Central Texas, 146; as Paint Rock artists, 153, 155; 156; mentioned, 175

Live Oak Hole: rock art at, 93

lizard: as food, 60; in rock art, 167

llama: in South American rock art, 33

Llano River: mentioned, 3; Paint Rock Springs site on, 12; Lehmann Rock Shelter near, 158

Llano River site: compared to Brownfield Ranch site, 166

Loma Pinta: name for Paint Rock, 155

longhorn cattle. SEE cattle

Lookout Shelter: rock art of, 58

Lower Paleolithic peoples: 23

lower Pecos, later art of. SEE Red Monochrome style

lower Pecos, primitive art of. SEE Pecos River style

lower Pecos River area: Western Archaic culture of, 40-41; Archaic culture of, 40, 111; cultural debris of, 41, 123; mescal bean in, 65, 70; miscellaneous art of, 92-95; lack of petroglyphs in, 98; historic Indians in, 100; painted pebbles in, 110; rock art of, compared to Big Bend, 111; southeastern trans-Pecos, 111; cultures of, 111; Panther Cave in, 112-113; art of Meyers Springs, 119, 121; post-Archaic of, 123; art of, compared to Fort Davis site, 131; compared to Central Texas sites, 143; Archaic point types of, 145; rock art of, 173; art of, as indigenous isolated style, 217; Amistad Reservoir, 219; mentioned, 19, 37-38

Lozier Canyon: and Indian Water Hole, 123

Luiseños: puberty ceremony of, 34

Magdalenian phase: of upper Paleolithic culture, 24; development of art in, 26

magic: rock art as, 26-27; in Arctic rock art, 27; in Levantine rock art, 28; in Bushman art, 31; in art of Nevada and California, 34; Pecos River style, 46, 218; Red Monochrome style, 92; Christian symbols, 123; hunting, 133-134, 216; at Fort Davis, 133-134; in Paint Rock art, 158; in Puebloan style, 202; handprints, 218; in Rocky Dell art, 216; in Panhandle petroglyphs, 216

mammoth: in lower Pecos, 39; Pleistocene, in Central Texas, 143

manos and metates: for grinding colors, 42-43; of Pecos River peoples, 40, 61, at Rio Grande Cliffs, 109

Mansos peoples: descendants of El Paso Phase peoples, 175

Maravillas Complex: Archaic occupation in Big Bend, 111

Marfa Lake Shelter: pictographs of, 127-129; historic art of, 129

Marsoulas, France: rock art at, 24

masks: in Colorado Plateau art, 35; at Hueco Tanks, 177, 185, 187, 189, 196-197, 198, 202; worn by Mescalero ceremonial dancers, 194; in Puebloan style, 196-197, 198, 202; kachina, 198. SEE ALSO costumes

Massachusetts: Dighton Rock in, 35-36

Matador Ranch: Brown's Camp on, 210

Mauritania, Africa: rock art sites in, 28

Maya civilization: and rock art, 33

medicine societies: and Pecos River style shamans, 65, 79; among Caddos, 75; deer hunting, 79; initiations into, 75

Mediterranean coast: rock art sites on, 28-29

Melanesia: and Australian rock art, 32

mescal: beans of, in historic Indian rituals, 61, 75, 79; cult of, and Pecos River style, 65, 70; range of, 65, 70; ritual use of, 70, 75; and peyote, 70-71; used by Caddos, 75; used by Tonkawas, 75; used by Coahuiltecans, 75; Caddo society of, 75; used by other Indian tribes, 75; as source of rock art, 80

Mescalero Apaches: historic pictographs of, 100, 107, 111; and missionaries, 108; defeated by Spanish, 175, 180; history of, 181-182, 189-190; and Comanches, 189; Puebloan influence on, 189; social units of, 190; religious beliefs of, 190, 194; and Chiricahuas, 194; rituals of, and rock art, 194; as Hueco Tanks artists, 202; Comanche Cave as sacred place of, 202; at Hueco Tanks, 199. SEE ALSO Mescalero style

Mescalero style: at Hueco Tanks, 198-203 *passim*; definition of, 199; other than at Hueco Tanks, 199; interpretation of, 202-203; in Comanche Cave, 202-203; Puebloan source of, 217

Mesillo Phase: peoples of, in Hueco Tanks region, 173, 175

Mesolithic period: decline of rock art in, 27

metate. SEE manos and metates

Mexicans: at Hueco Tanks, 180. SEE ALSO Spanish-Mexican influence

Mexico: valley of, archeological interest in, 33; Pecos River style in, 37; Coahuiltecans in, 60; mescal bean in, 65; Indian raids into, 107, 112; Tonkawas in, 146; Mescaleros and, 180

Meyers Springs: Kirklands at, 7, 115; Pecos River style in, 37, 111, 112-113; rock art of, 112-123 *passim*; early periods of, 112-113, 119, 121; use of, by men, 112; middle period of, 113, 119, 120, 121; miscellaneous designs at, 114; historic period of, 119-121, 123; evidence of periods of, 120; objects not assigned to periods, 121; methods of painting at, 121; as ceremonial site, 121; bird paintings of, 121; significance of red figures of, 121; significance of yellow pictures of, 121; red-outlined figures at, 121

midden. SEE cultural debris

Middle America: rock art of, 32-33

Mile Canyon: rock art of, 8; Eagle Cave in, 39; cultural debris in, 41

Mimis: in Australian rock art, 31, 32

minotaur: in Agua Fria Mountain rock art, 123

Middle Archaic culture: of Central Texas, 145

missions, Spanish: Caddos' use of mescal, 71; Coahuiltecans, 100; Texas Indians, 107, 108; historic period of Meyers Springs, 121, 123; Central Texas Apaches, 146; Lipans at Paint Rock site, 153, 155; in San Antonio, 155; along Rio Grande, 155

Mogollon: variant of Puebloan civilization, 173

monkey-like figure: historic, at Meyers Springs, 121

monochrome style: in evolution of Pecos River style. SEE ALSO Red Monochrome style

Montana: rock art in, 35, 200-201

Montezuma: figures as, at Rocky Dell, 205

Montignac, France: cave art near, 24

moose, pipe-smoking: in Canadian Shield rock art, 33-34

Moran Shelter: 176

Mormos (evil spirits): in Australian rock art, 31-32

Morocco: rock art of, compared to Levantine, 28

mortar holes: at Panther Cave, 58; at Pecos River-style sites, 61; of Pecos River-style peoples, and manos, 61; at Ingram Ranch Shelter, 74; at major Red Monochrome sites, 81, 89; at Pandale Crossing, 97; natural, 98, 213; at Rio Grande Cliffs, 109; at Meyers Springs, 112; at Blue Mountain Shelter, 141; at Paint Rock Springs, 161; at Fort Sterrett, 161; at Champion Creek, 164; at Hueco Tanks, 173; at Alibates Creek, 215

mountain sheep: in lower Pecos area, 38; in Puebloan style, Hueco Tanks, 196, 198, 202

Mountain Spirits: Hueco Tanks as home of, 194; and Mescalero religious beliefs, 190, 194; Comanche Cave as home of, 202

Mount Elgon: pictographs of, 29-30

Mount Livermore: rock art near, 130, 134

Mousterian culture: 23

Mujares Creek: historic petroglyphs on, 208, 210, 213, 214, 216

Murrah Cave: Archaic site, lower Pecos, 40; mescal beans in, 70

Mycenaen art: compared to Ethiopian, 29

mythology: in Bushman rock art, 31; in Australian rock art, 31; in Canadian Shield rock art, 33-34; in Washington rock art, 34; in Pressa Canyon rock art, 94; in Fort Davis rock art, 134; in Central Texas rock art, 146; of Mescaleros, 189-190, 194, 202; in Comanche Cave art, 202; of Pueblos, 205; in rock art, 218

Nachikufan culture: African rock art in, 30

Nahant: plumed serpent and, 205

narrative art: in Lehmann Rock Shelter, 159-160; rock art as, 218

Natal, Brazil: rock art near, 33

Navahos: rock art of, related to Puebloan, 34; and diffusion of Flute Player, 200; mentioned, 175

Navaho Reservoir District, New Mexico: rock art in, 18, 200

Neo-American peoples: in Central Texas, 145-146; Mesillo Phase as, in Hueco Tanks region, 173

Neolithic peoples: in Africa, rock art of, 29

Nevada: significance of rock art of, 18; rock art in, 34; Western Archaic sites in, 40

New England: petroglyphs in, 35-36

New Mexico: study of rock art in, 18; Spanish settlement in, and horses, 108; revolt of Pueblo Indians in, 175; Spanish campaign in, 175; Flute Player in petroglyphs of, 200

New South Wales, Australia: rock art of, 32

Newton Harrall Ranch: petroglyph site at, 210, 212

Nile Valley: rock art sites in, 28, 29

Northwest Coast culture: Pacific Coast rock art, 34

Norway: rock art of, 27

Nuclear American civilizations: rock art and, 33

Nueces River: rock art sites on, 143; mentioned, 155

Ohio: footprints in rock art of, 35

Omaha Indians: use of mescal bean by, 75

ornaments: bone, 61; in Pecos River style, 46, 61; in Red Monochrome style, 81; at Paint Rock, 152; at Mujares Creek, 208; of Plains Indians, 212

Osage Indians: use of Mescal bean by, 75

Otermin, Antonio de: 175

Oto Indians: use of mescal bean by, 75

overpainting: in Franco-Cantabrian art, 26-27; in Bushman art, 31; in Pecos River style, 41, 47, 54, 57, 58, 65, 79, 87; and Red Monochrome style, 41, 87; at Slick Trail Shelter, 58; in Panther Cave, 62; at Ingram Ranch Shelter, 74; at Pecos River, Cave 1, 77; at Pandale Crossing, 97; in Pressa Canyon, 108; at Meyers Springs, 121; at Fort Davis, 130-131; at Paint Rock, 148, 150, 152, 156; at Hueco Tanks, 195; in Mescalero style, 199; at Comanche Cave, 200; mentioned, 26

ox: in rock art, 29

Ozona-Langtry Road Crossing: rock art site near, 98

paintbrush: used for Mescalero style, 199; used at Hueco Tanks, 194, 195; use of, for pictographs, 42-43; used at Meyers Springs, 120; used at Hot Springs, 127; used at Fort Davis, 134; used at Balmorhea Shelter 1, 135, 139; used by Comanches at Blue Mountain, 142. SEE ALSO pictographs

Paint Canyon: Hanging Cave in, 70; Rio Grande Cliffs near, 109

Painted Cave. SEE Parida Cave

painted pebbles: discussion of, 107; of lower Pecos, 108-110; dates of, 110; distribution of, 110

Painted Rock Shelter: Red Monochrome site, 81, 87; Starr points at, 89

Paint Rock: Kirkland and, 3, 5-6, 7; compared to Rock Pile Ranch, 134; pictographs of, 146, 148, 150, 152-153, 155-158; possible artists of, 153, 155-157, 217; historic art of, 153, 155, 156; destruction of art at, 156-157; meaning of art at, 158; ceremonial site, 158; tallies at, 218

Paint Rock Springs: rock art of, 12, 161, 163, 166

Pair-non-Pair, France: rock art at, 24

Paleo-Indian cultures: of lower Pecos, 39-40; rock art of, 40; hunters of, 60; in Big Bend, 111; in Central Texas, 143, 145

Palo Duro Canyon: historic petroglyphs in, 210

Panama: rock art of, 33

Pandale Crossing: rock art at, 95, 97, 98

Panhandle, the (Texas): rock art of, 13, 34, 99, 173, 216, 217; map of, 204; Rocky Dell in, 203

Panther Cave: mortar designs at, 58; Lookout Shelter near, 58; figures in, 54; Pecos River style of, 62; panther picture in, 66; compared to Meyers Springs, 112

Parida Cave: art of, 54, 58

pastoral peoples: rock art of, 23, 29, 30; in Africa, 29; in Libyan Desert, 29; in Ethiopia, 29; in Kenya, 30

Patagonian group: of South American rock art, 32

Pawnees: use of mescal bean by, 75

Pearce, J. E.: 7

pebbles, painted: SEE painted pebbles

Pecos River Caves: paintings at, 77

Pecos River Focus style: ancient Pecos rock art as, 37

Pecos River region: rock art in, 8, 9, 12, 13, 20; Kirkland in, 9; Brown Ranch in, 9-10; Val Verde County art in, 12; rock art sites in, 24-25, 36, 68, 71, 72, 91; style of, 37, 217; Slick Trail Shelter near, 58; Lewis Canyon, 68; Pandale Crossing of, 95; black pictograph site on, 98; Apaches and, 107; mentioned, 113. SEE ALSO lower Pecos River area

Pecos River style: in Rattlesnake Canyon, 11; compared to Colorado Plateau art, 35; term for ancient Pecos rock art, 37; geographic area of, 37, 38; artists of, 39, 40, 41-43, 60-62, 64, 88; bison in, 40; local Archaic culture trait, 41; colors in, 41-43; shamans in, 43-58 passim; oldest, 47; periods of, 43, 46, 58, 75; Period 1 of, 47-48, 60, 94; evolution of, 47-48, 58; Period 2 of, 52, 54, 60, 108, 112; unassigned objects in, 58; outstanding features of, 58; dating of, 60; meaning of, 65, 70, 71, 75, 79-80;

ritual use of mescal bean, 70-71, 75; decline of, 80; Red Monochrome style, 81, 87, 88, 94; Pressa Canyon art, 94, 95, 108; at Pandale Crossing, 95; at Bee Cave, 97; at black-pictograph site, 98; painted pebbles, 109, 110; in Big Bend, 111; Meyers Springs early period, 112; possible extension of area, 113; Late Archaic of Central Texas and lower Pecos, 145; Brownfield Ranch art, 164, 166; Paint Rock Springs petroglyphs, 166; reason for painting of, 218; complexity of, 218; mentioned, 95

Périgordian: stage of Upper Paleolithic culture, 24; period, in Spain, 28

Peru: rock art of, 32, 33, 35

petroglyphs: at Fort Chadbourne, 6; in Lewis Canyon, 12; definition of, 14; in Nevada and California, 18; study of cultures, 22; in Arctic, 27-28; in Africa, 29, 30; of Bushmen, 30; in Australia, 31, 32; American, variation of, 32; in Chile, 33; in Colombian-Venezuelan region, 33; in North America, 33; in Nevada and California, 34; Pit-and-Groove, 34; along Pacific Coast, 34; in Great Basin region, 34; Puebloan, 34, 189, 200; in Texas plains, 35; on Dighton Rock, 35, 36; of lower Pecos, 37, 68, 218; at Lookout Shelter, 58; in Red Monochrome style, 89; in Lewis Canyon, 98-100; in Panhandle, 99, 173, 216; at Bee Cave, 123; in Davis Mountains, 130; in Central Texas, 143, 145, 146; at Paint Rock Springs, 161, 163; at Fort Sterrett, 161, 172; combined with painting, 161; in Nolan and Coke counties, 161, 164, 165; of Mescaleros, 189; Flute Player in, 200; in New Mexico, 200; at Rocky Dell, 205, 206; at Mujares Creek, 208; at Brown's Camp, 210; on Agua Piedra Creek, 210; at Newton Harrall Ranch, 210, 212; near Lahey Creek, 212; at Chimney Rock, 212-213; at Alibates Creek, 213, 214-215; at Gulf Camp, 213; survival of, in Texas, 217; study and preservation of, 219; mentioned, 3, 13

petrograph: defined, 14. SEE ALSO pictograph

phallus. SEE genitalia, male

pictographs. SEE ALSO rock art

—, colors used in: source of, 6; copying of, 19; in Levantine art, 28; at Tassili, 29; in Kenya, 29-30; in Australia, 31, 32; in Canadian Shield, 33; in California, 34; in Colorado Plateau, 35; in Texas plains, 35; of Basket Makers, 35; at Eagle Cave, 39; in Pecos River style, 41, 47-48, 48-49, 54, 56, 58; in Seminole Canyon, 46, 83; in Panther Cave, 62; in Val Verde County, 65; in Pecos River sites, 68, 70, 72; at Pecos River, Cave 1, 78; variation of, in Red Monochrome style, 81; at Ingram Ranch Shelter, 74; at Tardy Draw, 91; at Pandale Crossing, 95, 97; at Bee Cave, 97, 123, 125; at Pressa Canyon, 105; of painted pebbles, 107, 108; at Meyers Springs, 112, 113, 115, 120-121; at Agua Fria, 123, 125; at Chalk Draw, 125; at Comanche Springs, 126; at Study Butte, 126; at Hot Springs, 126-127; at Glenn Spring, 127; at Davis Mountains, 130; at Fort Davis, 130-131, 132, 134; at Rock Pile Ranch, 134, 135, 136, 218; at Balmorhea, 135, 139, 140; of Central Texas art, 146; at Paint Rock, 146, 148, 152, 157; at Frio Canyon, 160, 161; at Lehmann Rock Shelter, 159, 160; at Paint Rock Springs, 161; at Fort Sterrett, 161; at Brownfield Ranch, 165; at Breckenridge, 170; at Brady Creek, 172; at Hueco Tanks, 177, 178, 181, 182, 185, 187, 189, 190, 192, 194, 195, 196, 197, 198, 199, 201, 202; at Comanche Cave, 200; in Puebloan style, 196, 197; in Mescalero style, 199, 200, 201; at Rocky Dell, 203, 205, 206; at Mujares Creek, 208; at Tulia Canyon, 216; of crude rock art, 218; mentioned, 8, 10, 20

—, methods of applying color in: discussion of, 42-43; at Seminole Canyon, 83; for handprints, 85, 88, 131; at Meyers Springs, 119, 121; at Indian Water Hole, 122, 123; spraying of, 122, 123; at Bee Cave, 123; at Hot Springs, 127; at Fort Davis, 131, 134; at Balmorhea, 135, 139; at Blue Mountain, 142; at Paint Rock, 150; at Hueco Tanks, 194, 195, 197, 199

pipes, stone: used by Pecos River-style peoples, 61; figure at Pressa Canyon, 108

Pit-and-Groove petroglyphs. SEE petroglyphs

Plains Indians: bison hunters, 40; historic, 40, 108, 173, 218; "heart line", 84; use of horses, 108; in Meyers Springs art, 120; Tonkawas as, 146; Panhandle petroglyphs by, 173, 213-214, 216, 218; Mescaleros as, 181-182; as warriors, 212, 216; as Rocky Dell artists, 215

Plains (southern): Indians struggle for, 100; rock art of, 100

Pleistocene epoch: fauna of, in Africa, 28; late, in Central Texas, 143

plumed serpent: at Rocky Dell, 205, 215

pouches, fiber: in lower Pecos, 61; with Red Monochrome figures, 84

—, prickly pear: with Pecos River style shamans, 49, 52, 56, 57; use of, 61; in Meyers Springs early period, 112

Poncas: use of mescal bean by, 75

potsherd: from Brady Creek site, 172; Pueblo, at Rocky Dell, 205; Puebloan, at Antelope Creek, 214-215. SEE ALSO artifacts; cultural debris

pottery: associated with Red Monochrome style, 89; Leon Plain, 146, 153 and n.; Neo-American, in Central Texas, 146; Puebloan influence, 173; Puebloan, and Hueco Tanks pictographs, 195; Puebloan style, 197; Flute Player, 200

prayer sticks: in Pueblo shrines, 202

pre-Columbian art: in Southwestern U.S., 35

Pressa Canyon: rock art of, 12; shamans of, 47-48; Black Cave in, 66; rock art of, 12, 68, 92-95, 98, 105, 108

priests, Christian: in historic rock art, 108; in Frio Canyon art, 161; in Rocky Dell art, 205. SEE ALSO Christianity; missions, Spanish

projectile points: in lower Pecos, 39, 40, 44 n.; and Pecos River-style shamans, 56; in Wild Horse Creek area, 111; Archaic, of Central Texas, 145; in Lehmann Rock Shelter narrative, 159; in Lahey Creek petroglyphs, 212. SEE ALSO arrow points; dart points

puberty rites. SEE ceremonies

Puebloans: rock art of, 34-35; influence of, on El Paso Region peoples, 173, 175; of New Mexico, revolt against Spanish, 175; Mescaleros and, 189-190; diffusion of Flute Player, 200; shrines of, and Puebloan style, 202; at Hueco Tanks, 202; children of, and kachina dolls, 202; plumed serpent myth of, 205; at Rocky Dell, 205; traits of, and Antelope Creek peoples, 214; as rock artists, 217; potsherds of, at Rocky Dell, 205

Puebloan style: other than at Hueco Tanks, 195-196; of Hueco Tanks, 195-198; Hueco Tanks, as prehistoric, 195; Hueco Tanks, characteristics of, 196; Mescalero style compared to, 199; at Hueco Tanks, interpretation of, 202; at Hueco Tanks, as commemorative, 202; masks of, as ceremonial art, at Hueco Tanks, 202; peripheral, in Texas, 217; date of, in Texas, 217; as distinctive art form, 218; static nature of, 218

Puerto Rico: rock art of, 33

pyramids: in Puebloan style, Hueco Tanks, 198

Quinault, Indians: rock art of, 34

rabbit: as food, 60; in Red Monochrome style, 84; 92; jackrabbit, 84; cottontail, 60, 84; ears of, on figures, 200, 201

rabbit stick: in lower Pecos, 49, 52, 61; and male figures, Pressa Canyon, 94; in early period, Meyers Springs, 112. SEE ALSO atlatl

radiocarbon dates: of lower Pecos sites, 111

Railroad Tunnel: Pecos River-style site, 52

rain: design as, 198; Flute Player and, 200; Puebloan ceremonies for, 202; and snake, in Puebloan myth, 205

rainbow: in Puebloan style, Hueco Tanks, 198

Rattlesnake Canyon: rock art at, 9, 10, 11, 108

rattlesnake: in Mescalero style, 199; and Flute Player, 200; in Comanche Cave art, 200, 201; in Hueco Tanks art, 201

Red Canyon: outstanding site, 35
Red Linear: term for Pressa Canyon art, Site 3, 93
Red Monochrome style: of lower Pecos, mentioned, 37; and
   Pecos River style, 41; location of major sites of, 81; deterioration of, 81; figures in, 81, 84, 92; at Seminole Canyon, 83; animals in, 84-85; dating of, 89; evolution of, 89; artists of, 89; as
   commemorative art, 92; at Pandale Crossing, 95; painted pebbles, 109; Meyers Springs middle period, 113; Fort Davis art,
   133; Pecos River style, 217
religion: historic Indian rituals, 61; Pecos River style, 80, 218;
   dancing and, 121; rock art and study of, 291. SEE ALSO rituals;
   shamans
reptiles: in Bushman art, 30; in Australian rock art, 31
rheboks: in Bushman art, 30
rhinoceroses: in Bushman art, 30
Northern Rhodesia: rock art of, 30
Rio Grande Cliffs: 109
Rio Grande: rock art sites on, 9, 36, 37, 39, 52, 58, 113, 126, 217;
   painted pebbles from, 109-110; Wild Horse Creek route, 111;
   missions near, 155; Mescaleros on, 182 n., Pueblo peoples
   along, 189, 202; kiva murals at Kuaua, 198; mentioned, 173,
   175
rituals: fertility, 27, 93, 95, 202; puberty, 34, 121, 194; religious,
   of historic tribes, 61; Pecos River-style shamans, 65; mescal
   beans in, 75; scheduling of, 79; Puebloan, snakes in, 205
rock art: Kirkland's interest in, 3, 4; European, 3, 23-28; copying
   of, 8, 11, 12, 18-19, 22, 218; definition of, 14; as art form, 14,
   15-16, 22; evolution of, as art, 15, 16; study of, 17-18, 22, 23, 35,
   218-219; analogy of, to fossils, 17; subject matter significance,
   18, 24, 26, 27, 31, 32; of France, 23; of Spain, 23, 26; Franco-
   Cantabrian, 24, 26-27; of Arctic, 27-28, 33; of Australia, 31-32;
   of South America, 32-33; of Middle America, 32-33; of eastern
   U.S., 35-36; worldwide diversity of, 36; distribution of, in
   Texas, 217-218; as stimulus for further art, 217; crude, in Texas, 218; complex, in Texas, 218; need for preservation of, 218
—commemorative: of Pueblos, 34; Red Monochrome figures,
   92; meaning of rock art, 218
—, designs of: comb-like, 58, 98, 152, 198; smudging of, at
   Meyers Springs, 120; tower-like, 121; fence-like, 129, 141, 142;
   check marks, 129, 130; at Blamorhea, 139-140; disc-like, 159-
   160; check lines, 161, 163; cross-hatching, 166; zig-zag lines,
   185, 198; checkerboard, 197, 198, rake-like, 198. SEE ALSO
   rock art, geometric designs of
—, geometric designs of: significance of, 18; in Kenya petroglyphs, 30; in South American rock art, 33; in California rock
   art, 34; in Texas Plains rock art, 35; in Pecos River style, 57, 58,
   72, 87; in Red Monochrome style, 87, 88; at Pressa Canyon,
   94; line and circle, 99; in Lewis Canyon, 99; at Chalk Draw,
   123; at Comanche Springs, 126; at Hot Springs, 126; at Rock
   Pile Ranch, 135; in identification of Central Texas art, 146; at
   Paint Rock, 146, 148, 153; at Lehmann Rock Shelter, 159; at
   Champion Springs, 164; at Oak Creek Shelter, 169; at Hueco
   Tanks, 181, 196, 197-198; Puebloan style, 198; parallel lines,
   198; Mescalero style, Comanche Cave, 200; at Rocky Dell,
   203, 205; in crude rock art, 218
—, deterioration of: kerosene treatment, 19, 20, 158; at Hueco
   Tanks, 19, 20-24, 173, 181, 182, 187, 190, 192, 197, 198, 199,
   201; in Africa, 28; in North America, 33; in lower Pecos area,
   37, 39, 46, 47-48, 58, 68, 71, 72, 77, 91; in Seminole Canyon,
   83; in Painted Rock Canyon, 87; in Pressa Canyon, 95, 105,
   108; at Pandale Crossing, 97; in Lewis Canyon, 98, 100; at
   Castle Canyon, 105; at Rio Grande Cliffs, 109; in Big Bend,
   111; at Meyers Springs, 113, 115, 120-121; at Bee Cave, 123;
   at Agua Fria, 123; at Chalk Draw, 125; at Comanche Springs,
   126; at Study Butte, 126; at Hot Springs, 126; at Glenn Spring,
   127; at Blue Mountain, 141; in Central Texas, 143, 145; at
   Paint Rock, 148, 150, 156-157; in Lehmann Rock Shelter, 158;
   at Paint Rock Springs, 161; at Brownfield Ranch, 164; at Fort

Chadbourne, 166; in Oak Creek Shelter, 169; in Moran Shelter, 170; at Rocky Dell, 203, 205; of Brown Camp petroglyphs,
   210; of Agua Piedra Creek petroglyphs, 210; of Harrall Ranch
   petroglyphs, 212; of Chimney Rock petroglyphs, 212-213; of
   Lahey Creek petroglyphs, 213; of Alibates Creek petroglyphs,
   215; mentioned, 3, 10, 20, 24, 26, 48, 52, 54, 62, 78, 217
—, historic: of Puebloans, 34; in Great Basin, 34; at Hueco
   Tanks, 35, 199, 202-203; Dighton Rock as, 36; in lower Pecos
   47-48, 100, 108; in Red Monochrome style, 81; at Pressa Canyon, 105; and cowboys, 105; horses as clue to, 108; and Indians of Big Bend, 111-112; at Meyers Springs, 113; at Marfa
   Lake Shelter, 129; at Blue Mountain, 141-142; in Central
   Texas, 146; at Paint Rock, 148, 152, 156; at Frio Canyon, 161;
   at Lehmann Rock Shelter, 159, 160; at Ford Chadbourne, 167,
   169; at Brady Creek, 172; in Panhandle, 173, 218; Mescalero
   style as, 199, 200; at Comanche Cave, 200; shield-bearing warriors in, 201; at Rocky Dell, 203, 205; at Brown's Camp, 210;
   Harrall Ranch petroglyphs as, 210; Chimney Rock petroglyphs
   as, 213. SEE ALSO painted pebbles; petroglyphs; pictographs
Rock Pile Ranch: rock art of, 8, 134-135, 136; interpretation of
   art at, 135; colors used at, 218
Rocky Dell: Puebloan art in, 34; discovery of, 203; Whipple and,
   203; age of art of, 205; Pueblo Indians and, 205; artists of, 205;
   petroglyphs at, compared to pictographs of, 205, 207; pictographs of, discussed, 206, 215-216; mentioned, 13
Russia: rock art of, 27-28

Sahara Desert: rock art of, 29, 31
Sahara, Spanish: rock art of, 28
San Carlos Indians: mentioned, 175
San Elizario village: Mescaleros at, 180
San Saba Mission: Lipans at, 155
Santa Barbara, California: rock art of, 34
Santiago Complex: and Archaic tradition of lower Pecos, 111
scalp-shaped figure: at Marfa Lake Shelter, 129
Scandinavia: rock art of, 27-28
Seminole Canyon: rock art of, 43, 46, 52, 83, 92; Fate Bell Shel-
   ter, 46, 61; Lookout Shelter, 58; Panther Cave, 58; Red Mono-
   chrome site in, 81; Rio Grande Cliffs near, 109
Seminoles: historic, in lower Pecos, 107
sexuality: in Pressa Canyon art, 93; and Mescalero ceremonies,
   194; in Mescalero style, · Comanche Cave, 200; and Flute
   Player, 200. SEE ALSO genitalia, male
shaman: in Pecos River style, 43-58 passim; importance of, 43;
   distinguishing characteristics of, 44 (table), 57; phases of, 44,
   45 n.; schematic drawings of, 45; supernatural powers of, 46;
   overpainting of, 43, 46, 47-48, 54, 79; costumes and ornaments of, 46, 49, 75; first attempts at portraying, 47-48; abstraction of, 48; Period 2 of, 48-49, 52, 54, 58, 75, 79; in side view,
   49; anatomical features of, 49, 56; drawings associated with,
   46, 49, 52, 54, 56-57, 58, 79; of Period 3, 54, 56-57, 58, 79; of
   Period 4, 57-58; as leader of Archaic cultures, 64, 65, 75, 79, 80;
   interpretation of, 65; and modern mescal bean cults, 75; among
   Caddos, 75; as Pecos River style artists, 79-80; in Pressa Canyon art, 94; mentioned, 110
shamanistic societies: hypothesis of, and Pecos River style, 75,
   79-80. SEE ALSO medicine societies
Shawnees: in lower Pecos, 107; at Paint Rock, 156
sheep: in African rock art, 29
ship: in Rocky Dell art, 205
Shumla caves: Archaic site, lower Pecos, 40
Sierra Blanca Mountains (New Mexico): Mescalero art in, 199
Sierra Nevada Mountains: rock art barrier, 34
Sims, O.L.: 6, 7
Slick Trail Shelter: 58
Smith, Victor: 7, 10, 13